BIRTHING ETERNITY

BIRTHING
ETERNITY

A Different Perspective on the
Four Horsemen of Revelation

JANE ELIZABETH CODY

WESTBOW
PRESS
A DIVISION OF THOMAS NELSON

WestBow Press books may be ordered through booksellers or by contacting:

WestBow Press
A Division of Thomas Nelson
1663 Liberty Drive
Bloomington, IN 47403
www.westbowpress.com
1-(866) 928-1240

Because of the dynamic nature of the Internet, any web addresses or links contained in this book may have changed since publication and may no longer be valid. The views expressed in this work are solely those of the author and do not necessarily reflect the views of the publisher, and the publisher hereby disclaims any responsibility for them.

Any people depicted in stock imagery provided by Thinkstock are models, and such images are being used for illustrative purposes only.

Certain stock imagery © Thinkstock.

Cover image of author by Nancy Crawford Photography

ISBN: 978-1-4497-8336-5 (sc)
ISBN: 978-1-4497-8337-2 (hc)
ISBN: 978-1-4497-8335-8 (e)

Library of Congress Control Number: 2013901645

Scripture taken from the Authorized King James Version of the Bible.

Printed in the United States of America

WestBow Press rev. date: 4/8/2013

ENDORSEMENTS

Birthing Eternity is not answering the questions we all ready have answers to. It is a revelation on Revelation. God's word is true and faithful and all he has given us will be known in its time – it's time has come. This factual account of historical events, that could only have been achieved in a time when information was at our finger tips, has given insight into what has already happened in God's timeline. I am excited and apprehensive of the time we are in. A must read for anyone who wants to know and understand God's word.

Rick A. Pisani - CIO of Merging Streams Belize Limited, a Kingdom Company

I am really amazed by this step by step account according to the word of God. Birthing Eternity is amazing book! I would call it **"The Voice of the last Bell of Prophecies."** It is well organized not only Biblically, but also historically. The prophetic word comes through all generations step by step until the Lord comes back again. Good work and God bless this book.

Dr. Gabriel Bainesai, Minister, Evangelist, Licensed Counselor, Bible Teacher & Writer

Birthing Eternity is straight forward in its message, well documented historically and Biblically, and profoundly significant in its implication for people who are searching for the true meaning of life in today's complex social and economic environment! Jane's passion for unlocking the mysteries of little understood Biblical prophecy will take you to a new level of appreciation for the fact that God is fulfilling his word in shocking detail.

Throughout my three and a half decade career of helping raise support for prominent and internationally recognized evangelists and ministry organizations, I have been aware of what little most of us know about the prophetic message of Daniel and Revelation. After prayerfully considering Jane's insight and examining the result of her study, I can say with confidence and conviction that Birthing Eternity is a must read guide for anyone who has a lingering question about God's plan for His people.

Stephan Brown, Christian Broadcasting Network, Christ for All Nations, McConkey – Johnston Inc., Development Association for Christian Institutions, Assemble of God National Headquarters, Canvasback, Benny Hinn, Spokane Homeless Coalition, Valley Homeless Network, Union Gospel Mission, and Letourneau Ministries International

In memory of my dear mother,

Helen Mercia Tiers,

a faithful intercessor who has gone to see

Jesus face to face.

And to my beloved Father, Charles Tiers,

who has always supported and encouraged me.

And to my family in Messiah

who have prayed for this book.

ACKNOWLEDGMENTS

Writing a book is not something done alone, and I want to thank the many people who supported me. I am most grateful for those who helped me in preparing the manuscript for publication, particularly Stephan Brown, Ted Brown, Virginia Powers and Kimberley Brown. In addition, I want to thank Diana Reed, Linda Wallman, Molly Murphy, Sarah Murphy, Stacy Hollister, Joanne Lockwood, Lynda Zertuche, Laurie Denning, Joshua Thompson, Josephine Bergland, Olivia Zurtuche, Eva Zertuche, and Laural Brown for their help with editing. Josephine Bergland, Laural Brown and Nancy Crawford all lent their artistic talents to this project. I want to thank my parents Helen and Charles Tiers, my sons Sam and Israel Cody, Rick and Lisa Pasani, Robin McDonald, Vickie Blum, Carol Robison, Ron and Pat Slade, Jan Brown, Joanne Lockwood, Michelle Zerbst, Katrina Byrum, Josephine Bergland and members of my fellowship for their encouragement and prayer support.

Contents

Prologue: Why Language Is Important xiii

Part 1: The Scroll 1

   Chapter 1: Watch.. 3

   Chapter 2: Betrothal, Consummation, and Conception 7

   Chapter 3: Expecting... 17

   Chapter 4: The Scroll Opens 27

   Chapter 5: An Exponential Curve 37

   Chapter 6: "Come and See" 47

Part 2: The White Horseman 53

   Chapter 7: With a Bow.. 55

   Chapter 8: Given a Crown....................................... 63

   Chapter 9: Conquering and to Conquer—Europe 73

   Chapter 10: Conquering and to Conquer—the World........... 93

   Chapter 11: A Lion with Eagle's Wings 111

Part 3: The Red Horseman 123

   Chapter 12: A Horse of a Different Color 125

   Chapter 13: Two Sides of the Same Coin 135

   Chapter 14: The Bear and the Bull................................. 141

   Chapter 15: Taking Peace—Rumors of War 151

   Chapter 16: Taking Peace—A World of Constant Change 159

   Chapter 17: Kill One Another................................... 169

Chapter 18: Given a Sword..177

Chapter 19: A Bear with Three Ribs....................................185

Chapter 20: Devour Much Flesh..199

Part 4: The Black Horseman...203

Chapter 21: The Face of a Man 205

Chapter 22: The Black Horse 211

Chapter 23: The Yoke of Debt 223

Chapter 24: The Millstone of Inflation 237

Chapter 25: Oil and Wine...247

Chapter 26: Like a Leopard 257

Chapter 27: Four Heads..269

Part 5: The Green Horseman 283

Chapter 28: The Fourth Horse 285

Chapter 29: Death and Hades...295

Chapter 30: Power to Kill—Sword and Hunger 309

Chapter 31: Power to Kill—Death and Beasts 325

Chapter 32: A Fourth Beast..339

Part 6: Seals, Trumpets, and Bowls................................347

Appendix A: Early Jubilees...361

Notes 363

PROLOGUE:

Why Language Is Important

I once had the privilege of witnessing the completion of a *Sefer Torah*, or Torah scroll, an event I will never forget. The room at the synagogue was hushed in awe as the Israeli scribe lovingly unwrapped the scroll from its protective cloth and laid it on a specially prepared worktable. The scribe, a professional trained in the ancient art of writing and preserving scrolls, had handwritten the Sefer Torah, a scroll containing the five books of Moses. At that point, after more than a year of painstaking labor, the scroll was ready for the last phase in its creation: to be mounted on the wooden housing, called the *aitz chaiim* (עץ חיים, or Tree of Life), which would enable readers to open the scroll without touching it. Only the sounds of the scribe opening the scroll and lashing its edge to the spindle that formed the core of the Tree of Life punctuated the silence.

He unrolled the mounted scroll and revealed the final section of its contents for all to see. The parchment glowed amber. The inked letters that formed perfect rows of Hebrew calligraphy caught the light as they rose slightly from the page. The writing was exquisite, the perfect blend of ornament—the tops of most of the letters were adorned with *taggin*, crown-like embellishments—and meticulous clarity, making it highly readable even for a child versed in the aleph-bet.[1]

The Art of the Scribe

The Jews did an outstanding job of preserving the *Tanakh*, which roughly corresponds to what Christians refer to as the Old Testament and contains the Torah, the Prophets, and the Writings. Over the centuries, highly trained scribes spent their lives copying scrolls of sacred writings in highly standardized calligraphy, all without errors. However, this was only part of the story. The art of the scribe included processing the skins of kosher animals into parchment, which remained flexible far longer than paper. It also involved carving quill tips from prescribed feathers at just the right angle for transcribing calligraphy with the precision of a printing press and preparing ink that would remain black without fading for untold years.

These exacting standards of production combined with a ritualized code regarding the proper storage and handling of scrolls have allowed them to remain intact for as long as 800 years.[2] The Dead Sea Scrolls, created using similar technology, survived more than 2,000 years under extraordinary conditions. These ancient scrolls are testimony that the Jewish scribes have done an equally good job at preserving the words of Scripture over the centuries, ensuring each copy was perfect, without error. Once complete, a scroll was checked for mistakes by three rabbis; today's scribes can do an additional check of their work using computerized scanning.[3]

The Art of the Translator

Most of us don't read the Bible in its original languages, the Old Testament in Hebrew with a smattering of Aramaic, and the New Testament in an ancient dialect of Greek. We diligently pore over our favorite English translation—or translations—assuming the scholars who made them accurately preserved their meaning. Indeed, the art of the translator is as important as that of the scribe. The careful work of the scribes minimized several common pitfalls in document translation: text that is difficult to read or even illegible, words that are misspelled or miscopied, and source documents that are incomplete.

In many ways, the problems faced by Bible translators are more challenging than those of the scribes. Anyone who has studied a foreign language knows the source of difficulties: languages are not the same. Years ago, when I took my first foreign language class, I was frustrated by the fact that translation was *not* like math, that it was not simply a case of deciphering the French or Hebrew "code" into English. Worldwide Translation, a school for translators, explains the challenge this way:

> There are some particular problems in the translation process: problems of ambiguity, problems that originate from structural and lexical differences between languages and multiword units like idioms and collocations. Another problem would be the grammar because there are several constructions of grammar poorly understood, in the sense that it isn't clear how they should be represented, or what rules should be used to describe them.[4]

Sometimes a single word could be translated correctly into any of a dozen English words, each with its own nuance. For example, the Hebrew word *halak* (הלך) has been translated as "go, went, walk, followed, come, depart, gone, continually, enter, go forth, conversant, waxed, wrought, exercise, travail, run, move, pass away, traverse" and figuratively refers to a manner of living. Which is the correct one? Which best expresses the author's intent? The writers of the Authorized King James Version chose to translate halak as "go" 217 times, "walk" 156 times, "come" 16 times and a variety of other words more than a hundred times.[5] Similarly, half a dozen Hebrew words, each with its own inference, are translated as "go" in Genesis alone. The English word "praise" was used to translate nearly a dozen Hebrew words![6]

Compounding the problem is the fact that English has undergone significant changes since Tyndale and the King James translators worked. A quick review of Shakespeare, a contemporary of these scholars, should dispel any doubts on this score. Today, the word "keep" has a rather anemic meaning, and actually appears on a list of "weak" verbs best avoided. However, the word once referred to a castle keep, the most secure, most easily defended place in a fortress, used to store items of high value or essential for survival. In this context, the command to "keep" something is a command to guard it with every fiber of your being as if your very life depended on it.

Hebrew and Greek have grammatical structures very different from English, most clearly demonstrated by their sentence structure. In Hebrew, each verse is a sentence, and many would be marked incomplete in English. The preciseness of Greek, on the other hand, allows a complexity unthinkable in English. A Greek sentence can be pages long, functioning more like an English paragraph or chapter. A sentence is meant to convey a complete idea, with every detail and nuance woven together in an intricate web of dependent and independent clauses, prepositional phrases, and compound sections. This forces the translator to carve up these grammatical behemoths into more-manageable pieces, often losing sight of the meaning or intent of the original sentence. As a result, a verse that appears to be a complete sentence in English may actually be a subordinate clause of a subordinate clause and convey only a small portion of the whole idea being expressed.

Greek and Hebrew contain verb tenses that English can only approximate. For example, Hebrew includes a causative verb tense (*hiphil*) which refers to the subject *causing* action of the verb: instead of "he ate," it means "he caused to eat."[7] Greek often uses the aorist tense, which conveys the concept of a verb without regard for the timing of the action, past, present, or future.[8] When the original language uses a tense or phrase with no clear English translation or when the literal meaning is awkward in English, the translator often resorts to "ironing out" the cumbersome differences between the languages, sometimes inadvertently watering down the meaning.

Despite the numerous challenges in translating Scripture, those who took on the task were dedicated to giving others the Bible in their own languages. Over the centuries, godly scholars have wrestled with Scripture to produce clear, understandable translations while making every attempt to remain true to its original meaning and often under the most difficult of circumstances. These men, such as St. Jerome (c. 347–420), who translated the Latin Vulgate;[9] John Wycliffe (c. 1328–1384), author of an early English translation;[10] Jan Hus (1369–1415), who translated into Czech;[11] and the Renaissance and Reformation scholars who followed them are heroes of the faith.

Challenge for Today

I am convinced that the Bible is the inerrant Word of God. Nevertheless, because of the difficulties inherent in even the best translations, it is important to return to the Greek and Hebrew to confirm the meaning of key passages and ensure we do not build doctrine on faulty foundations. Ironically, end-time prophecies seem to have a higher rate of translation issues; Revelation, for instance, makes frequent use of the aorist verb tense that has no English counterpart. The good news is that God's Word in its original language is perfect. Each word, each verb tense, will be perfectly fulfilled in God's perfect time.

This book will examine various prophecies recorded by John, Daniel, and others. This will often include specifics about the meaning of key words and some of the verb tenses used. Resist the temptation to let your eyes glaze over during these discussions. Through the careful analysis of each word, a more complete picture of the prophetic vision emerges, a vision that has an overwhelming correlation with historical and current events on the worldwide stage. It is clear that God foreknew all things!

PART 1:

The Scroll

And I saw when the Lamb opened one of the seals, and I heard, as it were the noise of thunder, one of the four beasts saying, Come and see. (Rev. 6:1 Authorized King James Version)

Chapter 1:

Watch

It was Passover season, and all Israel was converging on Jerusalem for the feast. Passover was always important in the lives of the disciples of Jesus, but this year they felt an added edge of expectation. Jesus had received death threats and had escaped an attempt to kill Him by stoning only a few months earlier, which made Jerusalem a dangerous place for Him. Even more troubling were the comments Jesus Himself had been making about laying down His life and being raised up on the third day (Matt. 16:21, 17:23). What did He mean? What did He ever mean? Sometimes it was best not to ask.

All these concerns had been wiped aside by the string of amazing miracles Jesus had performed, from opening the eyes of the blind to dramatically raising Lazarus from the grave. The crowds continually surged around Jesus, desperately hoping for a touch from His hand, eager to see what the Master would do next.

Things had seemed so clear when Jesus and His disciples arrived at the home of Mary and Martha and their brother, Lazarus, who had recently been resurrected from the grave (John 11:17–46); Jesus seemed poised to become ruler of all Israel. Hadn't He ridden a donkey colt into Jerusalem with the procession that carried the Passover lamb into the temple courts? Hadn't the crowds sung His praises and called Him the Son of David? Hadn't He demonstrated His authority by driving the money changers from the outer courts, by answering the interrogations of the religious leaders of every party, and by healing all manner of diseases and afflictions right before their eyes (Matt. 21:1–16, 22:11–13)? Surely they would all know Jesus was the long-awaited Messiah.

And then, in a moment, all their hopes were dashed. Jesus pronounced a scathing judgment on the scribes and Pharisees, confronting them face-to-face and calling them hypocrites and whitewashed tombs. Without skipping a beat, He judged the nation (Matt. 23:37–39), turned on His heel, and departed, never to return to the temple. What could the disciples do but follow?

When they had retreated to a quiet place on the Mount of Olives, the disciples asked, "what [shall be] the sign of thy coming, and of the end of the world?" (Matt. 24:3b KJV). The answer they heard was double edged. Jesus described events that would take place in their own lifetimes—the fall of the temple system and their own persecution and martyrdom. He answered their next question by setting the context of events that would lead inexorably to His second coming, events that would happen hundreds of years in the future. As part of His discourse, Jesus told the tale of ten virgins.

> [1]Then shall the kingdom of heaven be likened unto ten virgins, which took their lamps, and went forth to meet the bridegroom. [2]And five of them were wise, and five [were] foolish. [3]They that [were] foolish took their lamps, and took no oil with them: [4]But the wise took oil in their vessels with their lamps. [5]While the bridegroom tarried, they all slumbered and slept. [6]And at midnight there was a cry made, Behold, the bridegroom cometh; go ye out to meet him. [7]Then all those virgins arose, and trimmed their lamps. [8]And the foolish said unto the wise, Give us of your oil; for our lamps are gone out. [9]But the wise answered, saying, [Not so]; lest there be not enough for us and you: but go ye rather to them that sell, and buy for yourselves. [10]And while they went to buy, the bridegroom came; and they that were ready went in with him to the marriage: and the door was shut. [11]Afterward came also the other virgins, saying, Lord, Lord, open to us. [12]But he answered and said, Verily I say unto you, I know you not. [13]Watch therefore,

> for ye know neither the day nor the hour wherein the
> Son of man cometh. (Matt. 25:1–13, KJV)

This parable is a picture of the church waiting for the return of the Messiah. Note that all ten virgins loved the bridegroom and were waiting for his arrival. They all had oil in their lamps and began the wait with the appearance of being equally prepared, but only five had vessels of additional oil. Interestingly, as the wait for the bridegroom took *much* longer than anyone had expected, all ten "slumbered and slept" (Matt. 25:5, KJV). A more literal translation might render the passage as "became negligent or careless"—*nystazo* (νυστάζω)[12]—and "indifferent to sloth and sin"—*katheudo* (καθεύδω).[13]

The return of our Bridegroom, Jesus, seems to be taking an exceedingly long time. Despite the fact that Jesus exhorted us to watch (Matt. 25:13), we have all stopped paying attention. We are indifferent. We have fallen asleep. Our lamps have gone out.

When the bridegroom finally arrived, all ten virgins were awakened by the announcement of his coming, and all ten began to trim their lamps. However, only the wise virgins were prepared for such a long delay. They had brought additional vessels of oil, while the foolish virgins assumed the initial contents of their lamps would be enough to carry them through.

Unfortunately for the foolish virgins, the wise virgins would not share their oil. So the foolish ones tried to remedy the situation by hurrying to the market for additional oil, little knowing that while they were gone the bridegroom would come, those waiting for him would enter the wedding feast, and the doors would be shut eternally. At one time, I thought the details concerning the time of Jesus' return were interesting but were not salvation issues. The crucial point remains, however, that the five foolish virgins were shut out of the wedding feast. When they knocked on the door, pleading to be let in, the bridegroom replied in essence, "I emphatically never, ever knew you" (Matt. 25:10–12).

Jesus summarized the parable's lesson for His disciples: "Watch therefore, for ye know neither the day nor the hour wherein the Son of man cometh" (Matt. 25:13, KJV). Jesus' command to watch—*gregoreo* (γρηγορέω) in Greek—means, "to take heed lest through remission and indolence some destructive calamity suddenly overtake one."[14]

The end-time prophecies such as those given in Matthew and Revelation are vitally important for today's church to know, to understand, and to use as a guide as we live through these end times. Revelation, which begins with instructions to read it, is the only New Testament book that specifically promises a blessing to those who do read it. "Blessed [is] he that readeth, and they that hear the words of this prophecy, and keep those things which are written therein: for the time [is] at hand" (Rev. 1:3, KJV).

The Greek word *tereo* (τηρέω), "keep," means "to attend to carefully, to guard."[15] You cannot guard something if you don't know what it is. This book does not examine all of Revelation, but focuses on the prophecy of the four horsemen in Revelation 6—verse by verse and word by word—to demonstrate, thoroughly and beyond dispute, by the overwhelming evidence of Scripture and historical events, that the "time of the end" has begun. It is now! The Bridegroom is coming, and we must be among the wise who watch for Him.

CHAPTER 2:

Betrothal, Consummation, and Conception

And the Spirit and the bride say, Come. And let him that heareth say, Come. And let him that is athirst come. And whosoever will, let him take the water of life freely. (Rev. 22:17, KJV)

The Bible uses betrothal, marriage, pregnancy, and birth to illustrate the relationship between God and His people and other spiritual concepts. Of these, none captures our imagination or communicates the essence of intimacy, love, and caring as well as the picture of the Bridegroom and His bride. The converse is also true. The prophet Hosea was commanded to marry a harlot to portray God's covenant love towards us and the pain our faithlessness causes Him (Hos. 1:2).

The writers of the New Testament called the church "the bride, the Lamb's wife" (Rev. 21:9, KJV) and commonly referred to the church as the bride of Christ. John the Baptist declared that Jesus was the Bridegroom and referred to himself as the "friend of the Bridegroom" (John 3:28–29, KJV). John the Apostle mentioned a heavenly wedding feast in Revelation 19. Long before this, Exodus recorded a marriage at Mt. Sinai, sealing the covenant between God and Israel.

During the Sermon on the Mount, Jesus used wedding language to describe His mission on earth, although English translations obscure much of it: "Think not that I am come to destroy the law, or the prophets: I am not come to destroy, but to fulfill" (Matt. 5:17, KJV).

The Greek word *katalyo* (καταλύω), translated "destroy," means to dissolve or disunite what has been joined together, whether stones of a building, government institutions, or contracts.[16] English uses different terms to describe this action; when we break apart the stones of a building, we say it is destroyed, but when we break a contract, we say it is annulled. Jesus is warning his listeners not to assume He is breaking apart the Law (Torah) and the prophets, the Old Testament covenant between God and His people. A better translation might replace "destroy" with "annul"—"Think not that I am come to *annul* the law, or the prophets: I am not come to *annul*, but to fulfill."

Similarly, the word translated "fulfill" has other nuances better suited to the context of covenant. The Greek *pleroo* (πληρόω) does indeed mean to make full or supply liberally so that nothing is wanting, but it can also mean "to consummate."[17] Thus, Jesus' words could be translated, "Think not that I am come to *annul* the law, or the prophets: I am not come to *annul*, but to *consummate*." Now that's marriage talk!

The significance of this change becomes clear when we understand the components of a biblical marriage still preserved in Jewish weddings today. Traditionally, a marriage was sealed in three ways: through a covenantal contract, through the payment of money (the bride price), and through intercourse. While exceptions were made for special circumstances, all three conditions were ordinarily met. Of course, God does all things with excellence, so His marriage to His people would have all components.

The Betrothal

The first component is the covenantal contract, called a *ketubah*, a legally binding document that lays out the rights and responsibilities of the husband to the wife during marriage, the conditions of inheritance upon his death, and obligations regarding the support of children resulting from the marriage. It also provides for the wife's support in the event of divorce. The ketubah was signed by the husband and two witnesses and given to the bride for safekeeping. Usually, this was done at the betrothal or *kiddushin* (קִדּוּשִׁין), which comes from the word *kadosh* (קָדוֹשׁ), meaning holy, sanctified, or set apart. The betrothal was as legally binding as marriage and could be only be annulled by a court-approved divorce.[18]

God presented His people with a ketubah on Mount Sinai and signed it with His own finger (Exod. 31:18, KJV). He introduced it by pointing out His care for them when He brought them out of Egypt with miraculous signs and wonders, and He promised continued blessing if they lived according to the terms of the covenant:

> [4]Ye have seen what I did unto the Egyptians, and [how] I bare you on eagles' wings, and brought you unto myself. [5]Now therefore, if ye will obey my voice indeed, and keep my covenant, then ye shall be a peculiar treasure unto me above all people: for all the earth [is] mine: [6]And ye shall be unto me a kingdom of priests, and an holy nation. These [are] the words which thou shalt speak unto the children of Israel. (Exod. 19:4–6 KJV)

The Torah has all the requirements of a ketubah. It clearly lays out God's responsibilities as a husband to Israel, both as a faithful wife and as an unfaithful wife, which Deuteronomy 28 sums up. The short version of the ketubah, the Ten Commandments (literally, the Ten Words), was written on stone tablets and signed by the bridegroom, God, with His own finger and in the sight of two witnesses, Moses and Joshua, son of Nun (Exod. 31:18. KJV).

A second component of a biblical wedding is the bride price, which could be anything from a significant sum of money or tract of land, reminiscent of marriages among the noble families in pre–twentieth century Europe, to a small coin with the value of our penny. In most cases, the bride price was a ring, a tradition still followed in Western culture. It was presented to the bride as part of the *kiddushin*.

God also provided a bride price for Israel before bringing her out of Egypt. When Moses received his instructions at the burning bush, he was told,

> [21]And I will give this people favour in the sight of the Egyptians: and it shall come to pass, that, when ye go, ye shall not go empty: [22]But every woman shall borrow of her neighbour, and of her that sojourneth in her house, jewels of silver, and jewels of gold, and raiment: and ye shall put [them] upon your sons, and upon your daughters; and ye shall spoil the Egyptians. (Exod. 3:21–22 KJV)

It is amazing that the Hebrew slave women went to their masters, requesting, "Give me jewelry and fancy clothes." It's harder still to imagine the Egyptians complying with this instead of rewarding such impudence with flogging or jail. It would have been an incredible act of faith to do this, and just as God had promised, the Egyptian women responded by generously granting their requests. No doubt many Egyptians responded not to their slaves but to that big, powerful God of the Hebrews pouring out plagues on their nation. Clearly this was not a God to be provoked.

As they left Egypt, the Children of Israel donned beautiful new outfits, better than anything they had worn in their lives, with more stashed among their possessions. This was their bride price, a small taste of the type of provision they would enjoy with their new husband.

Imagine the grief and anger of the Bridegroom as he watched His beloved bride take His "engagement ring" and melt it down to forge an offering to another lover even as the ketubah was being signed (Exod. 32). God chose not to destroy Israel and begin again with Moses (Exod. 32:10) but to go through with the marriage to the harlot from the seed of Adam. What an amazing picture of God's grace and lovingkindness!

There was an additional price paid for the bride of Israel— atonement for her sins. Foreshadowing the atonement wrought by the death and resurrection of Jesus, the Israelites were instructed to slay a Passover lamb and paint their doorways with its blood.

Obedience ensured that the angel of death would pass over their dwellings, leaving their families intact (Exod. 12).

Although the giving of the bride price and the signing of the ketubah are often done as part of a modern Jewish wedding ceremony, traditionally they were to be done as much as a year apart. The kiddushin is the moment when the bride is set apart for the bridegroom alone. At this time, the couple does not live together, but the groom prepares a home where they will live after the second phase of the wedding, the *nisuin*, or marriage ceremony.

The Wedding

In Exodus, the Bridegroom, God, gives Moses detailed instructions on how to construct His home on earth: the tabernacle, a tent version of the heavenly temple (Heb. 8:5). Once it was completed, God demonstrated His presence there by filling it with a cloud of glory so thick even Moses was unable to go inside (Exod. 40).

The nisuin, which includes reading the ketubah aloud, takes place under a canopy called a *chuppah* (חפה). Isaiah 4:5 is one of the few places in Scripture that uses this word.

> And the LORD will create upon every dwelling place of mount Zion, and upon her assemblies, a cloud and smoke by day, and the shining of a flaming fire by night: for upon all the glory [shall be] a defense (chuppah). (Isa. 4:5 KJV)

The Authorized King James Version translates chuppah as "defense," but this is not a military term; it is marriage talk. While the defense of the Lord is part of our inheritance, this is not what this verse is talking about. This is a promise of Israel's future nisuin, when it will again dwell with God as His bride. It parallels the promise of the church's position as the bride of Christ. No, God is not a bigamist. The Apostle Paul makes it clear that the church is a "wild olive tree," that has been grafted onto the cultivated olive tree that is Israel, "and with them partakest of the root and fatness of the olive tree" (Rom. 11). All who draw life from the olive tree of those who believe that are part of the heavenly bride.

The pillar of cloud by day and fire by night is the chuppah

under which God marries His people. In Exodus 20, God speaks the Ten Words to His beloved, while the chuppah of cloud and fire hovers over them. Scripture recounts that the people literally "saw his voice"—the King James calls it "thundering" (Exod. 20:18, KJV). I'm not sure what that was like, but it was terrifying in the extreme to this congregation of ex-slaves! Even after witnessing the plagues of Egypt, the parting of the sea, the provision of bread from heaven, the water that gushed forth out of solid stone, and the miraculous defeat of the army of Amalek, the Israelites were unprepared for the awesomeness of God (Exod. 4:1–20:26).

Israel had freely entered into the marriage; before the reading of the ketubah, they had proclaimed their acceptance.

> 7And Moses came and called for the elders of the people, and laid before their faces all these words which the LORD commanded him. 8And all the people answered together, and said, All that the LORD hath spoken we will do. And Moses returned the words of the people unto the LORD. (Exod. 19:7–8 KJV)

After God spoke forth the ketubah, the terrified bride of Israel sought distance between herself and her Bridegroom.

> 18And all the people saw the thunderings, and the lightnings, and the noise of the trumpet, and the mountain smoking: and when the people saw [it], they removed, and stood afar off. 19And they said unto Moses, Speak thou with us, and we will hear: but let not God speak with us, lest we die. 20And Moses said unto the people, Fear not: for God is come to prove you, and that his fear may be before your faces, that ye sin not. 21And the people stood afar off, and Moses drew near unto the thick darkness where God [was]. (Exod. 20:18–21 KJV)

Throughout Israel's wanderings in the wilderness, the cloud covered the encampment like a chuppah, a constant reminder of the marriage covenant between God and His people. Forty years later, the next generation reconfirmed the ketubah on Mount Ebal and Mount Gerizim (Deut. 27).

The Consummation

The *yichud*, or seclusion, is an important part of a biblical marriage. In modern Jewish weddings, this is fulfilled by arranging for the newlyweds to simply retreat to be completely alone for a time. However, this was traditionally a far more serious endeavor. The couple would go into a place set apart for the consummation of the marriage on a bed prepared with pristine white linen. Meanwhile, the guests and the wedding party would enjoy an extended time of feasting.

The purpose of this relatively "public" consummation was to ensure the bride's family ended up with proof of her virginity. The linen sheet, spotted with blood, would be presented to the bride's father before the entire assembly as evidence that she had been a virgin, and this finalized the marriage covenant. The bride's "tokens of virginity" were to be kept for legal proof in the event her husband accused her of harlotry instead of paying the price required in the event of a divorce. Without the "tokens of virginity," it was possible for the bride to be stoned (Deut. 22:13–21). This puts a different perspective on Jesus' words in Matthew, "Think not that I am come to annul the law, or the prophets: I am not come to annul, but to consummate" (Matt. 5:17).

The word "law" is the Greek *nomos* (νόμος), the word the Jewish authors of the Septuagint, a Greek translation of the Old Testament, used for "Torah." When we understand that the Torah or the Law is not some legal tome but actually a wedding ketubah, Jesus' declaration makes more sense; it is an expression of his tender love for us. Keep in mind he is talking to a Jewish audience that had been living according to Torah their whole lives. Jesus is assuring them, "Don't worry. I'm not annulling the ketubah. I'm consummating it."

The events surrounding the first coming of the Messiah completely illustrate the idea of consummation. Jesus shed the blood of the covenant on the cross. Seven weeks later, on the Feast of Weeks, when pilgrims streamed to Jerusalem from all over the world to celebrate the anniversary of God speaking the Ten Words on Mount

Sinai, the Holy Spirit was poured onto the infant (still Jewish) church with a "sound from heaven as of a rushing mighty wind" and "cloven tongues like as of fire" (Acts 2:2–3 KJV).

From that point, the church moved with a power and authority not seen before. It was clear that God was doing something new, turning the stony hearts of men into hearts of flesh and writing His word upon their innermost being, giving them the ability to walk in God's ways just as Jesus had. This fulfilled the prophecies given through Jeremiah and Ezekiel.

> [31]Behold, the days come, saith the LORD, that I will make a new covenant with the house of Israel, and with the house of Judah: [32]Not according to the covenant that I made with their fathers in the day [that] I took them by the hand to bring them out of the land of Egypt; which my covenant they brake, although I was an husband unto them, saith the LORD: [33]But this [shall be] the covenant that I will make with the house of Israel; After those days, saith the LORD, I will put my law in their inward parts, and write it in their hearts; and will be their God, and they shall be my people. (Jer. 31:31–33 KJV)

> [26]A new heart also will I give you, and a new spirit will I put within you: and I will take away the stony heart out of your flesh, and I will give you an heart of flesh. [27]And I will put my spirit within you, and cause you to walk in my statutes, and ye shall keep my judgments, and do [them]. (Ezek. 36:26–27 KJV)

Mary conceived Jesus when, "The Holy Ghost shall come upon thee, and the power of the Highest shall overshadow thee: therefore also that holy thing which shall be born of thee shall be called the Son of God" (Luke 1:35 KJV). In the same way, the marriage between Jesus and His bride was consummated by the pouring out of the Holy Spirit on the anniversary of receiving the wedding ketubah on Mount Sinai.

The Holy Spirit began a new thing on earth. The marriage

covenant between God and his people had been consummated. Something—the kingdom of heaven—was now in gestation, but for how long? Human gestation, the example every mother is intimately familiar with, takes approximately forty weeks, and this information is not irrelevant; it is a key to understanding the timing of His return.

Chapter 3:

Expecting

Christians around the world have been waiting for the second coming of the Messiah, although they have held widely divergent opinions about the timing of His return and the role of the church in the events that precede it. These opinions range from the belief that His return was an invisible, spiritual event in our past, to the more "normative" view that all this is squarely in the future, most likely the far distant future, something best left to the professionals and certainly nothing to worry about in daily life.

The early church awaited Jesus' imminent return, but as years turned into decades and decades into centuries, generation after generation died without seeing any sign of His coming. Now much of the church functions out of a "someday, far, far, away" mentality on the timing of the last days. Despite occasional outbreaks of panicked prognostications of impending doom, inattentiveness has been the norm. The Apostle Peter predicted this attitude.

> [3]Knowing this first, that there shall come in the last days scoffers, walking after their own lusts, [4]And saying, Where is the promise of his coming? for since the fathers fell asleep, all things continue as [they were] from the beginning of the creation. (2 Pet. 3:3–4 KJV)

Peter goes on to warn believers that the naysayers are wrong.

> [8]But, beloved, be not ignorant of this one thing, that one day [is] with the Lord as a thousand years, and a thousand years as one day. [9]The Lord is not slack concerning his promise, as some men count slackness; but is longsuffering to us-ward, not willing that any should perish, but that all should come to repentance. [10]But the day of the Lord will come as a thief in the night; in which the heavens shall pass away with a great noise, and the elements shall melt with fervent heat, the earth also and the works that are therein shall be burned up. (2 Pet. 3:8–10 KJV)

For those not paying attention, the events of the last days will be a shock, like "a thief in the night," but to those who are watching, as Jesus commanded, the signs are as evident as the approaching labor of a pregnant woman in her third trimester.

God's System of Timekeeping

The Torah contains instructions about many aspects of life, including the keeping of time. God's design for this is introduced in the creation account in Genesis: "And God said, Let there be lights in the firmament of the heaven to divide the day from the night; and let them be for signs, and for seasons, and for days, and years" (Gen. 1:14 KJV).

Most units of time are universal. A single orbit of the earth around the sun marks a year. The rhythm of day and night is the result of the earth's rotation. Many societies use the lunar phases as the basis of the month; our own calendar began that way in Rome but was adjusted according to the egotistical whims of various Caesars.

However, there are two units for counting time that have no basis in planetary orbits but were simply ordained by God. The week is the most familiar of these. There is only one reason to have a seven-day week—God said so. In fact, the keeping of Sabbath, or day of rest, every seventh day is the fourth of the Ten Commandments.

> [8]Remember the sabbath day, to keep it holy. [9]Six days shalt thou labour, and do all thy work: [10]But the seventh day [is] the sabbath of the LORD thy God: [in it] thou

shalt not do any work, thou, nor thy son, nor thy daughter, thy manservant, nor thy maidservant, nor thy cattle, nor thy stranger that [is] within thy gates: [11]For [in] six days the LORD made heaven and earth, the sea, and all that in them [is], and rested the seventh day: wherefore the LORD blessed the sabbath day, and hallowed it. (Exod. 20:8–11, KJV)

Leviticus 23 lists the Sabbath as the first of the *mo'edim* (מוֹעֲדִים) "a set time,"[19] one of the appointed times that were to be observed as part of the terms of the *ketubah*. God desired to meet intimately with His people each and every Shabbat. However, this was not a new revelation He was giving to Israel. This was as ancient as the prohibition against murder; in fact, it was older.

God's stated purposes for creating the lights in the heavens is that they would be "for signs, and for seasons, and for days, and years" (Gen. 1:14). Reading this in English, one might assume that "seasons" refers to winter, spring, summer, and fall, which are clearly a result of the angle of the sun as it hits the earth. However, this is a poor rendition of the Hebrew word mo'edim; the heavenly lights are there to determine the time of God's appointments. His celestial Day-Timer was in place before the appearance of Adam, who was designed to keep those appointments and have intimacy with his Creator.

While a week is commonplace, there is another unit of time ordained by divine fiat that has rarely been followed. It is the year of Jubilee, the *Yuvel* (ויבל), which occurred every fiftieth year. The theme of the Jubilee year was liberty from slavery, sin, and debt. It was about having inheritances restored to people and their families so each man could return to the possessions God had given him (Lev. 25:8–17).

An analysis of the demographic data recorded in Genesis indicates that the exodus took place approximately 2,500 years or fifty Jubilees after creation. (See Appendix A: Table of the Early Jubilees.) This was an event that was all about setting captive Israel free from its bondage to pharaoh, foreshadowing the liberation of mankind from its bondage to sin; it is fitting that it took place on the Jubilee of Jubilees.

Jesus inaugurated His ministry by standing in the synagogue to read, "as was his custom," and He didn't read some random passage, but the portion from the scroll of Isaiah that was read on the Day of Atonement at the start of a Jubilee year (Luke 4:16–21).[20] It would have been the thirtieth Jubilee since the exodus.

Almost 2,000 years have passed since the Jubilee that occurred during Jesus' first coming. The fortieth Jubilee is fast approaching. The next Jubilee must be significant. There will have been 40 Jubilees since the church was conceived, 70 since the ketubah was proclaimed at Mount Sinai and 120 since the creation of mankind. For 120 Jubilees God has been pleading with man to turn from his wicked ways, wooing His bride, longing for a holy people restored to the perfection He had envisioned as He fashioned Adam and Eve.

Just prior to the flood, God pronounced judgment on the human race: "And the LORD said, My spirit shall not always strive with man, for that he also [is] flesh: yet his days shall be an hundred and twenty years" (Gen. 6:3 AV). This cannot refer to a new limit on the life span of human beings; Psalms states a man generally lives 70 or 80 years (Ps. 90:10), while there are plenty of examples of men after the flood who significantly outlived 120 years. For instance, Abraham lived to be 175 (Gen. 25:7); Isaac 180 (Gen. 35:27); and Jacob 147 (Gen. 47:28).

However, the construction of this sentence is unusual, since the word "year" is singular; in Hebrew, such a distinction is like setting it in a bold font, pointing to something beyond the surface meaning. I believe that the "year" of mankind is 120 Jubilees, 6,000 years, and then God shall set up His throne of judgment as Daniel and John attest (Dan. 7; Rev. 19–20).

The Timing of the Birth

The bride has been betrothed, the marriage has been consummated, the Holy Spirit has come upon the bride, and she has conceived. Now we are in a time of gestation, waiting for the birth, an illustration of the plan of God demonstrated by every birth on the planet. The forty Jubilees coincide with the forty weeks of gestation. Interestingly, this pattern was repeated by the years that Israel wandered in the wilderness. From the time that Gods holy nation was conceived at the crossing of the Red Sea to the time it was birthed at the crossing of the Jordan River was forty years.

The growth of a baby from a multiple-celled zygote (the church of Acts 2) to the infant heading out the birth canal (Rev. 12) is a prophetic picture of this church age and God's plan for the fullness of time. The church is like an expectant mother nearing the end of her third trimester feeling like the baby will never come! However, you can be absolutely sure it will happen, and its timing is somewhat predictable. Granted, nobody knows the exact time. Even today, expectant mothers are confidently quoted an official due date, but it is considered "normal" to deliver as much as two weeks before or after.[21]

Jesus confirmed there is a similar "due-date window" for his return: "But of that day and hour knoweth no [man], no, not the angels of heaven, but my Father only" (Matt. 24:36 KJV). Even if we don't know the exact moment of His return, Scripture gives us enough information to estimate a due date. Like those doing modern prenatal care, we have an outline of what to expect in the last trimester of waiting; it's written in the scroll.

Just as there were two witnesses to the signing of the ketubah by our heavenly bridegroom—Moses and Joshua—there are two witnesses concerning the scroll—the prophet Daniel and the Apostle John.

Daniel and the Scroll

Daniel spent most of his life as a slave serving in the court of the kings of Babylon. Like Joseph before him, he was enslaved as a youth but became a top royal advisor thanks to the wisdom and blessing of God that was upon him. In the first half of his book, Daniel records the high points of his ministry in chronological order from his arrival in Babylon as a youth (Dan. 1) to his service under the Persian king Darius (Dan. 6). It is filled with visions concerning the city of Babylon and classic Sunday school stories: King Nebuchadnezzar's forgotten dream of a giant statue with a head of gold and feet of mixed iron and clay (Dan. 2); Daniel's three friends in the fiery furnace (Dan. 3); the disembodied handwriting on the wall (Dan. 5); and perhaps the most famous of all, Daniel in the lion's den (Dan. 6).

The seventh chapter of Daniel is pivotal. From this point, he recounts a series of prophetic visions (in Hebrew), including those concerning the "time of the end." However, Daniel chose to write both his testimony and chapter 7 in Aramaic, the most commonly used language before the conquest of Alexander the Great, the language in which commerce, trade, diplomacy, and communication were conducted throughout the Middle East.[22]

Daniel wrote his vision of four beasts rising up out of the sea in Aramaic because it pertained to worldwide events and was intended for all people. It is a brief overview of four global epochs in history that culminate with the Day of Judgment by the Ancient of Days and the Son of Man coming on the clouds of heaven. All the beasts are ravaging predators, but the fourth beast, which is so terrifying that Daniel can describe only its teeth and claws, rises up out of the world system with a specific agenda against the people of God (Dan. 7:7-28).

The rest of Daniel records prophetic visions in Hebrew, the language of God's communication with His people. At the end, Daniel is told to seal the scroll containing what God has shown him.

> [4]But thou, O Daniel, shut up the words, and seal the book, [even] to the time of the end: many shall run to and fro, and knowledge shall be increased. (Dan. 12:4 KJV)

> [8]And I heard, but I understood not: then said I, O my Lord, what [shall be] the end of these [things]? [9]And he said, Go thy way, Daniel: for the words [are] closed up and sealed till the time of the end. (Dan. 12:8–9 KJV)

The visions shown to Daniel were not to be revealed until the "time of the end"; only then would the scroll be unsealed and the events recorded by Daniel unfold.

John and the Scroll

Centuries later, Israel had returned to the land; the temple had been rebuilt; the Messiah had come, died, risen, and ascended into heaven; and the fledgling church was under Roman persecution. The Apostle John was shown a vision while he was held prisoner on the

Isle of Patmos, not a new revelation, but a more detailed version of Daniel's vision. John is shown the scroll of Daniel, the one written and sealed until the "time of the end."

> ¹And I saw in the right hand of him that sat on the throne a book written within and on the backside, sealed with seven seals. ²And I saw a strong angel proclaiming with a loud voice, Who is worthy to open the book, and to loose the seals thereof? ³And no man in heaven, nor in earth, neither under the earth, was able to open the book, neither to look thereon. ⁴And I wept much, because no man was found worthy to open and to read the book, neither to look thereon. ⁵And one of the elders saith unto me, Weep not: behold, the Lion of the tribe of Juda [sic], the Root of David, hath prevailed to open the book, and to loose the seven seals thereof. ⁶And I beheld, and, lo, in the midst of the throne and of the four beasts, and in the midst of the elders, stood a Lamb as it had been slain, having seven horns and seven eyes, which are the seven Spirits of God sent forth into all the earth. ⁷And he came and took the book out of the right hand of him that sat upon the throne. ⁸And when he had taken the book, the four beasts and four [and] twenty elders fell down before the Lamb, having every one of them harps, and golden vials full of odours, which are the prayers of saints. ⁹And they sung [sic] a new song, saying, Thou art worthy to take the book, and to open the seals thereof: for thou wast slain, and hast redeemed us to God by thy blood out of every kindred, and tongue, and people, and nation; ¹⁰And hast made us unto our God kings and priests: and we shall reign on the earth. (Rev. 5:1–9 KJV)

Daniel and John bear witness to this momentous, heavenly event. One testifies about the writing and sealing of the scroll, and the other about its opening, declaring to us who had the authority to unseal it. Both record the impact of the scroll on world events. Jesus, the

Lamb of God, has the authority to break open the seals but only at the perfect time, according to criteria revealed to Daniel. John watches as the scroll is handed to the Lamb of God, who opens it, seal by seal, triggering the ride of the four horsemen.

When did the "End Times" Start?

John said he was in the end times (1 John 2:18). Paul said he was in the end times (1 Cor. 7:29). Peter thought he was in the end times (1 Pet. 4:7). Many believers today feel we are in the end times too, so when did the end times actually start? Were the writers of the New Testament mistaken in thinking they were living in the last days? While this is a popular conclusion it is a dangerous one, since it implies that Scripture is not without err!

Perhaps there is an alternative explanation. What if being in the end times is like being pregnant? It can be asked, when does a pregnancy start? We know that life starts at conception, political rhetoric notwithstanding. A baby is a baby the whole forty weeks. So it is with the end times; the "time of the end" unfolds during the entire 2,000 years of "gestation."

Jesus used the language of pregnancy and birth to describe His return. He prophesied,

> ⁶And ye shall hear of wars and rumors of wars: see that ye be not troubled: for all [these things] must come to pass, but the end is not yet. ⁷For nation shall rise against nation, and kingdom against kingdom: and there shall be famines, and pestilences, and earthquakes, in divers places. ⁸All these [are] the beginning of sorrows. (Matt. 24:6–8 KJV)

This last phrase, "the beginning of sorrows," is the key to understanding this passage and parts of Revelation. The Greek word translated "sorrows" is *odin* (ὠδίν), meaning labor pains.[23] Thus, the "beginning of sorrows" refers to the contractions that get the body ready for labor and are responsible for false labor. Modern medicine calls them Braxton-Hicks contractions. The fact that Jesus says "the end is not yet" confirms that wars, rumors of wars, nation rising against nation and kingdom against kingdom are prelabor contractions and not the actual birth.

Braxton-Hicks contractions can start at twenty-eight weeks of gestation. *Taber's Medical Dictionary* defines Braxton-Hicks as "an intermittent, painless contraction that may occur every 10 to 20 minutes." While many mothers would argue the painless part of the Braxton-Hicks definition, some find them merely uncomfortable, and others barely notice them.[24]

When the timeline of the church history is marked into forty Jubilee periods (2,000 years) and compared to forty weeks of prenatal development, there is an amazing relationship. According to this timeline, we would expect to detect Braxton-Hicks contractions sometime in the latter half of the fifteenth century AD. In the following chapter, we shall survey events of the time to see if any might be signs of "the beginning of sorrows."

CHAPTER 4:

The Scroll Opens

> ⁴But thou, O Daniel, shut up the words, and seal
> the book, [even] to the time of the end: many shall
> run to and fro, and knowledge shall be increased.
> (Dan. 12:4 KJV)

The fifteenth century was a period of momentous change that
transformed Europe from a traditional medieval society into a
modern one. The "time of the end," when the Lamb of God opened
the scroll, was heralded by unprecedented and exponential increases
in the speed of transportation and the dissemination of knowledge.
These changes are not obscure events that only scholars and a few
conspiracy theorists know; these are events most of us studied in
elementary school. They are known as the Age of Discovery and the
printing revolution.

To and Fro: The Age of Discovery

Daniel's first criterion for the opening of the Scroll was that
"many shall run to and fro." The phrase "to and fro" is the translation
of the Hebrew *shuwt* (שׁוּט), which describes the actions of rowers
or the movements of the wings of birds. Thus, we have the image of
men traveling back and forth across the planet at the speed of birds'
wings. The Age of Discovery, also known as the Age of Exploration,
was marked by an unprecedented increase in travel and navigation
so significant it was like the opening of Pandora's Box. Some have

referred to it as a bridge between the Middle Ages and the modern world.[25]

The Age of Discovery was the result of the intersection several fifteenth century trends including political and economic pressures, a looming international financial crisis, and groundbreaking technological developments. These combined to overturn the status quo and provide both the motivation and the means for global circumnavigation. Led by Portuguese and Spanish explorers, Europeans embarked on worldwide quests to discover new trade routes to Asia. In the process, they explored previously unknown countries, set up overseas trade monopolies, and eventually established colonies in every corner of the globe.

The Fall of Constantinople

Constantinople had served as the eastern capital of the Roman Empire and had been the center of Byzantine (Eastern Orthodox) Christianity for centuries. When the city fell to the Ottomans in 1453, it closed the traditional Far Eastern trade routes and effectively cut off Europe from all access to the spice trade. The resulting crisis forced Europeans to search for new trade routes and to rethink the traditional business paradigm.

Before the Age of Discovery, intercontinental trade was limited to items that were small, lightweight, and extremely valuable. They were handled by a series of merchants, each of whom who transported goods over a relatively short leg of the total journey. The spice trade is a great illustration of this. For centuries, Arab sailors would export spices from India and the Far East and sell them at ports along the Persian Gulf and the Red Sea. Muslim caravans would then transport the spices overland to the Mediterranean, where they would be sold to Venetian traders, who in turn, sold them to European merchants for distribution in European market towns.

Today, we associate spices with the culinary arts, pleasurable but not essential for life. However, spices played a much more significant role in medieval Europe; they were of vital importance in medicine, food preservation, perfumery, and religious rituals. With the collapse of commerce with the Middle East, there was an urgent search for alternative trade routes to India and the Far East. The promise of lucrative profits for those who succeeded made voyages in unknown waters worth the risk.[26]

Financial Crisis

The European spice trade had been financed by the Venetian gold ducat, the most widely used coin in the world for over five centuries.[27] This system worked well as long as gold was plentiful. However, by the 1400s, European gold supplies were becoming increasingly scarce, and mines had failed to keep pace with the flood of gold traveling to Asia in trade. According to the theories of the day, the ownership of gold and silver was a necessary prerequisite for acquiring wealth and holding power.

The impending crises were both economic and political. On one hand, this bullion shortage spurred innovation, leading to the development of a complex banking industry; the first bank was established in Genoa in 1407, with branches in Flanders (Bruges), England, and Portugal.[28] On the other hand, kings were anxious to acquire gold from foreign sources by whatever means, including conquest. King Ferdinand of Spain ordered the Spanish explorers of the New World "Get gold, humanely if you can, but all hazards, get gold."[29]

Henry the Navigator's School of Navigation

Europeans were able to head off their looming crisis because of shipping and navigation advances fostered by Prince Henry the Navigator, third son of King Juan I of Portugal, at his school of navigation. This was not a school in the modern sense but a gathering of experts in the arts of navigation, cartography, and shipbuilding.[30]

Master navigators at the school developed techniques that allowed sailors to accurately navigate far from land; their tools included the quadrant, the astrolabe, and the dry compass. The latter innovation mounted the compass needle in a box rather than floating it in a bowl of water, making it easier to use in rough seas.[31] The metal astrolabe, developed by Abraham Zacuto of Lisbon, royal astronomer in the court of Henry's great nephew King Juan II, was significantly more precise than wooden ones. This, coupled with Zucuto's highly accurate astronomical tables, enabled Portuguese ships to navigate to Brazil and India.[32]

In the past, sailors had used portolan charts, which gave useful details about ports and coastal features, which limited their usefulness to relatively small bodies of water such as the Mediterranean; they were of little help on long ocean voyages. Cartographers at Prince Henry's school drew maps based on the new observations of returning explorers and data derived from new surveying techniques that combined readings from the compass, sextant, and later, the telescope. Because these maps took the earth's curvature into account, they were far more accurate than the portolan charts they replaced.[33]

In addition to his navigation center, Prince Henry sponsored numerous voyages down the coast of western Africa as far south as Guinea for the purpose of discovery and trade—and with the hope of finding an alternative spice route.[34] Under his direction, shipbuilders developed the caravel, a lightweight, easily maneuvered ship that used lateen sails, which allowed it to tack into the wind. Its small capacity limited its use as a merchant vessel, but its speed made it ideally suited for long-distance excursions.[35]

Navigating Around the Globe

These new shipping technologies triggered a flurry of overseas exploration. In 1488, Portuguese nobleman Bartolomeu Dias sailed around the southern tip of Africa (later named Cape of Good Hope), putting to rest the idea that the Indian Ocean was landlocked.[36] By 1498, Vasco da Gama, also Portuguese, had journeyed to India via this route.[37]

Spain was not about to be outdone by its Portuguese rivals. The Spanish crown sponsored a transatlantic voyage in 1492 in hopes of finding passage to the Indies via the Atlantic. Columbus, of course, accidentally discovered the New World, and other expeditions soon followed. In 1500, the Portuguese launched a transatlantic envoy of their own, laying claim to Brazil.[38] Finally, Ferdinand Magellan, a Portuguese captain serving the king of Spain, circumnavigated the globe it in three years (1519–22), the first to do so.[39]

In three short decades, the Age of Discovery had laid the foundations for European dominance and launched the world precipitately into unprecedented travel. Men were sailing "to and fro" over the entire globe!

Knowledge Shall Increase: The Printing Revolution

Daniel foretold a second prerequisite for the opening of the scroll: knowledge was going to "increase." The Aramaic word *rabah* (רבה) literally means to "to be multiplied."[40] During the fifteenth century, while the Age of Discovery was starting, the volume of knowledge was increasing exponentially, and the number of people who had access to information was expanding rapidly as well. However you looked at it, knowledge was on the rise!

During the Renaissance, it was believed that an accomplished man could do all things well. It was actually thought possible for a man to develop expertise in every field of knowledge as well as the arts, social graces, and athletics. Men such as Leonardo da Vinci, Michelangelo, and Francis Bacon were examples of Renaissance Men.[41] Today, the body of information in almost every discipline is multiplying daily, making it very difficult for people to remain current even in a single profession.

The invention of the printing press changed the world by allowing the widespread dissemination of information, ideas, and technology. The printing press has been called the most influential invention of the second millennium AD, comparable with the Industrial Revolution. Indeed, its impact on European society was so immense it is sometimes referred to as the printing revolution.

The printing press, invented around 1440 by Johannes Gutenberg in Mainz, Germany, featured movable type, die-cast letters that could withstand heavy use and be easily rearranged to print different material. The idea spread like wildfire across Europe. By 1500, over 20 million books had been printed throughout the continent. Within the century, European printers were capable of producing about 3,600 pages a day. In contrast, Chinese printers using manual methods had a maximum capacity of 40 pages a day.[42]

Francis Bacon declared that typographical printing had "changed the whole face and state of things throughout the world."[43] History confirms this; the printing press caused exponential growth in the availability of knowledge and the ability to exchange ideas. As a result, it was instrumental in the inception of the Renaissance, the Protestant Reformation, the scientific revolution, the democratization of knowledge, and the rise of nationalism.

The Renaissance

The Renaissance describes the cultural movement that ran from the fourteenth to the seventeenth centuries, starting in northern Italy and spreading throughout Europe. It was characterized by humanism, which studied of the accomplishments of man, the resurgence of classical writings, and the adoption of the ancient Greco-Roman educational system. In addition, newly published works written in the modern languages took their place alongside those written in Latin, the preeminent language of scholars since ancient times. [44]

The printing press played a key role in the Renaissance by making possible the dissemination of new ideas. Key writings from ancient Greece and Rome were widely circulated among western European readers for the first time thanks to Aldus Manutius, a Venetian and the leading book publisher of the High Renaissance. Greek scholars who had migrated west after the fall of Constantinople were hired to write Greek lesson books and to assist in the publication of the Greek classics. Manutius printed editions of classical writings, both Greek and Latin, in his octavo (pocketbook) format, using his patented *italic* print, increasing their accessibility.[45]

In addition, the writings of key thinkers of the period enjoyed wide distribution thanks to publication. For example, *The Prince*, written in Italian by statesman Machiavelli, was widely circulated in printed form despite its highly controversial content. He distinguished traditional political idealism from a new political pragmatism dedicated to acquiring and keeping power, and he laid the foundations of modern politics.[46]

Oration on the Dignity of Man, by Pico della Merandola, has been called the "Manifesto of the Renaissance." In it, Merandola argued that men could rise up in the "Chain of Being" through their intellectual capacities, which not only glorified humanity but also introduced the concept of promotion on the basis of people's merits rather than their stations at birth.[47]

The Reformation

Just as publishing the classics ignited the Renaissance, printing the Bible fueled the Reformation. The first volume to be printed was the Gutenberg Bible, an edition of the Vulgate (Latin) Bible.[48] The Greek New Testament *Textus Receptus* was published side by side with a Latin translation by Desiderius Erasmus of Rotterdam, a humanist scholar who had a profound influence on both Protestant and Catholic theologians. Erasmus' work made the Greek New Testament texts available to Northern Europeans for the first time, thanks to the printing press.[49] Other religious publications, including inexpensive theological pamphlets, soon followed.[50]

It is hard to overestimate the impact the increasing availability of Scripture had on the church. Previously, handwritten Bibles were rare and extremely expensive. In addition, Europe had experienced high levels of illiteracy for centuries, even among lower-ranking clergy. The printing press allowed Scripture and new theological ideas, including controversial ones, to spread quickly.

For example, when Martin Luther posted his Ninety-Five Theses on the door of Castle Church in Wittenberg on October 31, 1517, he initiated a formal protest against corruption in the church. Normally, such rebellion would have been suppressed and his writings burned, and Luther might have gone down as an obscure footnote in history. However, this is not what happened. By January 1518, his theses had been translated into German, printed, and widely circulated. Within two weeks, copies had spread throughout Germany; within two months they were disseminated throughout Europe.

The printing press provided the means for a local dispute to become the international controversy known as the Protestant Reformation. Luther's writings enjoyed wide circulation; in fact, he was the most extensively read author of his generation. Between 1518 and 1520, 300,000 printed copies of Luther's tract were distributed.[51] In 1534, Luther published his German translation of the Bible, which had a significant influence on the development of the German language and on the Protestant Church. [52]

Tyndale's Bible had a similar impact in England. He was the first to translate the Bible into English for a lay readership, using Hebrew texts and Erasmus' Greek *Textus Receptus*. Subsequent translations have borrowed heavily from Tyndale's work, including Henry VIII's Great Bible, published four years later, and the Authorized King James Version, published in 1611. It has been estimated that the King James' scholars took nearly 84 percent of the New Testament and 76 percent of the Old Testament from Tyndale's translation.[53]

The Scientific Revolution

The scientific revolution resulted from the publication of two works: Nicolaus Copernicus' *On Revolutions of the Heavenly Spheres* and Andeas Vesalius' *On the Fabric of the Human Body in Seven Books*. Both disproved scientific theories that had prevailed since their origin in ancient Greece. Together they laid the foundations of modern science.

Copernicus' book, published in Nuremberg in 1543, used planetary observations and mathematics to prove the heliocentric view that the planets, including earth, revolved around the sun. This was in direct opposition to the widely accepted geocentric idea that the sun, stars, and planets rotated around the earth.[54]

Vesalius was a physician who taught at the school of medicine in Padua, Italy. Contrary to traditional methods, he dissected corpses to demonstrate human anatomy in his lectures. His book series, published in 1546, duplicated these demonstrations using illustrations printed with high-quality woodcuts.[55]

The printing press also encouraged the scientific revolution by facilitating the exchange of information necessary for scholarly debate. Printing allowed hundreds or thousands of copies of a single work to be distributed all over Europe at a greatly reduced cost. Publication facilitated the exchange of ideas within a scientific community and eventually led to the establishment of academic journals.

In addition, printing rewarded authors financially, allowing them to receive a share of the profits. Previously, there were variations from copy to copy of the same work, but mass printing ensured that each copy was identical and clearly reflected the intent of the author. Since exact citations were now possible, it introduced the rule "one Author [sic], one work (title), one piece of information."[56]

Democratization of Knowledge

The printing press made knowledge accessible to an increasingly expansive readership. Presses that could print hundreds of pages per day were incomparably more efficient than manually copied books and prices fell accordingly. Books were printed in vernacular languages, so access to information no longer required a classical education and knowledge of Latin. For the first time in a millennium, someone could read literature, scientific works, or the Bible without first having to master a foreign language.[57]

Rise of European Nation States

The reinforcement of vernacular languages sowed the seeds of nationalism. People were bonded by common tongues, cultures, and traditions, as well as the stories were being published. By 1500, many parts of Europe was being transforming from a patchwork of feudal domains into modern nation states.

The burgeoning merchant class supported the development of national governments both financially (wealth was no longer based on land alone) and by providing a source of labor for the army of civil servants needed to run a large, modern bureaucracy. Thanks to the broadened tax base, kings could rely on professional infantry-based armies rather than small armies comprised of loyal vassal knights. Even the church was increasingly divided along national lines, with ecclesiastical appointments controlled by kings, who frequently took a percentage of church revenues.[58]

The Time of the End

The intersection of the Age of Discovery and the printing revolution brought about rapid changes that ensured nothing would ever be the same again; a thousand year-old culture and its rules for living were eroded within a couple of generations. The prophecy of Daniel 12 had been fulfilled.

These two movements ushered in the opening of the first seal of the scroll, followed closely by the White Horseman going forth "conquering and to conquer." The history of white imperialism, which marched around the globe until the whole earth was under its feet, demonstrates the truth and the breathtaking accuracy of God's Word.

CHAPTER 5:

An Exponential Curve

We live in a world where satellites spin about the planet, men in spacecraft traverse the United States in minutes and the globe in an hour and a half.[59] "The world's commercial jet airlines carried approximately 1.09 billion people on 18 million flights" in the year 2000, exceeding 49,000 flights per day,[60] and Boeing twin jets alone perform about 40,000 long-range overseas flights each month.[61] Clearly, the people of today are traveling "to and fro" as never before imagined.

At the same time, it is becoming increasingly difficult not to be connected. As of 2010, there were an astounding 5 billion cell phone subscribers globally.[62] The number of people who surf the Internet has swelled by more than 500 percent between 2000 and 2011, with current statistics showing 2.3 billion users around the globe, with over 1 billion in Asia alone.[63] Social media sites such as Facebook, Twitter and LinkedIn have proliferated. The statistics for Facebook are particularly impressive.

> With over 500 million users, Facebook is now used by 1 in every 13 people on earth, with over 250 million of them (over 50%) who log in every day … 48% of young people said they now get their news through Facebook. Meanwhile, in just 20 minutes on Facebook over 1 million links are shared, 2 million friend requests are accepted and almost 3 million messages are sent.[64]

Even the old-fashioned book continues to multiply, although an increasing number of readers prefer eBooks over print editions. According to the United Nations Educational, Scientific and Cultural Organization, almost 2 million books are published worldwide each year.[65]

All this makes Portuguese caravels and German printing presses seem pathetically inefficient and outdated. Clearly, the fulfillment of Daniel's criteria for the "time of the end" is not a static moment but an exponential curve streaking across the plane of time.

The Four Horsemen

When John witnessed the opening of the scroll, he saw four horsemen ride forth in succession: White, Red, Black, and Pale or Green. Just before each horseman was released, there were revolutionary changes in transportation and communication technology. In each case, these changes created a dramatic increase in the speed and the volume of global travel and the dissemination of information.

As we have seen, the first revolution in travel and communication occurred in the 1400s; it was followed by events that specifically fulfilled John's vision of the White Horseman. In the same way, the opening of the second, third, and fourth seals were heralded by equally impressive changes. These occurred during the 1800s, the early 1900s and since the 1970s. Each of these transitions ushered in events that fulfilled the prophecies about the three remaining horsemen.

Transformation in the Nineteenth Century

The 1800s began in the world of Jane Austen, captured in her novels such as *Pride and Prejudice*, a world that moved at the leisurely pace of a horse and carriage. Over the next half century, society changed beyond all recognition through the introduction of steam-powered vehicles built of iron and steel and the emergence of mass media marketed to a highly literate population.

Steam-Powered Transportation

The impact of the steam engine on Western society had far-reaching consequences. The concept of steam power had been around for a long time, but James Watt developed an efficient engine that quickly became the dominant power source.[66] It fueled the Industrial Revolution, its factories, and the mass production of affordable consumer goods.

Steam-powered transportation soon followed. Locomotives used steam engines to pull a series of carriages on iron rails. A newly developed manufacturing process made boilers strong enough to safely travel through cities. Steam-powered trains quickly dominated land transportation, carrying consumer goods rapidly and cheaply to new markets and making long-distance food shipments economical for the first time. Railways also allowed passengers to travel inexpensively and efficiently.[67]

The same technology in steam-powered ships drastically reduced travel times and made ocean voyages safe and economical. The early steamships were wooden-hulled hybrids of steam and wind power. The first of these to cross the Atlantic was the *Great Western*, which completed the westbound crossing in less than sixteen days, a fraction of the time taken by sailing ships. Further innovation reduced the transatlantic crossing time to about eight days in the 1870s and under a week by 1900.[68] This, coupled with reduced fares, allowed the mass emigration of Europeans around the world. For the first time, individuals from many geographical, cultural, and ethnic backgrounds lived in proximity and intermarried, fundamentally altering human society.[69]

Publications for the Masses

Nineteenth century innovations in the publishing world produced inexpensive reading materials for the masses. At the same time, literacy rates nearly doubled, possibly because access to interesting reading material provided motivation for mastering literacy skills. A study on literacy rates in Victorian England found that in 1840, only half of the brides and two-thirds of the grooms were able to sign their names on marriage registers, but by the end of the century, most couples were sufficiently literate to write their signature.[70] In fact, the period enjoyed the highest level of literacy of all time.[71]

Serialized fiction was the great innovation of Victorian publishing houses. Many of the era's most gifted authors, including Charles Dickens, George Eliot, Thomas Hardy, Rudyard Kipling, Robert Louis Stevenson, and William Thackeray published their novels in installments. Because they were printed either as pamphlets or in popular magazines and newspapers over a period of many months, the costs of production could be recouped over multiple editions, lowering the purchase price. Books became affordable even for the lower classes. As a result of the unprecedented demand, serialized publication became the preferred method for releasing original works.[72, 73]

The newspaper business also underwent revisions that made information more readily available. Newspapers had been around since the seventeenth century, but the Industrial Revolution brought technological advances such as rotary printing presses that made newspapers faster and cheaper to print. As early as 1814, *The Times* (of London) had a press that was capable of printing more than a thousand pages a minute.[74] Later, the Penny Press made daily newspapers inexpensive enough to be purchased by the general public.[75]

The penny post, another nineteenth century innovation, revolutionized written communication. Although postal service was available before 1840, it was expensive, costing more than a working man's wages for a day. Furthermore, since postage rates were paid by the recipient rather than the sender, there was no guarantee the letter would accepted, making the system haphazard at best. All this changed when Queen Victoria signed into law the uniform penny postage. Mail service was transformed from

> an expensive tax for revenue to a civic service affordable to all social classes … Cheap, uniform postage … allowed Victorians to transcend geographical boundaries. Suddenly, it became possible to stay connected with friends and family despite relocation, emigration, and travel. More remarkably, due to prepayment, Victorians could communicate and conduct business directly with those outside of their circle of acquaintance.[76]

Can anyone say junk mail?

Communication over Wires

Time is money, and so is information; accelerating communication is of economic importance. During the 1800s, innovations in the printing world were dwarfed by new technologies that allowed messages to be accurately transmitted of over vast distances. This allowed investors and news outlets to access financial updates and current events within a day or two.

In 1837, the electrical telegraph was independently developed and patented in both the United Kingdom and the United States. The American version, which used Morse code, quickly connected the Pacific and Atlantic seaboards; the first transcontinental telegram was sent in 1861. Five years later, the first commercially successful transatlantic telegraph cable was laid. By 1902, the globe was encircled with telegraphs with the completion of the transpacific cable.[77]

During the 1870s, attempts were made to improve telegraph technology to allow multiple messages to travel through the wire simultaneously. The solution, patented by Thomas Edison, was the acoustic telegraph, a device that transmitted messages as electrical pulses of a specific audio frequency.[78] Edison and others continued to experiment with the acoustic telegraph technology in hopes of transmitting voice-generated electromagnetic pulses over wires. In 1876, Alexander Graham Bell patented the immensely popular telephone. By 1904, the United States alone had over 3 million phones connected by manual switchboard exchanges.[79]

Inventors around the world continued to tinker with acoustic telegraph technology, hoping to achieve wireless transmissions. Finally, Marconi succeeded in 1895, building a wireless system capable of transmitting signals over long distances—the first commercially successful radio. By the turn of the century, Marconi had established a radio station and a "wireless" factory in England.[80]

Transformation during the 1900s

Jules Verne's *Around the World in Eighty Days* chronicles the adventures of a Victorian Englishman who circumnavigates the globe with steam-powered public transportation. The fictitious tale was taken as a challenge by some, inspiring several real-life journeys. The most famous was by *The New York Times* reporter Nellie Bly, who encircled the globe in just over seventy-two days, an astonishing record, but one that was soon broken.[81]

However, the invention of flight in the first half of the twentieth century ratcheted up both the speed and mode of travel, as one Jules Verne copycat clearly demonstrated. In 1991, Maxim Naviede flew around the world in eighty-five hours (sixty-five flying hours) in a Cessna Citation 2, setting a new—soon to be broken—world record.[82]

The increased speed was made possible by the airplane, which has reduced a vast globe into a village. The Wright brothers are generally credited with the first successful fight in 1903, and it became evident that flying was something more than a novelty during World War I. Following the war, commercial flights, airmail, and the first jet engines were introduced. After 1947, aviation technologies developed during the Second World War were used to build wildly popular commercial airlines.[83]

The automobile had even more impact, at least in the Western world. The car was originally a toy for the rich, and few believed it would ever replace the horse and buggy. However, when Henry Ford's Model Ts rolled off the assembly line at a price the American worker could afford, he sold over a million of them by 1920. The impact was an unprecedented level of mobility that caused radical changes in the physical structure of society. People were no longer bound to living near their work or even near the railroad stations but could move into the garden-like suburbs springing up around the city core. Decreased transit times blurred the distinctions between urban and rural areas.[84]

Mass Communication

Mass communication was perfected during the twentieth century. In addition to print publications, the new media of radio, motion pictures, and television allowed news and other programming to reach ever-growing audiences. For the first time, governments and advertisers could deliver their messages to a significant portion of the population with little opportunity for rebuttal.

Radio first became commonplace during the 1920s and 1930s. Families would gather around the radio the way they had once gathered around the fire, listening to their favorite programs and keeping abreast of current events. By the end of World War II, radios had almost become ubiquitous; a 1947 survey found that 82 percent of Americans were listeners.[85]

Although radio programming was generally free from state control, at least in the West, even the American government used it to massage public opinion for its own purposes. For example, Franklin Roosevelt broadcast his "fireside chats" to get the public behind his agenda.[86] Later, during World War II,

> Washington not only censored dissident voices and produced its own propaganda programs, but also created a master schedule, dubbed the National Allocation Plan, for advancing its messages in radio comedies, soap operas, and other series.[87]

If a picture is worth a thousand words, a moving picture is worth a thousand times more in its power to impact viewers. In addition to the parade of spectacular (and spectacularly bad) stories that graced the silver screen, film technology was used to make newsreels, short documentaries about news and other items of current interest. They usually ran as short subjects before a feature film and allowed ordinary people to witness events on the other side of the world—for the first time.[88]

Television combined the visual impact of movies with the intimacy of radio. When television brought the world into people's homes, it was hailed both as the "key to enlightenment" and understanding, and a surefire way to produce a nation of morons. Television has given us an eyewitness view of a man walking on the moon, glimpses of life in faraway places, and access to cultural events beyond our means. It has also brought violence, disasters, murders (real and imagined), and a host of other negative behaviors into our homes, transforming our view. However, television's biggest impact has been the amount of time people spend watching it—an average of four or more hours a day—hours once spent on more productive activities.[89]

Revolutionary Changes of the Turn of this Century

As the world hurtled toward the twenty-first century, new technologies continued to accelerate transportation and communication. Flight broke the sound barrier, and space launches became routine. The personal computer, the Internet, and the cell phone opened the information floodgates, pushing us toward a *Brave New World*.

Ever-increasing speed is the key factor in modern transportation developments, epitomized by supersonic jets racing at the speed of sound. The Concorde was the first plane designed for commercial use capable of breaking the sound barrier. Built jointly by Britain and France, it entered service in 1976. Its passengers crossed the Atlantic in less than half the time of other airliners; its fastest transatlantic flight from London to New York was 2 hours, 52 minutes, and 59 seconds from takeoff to touchdown. The Concorde also holds the record for the fastest trip around the world, circumnavigating the globe in 32 hours, 49 minutes, and 3 seconds, set on the 500th anniversary of Columbus' departure for the New World.[90]

Then men embarked on space travel, going to the moon and launching satellites. Once the space shuttle made the regular launching of satellites economically feasible, everybody wanted in. More than fifty countries currently have satellites in orbit for observation of the earth, communications, navigation, weather monitoring, and research. Space stations and manned spacecraft also orbit the globe.[91]

Satellites have made it possible to view events on the other side of the globe in real time. While I was teaching in Massachusetts, I took an elementary school class to observe the excavation of a Roman trading vessel sunk deep in the Mediterranean. Nautical archeologists used underwater robots to do the dig, sending film images via fiber-optic cable to the ship above, where they were relayed via satellites to observation points around the world in seconds. The awe I felt was reminiscent of my parents' reaction to the first moon landing years before.

Another paradigm-changing use of satellites is GPS, global positioning system technology, which uses multiple satellite readings to accurately pinpoint a position on the globe. GPS technology is now widely applied in the fields of commerce, scientific research, tracking, and surveillance. In addition, GPS readings can be used to calculate the precise time, a feature that facilitates everyday activities such as banking, mobile phone operations, and even the control of power grids by synchronized hands-off switching. GPS is a key component in cell phone function, enabling calls to be transferred from one station to the next. It is used to ensure that disaster relief and emergency personnel can get to the right location as quickly as possible, to assist in cartography and navigation, and to track aircraft flight paths.[92]

Information access exploded with the advent of the personal computer, its cousin, the Internet, and the cell phone. Personal computers displaced most of the large mainframe computers that once filled rooms and required a full-time staff to operate. The compact size of personal computers allowed individuals to enjoy the advantages of computers at home. Word processing replaced the traditional typewriter. Spreadsheets, databases, and mail-merge functions made record keeping more efficient.[93]

Web browsers also made every personal computer a portal into a vast array of information via the Internet. Users can read hundreds of different newspapers, magazines, and books. They can shop for almost any product you can imagine, many of which are not available in traditional stores. They can listen to music, watch TV and movies, play games, chat with someone across the room or across the planet, pay bills, do their banking, and perform a myriad other activities. Never before has any generation had access to so much information.[94]

Mobile phones allow users to make and receive phone calls wherever there is access to cellular networks. In addition to making calls and sending text messages, these phones also function as Day-Timers, calendars, watches, address books, cameras, and onramps to the information highway. With the introduction of media on cell phones, they became the "fourth screen" (after movie, TV, and PC screens), and it is estimated that paid media content on cell phones was worth $31 billion in 2006 alone, exceeding that on Internet or TV.[95]

We live in a world of dazzling speed in which many people think nothing of flying between continents for a brief visit or spending hours each day commuting to work, where we are being constantly bombarded with a barrage of information, and where it is as easy to talk to someone in Delhi as it is to talk to someone in the neighborhood. Daniel's criteria for the "time of the end" simply match the world in which we live.

Chapter 6:

"Come and See"

> One witness shall not rise up against a man for any iniquity, or for any sin, in any sin that he sinneth: at the mouth of two witnesses, or at the mouth of three witnesses, shall the matter be established. (Deut. 19:15 KJV)

> But if he will not hear [thee, then] take with thee one or two more, that in the mouth of two or three witnesses every word may be established. (Matt. 18:16 KJV)

> This [is] the third [time] I am coming to you. In the mouth of two or three witnesses shall every word be established. (2 Cor. 13:1 KJV)

God always establishes His Word through the testimony of two or three witnesses. As we have seen, there were two who witnessed God signing the wedding ketubah on tablets of stone: Moses and Joshua. Two witnessed the events that will unfold in the last days: John and Daniel. Both described four powerful systems that would dominate the globe in succession, and both make mention of God's glorious throne.

John begins his testimony about the opening of Daniel's scroll by giving us a portrait of the celestial throne room, where he is shown those "things which must be hereafter" (Rev. 4:1 KJV). He described a place of awesome wonder, majesty, and glory; there is the irresistible presence of the One seated on the throne, and round about the throne are four beasts or living creatures. Once again, there are two eyewitnesses who testify concerning the appearance of the four living creatures: John and the prophet Ezekiel.

The Four Living Creatures

Ezekiel described the living creature as "a wheel in the middle of a wheel" (Ezek. 1:16 KJV), while John's account said that the creatures seemed to be "in the midst of the throne, and round about the throne, [were] four beasts full of eyes before and behind" (Rev. 4:6). It is as if they form a part of God's throne in the same way the cherubim of beaten gold were of one piece with the covering of the Ark of the Covenant, enveloping the space above the "mercy seat" from where God promised to commune with his people (Exod. 25:17–22).

John was dismayed to learn there was no one worthy to open the scroll; he rejoiced with all heaven when the Lamb of God stepped from the "midst of the throne and of the four beasts" to take the book and open the seals one at a time (Rev. 5). As the Lamb opens the first seal on the scroll, John is commanded by one of the living creatures to "come and see," witnessing the White Horseman riding forth: "And I saw when the Lamb opened one of the seals, and I heard, as it were the noise of thunder, one of the four beasts saying, Come and see" (Rev. 6:1 KJV).

This command to "come and see" is repeated as Jesus opens the first four seals, revealing each of the horsemen. The four living creatures or beasts are described in Revelation 4.

> ⁶And before the throne [there was] a sea of glass like unto crystal: and in the midst of the throne, and round about the throne, [were] four beasts full of eyes before and behind. ⁷And the first beast [was] like a lion, and the second beast like a calf, and the third beast had a face as a man, and the fourth beast [was] like a flying eagle. (Rev. 4:6–7 KJV)

Ezekiel also gives a detailed description of the faces of the four living creatures.

> As for the likeness of their faces, they four had the face of a man, and the face of a lion, on the right side: and they four had the face of an ox on the left side; they four also had the face of an eagle. (Ezek. 1:10 KJV)

John and Ezekiel are clearly describing the same being but list the four faces in different order. Ezekiel's portrayal is geometric, giving details about how the faces are seen in relation to each other. Beginning with the face of the man and going counterclockwise, you would see the man, lion, eagle, and some sort of male bovine (bull, ox or calf—see Image 1).

On the other hand, John's description lists the faces numerically: the lion, the bovine, the man, and the eagle. Superimposing John's order onto Ezekiel's vision forms a cross, as shown in Image 2.

John presents the living creatures according to the order in which they will introduce the four horsemen. In John's account of the opening of the seals, he refers to the living creatures only by number since he has already listed them earlier in the passage. Thus, we can infer that the lion introduces the White Horseman, the calf/bull introduces the Red Horseman,

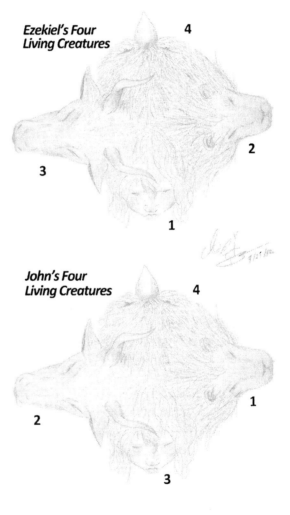

Ezekiel's Four Living Creatures

John's Four Living Creatures

the man introduces the Black Horseman, and the eagle introduces the Green Horseman.

In John's vision, four world systems are represented by four horsemen who ride forth as Jesus opens the seals of the scroll. In Daniel's account, the systems are symbolized by four beasts rising out of the sea. The first is a lion with eagle's wings, the second is a bear, the third is a four-headed leopard with four birds' wings, and the last is a terrifying beast with devouring teeth and stomping feet (Dan. 7:1–9).

As we have already seen, Daniel's criteria for the opening of the first seal started in the fifteenth century. In the next section, we will show how the prophecies concerning the kingly White Horseman, who went out "conquering, and to conquer," and the eagle-winged lion were perfectly fulfilled by the kings of Europe who set out to explore, colonize, and eventually dominate the whole world under white imperialism. The words of the prophets have been accomplished by the events of history in exacting detail.

Similarly, three successive world systems rise up, just as God predicted. In Part Three, we will see how Daniel's bear and the Red Horseman that takes peace from the earth and causes much killing have been fulfilled by Communism and the dominance of the Russian bear over global politics. Part Four will examine how the four-headed leopard and the Black Horseman are harbingers of the civil rights movement and bondage to debt and inflation. Finally, Part Five looks at Daniel's terrifying, nameless beast and the Fourth Horse, ridden by Death and followed by Hades. Going forth to kill in any way possible, this world system is in place until the return of Jesus.

The last days seem so terrible—so much a curse and so little a blessing. Many believers will respond in fear or behave like ostriches with their heads in the sand, pretending the second coming is something they need not think about. But Paul encourages us "For I reckon that the sufferings of this present time [are] not worthy [to be compared] with the glory which shall be revealed in us" (Rom. 8:18 KJV).

The fact is that there is not a person alive who has experienced life outside one or all these world systems. Life under the horsemen is normal to us, not an apocalyptic horror story, the stuff of nightmares. It is better characterized by the ever-increasing pain of contractions culminating in hard labor, as experienced by the "woman clothed in the sun," described in Revelation; "And she being with child cried, travailing in birth and pained to be delivered" (Rev. 12:2 KJV).

What the church needs is a prenatal guidebook, a spiritual Lamaze class of what to expect heading into the last days. Trust me—it is best to prepare for giving birth before you go into hard labor. That is the purpose of this book, to give us a clear picture of where we are in the timeline of the last days, so that we will not be among the foolish virgins who are unprepared for our Bridegroom's coming.

PART 2:

The White Horseman

¹And I saw when the Lamb opened one of the seals, and I heard, as it were the noise of thunder, one of the four beasts saying, Come and see. ²And I saw, and behold a white horse: and he that sat on him had a bow; and a crown was given unto him: and he went forth conquering, and to conquer. (Rev. 6:1–2 KJV)

³And four great beasts came up from the sea, diverse one from another. ⁴The first [was] like a lion, and had eagle's wings: I beheld till the wings thereof were plucked, and it was lifted up from the earth, and made to stand upon the feet as a man, and a man's heart was given to it. (Dan. 7:3–4 KJV)

CHAPTER 7:

With a Bow

¹And I saw when the Lamb opened one of the seals, and I heard, as it were the noise of thunder, one of the four beasts saying, Come and see. ²I saw, and behold a white horse: and he that sat on him had a bow. (Rev. 6:1-2 KJV)

Who Was the White Horseman?

While many have speculated about the identity of the four horsemen in Revelation, most conclude they represent future events; therefore, they fail to see the way God's Word lines up with world history. The purpose of this book is to demonstrate that the four horsemen represent four world systems or movements that are global in scope and influence. Each section will present historical, and later current, events as evidence that the criteria given in Revelation and corresponding passages in Daniel have been fulfilled. We will then use this criteria to sight these movements as they unfold.

John's description of the White Horseman indicates a system characterized by the following: it was ushered in by the explosive growth of knowledge and travel that began in the 1400s. The bow has significance in the movement and the color white is an integral part or somehow identifies it. Since the White Horseman is given a crown, political power must be held by royalty. He is introduced by a lion and Daniel's corresponding beast is a lion with eagle's wings, making the lion of symbolic importance.

The one group that fulfilled all these requirements was the Europeans. First, both the Age of Discovery and the printing revolution were birthed in fifteenth century Europe, beginning the process of modernization. It was the ability of the printing press to quickly disseminate new ideas and technology, particularly military technology, that gave Europeans the upper hand in their dealings with the nations they encountered in their travels.

Second, the color white epitomizes Europeans as a group. Even today, people of European origins are classified as white. Throughout the period of their domination, Europeans were largely confident of the superiority of the white race over others. For many colonists, dark skin was a sure sign of stupidity regardless of evidence to the contrary. Even within the Caucasian race, "fairness" was a highly sought-after trait. Northern Europeans often considered themselves superior to their swarthier brethren to the south. This prejudice was only entrenched by the fact that much of the royalty of southern Europe were fair skinned and blue eyed, unlike their subjects, thanks to years of intermarriage with northern royals.

Third, the lion was an important symbol, frequently used in European heraldry, despite the fact these animals had been extinct in Western Europe since 1 AD—the Romans were forced to import lions from northern Africa for their arena events.[96] Furthermore, "The Lion of Judah" was a title of Jesus, evoking the concept of the "divine right of kings" and increasing the lion's popularity as a symbol among European royalty.

Fourth, the White Horseman was given a crown; the political system of early modern Europe was based on hereditary monarchies and the absolute authority of kings. The medieval feudal system had ensured that only nobility could rule and that the rest of the population knew their "place." This system, or at least the appearance of it, remained intact until after World War I. Various styles of monarchy evolved in different parts of Europe: the absolutism of France, the constitutional monarchy of Britain, and the delicate balance of power between the monarch and his princes in the Holy Roman Empire. These nuances did not erase the conviction, held by most Europeans until the latter part of the 1800s, that monarchy was the only proper form of government.

The White Horseman and His Bow

> And I saw, and behold a white horse: and he that sat
> on him had a bow; (Rev. 6:2 KJV)

The first detail we are given about the White Horseman is that he carried a bow, which sounds pretty mundane. After all, the bow had been used as a weapon and hunting tool for centuries, with the earliest evidence for archers dating back to prehistory.[97] At the same time, the bow is hopelessly antiquated compared with military technology after the introduction of gunpowder.

This verse is the only New Testament reference to the bow, but the Greek word for "bow" was extensively used in the Septuagint in reference to the weapon. The verb "had" is in the past tense and active voice, which indicates that the horseman was actively in full possession of the bow at the time we first see him, before he is given a crown or goes out to conquer.

Archery was a highly valued skill in the ancient world and often attributed to the gods. In Europe, Apollo was one of the most important of the Greek and Roman pantheon. He was not only the god of the sun, medicine, and the arts but also the deity of archery,[98] aided by his twin sister, Diana or Artemis, the goddess of the hunt and childbirth.[99] Many ancient societies, including Israel, symbolized children as arrows in a man's quiver (Ps. 127:5).[100]

In ancient warfare, archers frequently formed auxiliary units that shot at the enemy from a distance. The bow was also used very effectively by the warriors of mounted nomadic groups such as the Mongols and the Germanic tribes that invaded the crumbling Roman Empire.[101] However, the bow fell out of favor as a military weapon in medieval Europe due to the rise of knights or armored men-at-arms.

The Middle Ages experienced ongoing improvement in armor and defensive weapons that rendered the bow increasingly ineffective. In addition, the use of the bow was discouraged, even after the introduction of a high-power crossbow, capable of piercing through heavy armor. In 1139, Pope Innocent II responded to the devastating effectiveness of the crossbow by decreeing that it could be used only on "infidels" and not on Christians.[102]

The backbone of medieval warfare was men-at-arms, professional soldiers who functioned as heavily armored cavalry. Because the men-at-arms were extremely expensive to equip, they came almost exclusively from the highest ranks of society, including royalty. For this reason, warring European factions often found it more beneficial to hold captured combatants for ransom than to kill them.

A mounted knight in a full suit of heavy armor was considered the ultimate war machine, the elite of both military prowess and social standing. On the other hand, the bow was viewed as the weapon of the poor man and of little value in combat.[103] However, all this changed with the introduction of the longbow.

> With the advent of the longbow (ca. 1400), for the first time the average combatant could single-handedly fire a weapon, from a distance, that would penetrate even the best of available, man-portable armor. This was a revolution that introduced a combination of distance and force that would continue in its basic format up until the present. The longbow began the process of rendering the knight extinct...[104]

The Welsh and English longbow played a key role in select battles during the Hundred Years' War, most notably the Battle of Crecy (1346) and the Battle of Agincourt (1415). The Battle of Crecy has been called the beginning of the end of the age of chivalry. The English won a stunning victory through their use of the longbow and innovative military tactics. The 4,000 English men-at-arms and 7,000 longbow archers were up against 29,000 French knights and 6,000 mercenary crossbow archers. Longbow archers proved that a shower of arrows could be effective against armored knights, with many dying after their mounts were shot from under them. As many as a third of the French men-at-arms were killed. The crossbow archers fared no better; the English archers used their greater mobility and position on higher ground to stay out of range while picking off enemy archers.[105]

The Battle of Agincourt, made famous by Shakespeare's *Henry V*, was particularly noteworthy because Henry had led a small army of mostly archers to victory over a significantly larger French force. In the resulting fray, the front lines of the French were bombarded by "a terrifying hail of arrow shot," forcing them to cross the battlefield with visors closed. This so severely restricted their oxygen supply, they arrived at the battle line exhausted, scarcely able to lift their weapons.[106]

Both these battles are prime examples of what military historian Clifford Rogers calls the "military revolution" of the Hundred Years' War (1337–1453). According to Rogers,

> The armies that dominated the battlefields of Europe from the mid-eleventh century through the early fourteenth were composed primarily of feudal warrior-aristocrats, who owed military service for lands held in fief. They served as heavily armored cavalry, shock combatants, relying on the muscle power of man and steed, applied directly to the point of a lance or the edge of a sword. They fought more often to capture than to kill. The armies which conquered Europe's first global empires, on the other hand, differed from this description on *every single count*. They were drawn from the common population (albeit often led by aristocrats); they served for pay; they fought primarily on foot, in close-order linear formations which relied more on missile fire than shock action; and they fought to kill. The tremendous revolution in warfare represented by these changes was well underway by the middle of the Hundred Years' War, and solidly in place by the end of that conflict.[107]

The medieval style of warfare was severely limited by the immense cost of outfitting men-at-arms, which was borne by feudal lords obligated to give military service in exchange for their lands. Only a man of significant wealth could afford a horse and armor, an expense equal to about thirteen years' worth of a laborer's wages at the time. This limited a king's ability to amass an army, placing France, the largest and wealthiest kingdom of its day, in a position superior to all its neighbors. Winning a war against France was impossible without employing infantry, which was traditionally limited to a defensive wall to protect knights as they readied for the real battle. The English use of longbow archers within their battle plan was a perfect example of the offensive use of infantry.

Other small nations bordering France used similar strategies. One of the earliest examples is the Battle of the Golden Spurs (1302), in which Flanders, home of the highly lucrative textile industry, soundly defeated the French cavalry with its guild-raised militia. The French king had added Flanders to his domains, but his centralist policies triggered resistance and revolt. When the French army arrived to suppress the Flemish rebels, they met a well-trained infantry militia organized by city guilds.[108]

The preferred weapon of the Flemish was a *goedendag*, a chest-height club that thickened to about four inches in diameter at the top, where a sharp iron dagger was fastened. The Flemish infantry was able to use this weapon so effectively that it was said that a "Fleming with his goedendag would dare to fight against two knights on horse."[109]

During the Burgundian Wars, the Swiss confederation repeatedly demonstrated the ability of commoner pikemen to resoundingly defeat noble men-at-arms. The pike square consisted of a hundred infantrymen in a ten-by-ten formation, armed with ten to twenty-five-foot wooden poles tipped with an iron spearhead, similar to the weapon used by the ancient Greek phalanx. Like the longbow, it required significant training to use effectively. However, the Swiss pikemen mastered the formation to the point they could turn on a dime and coordinate offensive charges against the enemy. [110]

The first battle that demonstrated the superiority of the Swiss pike square was the Battle of Laupen in 1339, when the outnumbered Swiss defeated a vast unit of cavalry. Shocked chroniclers recorded comments like "God himself must have become a Bernese citizen."[111]

More than a century later, the army of Charles the Bold, Duke of Burgundy, was devastated by the Swiss pike square in the Battles of Morat (1476)[112] and Nancy (1477),[113] finally convincing military strategists of the wisdom of incorporating infantry drawn from commoners into their ranks. Pikemen became a standard part of European armies.[114]

The increasing importance of infantry weapons such as the longbow had significant social consequences. This explains why the king of France refused to permit longbow training in his domains. There is a relationship between military and political power; the growing political influence of commoners in England and Switzerland was a direct result of the importance of infantry on the battlefield.

In England, for instance, the House of Commons first began to meet regularly under Edward I, the monarch credited with developing military tactics based on the longbow. Under the reign of Edward III, the House of Commons became equal in importance to the House of Lords "… just as the importance of the archers drew even with that of the men-at-arms on the battlefield."[115]

The incorporation of commoners into the military had another unexpected effect: battles became bloodier and deadlier. In the medieval style of battle, men-at-arms would be captured for ransom, and the class structure guaranteed "fellowship in arms" among combatants from different nations. Commoners, on the other hand, did not expect their lives to be spared by a conquering enemy, nor did they show such quarter by sparing the lives of their captives. On the contrary, the class distinction between knight and commoner ensured unbridled animosity on the battlefield, where the enemy was to be "cut down like dogs." Infantry weapons such as longbows and pikes were designed to disable the enemy from a distance and required tight formations to be effective, which made surrendering or taking prisoners difficult at best. [116]

The "European" way of warfare that evolved out of the infantry revolution continued with minor changes well into the modern period. It was based on tight formations of well-drilled foot soldiers armed with "pike and shot"—the bow was later to be replaced by firearms—who engaged in a kill-or-be-killed struggle. The result was a new, more lethal style of warfare that characterized European armies at home and abroad.[117]

The infantry revolution, epitomized by the longbow, was a necessary precursor to worldwide empire building. Without it, European kings would not have been able to spare the manpower needed to assert their dominion over a third of the earth.[118]

Because of its broader recruitment pool and lower costs of equipment and training, a military system based on common infantry—and only such a system—could turn surplus agricultural population into large numbers of soldiers for export to the world at large. Thus, the Infantry Revolution was a necessary precondition for the European conquests of the sixteenth through eighteenth centuries.[119]

Revelation states "behold a white horse: and he that sat on him had a bow" (Rev. 6:2 KJV). The bow was the most successful of the weapons that triggered the infantry revolution of the fifteenth century and the Western style of warfare that followed. Without the infantry revolution, the White Horseman could not have "gone forth conquering and to conquer." The bow and all it implied had to be in place before the first seal was opened, just as John had prophesied.

CHAPTER 8:

Given a Crown

> And I saw, and behold a white horse: and he that
> sat on him had a bow; and a crown was given unto
> him... (Rev. 6:2 KJV)

Knowing that the White Horseman's possession of a bow symbolized
the infantry revolution that had already taken place, it is reasonable to
conclude that the crown John saw is equally significant. "Crown"—
stephanos (στέφανος) in Greek—can refer to either the royal head
ornament commonly understood in English or a wreath awarded
to the victor in battle or an Olympic-style game.[120] In early modern
Europe, the person most qualified to receive a crown was usually
the king.

Of course, almost every nation in Europe was ruled by a
monarch or some other titled nobility. What is unique about the
White Horseman is that he did not inherit the crown, as would be
expected in a land in which primogeniture was the rule. The crown
was specifically given to him, literally, "and given to the same was
a crown." The verb tense of "given" is the indicative (meaning it is
a simple statement of the facts), passive (meaning the horseman did
nothing whatsoever to get the crown but merely received it from the
giver), and aorist (meaning the emphasis is on the action of receiving
the crown without regard for its timing). This is in stark contrast to
the previous verb, which demands that the rider took action to have
ongoing possession of the bow.[121]

It is time to examine the historical record to see if any European rulers had been given their crowns, and if so, if the receiving of their authority had any relationship to the rise of European exploration and conquest. Amazingly, there is. As many European powers embarked on building overseas colonial empires, they did so under the dominion of rulers who came to power in some unusual manner that might be described as being "given a crown."

The royal houses of Europe were very different from their subjects not only socially and culturally but also genetically. Their pattern of alternative inbreeding and dynasty building created an interwoven family tree that fell like a fish net across the continent.

Royal lines were kept "pure" through strict enforcement of rules forbidding the marriage of princes to people below their stations or ranks, which even included nobility from their own countries. These rules continued to be observed into the late nineteenth and early twentieth centuries. The marriage of Queen Victoria's fourth daughter, Princess Louise, to the heir to one of the most powerful aristocratic houses in all Great Britain required a special dispensation from the queen. It was the first time a marriage between a daughter of the monarch and a British subject had been permitted since 1515, and it met with strong opposition from all sides.[122]

In Germany, the children of royal sons who entered into a "morganatic" marriage suffered a legal status similar to children born of a mistress; they were forbidden to inherit anything from their fathers, which meant they were likely to live in genteel poverty or ruin unless they entered a profession and became self-supporting. This distinction was made as late as 1900, when the Archduke Franz Ferdinand, the heir to the throne of the Austro-Hungarian Empire, entered into a morganatic marriage with a Bohemian countess. Although the bride received the title of princess, their children took their mother's name and rank and were excluded from imperial succession.[123]

At the same time, marriage between dynastic houses was a diplomatic tool; treaties were often sealed by the personal union of royalty. These dynastic unions could build power in one of two directions. Some royal families, such as the Habsburgs, used intermarriage to concentrate their holdings into one vast empire. For instance, Charles V, Holy Roman Emperor, inherited the domains of three leading European dynasties: the House of Habsburg, rulers of the Austrian and Holy Roman Empires, through his father; the House of Valois-Burgundy, rulers of the Duchy of Burgundy and the Lowlands, through his maternal grandmother, Mary of Burgundy; and the House of Trastámara, rulers of the Spanish Empire, through his mother.[124]

Others sought to extend their influence and ensure their national interests through a campaign of marrying children into multiple royal houses. Masters of this strategy include Maria Theresa of Austria-Hungary, who married six of her children into other royal houses of Europe,[125] and Queen Victoria of Great Britain, who became known as grandmother of all Europe.[126]

Who Was Given a Crown?

Looking at these fascinating stories of the kings who started the process of European empire building, it is important to note that they are each deviations from the norm, events that many worked hard to ensure would never happen. It is difficult to discern this unusual pattern because the crowns were not given simultaneously but gradually, one by one over a period of more than 300 years. There are many examples, but the following five clearly illustrate how European global expansion began under kings who literally had been "given a crown."

Portugal: Juan I and Prince Henry the Navigator

Spain may have gotten top billing in the discovery of the New World, thanks to Christopher Columbus, but Portugal was the first to embark on the Age of Discovery. Expeditions were launched along the coast of northern Africa as early as 1419 in part to stop Barbary pirates from raiding Portuguese fishing villages for captives to sell into slavery. Once Portuguese explorers returned with tales of Africa, the search was on. Generations of sailors traveled ever farther down the African seaboard until Bartolomeu Dias found a trade route around the Cape of Good Hope in 1488. By1500, the Portuguese had colonial outposts as far away as India and Brazil.[127]

Prince Henry the Navigator, third son of Juan I of Portugal, sponsored many voyages of exploration and founded his school of navigation during the reign of his father. Juan, who ruled from 1385 to 1433, was known to his people as Juan the Good or Juan of Happy Memory. Outside of Portugal, however, he was sometimes referred to as Juan the Bastard because he was the illegitimate son of King Pedro I of Portugal and as such should never have come to the throne.

At Pedro's death, the crown passed uneventfully to his legitimate son, Ferdinand I, Juan's half brother, and it should have been inherited by Ferdinand's only surviving child, Beatrice. However, she was married to the King of Castile (Spain). If Beatrice came to the throne, the two kingdoms would become one, something unacceptable to the leading nobles and merchants of Portuguese society.[128] The Council of the Kingdom, or Portuguese Cortes, crowned Juan the king and embarked on a war against Castile to guarantee an independent Kingdom of Portugal.[129]

King Juan I of Portugal had been given a crown.

Spain: Isabella and Ferdinand

The year 1492 was a pivotal one in Spanish history. It marked the completion of the *reconquista* of the Iberian Peninsula with the fall of Granada. This was the final step in creating the Kingdom of Spain that had begun years earlier with the personal union of Isabella, Queen of Castile-Leon, and her husband, Ferdinand, King of Aragon. It was the year the Spanish Inquisition was established to ferret out any Jews or Muslims in the country who had refused to convert to Christianity. Most important, from our perspective, it was the year of the inception of the Spanish Empire as Christopher Columbus set sail in search of a transatlantic trade route to the Indies and stumbled onto the New World.[130]

Ferdinand and Isabella sponsored the Columbus expedition as part of a race with Portugal to see who would be the first to reach the South Seas and its lucrative spice trade. As new discoveries were made and tensions mounted, a series of papal bulls, or edicts, were issued in an attempt to keep the peace among the Catholic nations, culminating with the Treaty of Tordesillas. Authored by Pope Alexander VI and ratified in 1494, the treaty formally drew a north-south line halfway between the Portuguese colony of the Cape Verde Islands and the islands Columbus claimed on his first voyage. In effect, the treaty gave Spain exclusive rights to all the Americas except Brazil.[131]

When Queen Isabella was born, few would have dreamed she would one day oversee the creation of a unified Spain and its vast overseas empire. Isabella had two brothers, Enrique (Henry IV), who was twenty-six years her senior, and Alfonso, two years her junior. After years of civil war and dynastic disputes, the Kingdom of Castile had achieved unification through the marriage of Isabella's grandparents, Henry III of Castile and Catherine, the only child of John of Ghent and Constance of Castile.[132]

However, the discontent among the nobility was rekindled by the ineptitude of Henry IV, who many considered the worst king in the nation's history. The situation was aggravated by his failure to produce an heir after nineteen years and two marriages. When Henry's daughter, Joanna, was finally born, it did little to avert a crisis; rumors of her father's impotence and her mother's flagrant adultery cast doubts on Joanna's legitimacy.[133]

Rebellious nobles soon rallied around the child Alfonso, proclaiming him to be the true heir. A truce was reached with the arrangement of marriage between Joanna and Alfonso, but rebellion resurged when the boy died. The nobles then turned to Isabella as their new champion, but this she refused. She did, however, help negotiate a settlement in which she was made her brother's legitimate heir. Later, she wed Ferdinand of Aragon with a clear understanding that they would be joint regents; their marriage unified Spain for the first time since the eighth century. [134]

Queen Isabella of Spain had been given a crown.

England and Scotland: the Birth of the British Empire

Once the rulers of Europe saw the amazing wealth that poured into Spain from the New World, everyone wanted to create colonial empires, none more so than Queen Elizabeth I of England. Despite this, little was accomplished during her reign other than exploration. In 1581, Sir Francis Drake was knighted for his services to the queen's cause, which included the capture of Spanish treasure ships and the circumnavigation of the globe.[135, 136]

Elizabeth issued patents of "discovery and overseas exploration" to Humphrey Gilford. His first voyage (1578) ended before it even crossed the Atlantic, and a second attempt (1583) resulted in a claim on Newfoundland but no settlements. Similarly, Sir Walter Raleigh received a patent in 1584, but only managed to found the ill-fated colony of Roanoke on an island in the Colony of Virginia colony off the coast of present day North Carolina.[137]

All this changed when James VI of Scotland ascended to the English throne. In 1604, within the first year of his rule, he negotiated a peace treaty between England and Spain. This freed his fleets from endless naval conflicts to focus on the business of establishing English colonial outposts. He encouraged the expansion of international trade by issuing charters to mercantile companies such as the English East India Company, founded 1600; the Virginia Company, 1607; and the Newfoundland Company, 1610. He also pursued trade agreements such as the one negotiated with Tokagawa Japan.[138] Colonies were soon established throughout North America, including Jamestown, St. Kitts, Barbados, and Nevis.[139]

That James became king of England is truly remarkable considering he descended from not one but two lineages specifically barred from inheriting the English throne. John of Ghent's children by his mistress were granted legitimacy as young adults on the condition they were excluded from succession to the throne. Joan Beaufort, John's granddaughter through this line, married James I of Scotland, rendering all future Scottish kings ineligible to rule England.[140]

Generations later, Margaret Tudor, the elder sister of Henry VIII, married James IV of Scotland; she was the grandmother of Mary, Queen of Scots.[141] According to Henry VIII's will and the Act of Succession of 1543, the descendants of the Scottish royal family were once again excluded from the English throne.[142] Nevertheless, James the VI of Scotland became King of England thanks to the covert dealings of Queen Elizabeth's political advisors, who had worked to ensure a seamless transfer of power at the queen's death. The parliamentary bill "Union of the Crowns" confirmed that James was king of both England and Scotland, although the two nations remained separate.[143]

This was not the first time James had been given a crown. Shortly after his birth, his father was murdered, and three months later, his mother, Mary, Queen of Scots, wed the number-one murder suspect. The following month, outraged Scottish barons arrested the queen and forced her to abdicate in favor of her son, James, only thirteen months old.[144]

King James I of England and VI of Scotland was given a crown—twice.

France: Henry IV, Prince of the Blood

Like the English, the French were eager to build an overseas empire. During the early sixteenth century, under a charter from Francis I, Jacques Cartier set out to find a northwest passage to the lucrative markets of Asia. He explored the Gulf of St. Lawrence and the St. Lawrence River but was unsuccessful at settling a viable colony.[145] Internal strife coupled with Spanish vigilance in protecting its trade monopolies prevented the French from establishing successful colonies until the early 1600s.

France's colonial empire began in 1605 during the reign of Henry IV with the construction of Port Royal at Acadia in what is now Nova Scotia. Three years later, Samuel De Champlain founded Quebec and the fur-trading colony of New France, which was to spread as far south as Louisiana in the Mississippi basin.[146]

The story of how the French crown was transferred from Francis I to Henry IV is fascinating. Henry II, son of King Francis I, spent most of his reign embroiled in wars with Austria and internal battles against the Huguenots (French Protestants who followed the teachings of Calvin). However, he had four surviving sons by his wife, Catherine de' Medici, giving every reason to assume his family line was secure.

Unfortunately, events did not go as planned. In 1559, Henry II died at the age of forty after being stabbed in the eye in an unfortunate jousting accident.[147] Thirty years later, Henry's entire male line was gone. His eldest son, Francis II, had wed the young Mary, Queen of Scots when they were only teenagers. He ascended the throne of France the following year but died eighteen months later from a brain abscess caused by an ear infection.[148]

His younger brother, Charles IX, became king when he was only ten. During his rule, France continued to be wracked by wars foreign (with Austria) and domestic (with the French Huguenots). Charles married as part of the peace settlement with Austria but died from tuberculosis shortly before his twenty-fourth birthday and before he was able to sire a son. He did have a daughter, but Salic law, the ancient legal system of the Franks, banned females from succession, and she subsequently died in early childhood.[149]

A third brother was crowned Henry III, and his reign continued to be plagued by religious civil wars. Although he married, he also proved unable to father a child. The situation became more critical after his heir and only remaining brother died of malaria on the battlefield in the Netherlands.[150] It was becoming increasingly clear that Henry de Bourbon of Navarre, the king's cousin twenty-two times removed, would inherit the throne.

Henry de Bourbon, known at court by the title "Prince of the Blood," was a descendant of Louis IX (d. 1270), king of France ten generations earlier. Henry de Bourbon was also the leading French Protestant, and as such he was the favored candidate among the Huguenots. De Bourbon had made several attempts to end the wars of religion, including marrying the Catholic sister of Charles IX. The wedding did not end French hostilities but triggered a wholesale massacre of Huguenots in Paris. Eventually, de Bourbon was forced to flee to the neighboring Kingdom of Navarre.[151]

Unfortunately, the Catholic League, led by Henry I, Duke of Guise, another contender for the throne, was dedicated to doing everything possible to keep Henry de Bourbon from inheriting. They exerted great pressure on King Henry III, forcing him to flee Paris. The Duke of Guise was assassinated by Royalist supporters. Six months later, the King was also assassinated. As he lay dying, he named Henry de Bourbon of Navarre the rightful heir to the French throne.[152]

Remarkably, the French accepted Henry as their king. He put an end to the wars of religion that had plagued his predecessors by formally converting to Catholicism while enacting laws that gave religious freedom to the Protestants.[153]

King Henry IV of France had been given a crown.

The Netherlands: The Prince of Orange

Understanding the unique story of the Netherlands requires some background knowledge of the dynasty building of the Habsburgs. The Netherlands emerged from a loose confederation of seventeen provinces that had been gradually incorporated into the domains of the Duke of Burgundy.[154]

In 1477, Mary the Rich, only child of Charles the Bold, Duke of Burgundy and the Seventeen Provinces, became ruler of her father's domains. The king of France immediately launched a campaign to take possession of Mary's holdings. In desperation, she turned to her subjects for help, which they agreed to in exchange for a charter of rights called "The Great Privilege," signed in Ghent that same year.

Two months later, Mary was wed to Maximilian of Austria, heir to the Holy Roman Empire, effectively merging the Seventeen Provinces into the vast domains of the Habsburgs.[155] When the Habsburg territories were divided between Spain and Austria, the Netherlands came under Spanish rule.[156]

Conflicts between the Spanish king and his Dutch subjects led to the Eighty Years' War, which erupted in 1568. Dutch Protestants, unhappy with the Spanish policies of centralizing political power away from local authorities and of religious persecution, revolted against Spanish Catholic rule. Seven of the Seventeen Provinces united to form a republic under the leadership of a nobleman serving in the Habsburg court, William, Prince of Orange.[157]

The Dutch Empire began as a result of the ongoing war effort against Spain. A central component of its strategy was to divert Spanish military and financial resources from deployment against the infant Netherlands Republic by attacking Spanish holdings elsewhere. The Dutch used their formidable skills in shipping and trade to undermine established Portuguese and Spanish settlements.

In addition, the Dutch embarked on exploratory voyages that brought in vast new territories. Henry Hudson explored the Hudson River, where New Amsterdam (later renamed New York) was founded, and later discovered Hudson's Bay while searching for the Northwest Passage.[158] Willem Berentsz sailed north of Siberia in search of the Northeast Passage,[159] while Abel Tasman was the first European to explore Tasmania and New Zealand.[160] Like the British, the Dutch used the trade monopolies enjoyed by the Dutch East and West India Companies to build up their colonial possessions.[161]

The efforts to conquer overseas colonies began while William, Prince of Orange, was *Stadholder* or governor of the Dutch Provinces. However, William was not born a prince. When he was eleven, he unexpectedly inherited the Principality of Orange, a small state in the south of France, when his distant cousin died childless.[162]

William, Prince of Orange, had been given a crown.

Conclusion

John envisioned "a white horse: and he that sat on him had a bow; and a crown was given unto him" (Rev. 6:2 AV). The royal houses of Europe followed strict rules regarding the inheritance of royal power from generation to the next. Despite this, a handful of monarchs literally receive their crown with no effort of their own. Juan I of Portugal, Isabella I of Castile Leon, King James I of England and VI of Scotland, Henry IV of France and William, Prince of Orange had all been given a crown. In each case, their ascension to the throne triggered the successful beginning of their nation's overseas colonial empire.

CHAPTER 9:

Conquering and to Conquer—Europe

> And I saw, and behold a white horse: and he that
> sat on him had a bow; and a crown was given unto
> him: and he went forth conquering, and to conquer.
> (Rev. 6:2 KJV)

The final detail John gives us about the White Horseman is that "he
went forth conquering, and to conquer" (Rev. 6:2b). This passage
uses the verb "conquer" (*nikao; νικάω*), in two different tenses. The
first time it is in present participle, which is translated "conquering"
and is the subject of the verb "went forth." The text simply states that
the horseman is going forth out of his own volition (active voice) at
some undefined point in time (aorist tense) and will conquer. Since
both "went forth" and "conquering" are in the indicative mood, it
is a statement of fact. We may not know when the conquering will
happen, but we know it absolutely will.

In the second occurrence of nikao, the tense and voice are the
same, but it is in the subjunctive mood, conveying a very different
meaning. This is a mood of possibility; the action may or may not
actually happen depending on circumstances. In this case, the White
Horseman will do everything he can to conquer but might not
succeed.[163] Surveying the activities of the kings of Europe, it is clear
that both tenses are needed.

As the White Horse rode forth "conquering and to conquer," we would expect to see a significant increase in wars of conquest. It's not as if wars of conquest were unknown before the opening of the first seal. Wars, like poverty, seem to be one of those things that will always be with us until Jesus returns (Matt. 26:11). However, starting in 1492, Europe underwent a distinct change in both the frequency of wars and number of combatants involved. To understand the magnitude of this change, it is helpful to compare the frequency of wars after 1500 with that of the previous centuries.

During the first half of the second millennium AD, there were a total of eighty-nine wars worldwide. These included a series of conflicts on the borders of the Christian and Muslim worlds: the Crusades,[164] the efforts to drive the Moors out of Spain,[165] and to vanquish the remains of the Byzantine or Eastern Roman Empire, which culminated with the fall of Constantinople.[166] Wars disputing succession were also fairly common. Examples include William the Conqueror's famous invasion of England,[167] the Hundred Years' War (will the real king of France please stand up?),[168] and the War of the Roses (the great royal family feud).[169]

There were fourteen wars during the eleventh century, seven of which were in Europe. Nine wars began during the twelfth century, half of which involved Christian nations fending off Islamic jihadists. The 1200s saw eighteen wars around the globe, including numerous crusades and the Mongol conquests. There were sixteen wars during the fourteenth century, mostly in Europe. This was an average of 1.4 conflicts per decade over the first four centuries of the millennium. The 1400s experienced a record 33 wars, six of which were fought after 1492, an average of 3.3 per decade. This transitional time included the finalizing of the infantry revolution.[170] By contrast, the following century witnessed 72 wars, double the rate of the previous century, and most involving Europeans. This pattern continued during the 1600s (81 wars) and 1700s (83 wars).[171] The 1800s witnessed an astounding 314 wars.[172] See Chart 1.

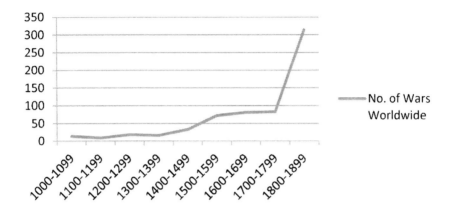

Chart 1: *Growth in number of wars per century.*

1492–1502: The Wars Begin

The year 1492 was a pivotal one. As every schoolchild knows (at least in North America), it was the year Columbus "sailed the ocean blue" searching for a transatlantic route to the East Indies. However, that was also the start of three centuries of wars between European nations wrestling to expand their dominions at home and consolidate monopolies on overseas colonies and trading routes.

Imagine eggs sitting in a pot of water getting hotter and hotter until the water reaches the boiling point. Suddenly, all the eggs start jostling each other, moving but not actually shifting position. The nations of Europe were like those eggs and 1492 was the year the water started to boil. Over the next thirty years, Moscow, Spain, France, the Holy Roman Empire, and the Ottomans pursued aggressive expansionist policies that immersed all Europe in multiple wars touching every corner of the continent. Consider the following.

- The Grand Duke of Moscow gathered the surrounding fiefdoms to form Russia and went to war with Poland, Lithuania, the Golden Horde, various khanates, and Sweden.
- Sweden, in turn, fought a war of succession with Denmark-Norway, as did various landgraves (feudal rulers) in the Holy Roman Empire.

- The Holy Roman Empire bubbled as various noble families, including the Wettins of Saxony, the Hohenzollerns of Brandenburg, and the Habsburgs of Austria, attempted to increase the size of their holdings.
- The Habsburgs wrestled for dominance with the French in the Netherlands, Brittany, Hungary, and Italy.
- In northern Italy, the Papal States, Milan, and Venice struggled for dominance but soon became a battleground in the struggle between France, the Habsburgs and Spain.
- In addition to fighting in the Italian Wars, Spain embarked on colonial ventures in North Africa and the New World.
- The Ottomans were engaged in a civil war in addition to wars with Spain, Venice, Hungary and the Knights of Rhodes.
- The Scottish and English entered the Italian Wars on opposing sides as a sort of proxy war of their age-old differences.
- Meanwhile, the Portuguese waged naval battles with the Ottoman and Mamluk empires for control of shipping in the Indian Ocean.

With the exception of a few minor feudal states, almost all Europe was immersed in war over the thirty years following 1492.

The Rise of Russia in Eastern Europe

Ivan the Great of Muscovy, nicknamed "gatherer of the Russian lands," had long pursued the goal of expanding his authority and dominions. Having seized control of the duchies and principalities surrounding Muscovy, including Novgorod and Belarus, he overthrew the Golden Horde, replacing their regimes with his own autocratic rule. He then embarked on a series of wars with Lithuania.[173] Three years later, Ivan formed an alliance with Denmark-Norway in a war against Sweden in hopes of gaining control of Finland.[174]

Ivan's policies were continued by his son Vasili III, who annexed the last remaining independent provinces in what became Russia by 1522. In addition, Vasili attempted to conquer Lithuania, capturing an important fortress, Smolensk, and successfully fended off the Crimean Khanate.[175]

Russia had gone forth "conquering and to conquer."

Scandinavia

Hostilities in Scandinavia were rooted in the Swedish desire for independence from Denmark-Norway. For the previous century, Scandinavia had been united under a personal union that began with the marriage of Margarite I of Denmark to King Haakon VI of Norway.[176] War erupted when the Sture family of Sweden laid claim to the Swedish throne. When Ivan III (the Great) of Russia allied himself with the Danish, the Swedes retaliated by capturing the fortress of Ivangorod. Ultimately, the war ended with no change in the status quo.[177]

Sweden had gone forth "to conquer" and had failed.

The Holy Roman Empire

The Holy Roman Empire, which had been in existence since the days of Charlemagne, was a hodgepodge of independent states bound by feudal allegiance to an elected emperor. Over the centuries, the emperor had been reduced to a figurehead while various leading families worked to amass power for themselves, scheming for domination. The Oldenburg family had already established a branch on the Danish throne, while branches of the Wittelsbach family did battle in the Landshut War of Succession. The House of Hohenzollern, Margraves of Brandenburg, and the House of Wettin, Electors of Saxony, capitalized on the unrest triggered by the Protestant Reformation to wrestle for political dominance.

The House of Habsburg was by far the most successful in rising to prominence in early modern Europe. This important dynastic family ruled as kings of the Germans, Holy Roman Emperors, and emperors of Austria. They pursued a highly successful plan of expansion using military and dynastic means, eventually controlling Burgundy, Spain, Bohemia, Hungary, and vast expanses of colonial territories.[178]

After the Habsburgs began their campaign of expansion in the Netherlands, they continued to the north with the invasion of Oldenburg and Brunswick. Their forces were countered by an alliance of several small Germanic states including Mecklenburg, Hesse, Saxony, and Brandenburg.[179]

The Habsburgs v. France

The Habsburg ambitions were also systematically opposed by the French, leading to disputes in Brittany, the Netherlands, Hungary and the Italian states.

When Maximilian I came to the Habsburg throne in 1493, he used military action to reestablish his claims on Luxemburg and the Netherlands, the hereditary lands of his first wife, Mary of Burgundy. When Mary inherited her father's lands in 1477, she was immediately courted by both the French and the Habsburgs. The French king pressured Mary, age twenty, to wed his seven-year-old son, while Frederick III, Holy Roman Emperor, offered marriage to his eighteen-year-old heir, Maximilian I. She chose the latter, inadvertently igniting two centuries of conflict that would end only with the War of the Spanish Succession in the early 1700s.[180]

The marriage was short-lived—the bride died in a riding accident—and Maximilian was wed a second time to Anne, Duchess of Brittany. The French interpreted this as a flagrant act of aggression despite the fact that Charles VIII, King of France, was betrothed to Maximilian's daughter. Charles laid siege to Brittany and forced the fourteen-year-old Anne, who had already wed Maximilian by proxy, to renounce her husband and marry him instead. Brittany was permanently annexed by France.[181]

Charles was successful only because Maximilian was in Eastern Europe and unable to intervene on Anne's behalf. Maximilian was negotiating with the king of Poland and the king of Hungary and Bohemia to arrange dynastic marriages for his grandchildren. His goal was to ensure these territories would eventually come under Habsburg control. Maximilian adhered to the family motto: "Let others wage war, but you, happy Austria, marry."[182]

The Habsburgs went forth, conquering in any way possible.

The Italian Wars, Part I

The French and the Habsburgs continued to collide in Italy. The Italian Wars began locally as a dispute between Milan, Naples, and Venice. The conflict expanded through the dynastic claims of the Habsburgs, the French, and the Spanish to involve every major power in Europe.

The trouble began when the king of Naples made an alliance with the pope in hopes of unifying Italy. The Duke of Milan, fearing a united south and the rising power of Venice, encouraged Charles VIII of France, who had a vague claim to the throne, to attack Naples. The resulting invasion was swift and brutal, with Charles laying claim to all Italy. The Duke of Milan then allied then himself with the Habsburgs, arranging for his niece, Bianca Maria Sforza, to marry Maximilian I, who desired to bring the Italian states back into the Holy Roman Empire. At the same time, Ferdinand II of Aragon entered the war in support of the deposed king of Naples, his nephew.[183]

The pope responded to the French invasion by forming the League of Venice, comprised of the Papal States, Milan, the Habsburgs (led by Maximilian I), Spain and Sicily (under Ferdinand II of Aragon), and the Venetian Republic, which hoped for assistance in their war with the Ottomans. England joined the league the following year. The combined armies of the league forced Charles VIII to abandon his conquests and retreat to France.[184]

However, the story of the White Horseman is not simply a story of conquests but also of efforts to conquer if at all possible. France may have failed to retain its victories, but it continued to make every effort to expand its reach over the small Italian territories. In 1498, Charles VIII died and was succeeded by his cousin Louis XII, who had a legitimate claim to the Duchy of Milan through his grandmother. By the following year, Louis had wrenched control of Milan from the Sforza family. He continued his wars of conquest by defeating the Venetian mercenary army, causing Machiavelli to comment that this great city-state had, in a single day, "lost what it had taken them eight hundred years' exertion to conquer." [185, 186]

French dominion over Italy was short-lived. It was contested by the Spanish king Ferdinand II of Aragon, who was also king of Sicily and had a claim to Naples. Ferdinand initially consented to divide Naples with Louis XII, but when the two failed to agree on terms, war resulted, and Naples fell to Spain. In one sense, this was also a victory for the Habsburgs, since Maximilian's son Philip was married to Joanna, daughter of Ferdinand and Isabella, and heir apparent.[187]

The Italian Wars, Part II

The peace in Italy was, once again, brief. The Italian Wars were restarted four years later (1508) when the pope formed the League of Cambrai for the purpose of limiting Venetian power in Italy. The conflict between France, the Papal States, and Venice continued until 1516, with virtually every European power joining the fray at some point. Ironically, the years of war made few changes to the political map except to reaffirm French claims in northern Italy.[188]

Wars to the East: Spain, Portugal, and the Ottoman Empire

The period starting in 1492 was one of great expansion for Spain thanks to Columbus' discoveries in the New World. However, the Spanish also made their presence known along the Mediterranean coast, competing with the Venetians, the Knights Hospitaller, the Barbary pirates of North Africa, the Mamluks of Egypt, and the Ottomans for control of trade routes.[189]

Meanwhile, the Portuguese, who were developing shipping routes into the Indian Ocean and Red Sea, attacked all other fleets that challenged their naval dominance. The Mamluk Sultan of Egypt sought the aid of the Ottomans in a failed attempt to halt Portuguese merchant ships and to protect the Muslim monopoly on trade between India and the West.[190] Although the Ottoman Empire was plunged into civil war at the time, it still managed to do battle with the Mamluks, the Hungarians, and the Safavid dynasty of Persia. By 1520, the Ottomans had established themselves in the Mamluk holdings in Egypt and the Middle East.[191]

The kingdoms of Europe had gone forth "conquering and to conquer."

1520–62: The Wars Continue

During the first part of the sixteenth century, Europe continued to experience paroxysms of wars, most of which lasted no more than five or six years. The few conflicts that lasted longer were generally fought with non-Europeans.

War with the Infidels

Jihad, Muslim holy war, continued to rage on the borders

of Eastern Europe. In 1522, the Ottoman ruler Suleiman the Magnificent besieged the Island of Rhodes and won control of the eastern Mediterranean.[192] In 1526, the Ottomans won a decisive victory over the Kingdom of Hungary and Bohemia, marking the end of the Ottoman-Hungarian War and the beginning of the Ottoman-Habsburg War. The most noteworthy change was the Franco-Ottoman alliance; Francis I of France joined with Suleiman against the Habsburg Emperor Charles V, who ruled both the Holy Roman Empire and Spain. This initiated nearly 200 years of almost constant battle between the Habsburg and Ottoman empires.[193]

After conquering Hungary, Suleiman turned his attentions to Vienna, the capital of the Holy Roman Empire and seat of Habsburg power. The Ottomans came close to capturing Vienna in 1529 but were driven back by the combined impact of the Habsburg cutting-edge weaponry (arquebuses and pikes) and the wet, autumnal weather.[194]

The Ottomans fought extensive wars along their borders, following the White Horseman pattern of "conquering and to conquer." In addition to their constant wars with the Habsburgs, they contested the Portuguese in a series of naval wars and were involved in the ongoing saga of the Italian Wars. In addition, they waged a jihad against the Ethiopian Empire, an Eastern Orthodox nation whose kings were descended from the House of Solomon (1529–43).[195]

The Ottomans engaged in a series of religious and territorial wars with the Persian Empire, which was ruled by the Safavid dynasty. The Ottomans were uncompromising in their devotion to Sunni Islam, while the Persians were followers of Shiite Islam; both considered the other a hotbed of heresy. In addition, both empires desired control of the Caucasus and Mesopotamian (Iraq) regions.[196]

The Ottomans had gone forth "conquering and to conquer."

Russia: the Making of a Czar

Under the reign of Ivan IV (the Terrible), Russia was transformed from a medieval principality on the fringes of Christendom to an empire encompassing over a million square miles and reigning over peoples of many ethnic and religious backgrounds. His empire building began with the complete subjugation of the Khanate of Kazan, in response to more than forty raids on Russian lands. Ivan added to his domains the khanates of Astrakhan and Siberia, all formerly ruled by the Golden Horde. Finally, he become the first to be crowned Czar of All Russia.[197]

During the 1500s, Russia continued its series of wars with Poland-Lithuania. During the fifth war (1534–37), Poland-Lithuania allied itself with the Crimean Khanate (modern-day Ukraine), a Muslim protectorate of the Ottomans, to fend off Russian advances.[198]

Russia also fought a series of border skirmishes with Sweden over the control of the lands edging the Baltic, especially Finland (controlled by Sweden at the time). In 1555, things went from an uneasy peace to all-out war when Russia invaded Finland. After two years of invasions into Finland and counter invasions into Russia, the Treaty of Novgorod preserved the pre-war status quo.[199]

Russia had gone forth "conquering and to conquer."

The Italian Wars, Part III

Italy continued to be the focal point of European hostilities. Once again, the war was part of the ongoing struggle between the King of France and the Habsburgs. Maximilian I nominated his grandson Charles of Spain to succeed him as Holy Roman Emperor, while Francis of France was also campaigning for the position. Charles won the election in part because the pope was looking for an ally to counter the rising influence of Martin Luther and partly because the German populace was outraged at the thought of submitting to a French emperor.

Francis opened hostilities by covertly supporting attacks on the Low Countries and on the tiny Kingdom of Navarre in the Iberian Peninsula. France soon found itself isolated, surrounded by the Papal States, England, and the Habsburgs, who controlled Spain and the Holy Roman Empire. In desperation, Francis sued for peace.[200]

Peace was short-lived—again. The League of Cognac was quickly formed as a check to the seemingly unstoppable power of Charles V, Holy Roman Emperor. The league allied the Papal States, Venice, Milan, Florence and France against Genoa and the Habsburgs. Although the war was a resounding victory for Charles, who drove the French out of Italy, the conflict between the Habsburgs and France was far from over.[201]

There would be two more rounds of warfare between the foes. The ensuing fighting devastated the Low Countries, the Rhineland, the Mediterranean, and Eastern Europe. The wars finally sputtered out for religious and financial reasons. In 1557, both the Spanish and French kings defaulted on their debts, and the rapid growth of Protestantism threatened to undermine the balance of power in the Habsburg homelands.[202]

Northern Europe, Part I

Significant changes were happening in northern Europe due to the Protestant Reformation. First, the ecclesiastical Teutonic States became the secular Duchy of Prussia. Traditionally, the Teutonic Knights had been a crusading military order formed to protect Christian pilgrims traveling to the Holy Land. Later, they had been rewarded with lands on the southeast Baltic and became vassals of the Polish king.[203] In 1511, Albert of Brandenburg, who owed feudal allegiance to the Holy Roman Emperor, became the Grand Master of the Knights, creating political tensions. However, in 1522, Albert became a Lutheran, the first German noble to do so, and in the following years, worked to secularize his estates into the Duchy of Prussia.[204]

Second, Sweden gained its independence, seceding from the Kalmar Union and deposing the Danish king under the leadership of Swedish nobleman Gustav Vasa, who was elected king in 1523. Gustav went on to "liberate" Finland from Danish rule and to convert the nation to Protestantism after prolonged political disputes with the pope.[205]

1558–1670: The Long Wars

The warfare grew in intensity during the latter part of the sixteenth and most of the seventeenth centuries. The wars that wracked Europe were long—many were measured in decades—and bloody. Whole stretches of the European countryside were destroyed as armies battled through. Since armies were expected to forage off the land, famine and devastation inevitably followed. Recovery was often brief as battling armies passed through within months of each other. Since many of the combatants had colonial trading monopolies, the battles also raged on the high seas and in remote outposts around the globe.

Northern Europe, Part II

Northern and Eastern Europe continued to be plagued by wars between the major powers as they wrestled for dominance. The Livonia War (1558–83) is an excellent example of this. The Livonian Confederation was a collection of estates held by two dozen Teutonic Knights and four Bishoprics, all governed independently and further divided by the influence of the Protestant Reformation. One historian described the situation this way: "Racked with internal bickering and threatened by the political machinations of its neighbours [sic], Livonia was in no state to resist an attack."[206]

Russia, still pursuing its expansionist policies, was one of the surrounding nations that plotted to carve up Livonia. Czar Ivan the Terrible saw Livonia as the gateway to trade with the West and was prepared to use military force if diplomacy failed. Sweden, having recently gained independence, desired to take their place on the European stage. According to the mercantilist thinking of the day, this meant expanding its borders. Meanwhile, the Duke of Prussia, whose brother was archbishop in Livonia, was making every effort to secularize the confederation as he had done in Prussia. Poland-Lithuania, concerned by the growing aggression of Russia, threw its support behind this effort.[207]

In the meantime, the Nordic Seven Years' War (1563–70) pitted Sweden against Denmark-Norway, Poland-Lithuania, and the Hanseatic League in a battle for control of trade in the Baltic Sea. When the war was over, no territory changed hands, but the king of Sweden implemented mandatory military service, requiring one in ten Swedes to report for duty. This was modern Europe's first standing army and it transformed Sweden into a great military power. [208]

Sweden had gone forth "conquering and to conquer."

The Conquering Ottomans

In 1571, Moscow was distracted from the European theater by threats from the south. The Crimean Khanate had been an ongoing threat since the 1400s, raiding the southern provinces to capture slaves and disrupt farming. This problem only ended when the Crimea was annexed in 1783. Perhaps sensing that Ivan IV was focused on the need to open Russia to the Baltic Sea and would not be able to reinforce his usual military presence along the borders, the Crimean forces swept across the countryside to Moscow, devastating all in their wake. Moscow was destroyed.[209]

The Crimeans were under the protection of the Ottoman Empire, which was also engaged in the latest installment in a series of lengthy wars with the Habsburgs. The appropriately named Long War, or the Fifteen Years' War (1593–1606),[210] pitted the Ottomans against the Habsburgs and their numerous allies from Eastern Europe, Italy and Germany. Poland-Lithuania entered the conflict to assert its claims over Moldavia.[211] Surprisingly, the Habsburgs were aided by Persia, who was struggling to gain hegemony over the Middle East.[212]

The Ottomans and the Persians had gone forth "conquering and to conquer."

Wars of Independence

While some princes fought to expand their holdings at the expense of their neighbors, others fought to gain their independence from the princes who had conquered them. Examples include the Dutch War of Independence, various uprisings against England, and the Portuguese Revolt.

The Dutch War of Independence (1568–1648), also called the Eighty Years' War, began as a revolt against Spain under the leadership of William of Orange. Unfortunately, even after the seven northernmost provinces succeeded in forming a republic in 1588, the battle was far from over; it merely expanded to include England and France. The war was fought globally, as the Dutch East India Company targeted Spanish and Portuguese colonial outposts (at the time, Portugal was under Spanish dominion).[213]

Meanwhile, the Portuguese staged a revolt, also known as the

Restoration War (1640–68), to regain their independence from Spain. The Spanish kings had claimed the throne of Portugal during a succession crisis sixty years earlier. When King Philip II tried to relegate Portugal to a province of Spain, Portuguese nobles staged a coup d'état and named a descendant of the royal line, the Duke of Braganza, as their new king. After almost thirty years with no decisive victory but much diplomatic maneuvering, Spain conceded Portuguese independence.[214]

England fought against Spain in both of these conflicts, giving rise to what came to be known as the Anglo-Spanish War (1585–1604). As a result, the English often found themselves battling Spanish mercenaries when quelling multiple rebellions within their domains. For instance, during the Desmond Rebellions (1569–84) and the Nine Years' War (1594–1603), ancient feudal lords of Ireland attempted to throw off English rule with the assistance of papal and Spanish armies.[215, 216]

War of Religion

The rise of Protestantism divided Europe. Generally, northern Europe became Protestant, while southern Europe remained Catholic. In between, intense wars raged over the issues of religion and politics, and in early modern Europe, wars of religion always involved politics.

In an era of secularism and religious pluralism, it can be difficult to understand the intense religious conflicts that characterized sixteenth-century Europe. The rise of Protestantism frequently led to war because there was no separation between an individual's religious beliefs and their loyalties to their rulers—subjects were expected to have the same faith as their princes. The Peace of Augsburg confirmed this, stipulating that a state's religion would be determined by the convictions of its ruler. This meant that any political disagreements frequently took on religious overtones.[217]

The Schmalkaldic War (1546–47) was a conflict between the Catholic Holy Roman Empire and the Schmalkaldic League, formed by Lutheran princes to defend themselves from the empire. Francis I of France also joined the league for a period despite his strong Catholic position, indicating the importance of the political element in this war. At the end of the war, Lutheranism was formally recognized as a valid state religion within the domains of the Holy Roman Empire.[218]

The French Wars of Religion (1562–98) were waged between the French Catholics and Protestants (the Huguenots) until they were ended by the ascension of Henry IV. By 1560, over half of the French nobility adhered to Calvinism. At the same time, power-hungry Catholic nobles were eager to expand their holdings at the expense of their Protestant peers. The Duke of Guise formed the Catholic League with the support of Spain, while the Huguenots, backed by the English and Scottish, rallied around the Duke of Bourbon.[219]

The Thirty Years' War

The Thirty Years' War (1618–48) was one of the most destructive ever waged in Europe. It was fought mostly in Germany between the Holy Roman Empire, aided by its Habsburg allies, against the states that sought to counter the growing hegemony of the Habsburgs over Europe.

As was the case with many other conflicts of the time, religion appeared to be a key motive for the war. The fighting was triggered by Emperor Ferdinand II's efforts to impose Catholicism on Protestant Bohemia. However, a close examination of key players shows that this was far from being the sole cause. Spain, France, and Scandinavia all harbored ambitions to control the German lands. By the time the war concluded, virtually every significant power in Europe was involved. The Holy Roman Empire was allied with Bavaria, the Catholic League, and Spain. They were opposed by most of the provinces of northern Germany, Sweden, England, Scotland, the United Provinces, France and the Ottoman Empire.

The devastation left in the wake of the Thirty Years' War rivals that inflicted during World War I both in terms of destruction and casualties as a percentage of the population (see Table 1). In many ways it was worse, because the civilian population was routinely attacked by marauding mercenary armies for three decades.[220] The Peace of Westphalia, sometimes called the "Peace of Exhaustion," put an end to both the Thirty Years' War and the Eighty Years' War, and laid the groundwork for modern nation-states.[221]

All of Europe had gone forth "conquering and to conquer."

TABLE 1	30 Years' War 1618-48	World War I 1914-18
Population of Europe 1600, 1920	78,000,000	485,000,000
Number of casualties	8,000,000	9,911,000 dead 39,000,000 total casualties
Casualties as percentage of population	10.26%	2.04% dead 8.04% total casualties
Number of years fought	30 years	4 years

Table 1: *Comparison of casualties in the Thirty Years' War and World War I.* [222, 223, 224, 225]

After the Peace of Westphalia: Nation States

England: Civil Wars, the Glorious Revolution and Rule by Consent

In England, a series of events transformed the country into a constitutional monarchy. These began with the English Civil Wars (1642–51) fought between the Roundheads (nonconformist parliamentarians) and the Cavaliers (Church of England royalists).[226] Later, the Restoration (Charles II was invited to return from exile in 1660 to rule as a constitutional monarchy)[227] and the Glorious Revolution (1688) gave Parliament authority over the monarchy and established the concept that the king could rule only by the consent of Parliament.[228] By limiting the traditional power of the English Crown, these acts laid the foundations for constitutional monarchy. From the time of the Restoration, conflicts over different views were expressed through political parties within Parliament rather than through battle.[229]

France: The Roadmap to Absolutism

Meanwhile, France suffered three civil or Fronde wars (1648–53), fought by the French aristocracy in defense of their ancient feudal liberties against increasing encroachment by the monarchy.[230] Louis XIV, king at the time, used the public desire for peace to transform the government of France into a highly centralized bureaucracy under leaders who owed their positions to the favor of the king. The French aristocratic claims to ancient feudal privileges were discredited by the Fronde. Louis XIV took advantage of the unpopularity of the Fronde to implement significant reforms. These included restructuring the tax code, implementing Colbert's new economic protectionist policies, modernizing the army, ending the ancient feudal monopoly over senior positions and implementing a uniform legal code with a government bureaucracy staffed by the bourgeois rather than the aristocracy.[231, 232]

Once Louis XIV had established himself as the absolute authority in France, he decided to pursue an expansionist policy by invading the Spanish Netherlands during the War of Devolution (1667–68). He claimed the area was rightfully due him as his wife's dowry. Louis soon found himself at war with the English and the Dutch as well as the Spanish.[233] The resulting Franco-Dutch War was the first of several that pitted Louis against William III, Prince of Orange, who eventually became King of England, Scotland and Ireland.[234, 235]

The First (Sometimes Called the Second) Northern War

While much of Europe was moving toward strong central governments at the expense of the aristocracy, the Commonwealth of Poland-Lithuania was ruled by powerful nobility and an elected king. This system initially served the nation well, keeping it out of the Thirty Years' War and ushering in a Golden Age. However, the commonwealth failed to develop a modern army or a tax system to pay for one, making it an inviting target for surrounding nations. A series of seventeenth century wars, known as the Deluge, began a period of steady decline for Poland-Lithuania. The commonwealth lost its standing as a major European power when parts of it were annexed piece by piece by its absolutist neighbors.[236, 237]

The undoing of the Polish-Lithuanian Commonwealth began with the Khmelnitsky Uprising (1648–55), an effort to create an autonomous Ukrainian state. As a result, the Commonwealth lost a third of its population and its position as a great power. The uprising initially appeared successful, but soon Polish rule was replaced by Russian rule. [238]

The Khmelnitsky Uprising in the Ukraine demonstrated the weakness of Poland-Lithuania against an attack by a modern, well-equipped army. Sweden, having become one of the most powerful nations in Europe by the close of the Thirty Years' War, invaded Poland. By the end of 1655, almost all Poland-Lithuania was occupied by either Sweden or Russia. Next, Brandenburg entered the fray to defend its claim on Prussia, a claim which was confirmed in the peace process, and laid the foundations for the great Prussian Empire. [239, 240]

Anglo-Dutch Wars (1652–54, 1665–67, and 1672–74)

The Anglo-Dutch Wars were fought almost entirely at sea over trade disputes. After the Thirty Years' War, the English and Dutch were no longer bound by their common enmity for the Habsburgs. The weakened condition of Spain and Portugal meant their former colonies were up for grabs and both the English and the Dutch fought for trade dominance around the globe.[241]

Ottomans and the Great Turkish War

Eastern Europe continued to struggle with the expansionist policies of the Ottoman and Russian empires. After the devastation of the Polish-Turkish War (1672–76), hostilities continued in the Russo-Turkish War (1676–81), in which the Ottomans attempted to take all of the Ukraine west of the Dnieper River. Meanwhile, the Russians sought to push southward into Turkish-held territory on the Black Sea in hopes of establishing a year-round port. Tensions culminated with the Great Turkish War (1683–99) when the Ottomans attacked the Habsburg's eastern flank. At this point the pope formed a Holy League to preserve Christendom; it included the Holy Roman Empire, Poland-Lithuania, Venice and Russia. After defeating the Ottomans in the Battle of Vienna, the league fought to drive them back, restoring Poland-Lithuania and creating Austria-Hungary. [242]

Conclusion

The Peace of Westphalia, which had put an end to both the Thirty Years' War and the Eighty Years' War, changed everything. It created the framework of the modern nation-state, in which citizens were subject only to their national governments and not to other powers. No longer was an individual's faith defined by his citizenship. In addition, the widespread use of mercenary armies was replaced by well-disciplined national armies, paid for by centralized tax systems. Most strikingly, it had the general effect of transferring the European powers' quest for new domains from Europe to overseas colonies around the globe.[243]

The kingdoms of Europe went forth "conquering and to conquer" just as John had prophesied.

CHAPTER 10:

Conquering and to Conquer—the World

The European lust for conquest continued unabated during the eighteenth century but with a twist. Wars between the European powers were frequently fought on the high seas, and in remote colonial outposts. The economies of the great powers of Europe came to depend more and more on the resources of their overseas holdings. Consequently, those colonies became strategic targets, increasing the odds that European conflicts would be fought globally.

1700s: The Road to World War

The 1700s opened with an explosion of military contests dominated by the Great Northern War centered on the Baltic Sea (1700–21), and the War of the Spanish Succession (1701–14). Although the war in the Baltic theater was longer, it was far more localized because the combatants were mostly landlocked with few overseas colonies. The War of the Spanish Succession, on the other hand, was fought at home and around the world.

The Great Northern War

The Great Northern War was a battle for control of the Baltic Sea, northern Europe's gateway to the world's oceans. In the rush to build empires by acquiring overseas colonies, this access was essential.

After the Thirty Years' War, Sweden was in control of much of the Baltic coastline, including territories that had once belonged to Denmark–Norway, but its triumph was, once again, short-lived. Sweden found itself facing war with a spectrum of enemies, including Denmark–Norway, Russia, Saxony, Brandenburg–Prussia, Hanover, Great Britain, and Poland–Lithuania. As Sweden receded from the international stage, Russia became the most powerful nation in Eastern Europe.[244]

War of the Spanish Succession

Meanwhile, Western Europe was submerged in the War of the Spanish Succession, fought to prevent the unification of the world's two most powerful nations, Spain and France. Charles II of Spain had failed to produce an heir, which meant the Spanish throne was going to be inherited by his cousin Philip, the grandson of Louis XIV of France. Initially, William III of England and the Netherlands was reluctant to contest the decision, but Louis' attempts to cut off English merchants from Spanish trade forced him to war. He was soon joined by the Habsburgs, Prussia, Savoy, and Portugal.

Although the war was fought mainly in Europe, it spilled into the colonies, including privateering in the waters around the West Indies and South America (See Map 1). Its American counterpart, Queen Anne's War, saw both sides solicit the support of the Native American tribes from Florida to Newfoundland. The resulting treaty permanently ended the threat of Habsburg hegemony over Europe and guaranteed that France and Spain would not be united, although they remained allies for years to come.[245, 246]

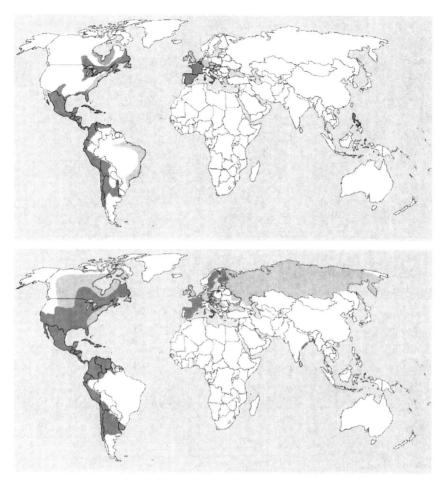

Above—Map 1: War of the Spanish Succession.[247]

Light gray: Great Britain, Dutch Republic, Portugal with more.
Dark gray: Spain, France with more

Below—Map 2: War of the Austrian Succession.[248]

Light gray: Great Britain, Habsburg monarchy with more.
Dark gray: France, Prussia, Spain with more

Russian Empire Building

At the close of the Great Northern War, Russia turned its attentions to its southern borders. The first of the Russo-Persian Wars (1722–23) foreshadowed the Great Game of the nineteenth century. Czar Peter I of Russia desired to extend his influence into the Caspian and Caucasus areas and to prevent Persia from falling into the hands of the Ottomans. As Russia attacked Persia from the north, the Ottomans attacked from the south, enabling Russia to win both a military and diplomatic victory. Then the Russians and Persians forged an alliance against the Ottoman Turks.[249]

With its southern borders secure, Russia turned its attention to the West. In the 1730s, they formed an alliance with Habsburg Austria and Prussia known as the "Alliance of the Three Black Eagles." The three empires conspired to influence the election of a king in Poland. After the Polish elections devolved into civil conflict, the War of the Polish Succession (1733–38) quickly expanded to include the Alliance and the European powers that opposed it.[250]

The Bourbon kingdoms of France and Spain took advantage of Austria's preoccupation to attack Habsburg holdings in the Rhineland and in Italy.[251] The Ottomans, allies of France, reopened their long-standing dispute with Russia in the Russo-Austrian-Turkish War (1733–39).[252]

During this period, western European nations continued to battle, staging wars in overseas colonies with native allies, especially in North America. The Chickasaw Wars (1721–63) were fought between the French and the British for control of the Mississippi from New Orleans to Illinois.[253] Similarly, the French and British fought with native confederacies for dominion over the lands between Nova Scotia and Massachusetts in Dummer's War (1722–25).[254]

The War of the Austrian Succession

Although the Habsburg dynasty had failed to produce a male heir, the Pragmatic Sanction of 1713, agreed to by most of the European powers, ensured the succession of Empress Maria Theresa.[255] However, women leaders were perceived as weak, and Habsburg weakness was an invitation to war.

The War of the Austrian Succession (1740–48) began when

Frederick II of Prussia led his highly disciplined, modern army into Silesia, a prize that would form a bridge between his duel holdings of Brandenburg and Prussia. He was soon joined by Saxony, Bavaria, and France. Spain fought to expand its Italian holdings at Austria's expense, and Russia battled with Sweden. In addition, wars were waged in the Alps and the Netherlands. After eight years of conflict, only one change was made on the European map; Silesia was transferred from Austria to Prussia.[256]

The fighting was not limited to Europe; it expanded into the colonies, as was so often the case (See Map 2, above). Britain and France continued their ongoing conflict in the Carnatic Wars of India (1746–63). There, both the French and British East India Companies sought to conquer the Mughal Empire, which had once dominated the Indian subcontinent.[257] During King George's War (1744–48), the two nations, allied with native tribes, feuded from New York to Nova Scotia.[258] The War of Jenkins' Ear (1739–48)—named for a British sea captain who had lost his ear to the Spanish coast guard—was fought between Britain and Spain from Georgia to Venezuela.[259]

The Seven Years' War

The second half of the eighteenth century began with the Seven Years' War (1754–63), a global conflict fueled by animosity between Great Britain and the Bourbons (France and Spain), between the Hohenzollerns of Prussia and the Habsburgs. It involved numerous theaters, including the Third Silesian War between Austria and Prussia (1756–63), the Pomeranian War between Sweden and Prussia (1757–62) and French-occupied sections of Hanover and Prussia. The war raged in North America as the French and Indian War (1754–63) and as the West Indies Campaign (1759–63). It was fought in India as the Third Carnatic War (1757–63). It was called the Spanish–Portuguese War (1761–63) in South America, and the Anglo-Spanish War (1761–63) in Central America (See Map 3).

The outcome of the Seven Years' War was indicative of how Europeans had come to dominate the globe, collecting colonies like poker chips. While European territories generally reverted to the prewar status quo, colonial possessions around the world changed hands between France, Britain and Spain.[260, 261]

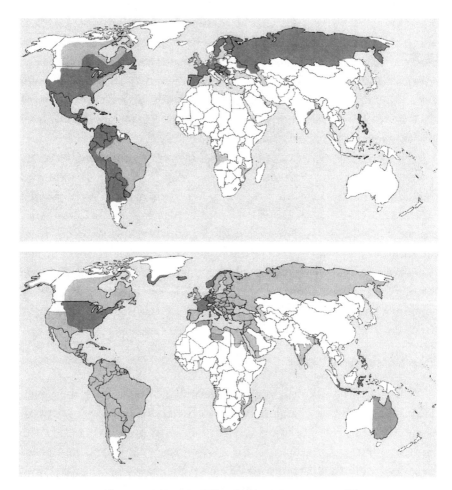

Above—Map 3: The Seven Years' War.[262]

Light gray: Great Britain, Prussia, and Portugal with more.
Dark gray: France, Spain, Austria, Russia, and Sweden with more

Below—Map 4: The Napoleonic Wars.[263]

Light gray: Great Britain, Prussia, Austria, Russia, Portugal Spain,
Sweden and Ottoman Empire with more.
Dark gray: France, French client states, Denmark-Norway, and USA with
more Medium gray: territory nominally claimed by Britain and Ottomans

Wars in the Colonies

During the period immediately following the Seven Years' War, there was a noteworthy moment: after almost 300 years of constant warfare, Europe experienced four years of peace (1764–67). There was a lull in the endless attempts of the great powers of Europe to "go forth conquering and to conquer." Actually, it was four years of almost peace: Britain was engaged in a couple of colonial disputes in North America (Pontiac's War, 1763–66),[264] and in India (Anglo-Mysore War, 1767–69).[265] Then Russia delved into another round of war with the Ottomans (the Russo-Turkish War, 1768–74) and the conquering continued.[266]

This was typical of much of the second half of the eighteenth century. Other than a few minor conflicts and another installment of Russian wars, most of the European drive for conquest was waged overseas until the outbreak of the French Revolutionary Wars in 1792. Colonial wars were fought in India (Anglo-Maratha Wars[267] and the Anglo-Mysore Wars[268]), in southern Africa (with the Xhosa[269]), in Australia (the Australian frontier wars[270]), and in the Americas (Revolt in New Granada[271] and border disputes with the Northwest Indian Confederation[272]). Of course, there was the curious instance of the American Revolutionary War,[273] in which European colonists broke from the motherland. However, that war soon fell into the established pattern of French-Anglo hostilities.

The Partitioning of Poland

The other exception was the partitioning of Poland. The triple alliance of Prussia, Austria-Hungary, and Russia continued to covet Polish lands. Poland-Lithuania had developed a system of government that allowed political policy to be enacted only after it had the unanimous agreement of every "gentleman," effectively rendering it powerless in the face of the empires that surrounded it. Indeed, foreign diplomats commonly bribed constituents of the Commonwealth parliament so that Poland functioned more like a vassal state than an independent nation. In 1772, armies from the allied empires simultaneously invaded and annexed about 30 percent of the nation according to a predetermined agreement. The second and third partitions inevitably followed as Poland sank into economic and political ruin.[274]

French Revolutionary and Napoleonic Wars

The relative European calm was shattered in 1792 with the outbreak of the French Revolution, followed by the French Revolutionary Wars (1792–1802) and the Napoleonic Wars (1803–15). The conflict shook Europe to its foundations. It began with the toppling of the French monarchy and escalated to a global scale hitherto unimagined (see Map 4, above).

The French Revolution (1789–99) was an attempt to duplicate the American Revolution by radical left-wing political groups, supported by the urban masses and peasants. The goal was to rid France of absolute monarchy and all vestiges of feudalism and replace them with a government based on the political ideals of the Age of Enlightenment, outlined in the *Declaration of Rights of Man and the Citizen*. The latter was a French version of the American Declaration of Independence, but was based on "natural rights" with no reference to God.[275]

Alexis De Tocqueville, a French political thinker and historian,[276] later commented (in 1835) on the folly of pursuing a republic without God.

There are persons in France who look upon republican institutions as a temporary means of power, of wealth, and distinction; men who are the condottieri of liberty, and who fight for their own advantage, whatever be the colors they wear: it is not to these that I address myself. But there are others who look forward to the republican form of government as a tranquil and lasting state, towards which modern society is daily impelled by the ideas and manners of the time, and who sincerely desire to prepare men to be free. When these men attack religious opinions, they obey the dictates of their passions to the prejudice of their interests. Despotism may govern without faith, but liberty cannot. Religion is much more necessary in the republic which they set forth in glowing colors than in the monarchy which they attack; and it is more needed in democratic republics than in any others. How is it possible that society should escape destruction if the moral tie be not strengthened in proportion as the political tie is relaxed? and what can be done with a people which is its own master, if it be not submissive to the Divinity?[277]

As the revolution progressed, other European powers stood by, debating whether to intervene. After all, France was one of the most powerful nations in the world, and no one was anxious for another pan-European war. The Habsburg king, brother to Marie Antoinette, made vague threats if anything should happen to the royal family. France responded by declaring war on Austria in April 1792, igniting the War of the First Coalition (1792–97).

In the beginning, the coalition consisted of Austria, the Holy Roman Empire, and Prussia. France initially experienced some military setbacks but gained the upper hand in the Austrian Netherlands. Four months later, Louis XVI was executed, and the Reign of Terror followed, during which between 18,000 and 40,000 were guillotined. All Europe, including Great Britain and Spain, was now united against the revolution, ringing France with modern armies. Nevertheless, France continued to wage a series of highly successful invasions of Italy, the Tyrol, and Germany until Austria was forced to sue for peace in the fall of 1797.[278, 279]

The secret of French military success was twofold. First, the French Republic used mass conscription to enlist hundreds of thousands of men into its army. Traditionally, army officers had been drawn from the ranks of the aristocracy, but most of them had either been executed or had fled into exile. The French solved the problem by assembling a vast army of raw recruits who would simply roll over the highly trained professional armies of the coalition by sheer force of numbers—up to 1 million.[280]

The second ingredient in France's success was the rise of nationalism. The military of all ranks was expected to be fiercely loyal to France and her national interests, and the government regularly distributed propaganda pieces to its troops so they would have the "proper opinions."[281] Nationalism added motivational force to the military discipline of the West.

> ... the new loyalties of the rank and file influenced tactics, logistics and strategy. Eventually, Napoleon demonstrated the potential implicit in the new form of warfare and thus altered the conduct of military operations forever.[282]

Napoleon harnessed this loyalty coupled with his military brilliance to inspire his men to not only to defeat enemy armies but to destroy them whenever possible.[283]

Even after 1797, when Austria signed a peace treaty conceding to France most of the territorial goals pursued by centuries of French monarchs, the hostilities did not end for long. France continued fighting with Britain, invaded Egypt, Switzerland, and Rome, and fought a quasi-naval war against the United States. Over most of the next two decades, France took its revolutionary army and attempted to conquer all Europe and possibly the world. A series of European coalitions, using national armies reinforced through mass conscription, first battled against the French Republic and later Napoleon's French Empire (Napoleon crowned himself Emperor in 1804).[284]

The Napoleonic Wars (1802–15) had far-reaching consequences in Europe and the world. Nationalism became the driving force that would lead to the unification of Germany[285] and Italy[286] in the late nineteenth century. Nationalism, coupled with the French occupation of Spain, led to the collapse of the Spanish colonial empire, as a tidal wave of wars of independence swept through South America (1808–33).[287]

The forces of nationalism coupled with unprecedented military superiority meant the White Horseman's lust for conquest would be played out on the international stage like a giant chess game.

1800s: The Game of World Conquest

After the Napoleonic Wars, the European powers desired two things: a guarantee there would never be a repeat of the devastation of a pan-European war and to carve up the remainder of the globe into colonial holdings. The race was on as the newly formed European nations (Belgium, Germany, and Italy) rushed to take their positions on the world stage. This New Imperialism (1830–1914) shifted the focus from trade monopolies and indirect rule to the formation of overseas territories ruled as extensions of the home country.

Economically, New Imperialism was designed to stabilize international trade which had become volatile by the glut of manufactured goods produced by industrialization. During much of the nineteenth century, Britain was by far the most efficient at making goods very cheaply and was able to undersell virtually all competitors. The spread of the Industrial Revolution to other nations—Germany, France, and the United States—and the high investment costs of industrial infrastructure, such as railroads, fueled a growing demand for protected markets. New Imperialism seemed to be the answer.

A comparison of Maps 5 and 6 underscores the success of New Imperialism. Map 5 shows the extent of all European colonial holdings in 1800, including the United States, which had been plucked from the British colonial empire through the American Revolution. Russia had enjoyed great success in absorbing khanates across northern Asia and had laid claim to Alaska. Spain still controlled vast holdings in the Americas. However, the majority of European colonies in Africa and Asia were narrow strips of territory along the coastlines, while much of the interior was either unknown or functioned as independent trading partners.

After the Napoleonic Wars, the attention of European leaders focused on enlarging their imperial domains in these untapped areas. This had little to do with the indigenous population or even the wealth and resources that could be siphoned from a colony—the most promising lands had already been engaged in trade monopolies. This was a game played between cousins, the royal houses of Europe. The point was to have the most territory on the map. It was like playing the game of Risk for real. By 1914, the Great Powers had successfully established large colonial empires around the globe.

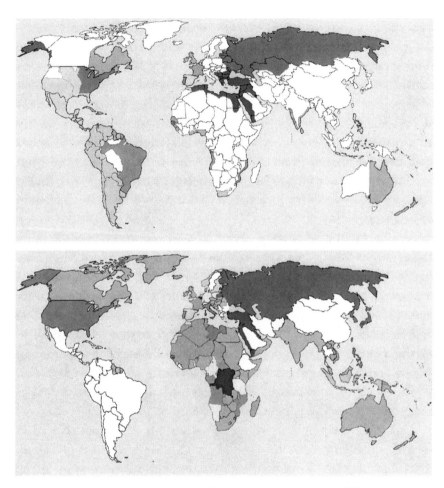

Above—Map 5: Colonial empires in 1800[288]

*Below—Map 6: World empires and colonies
in 1914, just before WWI*[289]

Almost the entire globe had been under European dominion.

The Great Game—Central Asia

The Great Game, also known as the Tournament of Shadows, was a strategic battle for supremacy in Central Asia waged from 1813 to 1907. The game began as Russia continued to expand its vast holdings into the southeastern khanates. Britain feared that Russia would use Afghanistan as a launching point for an invasion of India, the "Jewel in the Crown" of the British Empire. Thus, the first in a series of Anglo-Afghan wars began in 1838. By the 1890s, the game shifted east, with the focus on China, Mongolia and Tibet, as more khanates became Russian protectorates. The game ended with the Anglo-Russian Agreement of 1907.[290]

The crumbling Ottoman Empire, nicknamed "the sick man of Europe," was another theater for the Great Game. Since the end of the Napoleonic Wars, Russia had functioned very much like a "policeman of Europe," helping maintain the balance of power. Russia's interest in the Crimea, an Ottoman protectorate, was countered by an alliance of Britain, France, and the Ottomans.[291]

After the Russo-Turkish War (1877–78), in which Russia aided the nationalist aspirations of Orthodox Christians living in the Balkans, other European empires began to covet a piece of the Ottoman territories. Austria-Hungary occupied two Ottoman provinces, Bosnia and Herzegovina, for nearly thirty years. Meanwhile, Britain moved into Egypt and Cyprus in the name of "helping" the Ottomans, while France occupied Tunisia.[292]

**Political
cartoons
of the 1800s**

The Great Game

Carving up China

The Scramble for Africa

Above—The Great Game

Afghanistan between the Russian Bear and the British Lion[293]

Bottom Left—Carving Up of China

*"China—the cake of kings ... and emperors" Queen Victory
of the United Kingdom, William II of Germany, Nicholas II
of Russia with French Marianne in alliance, Meiji Emperor of
Japan dividing China as a Qing official tries to stop them.*[294]

Bottom Right—Scramble for Africa

*"The Rhodes Colossus"—announcing the Cape
to Cairo Railroad and telegraph line.*[295]

The Carving Up of China—the Open-Door Policy

By the early nineteenth century, the Qing dynasty of China was weak and unable to resist the colonial aspirations of Western Europe, Russia, and Japan. China had traditionally been closed to all outside influences, and what little foreign trade that did occur was strictly controlled by the government. The First Opium War (1839–42) ended in an unequal treaty that forced China to open its doors, awarding Britain control of Hong Kong Island and the ability to set tariffs governing Chinese foreign trade. This was the first of a series of land and trade concessions granted to foreign powers.[296, 297]

The Scramble for Africa

The final frontier of the New Imperialism was Africa. While Europeans had long held colonies rimming the coastlines of the continent, most of the interior was a vast, uncharted expanse that cried out to be explored, exploited, occupied, and annexed. Tensions ran high as emerging European nations such as Germany and Belgium sought overseas colonies as evidence they were taking their places beside established imperial powers such as Great Britain and France. Wilhelm II strived to make Germany the equal of Britain in every way, and by the early 1900s, Germany grew to be the third largest colonial power in Africa.[298]

World War I: The War to End All Wars

After the Napoleonic Wars, European governments pursued policies that maintained a Balance of Power through a network of diplomatic alliances. At the same time, the rising passions of imperialism and nationalism threatened to submerge Europe into yet another round of intense warfare on a global scale. By the early 1900s, all the major European powers were divided into two coalitions: the Central Powers or Triple Alliance consisting of Germany, Austria-Hungary and Italy, versus the Triple Entente of France, Russia, and Britain.[299]

The First World War was one of the deadliest conflicts in history thanks to the tactics and firepower made possible by the Industrial Revolution. The American Civil War and the Crimean War had offered glimpses of this new type of bloody and brutal warfare, but a pan-European war of this nature had previously been avoided. Modern weaponry made war more lethal, while industrialized infrastructure, including munitions factories and railways, ensured the front lines were constantly resupplied over long distances.[300] One historian summarizes it this way:

> In 1914 European armies confronted a technological revolution on the battlefield. The weapons developed over the previous decades—bolt-action rifles, machine guns, modern howitzers—provided firepower in unprecedented measure and presented insoluble problems to western military organizations. Modern weapons allowed armies to set up impregnable defensive positions, and neither the officer corps nor the general staffs worked out how to use modern technology or evolved tactical concepts to break through such defenses until 1918.[301]

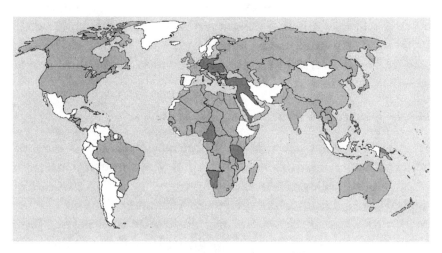

Map 7: The First World War[302]

Light gray: Entente and allies—
Dark gray: Central Powers White: Neutral Countries

By the outbreak of World War I, Europeans had conquered the world. Four years of intense fighting was the culmination of 420 years of nearly unceasing warfare and conquest. Ironically, World War I set in motion the events that ended the reign of the White Horseman, as we shall see.

CHAPTER 11:

A Lion with Eagle's Wings

> [3] And four great beasts came up from the sea, diverse one from another. [4] The first [was] like a lion, and had eagle's wings: I beheld till the wings thereof were plucked, and it was lifted up from the earth, and made to stand upon the feet as a man, and a man's heart was given to it. (Dan. 7:3–4 KJV)

As previously mentioned, Daniel's vision of the four beasts rising out of the sea and John's vision of the four horsemen foretell the same events. The White Horseman was introduced to John by the living creature with the face of the lion. Similarly, Daniel describes the first beast he sees as a lion with eagle's wings, a creature that was used as a Christian symbol and as a political emblem. In addition, the eagle and the lion were frequently used in the heraldry of the royal houses of Europe that had gone forth "conquering and to conquer."

Symbol of Mark the Evangelist—Symbol of Venice

Above—"The Lion of St. Mark" by Vittore Carpaccio (1516)[303]

Below—Flag of Most Serene Republic of Venice[304]

In Christianity, a lion with eagle's wings is used as a symbol of Mark the Evangelist, whom theologians credit with authoring the Gospel of Mark. As Europeans ventured around the world, the merchants and soldiers were followed by missionaries. Probably the best-known example was the Society of Jesus, better known as the Jesuits, founded for the purpose of Christian mission work in Portuguese colonies.[305]

Later, Protestant missionaries traveled from northern Europe and North America to areas where Christianity was previously unknown. For most of the world's inhabitants, whatever knowledge they have of Jesus was the result of this work, and certainly the presence of Christianity in so many non-European nations is a testimony to their efforts.[306]

The Venetian Republic, one of the great maritime powers at the start of the Renaissance, used the winged lion as its emblem. Venice was also one of the most important publishing centers during the early modern period thanks to Aldus Manutius. As a result, it played a pivotal role in spreading the ideas of the Renaissance and making the printed word the primary means of communicating knowledge.[307]

Between the late 1400s and World War I, the time represented by Daniel's lion with eagle's wings, the book and other printed materials, such as magazines and newspapers, were the primary source of information. Exceptions such as the telegraph were limited in the amount of information they could convey and were not useful as means of communicating to the masses. By the end of World War I, when the reign of the White Horseman ended, the importance of print in disseminating knowledge began to wane. Movies and radio grew rapidly in popularity, and by the end of the twentieth century, books were in danger of becoming irrelevant in the face of electronic media such as the Internet, Smartphones, and e-books.

A Lion with Eagle's Wings: A Picture of Europe

As the "king of the beasts," the lion symbolized bravery, strength, valor, and royalty, all characteristics that rulers wanted to emphasize in their coats of arms.[308] Likewise, the eagle, which evoked Imperial Rome, was a popular choice for royal shields. Shields featuring lions are scattered across the heraldry of Western Europe, while shields featuring eagles stretch out to the east, forming a pictorial version of Europe as a lion with eagle's wings. Even a cursory look at the distribution of lions and eagles in royal coats of arms will confirm this, as illustrated in the map of Europe (Map 8).

From Sweden[309] in the north, to Picardy in France,[310] to Castile and León in western Spain,[311] rampant lions were arranged diagonally in two quarters. The Duchy of Burgundy[312] used a similar arrangement with an additional rampant lion on a small shield in the center of the crest. A single rampant lion was used on the shields of Scotland,[313] the Netherlands,[314] Belgium,[315] the Duchy of Finland,[316] the Grand Duchy of Luxembourg,[317] Norway,[318] and the County of Flanders (now divided between France and Belgium).[319] A single rampant lion, topped by three fleurs-de-lis, was used on the shield of Lyon, the center of international trade in medieval France.[320]

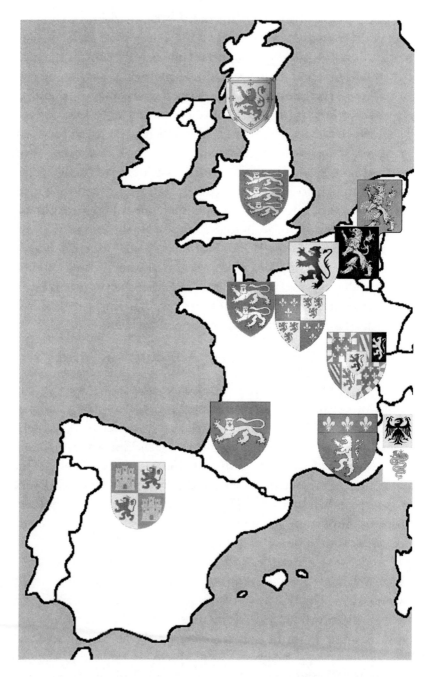

Map 8: Map of Europe with coats of arms arranged according to geographical location to the states they symbolized.[335]

Several coats of arms featured a lion passant (or walking lion), standing on three paws with the right forepaw raised.[321] The shield of Aquitaine featured one passant lion,[322] while that of Normandy had two,[323] and the shield of England had three.[324] The Danish coat of arms had a similar design—three passant lions in the unnatural shade of blue.[325]

The eagle figured prominently in the heraldry of central and Eastern Europe. The eagle, preeminent among birds and symbolizing courage, action, and protection, was used as an emblem long before the advent of heraldry. It was the sign of Horus in ancient Egypt and Jupiter in Rome. In addition, its history as an imperial symbol of both the Roman and Byzantine empires inspired the empire builders of continental Europe to adopt it as their own.[326]

Two types of eagles were used in European heraldry: those modeled after the Byzantine imperial eagle, and those modeled on the eagle of the Holy Roman Empire known as the *Reichsadler*. Because the czars saw themselves as the new guardians of Eastern Orthodoxy following the collapse of the Byzantine Empire, they based their coats of arms on the Byzantine eagle. Interestingly, the double-headed eagle featured on the Russian shield wears a breastplate bearing a white horseman slaying a dragon.[327] The Byzantine eagle was also adopted by the Kingdom of Romania, a new nation formed out of the medieval principalities of Moldavia and Wallachia, once part of the crumbling Ottoman Empire.[328]

The Reichsadler, German for "imperial eagle," was modeled after the Roman eagle and adopted by Charlemagne, Holy Roman Emperor. As a result, it was widely used throughout central Europe.[329] Both the Duchy of Prussia and the Electorate of Brandenburg used a single-headed Reichsadler making the choice of shields easy when the two merged to become the Kingdom of Prussia and later the German Empire.[330, 331] A white version of the Reichsadler was used by Poland,[332] while a black version was the insignia of the Austro-Hungarian Empire.[333] Both the German and Austrian shields were adapted from the double-headed Reichsadler that graced the imperial banner of the Holy Roman Empire.[334]

Lion Kingdoms versus Eagle Kingdoms

As you look at the map illustrating the coat of arms distributed across Europe (Map 8), you will notice the lion shields form a band from Spain to Scandinavia, with the British Isles lunging out like the paw of a rampant lion. To the east, eagle-bearing shields feather out across the continent like wings. Daniel then observes, "I beheld till the wings thereof were plucked, and it was lifted up from the earth, and made to stand upon the feet as a man, and a man's heart was given to it" (Dan. 7:4b KJV).

In order for this prophecy to be fulfilled, we need to see the kingdoms and empires represented by eagle shields removed from the rule of the royal houses of Europe, which characterized the White Horse system. At the same time, the nations with lion shields would need to be preserved to some degree, although not in their former glory.

Only twelve European nations are currently governed by some form of monarchy. They include Vatican City, an ecclesiastical state ruled by the pope,[337] three tiny principalities, a grand duchy, and seven kingdoms. The Vatican and the three principalities have never used lions or eagles in their heraldry. They are vestiges of the vassal estates of feudalism that barely function as fully independent modern nations. The Principality of Andorra, on the border between France and Spain, is ruled by co-princes, one of whom is the current president of France.[338] The Principality of Liechtenstein, between Switzerland and Austria, uses the Swiss franc as it unit of currency, relies on Switzerland for much of its diplomatic relations, and is one of the few countries in the world with no military.[339] The Principality of Monaco, off the coast of the French Riviera, has relegated its national defense to France.[340]

The remaining monarchies of Europe all have lions figuring prominently on their shields. They include the kingdoms of Britain, the Netherlands, Belgium, Spain, Sweden, Denmark, Norway, and the Grand Duchy of Luxembourg. Today, they all have some form of democratic government ruled over by a constitutional monarch.[341]

***Map 9: European republics (light gray) and
monarchies (dark gray) today.***[336]

Nations that used eagles as part of their crests are conspicuous by their absence in the current list of monarchies. Every one of them has some form of republican government. When you consider that most of Europe was under some type of monarchy at the turn of the twentieth century, this is remarkable. The powerful empires of Europe had been "torn off" just as Daniel prophesied. The first to go was Poland, consumed by the "Alliance of the Three Black Eagles," Russia, Prussia, and Austria-Hungary.[342]

The Russian Empire, which was one of the five Great Powers of Europe before the outbreak of World War I, was destroyed by the impact of the war and the Russian Revolution. The war caused food and fuel shortages, along with mounting inflation at home, and devastating casualties on the front lines. As workers staged a general strike and socialists exercised their political muscle within the government, Czar Nicholas II abdicated in the spring of 1917. He and his family were later murdered in the Russian Revolution and Civil War. The eagle wings of Imperial Russia had been torn from the lion.[343]

By the time World War I occurred, the great Habsburg Empire had been reduced to a fraction of its former glory, but Austria-Hungary was still numbered among the Great Powers of Europe. Like the Russian Empire, the dual kingdom had been economically and militarily strained by the challenges of World War I. In the fall of 1918, the monarchy collapsed, and the power vacuum was filled by leftist and liberal political movements demanding independence for the many ethnic groups that had made up the empire. Emperor Karl I was forced to step back from government; later the British removed Karl and his family into exile. The eagle wings of the Austro-Hungarian Empire had been torn from the lion.[344]

The last of the great empires symbolized by the eagle was Germany. Under the guiding hand of Otto von Bismarck, a Prussian statesman in the service of the king, Germany was hobbled together out of the hodgepodge of principalities that had once made up much of the Holy Roman Empire. In fact, the German Empire was known as the Second Reich, alluding to its status as the successor of the first. The impact of World War I destroyed the people's confidence in the political system, leading to the November 1918 revolution and the collapse of the monarchy. A new republican government emerged, forcing the kaiser to abdicate. The eagle wings of the German Empire had been torn from the lion.[345]

A Lion Like as a Man

> I beheld till the wings thereof were plucked, and it was lifted up from the earth, and made to stand upon the feet as a man, and a man's heart was given to it. (Dan. 7:4b KJV)

After World War I, the remaining monarchies functioned very differently from their predecessors. No longer were kings seen as divinely appointed rulers who wielded absolute power over their subjects. In fact, these kingdoms were transformed into constitutional monarchies in which kings had little real political power and were expected to remain above the political wrangling of the day. Royalty became the first families of their nations rather than part of an elite network of houses that forged diplomatic alliances through marriage.

The change in suitable marriage partners for members of royal families, particularly those of heirs apparent, illustrates this well. In Britain, Queen Victoria married a German prince in 1840. Eight of her nine children married into royal houses around Europe, although this was clearly not done by personal preference but rather out of a sense of duty. Victoria so disliked the fact that her three eldest daughters lived abroad that she allowed her youngest daughter, Beatrice, to marry Prince Henry of Battenberg only after he agreed to take up residence in Britain. She also allowed her daughter Louise to enter a morganatic marriage.[346]

This pattern became customary within the royal family. The British consorts of the earlier twentieth century were initially drawn from people of royal blood raised in the United Kingdom, including Princess Mary of Trek (consort of George V)[347] and Prince Philip, Duke of Edinburgh (consort of Elizabeth I).[348] Later, consorts came from the higher ranks of the commoners. Although Lady Elizabeth Bowes-Lyon (consort of George VI) was from a noble family, she was technically a commoner, the first to be married to a British ruler in centuries.[349] Lady Diana Spencer, who married Charles, Prince of Wales, came from a similar background.[350] Most recently, Prince William, who is expected one day to become king, married Kate Middleton, a commoner whose ancestors include laborers and miners. Such a marriage would have been inconceivable even fifty years ago![351]

It is interesting that the increasing tolerance of nondynastic marriages contributed in part to the undoing of the White Horseman. Recall the morganatic marriage of Archduke Franz Ferdinand of Austria-Hungary to Sophie, a mere countess, mentioned earlier.

In 1914, the Archduke and his wife were assassinated in Sarajevo, triggering World War I and unleashing forces that proved the undoing of the Great Powers of Europe and the kings behind them.[352]

The Ride of the White Horseman

The time of the White Horseman was proceeded by three momentous transitions that paved the way for European world dominance; the start of the Age of Discover, the invention of the printing press and the infantry revolution. While first two fulfilled Daniel's criteria that "many shall run to and fro, and knowledge shall be increased" (Dan. 12:4 KJV), the infantry revolution was an necessary pre-condition for the White Horseman. The infantry revolution, which began the Western style of warfare based blocks of foot soldiers armed with pike and shot, was epitomized by the bow—"he that sat on him had a bow" (Rev. 6:2 KJV).

From 1492, Europeans began a campaign of conquest, fulfilling John's prophecy that "he went forth conquering, and to conquer" (Rev. 6:2 KJV). They fought each other, attempting to conquer each other, which led to the emergence of handful of powerful nation states. At the same time, they made every effort to expand their influence around the globe, first by developing trading monopolies and establishing colonies on every continent, and then be subjecting the world into their colonial empires. Remarkably, the conquest generally began under a monarch who had been come to the throne in an unusual way, fulfilling the word, "a crown was given unto him" (Rev. 6:2 KJV).

PART 3:

The Red Horseman

³And when he had opened the second seal, I heard the second beast say, Come and see. ⁴And there went out another horse [that was] red: and [power] was given to him that sat thereon to take peace from the earth, and that they should kill one another: and there was given unto him a great sword. (Rev. 6:3–4 KJV)

And behold another beast, a second, like to a bear, and it raised up itself on one side, and [it had] three ribs in the mouth of it between the teeth of it: and they said thus unto it, Arise, devour much flesh. (Dan. 7:5 KJV)

Chapter 12:

A Horse of a Different Color

³And when he had opened the second seal, I heard the second beast say, Come and see. ⁴And there went out another horse [that was] red: and [power] was given to him that sat thereon to take peace from the earth, and that they should kill one another: and there was given unto him a great sword. (Rev. 6:3–4 KJV)

Who Was the Red Horseman?

The identity of the Red Horseman is easily recognized—once it is pointed out. It signifies a worldwide movement identified with the bear and the color red, a movement that takes peace from the earth, killing many. A key person associated with the movement is given a sword. Finally, the timing of the movement must follow the period of nineteenth century innovations that exponentially sped up communication and transportation.

Communism is the embodiment of all these requirements. Red is the color that epitomizes socialism or communism. Reds, pinks, commies—they all meant the same in American slang, especially during the Cold War. Red was used on communist flags and other national emblems. For example, the Soviet Union was symbolized by a red flag bearing a golden star over a hammer and sickle. Russia was also symbolized by a bear, usually called Mishka, which connects communism to the bear in Daniel's vision.

Communism and the fear it inspired absolutely took peace from the earth, as anyone who has lived through the Cold War knows. Most of the wars of the twentieth century were fought between communists and anticommunists. Fear of communism permeated the minds of an entire generation; there was a foreboding that a nuclear war might break out any day, one that truly would be the war that ends all wars because no one would survive.

The Red Horseman follows the second wave of exponential increases in knowledge, made possible by near universal literacy, the development of mass communication, and the revolutionary advances in transportation that began in the 1800s. It is likely that without these dramatic changes associated with industrialization, the Communist Revolution in Russia would have had little more success than all the other peasant revolts before it.

The Horse of Another Kind

> And there went out another horse [that was] red....
> (Rev. 6:4 KJV)

The Red Horseman is mounted on a horse of "another kind," a horse distinctly different from the White Horse. Unlike English, the Greek language specifies whether something is "another of the same kind" or "another of a different kind." In this case, John tells us that the Red Horseman is *allos* (αλλος), from which we get the word "else"—another of a different kind.[353] Therefore, the Red Horse must be fundamentally different from the White. The White Horse system ruled through the royal houses of Europe while the Red Horse system put power into the hands of the common people.

In addition, John describes the color of this second horse with the Greek word *pyrros* (πυρρός), the root of "pyrotechnic," "pyromaniac," and "pyre."[354] This is not the earthy red we see in actual horses, but the fiery red adopted as the color of communism. Perhaps the fiery shade is emblematic of the Red Horse system because it took all that had gone before it—conventions, traditions, and the structure of authority—and tossed it into the flames of change like a useless corpse on a funeral pyre.

This brings us to the spring of 1848.

The Spring of Revolutions

Europe was a political powder keg, with the embers of republicanism and revolution smoldering in the hearts of the people. The American and French revolutions had caused many to believe that all their problems would be solved if only their current governments were deposed. Discontent was rampant, and not just among the working classes. Many in the lower ranks of the aristocracy resented the current conditions sufficiently to be willing to revolt against the status quo.

On the other hand, after the French Revolutionary and Napoleonic Wars, many senior ranking authorities made it a high priority to avoid another such event. To ensure that any rumblings of revolution were silenced, Prussia, Russia, Austria-Hungary, Britain, and later France formed a Quintuple Alliance to put down any opposition to strong monarchies. The alliance successfully quelled revolts in Italy (1821) and Spain (1823)[355] but was powerless to stop the wave of revolutions that swept throughout the Spanish colonial holdings in South and Central America.[356] Interestingly, the alliance actually assisted the Greeks in their effort to overthrow their Ottoman overlords.[357]

However, diplomatic alliances between the Great Powers could not change the hearts and minds of the people. Localized rebellions continued to bubble up, and a handful achieved some measure of success. In France, the July Revolution (1830) led to the formation of a constitutional monarchy headed by liberal politicians.[358] A month later, the Belgian Revolution (1830) erupted as the people of the Spanish Netherlands broke away to form the independent Kingdom of Belgium under the newly elected King Leopold of Saxe-Coburg.[359]

The revolutions of 1830 were generally squelched by one of the Great Powers that formed the Quintuple Alliance. For example, the Polish bid for independence of November 1830, which began among the officers of Poland's military academy and spread into much of

Poland, Lithuania, Belarus, and the Ukraine, was soon quelled by the imperial Russian army.[360]

The Spring of Revolutions was different. In 1848, a series of grassroots rebellions erupted throughout Europe. Starting in France in February, political revolts spread like a tidal wave, impacting more than fifty countries across Europe and parts of Latin America. For the first time, there was a pan-European dispelling of traditional authority.[361]

The reasons for discontent varied. The nobility was frustrated with the rise of royal absolutism that destroyed its traditional privileges. The middle classes, pushing for universal suffrage and fueled by the new ideas of classical liberalism and nationalism, provided the intellectual impetus needed to stage an organized revolt. Social conditions were intolerable as traditional artisans found their livings undercut by factory-produced goods, and urban laborers worked long hours in squalid slums for wages so low they could barely subsist. The situation was exacerbated by high unemployment and rising food costs.[362]

The decade preceding the Spring of Revolutions came to be known as the Hungry Forties. Population growth coupled with years of crop failure led to prohibitively high food prices and caused great hardship among both urban and rural workers. When the potato blight struck northern Europe in the 1840s, the impact was devastating. Because the potato produced higher crop yields per acre compared to grains, it had become the staple of the lower classes. Years of blight were followed by severe famine, of which the Great Irish Famine is the most notorious. The failure of authorities to effectively address this situation only fueled antagonism toward government.[363]

Revolution on the Italian Peninsula

The Spring of Revolutions began in January 1848 in the Italian states with the Sicilian revolution for independence. The Kingdom of the Two Sicilies (Sicily, Naples and most of southern Italy) had once been ruled by the kings of Aragon and had become part of the Bourbon domains after the War of the Spanish Succession. The Italian population balked under the Bourbons and staged a revolt that gave Sicily independence for sixteen months.

Likewise, the northern Italians living under the control of the Austrian Empire staged a March uprising in a fight for freedom from foreign rule. Revolutionary forces were able to push the Austrians out of Milan and Venice, but the results were temporary. Austrian rule was restored by the end of the summer. [364]

Revolution in France

France experienced two insurrections in 1848 that ended the French monarchy and established the French Second Republic. The first revolt in February was a continuation of the July 1830 Revolution that sought to address the grievances of the working class, conditions that had only worsened with time. Despite the fact that the new republican government met protesters' demands, including the right to work and relief for the unemployed, a second workers' uprising known as the June Days erupted in yet another round of bloody insurrection.[365]

Revolution in the German States

The "March Revolution" referred to the revolts that convulsed the states of the German Confederation. The middle classes demanded the unification of Germany into a nation-state with a representative parliament and guaranteed civil liberties, while workers sought to improve their living conditions. In most cases, news of the February Revolution in France triggered the revolts in Germany.

Revolution first broke out in Baden in late February, despite the fact it had one of the most liberal political climates among all the German states. Protesters demanded a bill of rights and an elected representative government, a demand soon taken up in other parts of Germany with immense popular support. Unfortunately, liberal reforms within Baden and the formation of a national assembly were not enough to satisfy the radicals, and disorder continued. When a military mutiny broke out in early 1849, the Prussian army invaded, signaling the end of revolutionary fervor in Germany.[366]

Similar uprisings occurred across Germany. Events in the Palatinate paralleled those of neighboring Baden but with less support from its people. In Saxony, revolutionaries calling for a constitution took to the streets in May. Even in conservative Bavaria, public demonstrations protesting the king's mistress were hijacked by students demanding liberal reforms; order was restored only when the king abdicated.

Prussia was not immune to fomenting insurgency. In March 1848, crowds gathered in Berlin to present their demands in an "address to the king." Although the king verbally assented to all their demands, he responded with military force when rioting broke out. He then imposed a monarchist constitution on Prussia with an elected legislature.[367]

Revolution in Denmark

In Denmark, the push for a constitutional monarchy was easier since the king had just ascended the throne earlier that year. The Danish implemented a new constitution modeled on the American system, with the king as the head of the executive branch of government. The legislative branch consisted of two houses, one elected by landowners and a second elected by the general population.[368]

Revolution in Schleswig

Traditionally, Schleswig had been ruled by the Danish king but was actually a separate duchy with a mixed population of Danes and Germans. The new National Liberal government averted bloodshed in Denmark, but the Germans of Schleswig wanted no part of it and took to the streets in protest. Various German principalities sent armed forces in support of the revolutionaries but were subjugated by the Danish. The resulting peace settlement reaffirmed the pre-1848 borders.[369]

Revolution in Habsburg Austria

Austria had been a proponent of conservatism for generations, but nationalist feelings threatened to tear the empire apart. After generations of Habsburg conquests and dynastic marriages, the Austrian holdings were home to dozens of ethnic groups. Hungarians, Slovenes, Poles, Czechs, Slovaks, Romanians, Croats, Italians, and Serbs all sought to win some level of autonomy or independence over the course of the revolutions.

Recall, for example, the efforts in northern Italy to break away from Austria and form a unified Italian nation. In Bohemia, tensions erupted between Germans working to be included in a unified Germany and Czechs, who rallied for the independence of Austro-Slavs while hosting the Pan-Slavic Congress in Prague. The Habsburgs deployed military force to suppress the first round of rebellions across the empire. However, after radicals attempted to overthrow the monarchy in Vienna, the Prussian army was forced to intervene to put down the rebels. At this point, the Austrian chancellor fled to London for his own safety and the emperor abdicated in favor of his young nephew.[370]

Revolution in Hungary

The revolution took a different form in Hungary. The Hungarian Diet, founded in 1825 to handle the financial needs of the kingdom, grabbed the opportunity presented by the Spring of Revolutions to pass sweeping reforms, including the requirement that taxes collected in Hungary must be spent in Hungary. As a result, the country faced civil war on three fronts: Croatia to the south, Romania to the east (both were considered part of Hungary at the time) and Austria to the west. The Hungarian army enjoyed remarkable initial success, driving back the Austrians and 300,000 invading Russian troops, but suffered defeat after one and a half years of fighting. In the aftermath, Austria implemented brutal martial law and a program of Germanization designed to end ethnic resistance.[371]

Revolution in Switzerland

Switzerland, an alliance of independent republics, seemed an unlikely place for revolution. However, radicals from the unban middle class were pushing for a new constitution that would centralize the Swiss government. Seven cantons protested and formed the Sonderbund, or Separate Alliance, and civil war followed. When the fighting stopped, the new Swiss federal constitution created a unified nation, and the virtual independence of the Swiss cantons became a thing of the past.[372]

Revolution in Poland

In the face of revolution on the home front, the King of Prussia encouraged Polish prisoners released from Berlin to form a Polish Legion. Initially, the Prussians tolerated the idea of Polish autonomy, hoping to create a buffer zone that would keep Russia from interfering in the unification of Germany, but the Germans living in the area complained of Polish oppression. When war broke out in April, the Prussian forces terrorized the inhabitants, massacring six hundred prisoners, which in turn, triggered Polish insurgence. The Prussian army crushed the guerilla forces, ending Polish hopes for autonomy.[373]

Revolution in Wallachia

In Wallachia, a group of intellectuals and military officers attempted to overthrow Russian rule and establish a Romanian republic. Fearing Russian hostilities, the Wallachians sought an alliance with the Ottomans, which might have succeeded if the French and British, who feared another Russo-Turkish War, had not intervened. As the radicals overturned the provisional government, the Ottomans marched into Bucharest and the Russians occupied Transylvania (now Romania).[374]

Britain: the Dog That Didn't Bark

During this period, Britain certainly had its share of revolutionaries and radicals. The Chartists, possibly the first mass working-class labor movement, were calling for social and political reforms and backed their demands with a general strike in 1842. In April 1848, while much of Europe was awash in bloody revolts, the Chartists staged a mass demonstration to present another in a series of petitions to Parliament. A nervous government prepared for the worst, but the event proceeded without incident. Although the petition had no immediate impact, over the next twenty years, all but one of the Chartists' demands were passed into law. Remarkably, Britain avoided revolution.[375]

The Opening of the Second Seal

The Spring of Revolutions was a watershed event in world history. The common people of the most powerful continent in the world rose up en masse against the governing authorities. What made this even more remarkable was that there was no planned coordination among the revolutionaries; generally, each location staged its own revolt independent of others. It was as if a tap had been turned on and revolution had flowed like water throughout Europe. Although there was little in the way of long-term changes in the political structure, the social and cultural changes it began were profound. I argue that the revolutionary fervor that overtook Europe was spiritual in origins and that the event that allowed it to flow was the opening of the second seal. The Red Horseman rode forth.

CHAPTER 13:

Two Sides of the Same Coin

The Red Horseman was characterized by the rise of the common man to a position of leadership, completely transforming the Western world politically and economically. On one hand, there was the proliferation of communism, with its utopian vision of a classless society, the common ownership of the means of production, and the "distribution to all according to their need."[376] On the other hand, there was liberalism, with its broad-based democracy, appeal to the demands of the working classes, and nation-states based on the alliances of national people groups rather than the territorial holdings of the aristocracy.[377] Communism and liberalism are two sides of the same horse.

Karl Marx: Father of Communism

Karl Marx was the first to define communism; he and Friedrich Engels outlined its principles in a pamphlet entitled *The Communist Manifesto*, published in February 1848 during the Spring of Revolutions. Marx was both an influencer and a product of his time. As a young man, he studied philosophy at the Universities of Bonn and Berlin. He was involved with the Young Hegelians, a radical group of philosophers with a passion for tearing down anything they deemed irrational or restrictive of their freedom.[378] Marx, like thousands of other students across Europe, called for the overthrow of the established forms of government, particularly of the of Prussian absolutist monarchy.

As an author and journalist, Marx profoundly influenced the ideas of his generation and all that came after him. His articles in radical newspapers also attracted the unfavorable attention of the authorities; he was censored by the Prussians and the Russians (1843), expelled by the French—twice (1845 and 1849)—and was charged with revolutionary activities in Belgium (1848). Eventually, he landed in London, where he established the headquarters for the Communist League.[379]

Marx embraced a materialistic view of social change, reducing all of history to a record of class struggles between the "haves" and the "have nots," between those who owned the means of production—the bourgeois—and those who were brutally exploited for their labor—the proletariat. He argued that society must evolve through an inevitable series of economic systems, from feudalism to capitalism to socialism and ultimately to communism. Through this lens, he interpreted the revolutions of 1848 as the bourgeois rising up and pulling down the vestiges of the old feudal system, a necessary precondition for the proletariat revolution that would bring communism into effect.[380]

The Communist Manifesto is one of the most influential political works ever published. It was a short work designed to engage the masses rather than the intellectual elite. According to Cyril Smith, professor at the London School of Economics,

> Marx and Engels had encountered the ideas of the various groups of socialists and communists, and had also studied the organisations [sic] of the rapidly-growing working class. Hitherto, these two, socialism and the working class, had been quite separate from, or even hostile to each other. The achievement of the Manifesto was to establish the foundations on which they could be united.[381]

The Communist Manifesto called for the abolition of private property, arguing that its existence motivated the exploitation of the proletariat so the bourgeois could accumulate wealth. It called for a progressive tax to help redistribute wealth and a state central bank that would control all credit and currency. The centralized state would also control communication, transportation and all means of production, from factories to farms. Marx envisioned a state in which the distinction between town and country would be blurred and all children would educated in free schools. The workload would be equally distributed through the establishment of industrial armies.[382]

Although the pamphlet had no immediate effect, it impacted the thinking of future generations and became one of the most widely read documents of the twentieth century. It has inspired many to strive to bring about Marx's vision either through gradualist reform, like the Fabian Society,[383] or through revolution, like Leninism.[384] Either way, its anti-utopian perspective, claiming the ends justify the means, gave radicals justification for using brutality to implement the communist system.[385]

Marx expounded the principles of communism in his masterpiece, *Das Kapital.* The first volume was a critique of capitalism as a political-economic system built on the backs of the proletariat or urban workers. He argued that the capitalist who owns the means of production is able to charge his customers the "use value" of a commodity while paying his workers less than the value of their labor, and he keeps the "surplus profit" for himself.[386] Marx believed that the capitalist mode of production would necessarily result in a cycle of depressions and inflations, eventually causing capitalism's collapse. When that happened, he argued, communism would arise, bringing freedom and abundance to all. This was the ideology of communism, one side of the Red Horseman.[387]

Liberalism

To understand the connection between the Red Horseman and liberalism, it is necessary to distinguish between classical liberalism, which was popular in the eighteenth and much of the nineteenth centuries, and social liberalism, which had a huge impact on the twentieth century.[388] Classical liberalism was not new in 1848. During the Age of Enlightenment in the late 1600s, John Locke wrote of its fundamental premises, including the concepts of natural rights, social contracts and the rule of law over the rule of king.[389]

Classical liberalism defines liberty as freedom from harm. Therefore, the ideal government was small, with limited powers to ensure it could not do any harm to its citizens. Government was necessary only to protect against foreign invasion, provide police to protect citizens from being harmed by others, and to build and operate public works and institutions that did not provide a profit motive to the private sector.[390] The American Constitution, framed upon these ideals, used checks and balances to guarantee that no one individual or branch of government would have sufficient power to cause harm to its citizens or infringe on people's liberties to pursue their self-interests.

Economically, classical liberalism agreed with Adam Smith's concept of an "invisible hand," market forces that ensured the ambitious individuals pursuing their own interests would have a positive impact on society as a whole. The best thing the government could do was to leave the economy alone, a policy that came to be known as laissez-faire.[391] These ideas influenced much of public policy during the first half of the nineteenth century, exacerbating the problems already plaguing Europe. For example, the repeal of the Corn Laws in Britain (1846) was followed by a significant drop in the price of grain. This was beneficial for urban workers, who relied on food purchased with wages, but it devastated farmers. As a result, many were forced to migrate to the cities or overseas.[392]

Social liberalism, on the other hand, embraced a positive concept of liberty—the freedom to develop. Social Liberals, sometimes called New Liberals, believed that individual liberty could happen only under favorable social and economic circumstances and was impossible under the squalid conditions in which the majority of people lived. Therefore, they called for extensive government intervention aimed at improving the welfare of the poor. Social liberalism would give rise to the social welfare–oriented governments that dominate much of the Western world today.[393]

John Stuart Mill

John Stuart Mill (1806–73), whom some consider to be the father of modern liberalism, played a key role in the inception of social liberalism. He was the first to develop a liberal political-economic philosophy, believing that it was necessary not merely to criticize the traditional social order as most radicals did but to work toward replacing it with something better. He viewed history as a struggle between Liberty and Authority, a "contest … between subjects, or some classes of subjects, and the government." Mill defined social liberty as freedom from the "tyranny of the political rulers."[394] He also was the first to identify the tyranny of the majority.

In 1848, Mill published his monumental work *Principles of Political Economy and some of the applications to Social Philosophy*, which defined liberalism for the next quarter-century and became the leading economic textbook for years. In it, Mill made a distinction between production and distribution, and the different laws that govern them. He argued,

> The laws and conditions of the production of wealth, partake of the character of physical truths. There is nothing optional, or arbitrary in them … It is not so with the Distribution of Wealth. That is a matter of human institution merely.[395]

According to Mill, because institutions determined wealth distribution, changing the institutions would make possible a more equitable distribution of resources.

Philosophically, Mill was a transition between the classical liberalism he had studied as a young man and the social liberalism that would guide the policies of left-leaning liberals and social democrats of the twentieth century. As one scholar commented,

> Mill summed up his objective in his *Autobiography* (1873): "how to unite the greatest individual liberty of action, with a common ownership in the raw material of the globe, and an equal participation of all in the benefits of combined labour." (p. 239) In his economic theory Mill no doubt appears to the

modern socialist to be a follower of Ricardo and the classical liberal economists, but to the latter, and no doubt to himself, he was clearly a socialist.[396]

The impact of the writings of Marx and Mill cannot be overstated. At the beginning of the twentieth century, virtually all Europe was governed by some form of monarchy, with only three republics,[397] including the Third French Republic, established in 1870,[398] Switzerland[399] and San Marino, the oldest republic in Europe, founded in 301 AD.[400]

By the close of the twentieth century, the political structure of Europe had completely changed. The twelve monarchies still in existence have incorporated the ideals of social liberalism into their government policies. The rest of Europe is under some form of republican government with a history of either social liberalism and/or communism. Within a century of the Spring of Revolutions that opened the second seal, the entire Western world was permeated by the twin philosophies of the Red Horseman—communism and social liberalism. It was a world in which the White Horse royalty was removed from positions of power and replaced by the leadership of the common man. Undoubtedly, this was the fulfillment of "another horse of a different kind [that was] red" going forth (Rev. 6:4 KJV).

CHAPTER 14:

The Bear and the Bull

In John's vision, the Red Horseman is introduced by the second of the four living creatures listed in Revelation 4:7, the one with the face of a calf. The Greek word in this passage, *moschos* (μόσχος), implies a young bovine or "calf." Ezekiel's description of the living creatures uses the word *showr* (שׁוֹר), a male bovine often translated "bull" or "ox." Clearly, these two creatures—calf and bull—are one and the same.

In Daniel 7:5, the corresponding second beast that rises out of the sea is "like to a bear." While Daniel's first beast was the same type of animal as the living creature that introduced the White Horseman, this one is not. At first glance, a bear isn't remotely like a bull. However, this pairing was no accident.

The Stock Market

The bull and the bear are used as symbols of long-term stock market trends. A bull market refers to an upward trend such as that experienced in the United States before the dot-com bubble burst; it reflects investor confidence in the economy and the likelihood of rising stock prices in the future.[401] A bear market, on the other hand, is a general downward trend in the stock market that fosters a pessimistic mood among investors. The Wall Street Crash in 1929 is a classic example.[402]

Stock markets have been around since the Dutch East India Company was founded in 1602. Other nations soon followed suit; the New York Stock Exchange traces its beginnings to 1792. By the mid–1800s, the Industrial Revolution fueled rapid economic growth, forcing companies to search for new ways to fund expansion. The stock market provided the answer. By 1900, millions of dollars' worth of stock was being traded on Wall Street, only one of several stock exchanges.[403]

Although many consider the stock market as a plaything of the rich, it impacts all levels of society. The merchant class used it to acquire wealth in a new way (as opposed to the traditional means of land and inheritance). Stock market swings have a significant bearing on employers' ability to pay their workers. For example, during the panic of 1893, thousands of businesses failed, and "nearly one in six Americans lost their jobs."[404]

Russia: The Bear and the Communist Revolution

The bear has long been used as a symbol of Russia, and later, of the Soviet Union. Political cartoonists customarily used a bear to portray Russia and its communist successors. In fact, Misha or Mishka the Bear was used as the mascot of the XXII Summer Olympic Games, held in Moscow in 1980.[406]

It is no accident that Russia was the first nation to come under Communism. During the October Revolution of 1917, the Bolsheviks (majority), led by Vladimir Lenin (a.k.a. Nikolai Lenin), took control from the Russian government, the first openly Marxist seizure of power. Their intentions were to stage a socialist revolution before bourgeoisie capitalism had a chance to fully develop, thereby saving Russia from suffering through that stage of economic progression.

Mishka, the Russian bear as portrayed in a **Punch** *cartoon from 1911.*[405]

Ironically, Russia had already experienced a fairly quiet revolution earlier in the year (February Revolution), which resulted in the abdication of the czar and the formation of a provisional government intent on implementing the extensive democratic reforms demanded by moderate socialists. Unfortunately, the new government destroyed its credibility with the Russian people by continuing to participate in the immensely unpopular World War I.

Lenin, who had been living in exile in Switzerland, was granted permission from the German government to travel to Russia in June 1917. The German government hoped Lenin's presence would subvert the provisional government's will to continue fighting. The ploy worked spectacularly well, and by November, Lenin and the Bolsheviks were in charge, at least in theory. It soon became apparent that the Bolsheviks had virtually no support outside of the industrialized areas of St. Petersburg and Moscow.[407]

When the results of the first Russian election came in, the people "...voted overwhelmingly against the Bolsheviks and gave Communist candidates only one-quarter of the seats in the Constituent Assembly." After one day, Lenin forced the Assembly to close and unleashed the reign of "Red Terror" upon the country, using "arrest, torture, and death or imprisonment" to ensure compliance.[408]

Lenin's actions make sense if you understand that his motive was not political freedom and better conditions for the Russian people, but a desire to spark an international communist revolution.

> The Bolsheviks did not cause the overthrow of the Russian government; they came in after the overthrow with the plan of putting Marxist revolutionary theory to practice. Their plan from the beginning was to develop Russia in such a way as to spread social revolution throughout Europe and eventually the world. The biggest political opponents of the Bolsheviks in Russia, aside from the Czars, were the Mensheviks and Social Democrats, both Marxist groups who also supported Socialism, but were less militant. What is important to understand about the Russian Revolution is that some of the biggest opponents to the Bolsheviks were other Communists.

> The "brand" of Communism that was promoted by the Bolsheviks was by no means representative of all Communist ideology. Bolshevik ideology was the least tolerant and most revolutionary form of Marxist ideology.[409]

Lenin's goals were consistent with Marx's vision of the transformation of a capitalist society into a communist one.

> Between capitalist and communist society there lies the period of the revolutionary transformation of the one into the other. Corresponding to this is also a political transition period in which the state can be nothing but *the revolutionary dictatorship of the proletariat.*[410]

Lenin positioned himself as that "revolutionary dictatorship of the proletariat" and carried out his reign of "Red terror" through a secret police force called the All-Russian Extraordinary Commission, or Cheka. In July 1918, Felix Dzerzhinsky, who headed the organization, declared, "We stand for organized terror—this should be frankly admitted. Terror is an absolute necessity during times of revolution. Our aim is to fight against the enemies of the Soviet Government and of the new order of life."[411]

John Bull and Social Liberalism

Russia has Mishka the bear, the United States has Uncle Sam, and England has John Bull. Portrayed as a prosperous farmer, he came to stand for the loyalty, honesty and decency of the ordinary man on the street, ready to stand up for what he believed in, including criticizing the royal family or government if needed.[413]

Just as communism was first implemented in Russia, land of Mishka the Bear, the ideas of social liberalism were first put into practice in Great Britain, land of John Bull. From 1906 to 1914, the Liberal Party passed a series of reforms implementing the ideas of social liberalism. These included old-age pensions, and health and unemployment insurance paid for by a progressive taxation system. Although the reforms were initially resisted by big business, they were eventually accepted as a humane solution to the inevitable boom-

and-bust cycles that had plagued the economy in the nineteenth century. Other Western nations did not follow suit until the crises triggered by the Great Depression and the postwar era.[414]

Late-nineteenth-century Britain also saw the rise of the Labour Party, which was dedicated to giving a political voice to the urban proletariat. Herbert Asquith, leader of the Liberal Party, made an effort to work with the Labour Party. Initially (1903–14), the two parties collaborated during election campaigns to defeat the Conservative Party and pass the reforms of social liberalism.

During World War I, Prime Minister Asquith was the first to appoint members of the Labour Party to ministerial office as part of his strategy to guarantee trade union cooperation with the war effort. This experience convinced the Labour Party that it was possible to implement social change through Parliament rather than through revolution. It also marginalized demands by the Communist Party of Great Britain for a Soviet-style revolution. The Labour Party was rewarded at the polls. They became the official opposition to the Conservative administration in 1922 and won the general election the following year.[415]

John Bull, from a World War I recruiting poster.[412]

During the twentieth century, most Western nations implemented some form of social liberalism into government policy. In fact, liberalism has been called the dominant ideology of the modern world. In the United States, the values of social liberalism are most closely associated with the Democrat Party in the tradition of Franklin Delano Roosevelt's "New Deal" and John F. Kennedy.[416]

Social Democracy—Socialism through Liberal Means

In the early twentieth century, liberalism fell out of favor with European voters, who increasingly embraced some form of socialist ideology. After a half century of political and social upheaval, Europe embraced social democracy, an ideology that blended democracy and the gradual transformation from capitalism to socialism. The triumph of social democracy was fueled by the growing frustration that the long-awaited, "inevitable" collapse of capitalism as predicted by Marx seemed nowhere in sight.[417]

Lenin had tried to solve this disconnect between theory and reality by imposing communism through revolutionary means. His policy was an adaptation of the philosophy of Georges Sorel, expressed in his popular book *Reflections on Violence* (1908). Sorel, who advocated the use of violence as the tool of militant trade unionism, believed that a general strike was the essence of socialism and class struggle. He argued that only by constantly disrupting capitalism through boycotts, general strikes, and other modes of catastrophic revolution could workers achieve control over the means of production.[418] [419]

On the other hand, social democrats sought to achieve the goals of socialism by applying the ideas of Eduard Bernstein, a German socialist who worked with Engels and the Fabian Society. According to Bernstein, the best way to implement socialism in an industrialized nation was through a blend of trade union activity and party politics as explained in his highly influential book, *Evolutionary Socialism* (1899).[420, 421]

Although Bernstein's ideas were initially rejected by socialists, the upheaval caused by World War I and the Great Depression underscored their practicality. Socialist parties that remained true to Marx found themselves ousted by other radical political groups. During the interwar years, Swedish politicians laid out a practical roadmap for social democracy. Having sold the electorate on the importance of working for the common good, they were able to implement the revisionist version of socialism developed by Bernstein. As Sheri Berman, political science professor at Columbia University, stated,

> After 1945, therefore, Western European nations started to construct a new order, one that could ensure economic growth while at the same time protecting societies from capitalism's destructive consequences ... the state became generally understood to be the guardian of society rather than the economy,

... explicitly committed ... to managing markets protecting society from its most destructive effects, with the two most oft-noted manifestations of this being Keynesianism and the welfare state.[422]

What about Fascism?

To more radical leaders, such as Lenin, Stalin, and Hitler, the needs of society were best served by following the Georges Sorel model of using violence to achieve political ends. Sorel, who wrote several articles praising the actions of Lenin and the Bolsheviks, was honored by early communists as a great theorist. At the same time, he was also honored by fascists as a forefather of their political movement.[423] Oswald Mosley, founder of the British Union of Fascists, explained, "Georges Sorel's passion for revolutionary activity in place of rational discourse made him most influential in shaping the direction of fascism, especially in Mussolini's Italy."[424]

According to the *Merriam-Webster Dictionary*, fascism exalts the nation and race above the individual, while communism focuses on the camaraderie of all members of the proletariat around the world; it is easy to assume that the two are unrelated.[425] However, fascism blends political elements from the left and the right, forming what some have termed a revolutionary centrist view. Mussolini commented that fascism was developed to counter both the "backwardness of the right and the destructiveness of the left."[426]

Many of Hitler's key ideas came from Marx and Engels, as documented by Dr. John Ray. "The thinking of Hitler, Marx and Engels differed mainly in emphasis rather than in content. ... practically all Hitler's ideas were also to be found in Marx & Engels."[427]

The Nazi party platform was in line with those of most socialists, including the confiscation of all income not earned by work, the nationalization of business, profit sharing, government old-age pensions, and the communalization of department stores and land.

Hitler justified everything he did in the name of "the people" (*Das Volk*). The Nazi State was, like the Soviet State, all-powerful, and the Nazi party, in good socialist fashion, instituted pervasive supervision of German industry. And of course Hitler and Stalin were initially allies.[428]

In fact, the Nazis were called Brown Bolsheviks by their critics, including the German socialist Otto Rühle. In an article published in 1939, he argued that

> Russia was the example for fascism ... Whether party "communists" like it or not, the fact remains that the state order and rule in Russia are indistinguishable from those in Italy and Germany. Essentially they are alike. One may speak of a red, black, or brown "soviet state," as well as of red, black or brown fascism. Though certain ideological differences exist between these countries, ideology is never of primary importance ... On the contrary, because Russia calls itself a socialist state, it misleads and deludes the workers of the world ... This delusion hinders a complete and determined break with fascism, because it hinders the principle struggle against the reasons, preconditions, and circumstances which in Russia, as in Germany and Italy, have led to an identical state and governmental system.[429]

The Bear and the Bull Continuum

The social, political, and economic trends that characterized the Red Horseman ran the gamut from radical totalitarian regimes (Lenin and Hitler) to the more subtle shades of socialism and liberalism of the West. What all these "isms" have in common is that they were reactions to the social impact of the dominance of the White Horseman, in which the hereditary elite ruled over every aspect of society without regard for the needs or desires of the common people. They all attempted to give power to the people and implement some type of system to distribute society's resources more equitably.

The Red Horse political systems are a continuum between the bear's Bolshevik brand of communism of the extreme left to John Bull's centrist liberalism. Just as the stock market shifts from bull market to bear market and back, so the political pendulum of the Red Horseman swings from left to right and back in most Western nations. Other than the totalitarian extremes of communism or fascism, political parties of various shades—socialist, liberal, libertarian (who are conservative economically but liberal on social issues)[430] and even conservative—all compete at the ballot box for the votes of the commoners. Politicians who ignore the will of the people do so at their own peril.

CHAPTER 15:

Taking Peace— Rumors of War

> And there went out another horse [that was] red: and [power] was given to him that sat thereon to take peace from the earth... (Rev. 6:4a KJV)

The Red Horseman has the power to take away peace, but what does that mean? The obvious answer is war, but this is far from a complete answer. International wars, civil wars, revolutionary wars, and cold wars may take away peace, but so can fear and anxiety. Peace evaporates in the face of rapid upheavals in social relationships, including changes in the structure of authority, of marriage and family, and of gender roles in society. Ironically, the quests for utopia or some version of what society should be may have been the greatest threat to peace on earth. We will look at these more subtle stealers of peace in the next chapter, but for now we will look at how war impacted peace during the Red Horseman's reign.

The Specter of Modern War

Although the time of the Red Horseman experienced plenty of wars, the frequency of military conflicts in Europe actually went down after the conclusion of the Napoleonic Wars. In fact, the goal of the European Great Powers during the second half of the nineteenth

151

century was to avoid wars through the judicious use of diplomacy and political alliances.

The nature of war certainly changed during the 1800s due to the industrialization of weaponry and army supply lines. The Crimean War (1853–56) and the American Civil War (1861–65) left an indelible impression of the carnage that was now possible. World War I (1914–18), "the war to end all wars," reinforced the understanding that industrialized warfare left a trail of endless annihilation in its wake.[431]

At the same time, the new focus on the masses as essential units of production led to the realization that civilians working in factories and agriculture were as vital to the war effort as soldiers on the front lines. This was total war, in which the whole country was an essential part of the battle.[432] As a result, civilians became military targets. For example, during the Battle of Britain in World War II, London was bombed for seventy-six consecutive nights, destroying or damaging more than a million homes. Other urban centers all over the country were also targeted to damage the British war economy and demoralize the people into surrender.[433]

Rumors of Wars

When Jesus instructed his disciples about the end times, he said,

> [6]And ye shall hear of wars and rumors of wars: see that ye be not troubled: for all [these things] must come to pass, but the end is not yet … [8]All these [are] the beginning of sorrows." (Matt. 24:6–8 KJV)

He foretold that the first stage of Braxton-Hicks contractions, starting early in the third trimester of pregnancy, would be characterized by wars. As we have seen, the White Horseman brought a never-ending cacophony of wars across Europe and around the globe. The second phrase, "rumors of wars," characterizes the Red Horseman. A rumor is defined as "talk or opinion widely disseminated with no discernible source; a statement or report current without known authority for its truth."[434] Some scholars define rumor as a type of propaganda, communication designed to control the opinion of the masses or a group of people. Rumor also includes misinformation (false information) and disinformation (deliberately false information usually from a government source given to the media or a foreign government).[435]

The concept of government efforts to massage the truth during wartime was not new. However, the wartime use of propaganda and disinformation exploded in the late nineteenth and twentieth centuries. In part, this was due to emerging communication technologies such as the telegraph that allowed information from the front lines of a war to reach the home front within hours. Mass media outlets such as newspapers and later radio relayed it to the public soon thereafter. Visual modes of communication—photography and film—gave the impression of conveying the absolute truth, making them very difficult to refute.

Furthermore, the use of propaganda evolved over the nineteenth century in direct response to the expanding number of eligible voters and the tyranny of "public opinion." Historian Paul Jonathan Meller observed,

> Although traditional liberal ideas survived, the embodiment of public opinion was moving away from the iconic John Bull to the "man in the street," who in many eyes could be both irrational and belligerent … J.S. Mill had expressed a fear of mass opinion in his seminal work, *On Liberty*, which argued that not only over-bearing state intervention, but the conformity of the masses was stifling individualism in society, and, as a result, "At present individuals are lost in the crowd. In politics it is almost a triviality to say that public opinion now rules the world."[436]

The Crimean War

The issue of public opinion came to a head during the Crimean War. *The Times*, a highly influential London daily newspaper, pioneered the use of war correspondents on the front lines. Their reporters and photographers would send daily updates by telegraph to London for immediate publication.[437] *The Times'* dispatches gave the press a distinct advantage over the government in shaping public opinion about the war; it resulted in the resignation of the sitting government due to public dissatisfaction over the performance of the British army. It also forced the military to make reforms, including the abolition of the selling of commissions.[438]

The rapid flow of information via the telegraph from the Crimea created a significant problem for the government. The public's thirst for daily news from the front combined with the government's failure to provide relevant updates allowed *The Times* to serve as the main source of updates for the general public and government officials alike.

Eventually, the government saw the need to counter the propaganda of *The Times* with some of its own. The War Office sent a photographer to produce images that would counter the newspaper's negative accounts of the state of the army and the horrors of war. The experience of the Crimean War showed that even the most liberal of governments needs to exercise some level of censorship to ensure the ongoing support of public opinion and to guarantee that no information helpful to the enemy was published in the media.[439]

The Crimean War was fought with "rumors of wars."

World War I

By World War I, the British government had mastered the manipulation of the media sufficiently to ensure public support for the war. The Defense of the Realm Act forbade British correspondents from publishing any sensitive information about munitions, the number or location of British troops and ships, and any plans for future action. As a result, even the most devastating of battles was reported in the best possible light. Germany had a similar relationship with its press.

At the same time, newspapers from both sides freely printed disinformation designed to muster passionate hatred for the enemy. Propagandistic stories in the British Press included: "Belgium child's hands cut off by Germans" and "Germans crucify Canadian officer." Meanwhile headlines such as "French doctors infect German wells with plague germs" and "German prisoners blinded by Allied captors" screamed across the papers of Germany.[440]

World War I was fought with "rumors of wars."

World War II

The government propaganda machine was in full gear before World War II even began. In addition to the usual pro–allies, anti–enemy claptrap, governments launched a campaign to encourage behaviors that aided the war effort and increased industrial production. For example, the U.S. government admonished citizens to conserve supplies, grow victory gardens, and buy war bonds. Major campaigns were launched to convince married women (and their husbands) to enter the work force. Later, women were encouraged to sign up for the female branches of the service.[441]

Of course, one of the most widely used propaganda tools was the radio. President Roosevelt used his "Fireside Chat" broadcasts to prepare Americans for the possibility of entering the war in Europe, to announce the declaration of war on Japan, and later to provide encouragement and commentary about the ongoing war effort.[442] In Britain, King George galvanized his subjects with speeches over the radio. The heroic efforts he made to overcome his speech impediment illustrate how vital radio broadcasts were to the war effort![443, 444]

However, the award for most masterful use of radio for propaganda goes to the Nazis. Early on, Goebbels foresaw the effectiveness of radio broadcasts in shaping public opinion, and he distributed millions of subsidized radios throughout Germany. He referred to radio as the "Eighth Great Power," saying,

> It would not have been possible for us to take power or to use it in the ways we have without the radio... It is no exaggeration to say that the German revolution, at least in the form it took, would have been impossible without the airplane and the radio... [Radio] reached the entire nation, regardless of class, standing, or religion. That was primarily the result of the tight centralization, the strong reporting, and the up-to-date nature of the German radio.[445]

Germany and Japan made extensive use of English-language radio broadcasts designed to undermine the morale of Allied forces. *Tokyo Rose* gave propaganda reports sandwiched between popular American music and slanted news shows. It is claimed that "*Tokyo Rose* could be unnervingly accurate, naming units and even individual servicemen; though such stories have never been substantiated by documents."[446] Similar rumors circulated about Axis Sally, the nickname given to American radio personalities, Mildred Gillars, broadcasting from Berlin, and Rita Zucca, from Rome.[447] [448] American William Joyce was the voice of Lord Haw Haw, who presented the British Isles with discouraging accounts of high losses and casualties among Allied forces.[449]

For the first time, propagandists were able to use film to spread their message, knowing it would be very difficult to refute film footage as a lie. Leni Riefenstahl's *Triumph of the Will* was one of the Nazis' most memorable propaganda films, depicting Hitler's 1934 rally in Nuremberg with powerful imagery designed to inspire followers and intimidate enemies.[450] In fact, Germany produced an English-language propaganda film to convince Americans that the invasion of Poland was both justified and provoked.[451] Leading Hollywood director Frank Capra funneled his war efforts into the production of a series of Academy Award–winning informational films entitled *Why We Fight*.[452]

World War II was fought with "rumors of wars."

The Cold War

The Cold War was the pinnacle of battling with propaganda. Near the close of World War II, atomic bombs were dropped on Hiroshima and Nagasaki, wreaking a previously unfathomable level of devastation.[453] Finally, the nuclear weapons made war such a frighteningly terrifying prospect that even generals and politicians searched for ways to avoid total war. The concept of MAD (mutually assured destruction) resulted in the Cold War, which was just as effective at taking peace from the earth as any hot war before it.

The Cold War conflict was between the "communist bloc" and the "free world," led by the United States. Since total war was not an option, the Cold War was expressed through the arms race, competitions at international sporting events, and technological rivalry such as the space race. The fear that communism would spread over the entire earth seemed to be a very real possibility during the

1950s and '60s. After all, the establishment of the Soviet puppet states in Eastern Europe and revolution in China had put almost a quarter of the globe under the rule of communist dictators (see Map 10). The West responded with the twin policies of "rollback" and "containment."[454]

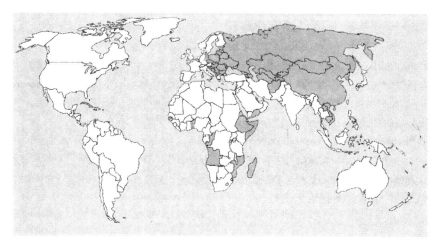

Map 10: The maximum territorial extent of countries under the direct influence of the Soviet Union in 1961.[455]

The Cold War was also expressed through proxy wars, in which the Soviets supported and fostered communist revolutions, while Western nations sent foreign aid to counter Marxist insurgents. The most famous were the Korean War (1950–53),[456] and the Vietnam War (1959–75),[457] but there were many others.[458]

The mood of distrust and suspicion that characterized the Cold War had started long before the 1940s. The Bolshevik rhetoric about capitalism coupled with Soviet funding of the British general strike of 1926 severed all Soviet-British diplomatic relations. The Soviets, on the other hand, were wary after the West supported the White Army during the Russian Civil War. They made frequent accusations of sabotage and espionage by enemies real or imagined in the Soviet Union.[459] For instance, Stalin accused Western capitalists of attempting to weaken Russia

> by means of invisible economic intervention, not always obvious but fairly serious, organizing sabotage,

planning all kinds of "crises" in one branch of industry or another, and thus facilitating the possibility of future military intervention.[460]

Accusations about espionage were not limited to the communist bloc. In the late 1940s and '50s, the United States experienced the Second Red Scare. There was concern that communists, both American and foreign, were infiltrating the federal government or influencing society in order to bring down American democratic capitalism and replace it with communism. These fears intensified during the trial of Julius and Ethel Rosenberg, the erection of the Iron Curtain around Eastern Europe, and the Soviet Union's possession of nuclear weapons. The result was a political witch hunt by the House Un-American Activities Committee, blacklisting, and political loyalty review boards that determined just how "American" federal employees were.[461]

The Cold War was fought with "rumors of wars."

Conclusion

The Red Horseman undoubtedly took peace from the earth. Far from creating a utopia of liberty, brotherhood, and equality, it produced a world filled with fear and suspicion. Instead of liberty, totalitarian regimes crushed individualism with their imposed visions of the common good. Instead of brotherhood, there was an underlying current of distrust, in which your neighbor could turn you in as a spy or traitor on nothing but a hunch, with or without evidence. Instead of equality, a new, unpredictable elite arose to power. The world became a giant game of Mao, in which the rules were constantly changing and those who broke the rules could lose everything, even their lives.

CHAPTER 16:

Taking Peace—A World of Constant Change

> And there went out another horse [that was] red: and
> [power] was given to him that sat thereon to take
> peace from the earth... (Rev. 6:4a KJV)

The Greek *eirana* (εἰρήνη), translated "peace," doesn't refer simply to the absence of war. It is also defined as "peace between individuals, i.e., harmony, concord."[462] Using this definition, dysfunctional relationships and stress in its many forms can result in discord and take away peace. As mentioned before, every facet of society underwent a complete restructuring that induced a subtle, but devastating corrosion of mental and emotional well-being.

There is a link between change and stress. Psychologists Thomas Holmes and Richard Rahe have developed a stress scale that documents the most common stressors. The highest levels of stress are caused by transformations within marriage or childrearing and other family dynamics. Stress can also be triggered by changes within the structure of authority. During the late 1800s and early 1900s, the social conventions governing all three of these relationships underwent monumental changes.

The other common thread in the stress-inducing elements listed by Holmes and Rahe is change—change in the workplace, change in living conditions. Even positive changes, such as getting married, have a stressful impact on the human body.[463] With the arrival of the Red Horseman, the world underwent a series of upheavals in virtually every area of life. It was as if the realm of the White Horseman was invaded by a strange race governed by a completely different set of rules.

Changing Social Relationships

Changing Authority Structure

One way to remove peace from the earth is to demolish society's authority structure. The Red Horseman did just that. Under the White Horseman, society was generally ordered according to the Great Chain of Being. This hierarchical ladder, which was developed in the medieval period, showed the relative position of all creation, from God at the top to base elements at the bottom. Everybody knew his or her relative rank in society, knew his or her place, as the Victorians would say, and believed it was God's divine will that he or she should remain in his place.[464] Although the rules might be broken, at least within the upper ranks of society, everybody knew who was in charge. There were clear guidelines regarding the chain of command and the passing of authority from generation to generation.

With the release of the Red Horseman, this system was overturned and society was ruled by the common man. The leaders were then drawn from the middle class, from the bourgeois, or possibly even the proletariat rather than from those who ruled by virtue of birth. Once this process began, anyone could ask "Why not me?" and revolt against the current government. For example, in Russia and China, the communist revolutions occurred shortly after royal dynastic rule had been replaced by a republican form of government.[465, 466] The rapid changes in the structure of government and the governing authorities created uncertainty and stress for those who lived under them.

Government upheaval took "peace from the earth."

Socializing Children

Traditionally, child-rearing had been considered the responsibility of parents. They may have arranged for others to care for their children, but ultimately they had full authority over their offspring. Education was not compulsory and was frequently done privately at home. Those who could afford to hire a governess or tutor did so. Some boys from wealthier homes went to boarding schools (called public schools). Others sent their children to village grammar schools or arranged for apprenticeships to teach them trades.

Although a primary education was highly desired, the vast majority of children did not attend school because their labor made an essential contribution to the family's income. Social reformers, both liberal and communist, believed that most of society's ills had their roots in the ignorance and vice caused by the lack of education, and they saw early intervention by schools as the best way to improve things. This was the motive of Robert Raikes, who began Sunday schools in the late 1700s.[467] Classes in reading and other basic skills were held on Sundays, when children would be free from their weekday work obligations.

In the late 1800s, Britain introduced the concept of compulsory education for children up to the age of ten. If attendance proved to be a problem, elected school boards could fine the parents of truants.[468] In the United States, school was compulsory in half the nation by 1900 and in every state by 1918.[469] John Dewey, the leading proponent of Progressive Education, argued that schooling was

> ...a regulation of the process of coming to share in the social consciousness; and that the adjustment of individual activity on the basis of this social consciousness is the only sure method of social reconstruction.[470]

In the years preceding the 1800s, the church played a significant role in ensuring uniformity within society. The proliferation of church denominations and the increasing rejection of Christianity by social and political reformers meant the church was no longer the social binder. Reformers such as Dewey and Lenin turned to state education as a tool for socialization. Anthropologist Dennis O'Neil points out,

> If all children receive the same socialization, it is likely that they will share the same beliefs and expectations. This fact has been a strong motivation for national governments around the world to standardize education and make it compulsory for all children. Deciding what things will be taught and how they are taught is a powerful political tool for controlling people.[471]

The rise of mandatory education by state schools began the efforts to transform a child's values and allegiances from his family's to the state's. Certainly, this was the philosophy of Lenin, who declared, "Give me four years to teach the children and the seed I have sown will never be uprooted ... Give us the child for 8 years and it will be a Bolshevik forever."[472]

Progressive educators saw long term exposure to state-designed schooling as an essential component of molding society to their utopian vision. This desire to "socialize" children into model citizens is partially responsible for the ever increasing number of completed years in "basic" schooling. When compulsory education was first introduced, four years of schooling was mandated and few progressed past the eighth grade. In 1910, only 13 percent of the U.S. population completed high school; by the end of the century, that figure had risen to 83 percent. [473]

During the second half of the twentieth century, formal schooling began at increasingly early ages. The name Kindergarten was coined by Friedrich Fröbel in 1840 to honor of the four hundredth anniversary of the invention of the Gutenberg printing press. During the nineteenth century, privately run Kindergarten classes supplemented the education system in much of the western world.[474] Enrollment was limited to a small portion of the population (less than 10 percent of the eligible children) until the mid-1960s, when Head Start and other federally funded pre-schools programs were introduced. By 1980, one in three children was enrolled in some type of pre-school, increasing to 53 percent by 1997.[475]

The importance of schools as instruments of social reform is underscored by the hostility shown toward those who don't comply. For example, home schooling is routinely criticized for failing to provide children with social skills, a charge that persists despite evidence to the contrary. The *Washington Times* reported that longitudinal studies on home-education "... should cause many critics to rethink their position on the issue of socialization. Not only are home-schoolers actively engaged in civic life, they also are succeeding in all walks of life."[476]

The rise of socializing children took "peace from the earth."

The Rise of Romantic Love and Marriage

With the Red Horseman came far-reaching changes in the patterns of marriage and courtship. The story of *Fiddler on the Roof* examines the impact of abandoning the traditional approach to marriage in favor of a new one based on romantic love. When Motel, the tailor, personally proposes marriage rather than using a matchmaker, his future father-in-law, Tevye, responds,

> They gave each other a pledge. Unheard of, absurd.
> You gave each other a pledge?
> Unthinkable. Where do you think you are?
> ... And what do you think you're doing?
> ... This isn't the way it's done, not here, not now.
> Some things I will not, I cannot, allow.
> Tradition—Marriages must be arranged by the papa.
> This should never be changed.
> One little time you pull out a prop, and where does it stop?
> Where does it stop?[477]

The answer given by the play is it doesn't stop until Tevye's whole world is pulled down by revolution, deportation and the "loss" of his daughter through marriage to an outsider.

Traditionally, marriages were arranged in all but the lowest levels of society. Marriages were about economics and ensuring the well-being of the next generation. In the world of the White Horseman, it was possible to improve one's position but only over the course of several generations and only through the careful forging of alliances through matrimony. This was just as true for the lower classes as it was for the royal houses; the difference lay in what was negotiated—manure piles and bed linens versus estates and houses.

Under the old system, nuptials were arranged between people in the same community and were enforced by the whole community. Once a couple was betrothed, if the groom failed to marry his fiancée, he would often be compelled by force, even if it meant being dragged to the altar. This was the origin of the shotgun marriage. As urbanization and industrialization removed young women from the protection of their communities, there was a surge of illegitimate births. "By the 1840s, as many as one birth in three was occurring outside of wedlock in many large cities."[478]

Over the course of the 1800s, the traditional view of holy matrimony was replaced with the ideal of marriage based on romantic love. While some form of romantic love had long been recognized, before the twelfth century it was seen as a sign of a character flaw.[479] For instance, Shakespeare's *Romeo and Juliet* was not a romance but a tragedy, in which the main characters bring disaster on themselves through their own weaknesses. More recently, romantic love was portrayed as heroic. Sociologist Anthony Giddens argues that the emergence of the novel is linked with the ideal of romantic love and its role in the marriage relationship.[480]

If novels such as Jane Austen's *Sense and Sensibility* brought the idea of marrying for love to the table for consideration, Hollywood movies seared it into the minds of Western youth. One young man blogged,

> Hollywood has berated us since we were young with "romantic love," that guy and girl experience love at first sight and everyone lives happily ever after. In the end, this Hollywood "love" myth has messed up many guys' minds.[481]

It is difficult to estimate the impact of Hollywood movies on the lives of viewers. How many were made discontent because things didn't measure up to the dysfunctional romantic ideal of love and family shown in the movies? While some may find romantic movies inspiring and uplifting, *Time* magazine cited studies that found many couples experience difficulties in their relationships because of misconceptions gleaned from Hollywood films.[482]

The rise of romantic love took "peace from the earth."

A Changing World

Change is a normal part of the modern world, but it was decidedly not expected or welcomed before the 1800s. Between 1850 and 1950, the world underwent rapid, revolutionary change, giving everyone reason to be stressed. Even the noise that the forms the background of our lives has escalated. Musician and relaxation specialist Steven Halpern points out,

> When Mozart was composing at the end of the eighteenth century, the city of Vienna was so quiet that fire alarms could be given verbally, by a shouting watchman mounted on top of St. Stefan's Cathedral. In twentieth-century society, the noise level is such that it keeps knocking our bodies out of tune and out of their natural rhythms. This ever-increasing assault of sound upon our ears, minds, and bodies adds to the stress load of civilized beings trying to live in a highly complex environment.[483]

The world in 1800 was the world of Jane Austen, in which the majority of people lived their lives in the country. Farming was the number-one vocation, and much of what a family consumed was made at home. The processes of urbanization and industrialization overturned all that.

Urbanization brought an increasingly large segment of the population from the countryside into the cities. For centuries, the majority of people were needed as farm laborers to ensure adequate food supplies. The agricultural revolution of the 1700s dramatically improved farm efficiency and put an end to customary land use. The resulting enclosure of fields forced countless peasants off the land. The establishment of factories in the 1800s, with their incessant demand for unskilled labor, drew thousands of displaced farm workers into the cities.

By 1950, 30 percent of the world's population lived in urban areas, and today, that figure has grown to approximately 50 percent. The proportion is much higher in industrialized nations; currently more than 80 percent of Americans are urban dwellers, and more than three-quarters of the U.S. population lives in just 3 percent of U.S. territory.[484] The early stages of urbanization created vast, squalid "morasses of misery" that served as homes for the urban laborers on the East End of town, which contrasted sharply with the upper-class West End where the bourgeois made their homes.[485]

Life in a country cottage, however small, was vastly different from life in urban slums, featuring damp, overcrowded, badly built houses with no windows, no drainage, no sewage and no running water. Instead of toilets, families shared outhouses that frequently overflowed into the surrounding structures, and at times into well water.[486] In London, the Thames River served as both a sewer and the drinking supply for many families. A bucket filled with untreated river water was left to sit for two or three days so the sewage sediment could settle to the bottom. Water for drinking and bathing would then be skimmed off the top.[487]

Industrialization was another agent of change, significantly transforming modes of production and economic relationships. Although the beginnings of the Industrial Revolution could be traced to the 1700s, 1850 marked the start of a Second Industrial Revolution, sometimes called the Technical Revolution. The introduction of the Bessemer steel smelting process allowed high-quality steel to be produced from inexpensive pig iron. Other developments significantly increased productivity, including the assembly line, Frederick Taylor's scientific management, which transformed crafts into mass production, and industrial engineering such as time-and-motion studies pioneered by Frank Gilbreth, Sr. Eventually, whole industries were restructured.[488, 489, 490]

During the nineteenth century, virtually every area of society was transformed, especially in England. Universal public schooling was followed by near-universal literacy. Communication through the postal service and telegraphs allowed people to keep in touch with their loved ones. As the world moved into the twentieth century, households enjoyed electric lights, city gas, and a constant parade of newly patented gadgets designed to make life easier. Medicine was changing the world too. Joseph Lister introduced anesthesia and sterile procedures to the surgical world,[491] while Florence Nightingale almost singlehandedly invented the profession of nursing.[492]

Changes continued at a breathtaking pace into the twentieth century. From 1900 to the 1950s, the citizens of the Western world experienced two world wars and the Great Depression. Horse-drawn transportation was replaced with cars, clothing was factory produced instead of homemade, and fashions changed annually instead of over the course of a decade or more. Change was so far reaching and pervasive that it has been said a person from 1890 would be more at home in the Roman Empire than in the modern world. All this change has added incredible amounts of stress to our lives in ways that our ancestors could not have perceived.

The Red Horseman was indeed given the power to take "peace from the earth."

CHAPTER 17:

Kill One Another

> And there went out another horse [that was] red: and [power] was given to him that sat thereon to take peace from the earth, and that they should kill one another: (Rev. 6:4a KJV)

The time of the Red Horseman is characterized by men killing each other. Murder is not new. The first murder was committed by the son of Adam and Eve only one generation after creation. War was not new, either, when the first seal was opened. Just as the White Horseman was accompanied by an exponential rise in the frequency and intensity of warfare, the Red Horseman ushered in a time of murder on a massive scale. The concept of Social Darwinism justified the killing of the "useless" and the "unfit" for the greater good of human society. The social application of the "survival of the fittest" allowed totalitarian states to implement large-scale democidal campaigns.

Evolution—Development of a Theory

It is impossible to understand the killing under the Red Horseman without first considering the ideas proposed by Darwin. In many ways, he and his followers laid the philosophical groundwork of the Red Horseman as surely as the "Great Chain of Being" had been the blueprint of the White.

Charles Darwin and ***Alfred Russel Wallace*** were the first to hypothesize the concept of evolution. Darwin presented his theory of natural selection in his seminal work, *On the Origins of Species*, published in 1859 twenty years after its inception. Surprisingly, it was received with general assent and proved immensely popular. The work was translated into several languages and widely disseminated through Western society. Darwin's name would become synonymous with evolutionary ideas. By 1870, a majority of scientists were convinced that some form of evolution had occurred, although few agreed with Darwin's mechanism of natural selection.[493]

Alfred Russel Wallace, a British naturalist, had developed a slightly different version of natural selection independent of Darwin, although the two men had exchanged their ideas before they were published. Wallace later spoke out in opposition to both Social Darwinism and eugenics. Like John Stuart Mill, he argued that society was too corrupt and unjust to be allowed to determine who was fit or unfit.[494]

Herbert Spencer was another enthusiastic supporter of the concept of evolution. An atheist philosopher and political theorist, he had a significant influence on both the politics and literature of his day. It was Spencer who coined the phrase "survival of the fittest." He is credited with inventing Social Darwinism, the application of the concept of survival of the fittest to human society. His book *Principles of Biology* (1864), presented a version of evolution with a capitalist twist, arguing that competition between men improved the well-being of the rest of society.[495]

Darwin's ideas were reinforced by the work of several prominent Victorian scientists, including *Charles Lyell*, a leading geologist. His book *Principles of Geology* (1833) popularized uniformitarianism, the theory that the earth's physical features had been formed gradually over millions of years through forces that could still be observed. This book had had a profound influence on Darwin in his youth, and later, the two had become close friends. In 1863, Lyell published another landmark work, *Geological Evidences of the Antiquity of Man*, which integrated data from human and geographical history to argue for evolution and the ancient origins of the human race. Lyell's book was quickly followed by others on the topic, including Darwin's *The Descent of Man* (1870).[496]

Thomas Henry Huxley, a biologist, spent much of his career on the study and classification of invertebrates, and was considered by some to have been one of the finest comparative anatomists of his generation. Although he was slow to accept evolution at first, Huxley became one of the most vocal public supporters of Darwin and natural selection, earning him the nickname "Darwin's Bulldog." His book *Evidence as to Man's Place in Nature* (1863) presented arguments in support of the evolution of man and apes from a common ancestor.[497]

Evolution—Life Without God

A theory is logically deduced from axioms that are not proven but are considered to be self-evident. One of the axioms behind evolution was "there is no God" or, at the very least, "the Bible is an inaccurate and a fanciful account." By 1879, Darwin considered himself an agnostic,[498] as did Huxley.[499] Wallace advocated spiritualism and the use of mediums to commune with the dead.[500] Spencer was an avowed atheist.[501] Only Lyell remained a Christian, and he struggled to reconcile his faith with evolution.[502]

Darwin and his contemporaries developed several interconnected theories that not only dismissed the Genesis creation account but eliminated the need for God. Evolution replaced the Creator with an invisible hand of natural selection, reminiscent of Adam Smith's invisible hand of market forces. Uniformitarianism provided the millions of years necessary for evolution to occur. These theories helped to sever Western culture from Christianity, an important step in implementing communism. As Lenin wrote, "The most important thing is to know how to awaken in the still undeveloped masses an intelligent attitude toward religious questions and an intelligent criticism of religions."[503]

Laissez-Faire, Eugenics and Social Darwinism

From the 1870s until World War II, many applied the ideas of evolution, particularly the "survival of the fittest," to sociology and politics, creating Social Darwinism. Later, the ideas of Social Darwinism were instrumental in developing eugenics, scientific racism, imperialism, fascism and Nazism.

The idea of unrestrained competition and the elimination of

the weak had already been demonstrated by laissez-faire capitalism. Darwin and his colleagues did not create their theory in a vacuum. Laissez-faire capitalism advocated giving market forces unfettered freedom on the assumption that competition between individuals and firms would produce the best results for society as a whole, even if some suffered. This theory was the basis of government policy during the Irish famine of the late 1840s, in which over 1.5 million people died of starvation. It was feared that natural laws and the mechanisms of laissez-faire would be violated if the government supplied free food to the starving Irish.[504]

Laissez-faire justified men "that they should kill one another."

Social Darwinism and Eugenics

Eugenics, or "good genes," was a biosocial movement that attempted to improve the human gene pool. It incorporated Gregor Mendel's theories of hereditary characteristics[505] and August Weismann's research on gametes as the sole agents of hereditary change.[506] Eugenics was widely popular in first part of the twentieth century. In the United States, studies documenting the genetic component in certain mental illnesses, including schizophrenia, bipolar disorder and depression, were used to enact laws prohibiting the marriage of the mentally ill and forcing them to be sterilized.[507]

Although eugenicists were found on both sides of the political aisle, conservatives generally believed the mechanism of natural selection would take care of the problem, while socialists and progressives felt natural selection was too slow. They pushed for compulsory sterilization,[508] and applied eugenics to immigration restrictions in an effort to maintain the quality of the American gene pool. The work of American eugenicists Harry H. Laughlin and Margaret Sanger were directly related to the Nazis' Law for the Prevention of Hereditarily Diseased Offspring and the Ku Klux Klan's efforts to "exterminate the Negro population."[509, 510]

Eugenics justified men "that they should kill one another."

Social Darwinism and Scientific Racism

Social Darwinism put a scientific veneer on racism. For example, evolutionists of the early 1900s displayed a pygmy in the Bronx Zoo, claiming he was the "missing link."[511] Eminent German biologist Ernst Haeckel argued that the toe structure of Negros proved they were more closely related to apes and therefore inferior. [512] Haeckel and other scientific racists set great store on the popular pseudoscience of phrenology, which used bumps on the skull to infer a person's character and behavior.[513] Physical anthropologist Samuel Morton hypothesized a relationship between skull sizes and shapes with superior intellectual capacity. He then used his theory to "prove" the superiority of the white race.[514] Adherents of scientific racism used the assumption of racial superiority to justify imperialism, arguing it was the "white man's burden" to colonize the rest of the world for the benefit of all mankind.[515]

Scientific racism justified men "that they should kill one another."

Social Darwinism and the Final Solution

Social Darwinism reached its logical extreme under the Nazi regime. Hitler adapted the recommendations of American eugenicists in his efforts to exterminate the Jews and all "useless eaters." Once the Nazis were in power, one of their first acts was to mandate the sterilization of persons with a variety of genetic markers. The list included anyone with mental retardation, schizophrenia, Huntington's chorea, epilepsy, blindness, hereditary deafness, grave bodily malformation, or alcoholism. By 1938, a policy of extermination had begun. Initially, executions were done one at a time under the guise of euthanizing the terminally ill, but soon gas chambers were installed in hospitals to carry out the large numbers of killings.[516]

Hitler and his followers were fully convinced of the superiority of the "Aryan race" over all other races, especially the Jews. From 1933 until the outbreak of World War II, the Nazis passed increasingly invasive laws that targeted the Jews for persecution. By 1938, Jews were isolated in ghettos and later sent to concentration camps for extermination, using the gas-chamber techniques that had been perfected in hospitals in the previous years.

The number of people involved was enormous. It is estimated that 11 million people were killed during the Holocaust, including about 1.1 million children. Approximately 6 million of the victims were Jews, two-thirds of the European Jewish population. The rest were "undesirables" and those who simply refused to comply with the Nazi agenda. Hitler's "final solution" had begun.[517]

The "final solution" justified men "that they should kill one another."

Democide

The Nazi holocaust was an example of democide, the premeditated killing of people by their own government either in cold blood or by wanton disregard for their lives. The word was created to describe conditions under some of the totalitarian regimes of the twentieth century. Democide was so prevalent in the 1900s that the number of those who died at the hands of their own governments greatly exceeded the casualties of war during the same period.[518]

Stalin's policy of forced collectivism in the Ukraine is a perfect example of murder by a government's disregard for the lives of its citizens. Stalin systematically confiscated all grain, livestock, and other foodstuffs from the Ukraine and sold the produce abroad to finance Soviet industrial development. Despite the fact that an estimated 25,000 Ukrainians were dying of starvation daily, the government continued to set high grain quotas that had to be met before farm workers could eat. Between 6 and 7 million died of starvation during the winter of 1932–33.[519] Far from seeing this as a disaster, Stalin viewed the famine as a great success. By forcing peasants to comply with collectivism, Stalin gloated: "It showed the peasants 'who is the master here. It cost millions of lives, but the collective farm system is here to stay.'"[520]

The intentional starvation of Ukrainian farmers is just one example of the official policy of democide under the Soviet regime. It is estimated that communist governments murdered approximately 110 million of their citizens, 62 million in the Soviet Union alone. Communist China boasts an efficient record of democide, with nearly 77 million dead, including the impact of Mao's famine of 1958–62.[521] Khmer Rouge, the communist party of Cambodia, managed to murder between 1.5 and 2 million citizens, including most of those with professional and technical training, in just four years.[522]

The communists were not the only ones practicing democide during the twentieth century, but they were the most prolific; more than two-thirds of all those killed by governments, quasi-governments, and guerrillas were killed by communists. The best known of the noncommunist megakillers were the Nazis. During the brief existence of the Nazi regime, the chances that a European would be killed by its orders was about one in fifteen, 2.5 times more likely than death at the hands of the Soviets since 1917, and nine times more likely than dying in communist China since 1949. The death toll includes the thousands slaughtered during Nazi occupation: citizens of Poland, the Soviet Union, Yugoslavia, Czechoslovakia, Greece, the Lowlands and France.[523]

The number of people who have been victims of democide worldwide during the twentieth century is truly shocking. It is many times higher than the number who died in battle, although the century has also produced some of the deadliest wars. It is estimated that 38 million have been killed in all this century's international and domestic wars, a small fraction of the conservative estimate of 170 million victims of democide.[524]

The twentieth century has conducted one of the greatest social engineering experiments ever seen based on the ideas of Karl Marx. Communism has failed utterly in its promise of creating a better life for the common man. Instead, it left a trail of death and suffering of all kinds, from the gulag-slavery system instituted by Lenin and Stalin to government-sponsored famines to simply being taken out and shot. As historian R. J. Rummel sums it up,

> In total, during the first eighty-eight years of this century, almost 170,000,000 men, women, and children have been shot, beaten, tortured, knifed, burned, starved, frozen, crushed, or worked to death; or buried alive, drowned, hanged, bombed, or killed in any other of the myriad ways governments have inflicted death on unarmed, helpless citizens or foreigners. The dead even could conceivably be near a high of 360,000,000 people. This is as though our species has been devastated by a modern Black Plague. And indeed it has, but a plague of absolute power and not germs.

Adding the human cost of war to this democide total, governments have violently killed over 203,000,000 people in this century.[525]

The common thread that links all this murder is power—absolute power in the hands of the government. Totalitarian governments can murder its citizens with impunity since by definition the state recognizes no limits to its own authority.[526] It is said that "power corrupts, and absolute power corrupts absolutely." The experience of the twentieth century has demonstrated that "power kills, and absolute power kills absolutely."

Democide justified men "that they should kill one another."

Of course, there have been plenty of megalomaniac dictators in the past who were just as eager to dominate the world, just as indifferent regarding the lives of their subjects and just as willing to kill or torture on a whim. Under the Red Horseman, these types of rulers could inflict their visions on far more people and do so far more efficiently thanks to the vast strides made in transportation, communication, recordkeeping and technology. The great lesson for today is that no one can be trusted with power. The Red Horseman absolutely gave men the power to "kill one another."

CHAPTER 18:

Given a Sword

> And there went out another horse [that was] red: and
> [power] was given to him that sat thereon to take
> peace from the earth, and that they should kill one
> another: and there was given unto him a great sword.
> (Rev. 6:4 KJV)

John's description of the Red Horseman concludes with one last
detail: he was given a great sword. The verb "given" is exactly the
same tense used when the White Horseman passively received a
crown. Once again, there is no clear indication of the timing of this
event (aorist tense), but we know he was given the sword (indicative
mood) and that he did nothing to get it but merely received it (passive
voice). The rider of the Red Horse was given a *machaira megala*
(μάχαιρα μεγάλη); a machaira is an ancient sword or knife-like weapon
often with a curved, short blade. Although military historians debate
the specifics of the weapon, the scriptural use is a generic reference
to an unspecified type of sword.[527, 528]

It seems odd that the Red Horseman would be given a sword
in an era long after the introduction of gunpowder. During the
American Civil War, which happened early in the period, the armies
used rifles and pistols that far outstripped the killing power of the
weaponry used as recently as the Napoleonic Wars.[529] By World War
I, armies had added machine guns, flamethrowers, grenades, and
mortars to their arsenals,[530] and in World War II, submachine guns

were available.[531] What use would a sword be compared with these types of weapons?

Sword of Honor

During the American Civil War, soldiers, especially officers, often carried swords. They were commonly presented in recognition of bravery or other displays of excellence.[532] This tradition dated back to the Revolutionary War when the United States military was in its infancy. George Washington's sizable collection of swords was among his most prized possessions. Civil War historian Donald Moran noted,

> To the civilian it [his sword] was the symbol of his standing in a highly systemized Society. To a military officer it was an emblem of his rank and often a reward for gallantry, having been presented to him. To the common soldier or sailor it was the weapon of "*last resort.*"[533]

An officer would have at least two swords, one for use on the battlefield and a second that was worn on formal occasions, called a presentation sword or sword of honor. These swords were highly ornate affairs, especially during the Victorian era. They were often given to officers in recognition of bravery or other service. In fact, Congress awarded several officers presentation swords in recognition of their service in the Revolutionary War.[534]

During World War I, swords continued to be used as a part of an officer's ceremonial uniform,[535] although the practice of presenting a sword of honor was falling out of favor.[536] However, even today a ceremonial sword is part of dress uniforms of many officers. When an officer is commissioned, it as assumed that he would behave with fidelity, honor, courage, and virtue and maintain a standard of behavior higher than that expected of enlisted men.[537] The sword, once symbolic of being a gentleman, is worn as a reminder of this higher code of behavior.

This is why convention required that any officer who surrendered on the field of battle had to relinquish his sword to the victor. It was assumed that a man who had led his troops to defeat had lost the right to wear the sword with honor. An exception was made when General Lee, head of the Confederate forces in the American Civil War, surrendered to General Grant of the Union Army. Lee was permitted to keep his sword because Grant held him in high esteem for both his military ability and his outstanding character.[538]

The Presenting of a Samurai Sword

A charming example of an international presentation of a sword of honor took place on July 4, 1918, in Fairhaven, Massachusetts. The town selectmen were presented with a fourteenth-century samurai sword by Viscount Ishii, Japan's ambassador to the United States, on behalf of Dr. Toichiro Nakahama of Tokyo. It should be noted that Japan and the United States were allies at the time.

Dr. Nakahama's father, Manjiro Nakahama, was one of five Japanese fishermen rescued from a rocky islet in the Pacific by an American whaling vessel commanded by Captain Whitfield of Fairhaven. Manjiro, who was only a boy, was raised and educated by Whitfield. He would later return to Japan, where he served as the translator for the shogun and Commodore Perry. According to the "permanent record" of the presentation, this sword

> ... commemorates the rescue of his father and the kindness shown him during his residence in Fairhaven.... There is deep significance in the thought that the thread of sentiment connecting Manjiro Nakahama and Fairhaven has never been broken and that to the second generation, it remains strong and steadfast. In the phrase of one of the speakers of the day, "We are here because a brave American was kind and a loyal Japanese remembered."[539]

Ambassador Ishii went on to express the meaning of the highly symbolic gift and why it was appropriate to present it "to this peace-loving town in recognition of an act of mercy."

> There is another sense in which it [the sword] stands for the loftiest conceptions of chivalric honor and virtue. To the old Samurai of Japan, whose spirit

is reflected in the act of Dr. Nakahama, the sword was the symbol of spotless honor. His right to wear it signified his worthiness to use it aright. What he carried at his belt was a symbol of what he carried in his mind and heart—honor, loyalty, courage, self-control. No unworthy man might carry this sacred token of responsibility. To possess it was to be recognized as worthy to use it aright; to use it amiss constituted the brand of deepest dishonor.[540]

These words sum up the significance of the presentation sword.

Stalin and the Sword of Stalingrad

In 1943, World War II was raging. The nonaggression pact between the Soviet Union and Germany, signed at the start of the war, had been shattered when the Germans invaded in June 1941.[541] For a while, it had seemed as if Hitler and his German army were unstoppable in their quest for world dominance. Unstoppable, that is, until the Battle of Stalingrad, the long (164 days) and bloody (between 1,250,000 and 1,800,000 casualties) struggle for the defense of the city. Despite the fact that the German army conquered 90 percent of the city, the Soviet launched a counterattack that saved the town and left the world in awe of the fortitude of its citizens. The battle proved to be a pivotal moment in the war.[542]

During the war, the Big Three—Franklin D. Roosevelt, Winston Churchill, and Joseph Stalin—met to plan and coordinate their strategies to defeat the Axis powers. The first meeting, the Tehran Conference, was held at the Soviet Embassy in Tehran, Iran, in late November 1943. The trio met again in the better-known Yalta Conference in 1945.

It was at the Tehran Conference that Stalin was presented with the Sword of Stalingrad by Roosevelt and Churchill.

Then the officer of the British guard approached the large black box on the table and opened it. A gleaming sword lay on a bed of "claret-coloured [sic] velvet." He handed it to Churchill, who, laying the sword across his hands, turned to Stalin. "I've been commanded by His

Above—The "Big Three" at the Tehran Conference: Joseph Stalin, Franklin D. Roosevelt and Winston Churchill.[543]

Below—The Sword of Stalingrad.[544]

Majesty King George VI to present to you ... this sword of honour [sic].... The blade of the sword bears the inscription: "To the steel-hearted citizens of Stalingrad, a gift from King George VI as a token of the homage of the British People."

Churchill stepped forward and presented the sword to Stalin who held it reverently in his hands for a long moment and then, with tears in his eyes, raised it to his lips and kissed it. Stalin was moved.

"On behalf of the citizens of Stalingrad," he answered in "a low husky voice," "I wish to express my appreciation...." He walked round to Roosevelt to show him the sword. The American read out the inscription: "Truly they had hearts of steel."[545]

To understand the significance of this act requires understanding the interplay between the Big Three. Stalin was currently the leader of the communist world and absolute dictator of the Soviet Union. From 1929, when he assumed power after the death of Lenin, Stalin (meaning "steel") had presided over Russia like a "Red Czar." Historian Montefiore describes Stalin and his oligarchs as functioning like

> ... members of a military-religious "order of sword-bearers" explain[ing] much of the inexplicable [including] many of his views and features, such as dependence on death as a political tool, and his paranoia....[546]

On the other hand, Churchill had

> ...spent the years before the attack on Pearl Harbor persuading Roosevelt to support Britain's war effort. Although Britain's Prime Minister was vehemently anti-communist, he was not about to refuse the gift of another powerful ally against Hitler ... Churchill had no hesitation in sending aid to Russia and defending Stalin in public. "If Hitler invaded Hell," he once remarked, "I would at least make a favourable [sic] reference to the Devil in the House of Commons."[547]

While Churchill was fairly conservative, Roosevelt followed policies that were left of center; his famed New Deal significantly increased the regulatory powers of the U.S. government.[548] Roosevelt was eager to develop a close relationship with Stalin and believed he was the best choice to deal with the Soviet leader. In March 1942, he sent a message to Churchill, asserting,

> I know you will not mind my being brutally frank when
> I tell you I think I can personally handle Stalin better
> than your Foreign Office or my State Department.
> Stalin hates the guts of all your top people. He thinks
> he likes me better, and I hope he will continue to do
> so.[549]

Despite Roosevelt's multiple attempts to meet with Stalin, the Russian leader refused until the Tehran conference, and even then, the meeting was held on Stalin's conditions. Once the Big Three convened, Stalin pushed his agenda in several areas. Most notably, Roosevelt and Churchill agreed to cede the eastern portion of Poland to the U.S.S.R. and gave consent to the establishment of Soviet puppet communist states in Eastern Europe, including Poland, Czechoslovakia, Romania and the Baltic nations.[550] These concessions deprived Eastern European nations of liberation at the conclusion of World War II and paved the way for the Cold War for the next half century. Roosevelt and Churchill "surrendered" to Stalin over other significant issues, essentially granting the Soviets control over Eastern Europe, including East Germany, which was to be divided from Western Europe by the Iron Curtain.[551]

Stalin, as the human representative of the Red Horse, was given a great sword. On the surface, this was a sword of honor given by King George VI of Britain to the people of Stalingrad in recognition of the courage they displayed against the Nazis. However, other nations, including Poland and Czechoslovakia, fought with equal valor but were rewarded with decades in the iron grip of the Soviets. In retrospect, the presenting of the sword seems more like surrender to the Red Horseman, who would dominate both sides of the Iron Curtain, and in the process transform the spiritual life of the Western world from Christianity to materialism.

CHAPTER 19:

A Bear with Three Ribs

> And behold another beast, a second, like to a bear, and it raised up itself on one side, and [it had] three ribs in the mouth of it between the teeth of it: (Dan. 7:5a KJV)

As mentioned previously, Daniel's second beast is "like to a bear," the national personification of Russia and the Soviet Union. The bear had been a powerful pagan symbol in pre-Christian Russia, representing womanhood in all its forms. It was synonymous with Mother Russia and Mother Earth. Similarly, the ribs that the bear holds in its mouth also represent women in Biblical symbolism.

The Russian Bear

A trio of goddesses dominates Russian mythology: Mother Earth; Rusalka, the virgin and patroness of embroidery; and Baba Yaga, the witch and spinner, ruler of fertility. According to folklore specialist Joanne Hubbs, the bear is associated with the goddess in all her forms. Rusalka is sometimes shown as a bear surrounded by deer or horses.[552] When Baba Yaga, the goddess who controls the fertility of both land and humans, appears with the bear, "she demands human sacrifice of her worshippers; in return for life she requires death."[553]

The phrase "like to a bear" evokes the idea that the bear is not what it appears to be but hides something else. In Russian mythology, the bear was sometimes nothing more than a skin disguising a witch beneath.[554] It was thought that the spirit of a dead animal could take on human forms and vice versa so that "…a body may be inhabited by a soul; it can be a wolf, a snake or a bear."[555]

The Bear in Scripture

The Bible makes a dozen references to the bear, eight of which also refer to the lion. The bear is associated with uncontrollable anger (2 Sam. 17:8) and unbridled foolishness (Prov. 17:12). David was trained to do battle with Goliath by killing both a lion and a bear (1 Sam. 17:36). Scripture uses the lion and bear as metaphors for bad government: "[As] a roaring lion, and a ranging bear; [so is] a wicked ruler over the poor people" (Prov. 28:15 AV). Amos says something similar in the context of the end days.

> [18]Woe to you that desire the day of the LORD! to what end [is] it for you? The day of the LORD [is] darkness, and not light. [19]As if a man did flee from a lion, and a bear met him; (Amos 5:18–19a AV)

The reign of the White Horseman brought suffering to the common people of Europe as kings tried to conquer the surrounding principalities like roaring lions, leaving devastation in their wake. Amos describes a man desperately attempting to escape the lion only to meet a bear. The Hebrew verb here is *paga* (פָּגַע), which means "to encounter, to meet, to entreat, or to strike upon."[556]

Envision a man tired of the wars and injustices perpetuated by his king, the lion, who encounters a bear promising a better way. The man entreats the bear to rescue him from the lion, thinking anything would be better than what he has experienced. And then he discovers that the Red Horse dictator is just as evil as any White Horse king. The ranging bear or the roaring lion—the poor man suffers under both.

Raised Up on One Side

In Daniel's vision, the bear—Russia—"raised up itself on one side" (Dan. 7:5). The verb translated "raised up" is *qum* (קוּם), the same verb used in the previous verse to describe the lion, now without eagles' wings, standing up like a man. However, in this instance, the verb is in a different tense, the aphel or causative form, which could be translated "to set up, to lift up, to establish, to appoint."[557] Thus we could say the bear set itself up or established itself on one side.

One possible interpretation of this verse is geographical; a topographical map of the Soviet Union shows significant mountain ranges to the southeast while plains dominate its west.[558] (See Map 11).

Map 11: Topographical map of Russia. [559]

Similarly, Russia has long been pictured as a sleeping bear that occasionally rises up to terrorize its neighbors. After centuries of conquering the khanates to the east and toying with Persia to the south, Russia, now the Soviet Union, rose up to dominate Eastern Europe through the establishment of puppet regimes following World War II. During the Cold War, the Soviet bear rose up in support of communist insurgents in remote corners of the globe.

A Bear with Three Ribs

Conversely, Daniel's vision of the bear rising up on one side could refer to the women's movement that elevated the position of women—one half of the human race—during the time of the Red Horseman. As mentioned, Russian mythology associated the bear with all forms of the woman as goddess. Daniel saw the bear holding three ribs in its mouth. In Scripture, the rib also represents women, since Eve was fashioned out of a rib taken from Adam (Gen. 2:21–23).

The fact that the bear holds the ribs carefully between its teeth indicates that it is not trying to destroy them but to control and exploit them. Between 1848 and the 1980s, the position of women in Western society was transformed in three distinct stages, corresponding with the three ribs in the bear's teeth. The first period was characterized by the suffragettes and their demands for women's rights, especially the right to vote. The second period saw the emergence of the modern woman, epitomized by the flapper, at least in the non-communist West. The third era saw the rise of women's liberation with its push for gender equality.

Three Ribs—Three Reforms in Women's Dress

Interestingly, each development in the position of women went hand in hand with efforts to reform women's clothing, particularly undergarments, reforms that were highly controversial and fraught with political significance. During the Victorian era, women's liberation from the societal constraints was symbolized by the abandonment of the corset and other "rational dress" reforms.[560] Though many of the changes in undergarments seem subtle to us, they were considered quite radical at the time and were closely connected with changing ideas of beauty and health.[561]

In the twentieth century, underwear continued to take on political significance. In the Soviet Union, the state designed patriotic underwear—the only kind allowed—which was uncomfortable, unflattering, and in some cases a danger to health. A scholarly exhibition on undergarments from the era of Lenin and Stalin includes an entire room of "…photographs of female bodies scarred by the effects of rough and ill-fitting bras and corsets."[562]

In the West, women began abandoning the corset in the 1920s but were persuaded by advertisers that the corset and later the bra were essential supplements to the female body. During World War II, bra manufacturing was given high priority when women complained they "…could not do the work required of them in munitions work if they didn't have more supporting corsets and brassieres."[563] In the late 1960s, the feminist movement labeled the bra as a "ludicrous invention" and a tool of the oppression of women.[564]

1848 Revisited

The changing role of women in society was a key component of the Red Horseman. As we have seen, Karl Marx, father of communism, and John Stuart Mill, father of social liberalism, both published key works in 1848. Both men wrote about women. Communists viewed women as essential additions to the labor force, somehow overlooking the fact that most women outside of the upper classes had always done essential work. For Marx, there was to be no distinction between the sexes, and women were only exploited as members of the proletariat. He believed that women were essential to social progress.

> Everyone who knows anything of history also knows that great social revolutions are impossible without the feminine ferment. Social progress may be measured precisely by the social position of the fair sex (plain ones included).[565]

Mill, who was known for his strong support of women, viewed their role from a utilitarian perspective, arguing that the emancipation and education of women would improve society for everyone. His essay, "The Subjection of Women" (1859), was the first work published by a male author to address the subject. He wrote,

> That the principle which regulates the existing social relations between the two sexes—the legal subordination of one sex to the other—is wrong itself, and now one of the chief hindrances to human improvement; and that it ought to be replaced by a principle of perfect equality, admitting no power or privilege on the one side, nor disability on the other.[566]

Like communism and modern liberalism, feminism was birthed in 1848. Elizabeth Cady Stanton organized the first women's rights meeting, which was held July 19 and 20 of that year in Seneca

Falls, NY. The highlight of the convention was Stanton's reading of her "Declaration of Sentiments and Resolutions," which was then debated. Signed by sixty-eight women and thirty-two men, including Frederick Douglass, this document served as a roadmap for the women's movement that followed. [567, 568]

1848–1920: The Suffragettes

The feminist movement was not independent of communism but another interwoven thread in the time of the Red Horseman. The feminist movement was intimately connected to socialism, and could not have existed without it. Looking at the biographies of the leading lights of the suffragette movement, their connections with socialism are astonishing!

Elizabeth Cady Stanton (1815–1902), who is credited with founding the woman's suffrage movement, had close ties to socialism. *The New York Times* quoted her as saying "if men did not grant women what they wished they would rise up as labor, the Socialists, and the Anarchists had done."[569] She also published an impassioned plea for socialism, entitled "Elizabeth Cady Stanton on Socialism," in *The Progressive Woman* magazine. In it, she wrote,

> We must now, at the end of fifty years of faithful service, broaden our platform and consider the next step in progress... namely, co-operation, a new principle in industrial economics.... Agitation of the broader questions of philosophical Socialism is now in order.[570]

Susan B. Anthony (1820–1906) worked hand in hand with Stanton as an abolitionist and campaigner for women's suffrage. Like Stanton, Anthony was a strong supporter of socialism. She published a newspaper, *The Revolution*, which carried the masthead "Men, their rights, and nothing more; women, their rights, and nothing less." In it she advocated for various socialist causes including the eight-hour day and equal pay for equal work.[571] In addition, Anthony was friends with Eugene Debs, five-time presidential candidate for the Socialist Democratic Party and later part of the Socialist Party of America. In 1905, the following exchange between them was recorded: "'Give us suffrage,' Anthony said with good humor, 'and we'll give you socialism.' Debs' good natured reply was: 'Give us socialism and we'll give you the vote.'"[572]

Ella Reeve Bloor (1862–1951), a longtime reformer, worked tirelessly on behalf of the Women's Christian Temperance Union, women's suffrage, and trade-union organizing. She helped Upton Sinclair gather materials for his classic book *The Jungle*. She also had a lively political career, first as a founding member of the Social Democracy of America (later the Social Democratic Party), then with the Socialist Party of America, and finally with the Communist Party of America. She was an admirer of the Soviet system, particularly their policy on childcare and women, which she expressed in her book, *Women in the Soviet Union* (1937).[573]

Margaret Sanger (1883–1966), founder of Planned Parenthood, worked with socialists such as Upton Sinclair and H. G. Wells to establish the Worker's Birth Control Group. She argued that birth control was an essential weapon in the arsenal of the cause of labor because it allowed the working class to keep its numbers low and thus increase its wages. She wrote,

> No Socialist republic can operate successfully and maintain its ideals unless the practice of birth control is encouraged to a marked and efficient degree … until labor finds its real enemy … the reproductive ability of the working class which gluts the channels of progress with the helpless and weak, and stimulates the tyrants of the world in their oppression of mankind.[574]

Florence Kelley (1859–1932), a friend of Friedrich Engels, was a crusader for a wide variety of reforms, including women's suffrage, child labor and educational reform, and African-American civil rights. While working at Hull House in Chicago, she was made Chief Factory Inspector for the state of Illinois. She later worked to establish an eight-hour workday and a minimum wage. In 1905, Kelley worked with Rose Pastor Stokes, Upton Sinclair, Jack London, and Clarence Darrow to found the Intercollegiate Socialist Society, the student branch of the Socialist Party of America. They hoped to organize members of the college community, including teachers, students, and alumni, in support of socialism.[575]

Mary White Ovington (1865–1951) was a suffragette, a socialist, and a champion of civil rights. After a decade of studying the employment and housing problems in black Manhattan, she joined the Socialist Party, in which she argued that racial problems were as much about class as they were about race. She was a founding member of the National Association for the Advancement of Colored People (NAACP), serving on its board for over forty years.[576]

Helen Keller (1880–1968) never did anything in a small way. Most people remember her as the blind and deaf girl whose amazing story was immortalized in the movie *The Miracle Worker*. Few know she went on to live her adult life as a political activist and lecturer who campaigned for workers' rights, women's suffrage, and the American Foundation for the Blind. She was a member of the Socialist Party (from 1909–1921) and a founding member of the American Civil Liberties Union (in 1920), but political action alone could not satisfy her. In 1912, she joined the Industrial Workers of the World, believing that "direct action"—strikes, propaganda, and boycotts—would have greater effect in achieving gains for the working class than politics.[577, 578] Marxist historian Philip S. Foner has argued,

> No matter what social cause she espoused, Keller was always on the radical side of the movement. As a left-wing socialist she disliked "parlor socialists" who quickly abandoned the struggle when the situation became difficult and later became "hopelessly reactionary."[579]

Emmeline Pankhurst (1858–1928), who was on *Time*'s list of the "100 Most Important People of the 20th Century," led the British suffragette movement. She came from a family of activists; her father was a friend and supporter of John Stuart Mill, and her mother was a passionate feminist who started bringing Pankhurst to suffragette meetings when she was only ten. She married Richard Pankhurst, a committed socialist who drafted a bill that would have granted the vote to unmarried female property owners. Together, the Pankhursts helped found the Independent Labour Party. Pankhurst later formed the Women's Social and Political Union, a group that became infamous for its campaign of direct action, including smashing windows and assaulting police officers, to further its political goals.

She is best remembered for her use of hunger strikes while in prison. Pankhurst had a surprising response to World War I and the threat of bolshevism: she abandoned socialism to join the Conservative Party, shocking many of her followers, including her own daughters.[580]

1920–1965: Women Under Communism

Lenin argued that women were victims of the bourgeois system that treated them like illegitimate children. Believing that the Soviet system was the solution to all society's ills, including the grievances of women, he declared,

> In the course of two years Soviet power in one of the most backward countries of Europe did more to emancipate women and to make their status equal to that of the "strong" sex than all the advanced, enlightened, "democratic" republics of the world did in the course of 130 years.[581]

Similarly, Mao viewed the subjugation of women to their husbands' authority as vestiges of feudalism and something to be undermined as quickly as possible. He saw women as the solution to China's labor shortage and demanded that they take their place as equal laborers along side men.

> In order to build a great socialist society it is of the utmost importance to arouse the broad masses of women to join in productive activity. Men and women must receive equal pay for equal work in production. Genuine equality between the sexes can only be realized in the process of the socialist transformation of society as a whole.[582]

Communism's boast of liberating women makes perfect sense if you agree with Marx: "Differences of age and sex have no longer any distinctive social validity. All are instruments of labor."[583] Thus, Marx reduced human beings to their usefulness as modes of production. At the same time, he viewed marriage and family as bourgeois institutions that needed to be uprooted as quickly as possible.

The Bolsheviks passed a series of laws aimed at achieving this. In

1918, women aged 17 to 32 were deemed the property of the State, while the traditional rights of husbands and fathers were abolished.[584] In order to equalize the legal status of children, the concept of illegitimacy was eliminated and divorce laws were revised to make divorce obtainable within minutes. The immediate impact was to leave thousands of children homeless after they had been abandoned by their parents. One witness wrote:

> "Chaos was the result. Men took to changing wives with the same zest which they displayed in the consumption of the recently restored forty-per-cent vodka … Peasant boys looked upon marriage as an exciting game and changed wives with the change of seasons. It was not an unusual occurrence for a boy of twenty to have had three or four wives, or for a girl of the same age to have had three or four abortions."[585]

1920–1960s: The Modern Woman

In the West, militant feminism fell out of favor once women were granted voting rights in the 1920s. However, forces of modernization combined with a devil-may-care attitude among the postwar generation greatly impacted women's roles. Young women and men returning from World War I saw no reason to conform to the standards of their parents and pushed the boundaries of socially acceptable behavior. The flapper emerged as the epitome of the modern woman.

Popularized in the 1920 movie of the same name, the flapper came to symbolize the thoroughly modern woman of the Roaring Twenties. She wore makeup, short "bobbed" hair, high heels, and scanty clothing with short skirts, flattened breasts, and straight waists. She was also associated with jazz, drinking, smoking, promiscuity, and other challenges of social norms. In short, she was a complete departure from her Victorian grandmother.[586]

The widespread popularity of the rebellious flapper was fueled in part by Prohibition, which put a large portion of otherwise law-abiding citizens at odds with authority. The flappers were prime examples of women shedding their traditional roles and embracing independence from men and their elders. Many suffragettes felt betrayed by the flappers' lack of political participation, but others viewed them as the ultimate fulfillment of women's sexual and economic emancipation.[587, 588] Although the average woman remained indifferent from politics, many intellectual women were advocates for communism.

Simone de Beauvoir (1908–86) was a feminist-existentialist and political activist, best known for her treatise *The Second Sex* (1949), an analysis on the oppression of women. She believed that women who wanted to stay home and raise children were victims of conditioning by a male-dominated society and did not know what was good for them. She wrote,

> We don't believe that any woman should have this choice. No woman should be authorized to stay at home to raise her children. Society should be totally different. Women should not have that choice, precisely because if there is such a choice, too many women will make that one.[589]

Marie Carmichael Stopes (1880–1958), a British physician, was an advocate for family planning and sex education. She was also an enthusiastic crusader for eugenics, supporting Hitler's policies. In fact, she disinherited her son for marrying a short-sighted woman.[590] Her sex manual, *Married Love or Love in Marriage* (1918), was extremely popular despite being censored. In 1935, academics believed it held more influence than the writings of Albert Einstein, Sigmund Freud, Adolf Hitler, and John Maynard Keyes.[591]

Feminism in the 1960s

Women's liberation, also known as the second wave of feminism, sought to right the inequities documented in Simone de Beauvoir's *Second Sex*. It focused on eliminating targeted areas of discrimination in the workplace, calling for equal pay and the end of the glass ceiling. Women's libbers also championed reproductive rights.

Most agree that the feminist movement began with the publication of *The Feminine Mystique* (1963) and the release of Kennedy's Presidential Commission on the Status of Women (1964). The movement dwindled in the 1980s, as many supporters felt feminist goals had been accomplished and the Equal Rights Amendment was added to the U.S. Constitution.[592]

There was a strong correlation between the goals of women's liberation and the goals of Marxism, and this was no accident. American communism was the underpinning of the feminist movement. For example, a pamphlet written by Mary Inman asserted, "Rape is an expression of ... male supremacy ... the age-old economic, political and cultural exploitation of women by men." Inman was not a radical feminist; the work was published in 1948 by the American Communist Party.[593]

Mary Inman was one of several women's activists within the Communist Party who fought to overturn the conventional leftist understanding of women's oppression as the product of bourgeois decadence. Kate Wiegand, author of *Red Feminism: AMERICAN COMMUNISM and the Making of Women's Liberation,* argued that communist women were the most radical feminists of the 1950s and that their writings had great impact on the feminist movement of the 1960s and 1970s. She asserted that "ideas, activists and traditions that emanated from the communist movement of the forties and fifties continued to shape the direction of the new women's movement of the 1960s and later."[594]

Many feminist leaders were "red-diaper babies," the children of communists. According to Wiegand, red-diaper babies were surrounded by progressives who "talked to them routinely about women's issues," including the ideologies that women were equal to men and that "the Bible was a book written by men to oppress women." Red-diaper babies also reported childhood awareness that housework, motherhood, and sexuality were not simply personal matters but political issues to be worked on by activists committed to reshaping the culture of the capitalist world. When these daughters of communists entered adult life, they were shocked by the chauvinism they encountered, even among the old left, and set out to combat it. The second wave of feminism had arrived.[595]

Betty Friedan (1921–2006) exposed the "problem that has no name" in her controversial book *The Feminine Mystique* (1963). In it, Friedan charted "... a gradual metamorphosis of the American woman from the independent, career-minded New Woman of the

1920s and '30s into the vacant, aproned housewife of the postwar years."[596] Freidan, who went on to found the National Organization for Women, was a longtime participant in the American communist movement.[597] She associated with known radicals during her university years and worked as a labor journalist in the early 1950s. In 1952, Freidan wrote a pamphlet, *UE Fights for Woman Works*, which has been called a "remarkable manual for fighting wage discrimination."[598]

According to historian Daniel Horowitz, Friedan's research notes of *The Feminine Mystique* include a quote from Engels' essay "The Origin of the Family, Private Property, and the State," which proposed that,

> equality of the sexes would only happen when women abandoned their homes and become worker-drones … That revolutionary passage would become the inspiration and guiding principle for Friedan's book, and eventually for the entire feminist movement.[599]

Gloria Steinem (b. 1934), cofounder of *Ms.* magazine, was one of the leading activists and spokespersons for women's liberation. A self-described "radical Feminist,"[600] she advocated for abortion and same-sex marriage. She believed that gender rather than race was "the most restricting force in American life."[601] Although Steinem has been heavily involved in the Democratic Party, she was a member of the Democratic Socialists of America, which sought to bring about social justice and the goals of socialism through gradual implementation and democracy.[602]

Barbara Ehrenreich (b. 1941) a feminist writer and leader who was a co-chair of the Democratic Socialists of America.[603] She claimed that socialist feminism was an abbreviation of what it truly embodied: "socialist internationalist anti-racist, anti-heterosexist feminism." In addition to campaigning that women be allowed to enter the workforce with the same opportunities and pay as men, she touted alternative views of gender and sexuality.[604]

Germaine Greer (b. 1939), author of *The Female Eunuch* (1970), became the voice of the women's liberation movement in the 1970s. She argued that while the suffragettes had called for reform, the new feminists were, calling for revolution. For many of them, the call for revolution came before the call for the liberation of women. The New Left has been the forcing house for most movements, and for many of them liberation is dependent upon the coming of the classless society and the withering away of the state.[605]

At the root of Greer's own call for revolution was her belief in anarchy. By 1972, her political identity was "anarchist communist," a stateless version of Marxism.[606] One biographer quotes Greer as saying, "I was already an anarchist ... I just didn't know why I was an anarchist. They put me in touch with the basic texts and I found out what the internal logic was about how I felt and thought."[607]

Many of the names of feminist organizations and publications reveal the socialist leanings of their founders. The most obvious of these was *Red Rag: A Magazine of Women's Liberation*, which was published during the 1970s by a collective of Marxist feminists.[608]

Redstockings was an early feminist group that represented the union of two traditions: the "bluestocking" label disparagingly pinned on feminists of earlier centuries—and "red" for revolution. They argued that institutional change alone would never be enough because the "male supremacy" practiced by all men on all women was at the root of female oppression.[609]

Perhaps the most extreme variation of feminism was S.C.U.M. or the Society for Cutting Up Men. The S.C.U.M. Manifesto advised women to "overthrow the government, eliminate the money system, institute complete automation and eliminate the male sex."[610] Although many believed the manifesto was a parody or satire, it should be remembered that its author, Valerie Solana, did attempt to murder artist Andy Warhol.[611]

Daniel's vision of the bear rising up on one side with the three ribs was fulfilled by the rise of feminism. Each stage of the woman's movement—from suffragettes to the New Woman to Women's Liberation—was led by women who were socialists or communists. Just as the bear controlled and dominated the ribs, the political philosophies of the Red Horseman promised freedom while molding women into the image of men.

CHAPTER 20:

Devour Much Flesh

> And behold another beast, a second, like to a bear, and it raised up itself on one side, and [it had] three ribs in the mouth of it between the teeth of it: and they said thus unto it, Arise, devour much flesh. (Dan. 7:5 KJV)

Daniel prophesied that the ribs—feminists—would tell the bear to "Arise, devour much flesh." Throughout the time of the Red Horseman, the various waves of feminism have considered family planning and reproductive rights a key issue. Feminists campaigned for sexual freedom and equality, for legalizing safe and effective contraceptives, and for abortion, which, in particular, fulfills the ribs' demand to "devour much flesh." And throughout the world, communists, socialist and feminists have combined forces to fight for legalized abortion.

Contraceptives

Margaret Sanger founded *Planned Parenthood*, the organization most closely aligned to the feminist goal of sexual freedom. Sanger's work as a New York public health nurse frequently brought her into contact with women suffering the results of poor nutrition and too many pregnancies with little time in between for recovery. Often, these women, when faced with yet another unwanted pregnancy, had used one of several risky methods for "restoring the menses" or procured a back-alley abortion, and Sanger was called in to clean up the aftermath.

Sights of suffering women added to her bitterness from watching her mother die of tuberculosis, which she attributed to the effects of too many children. The combination ignited a militant passion for ensuring that women had access to safe, effective birth control.[612]

Sanger founded the American Birth Control League, eventually called Planned Parenthood, to educate women about controlling their fertility and to distribute whatever contraceptives were available at the time. The organization also conducted studies of the use and effectiveness of contraceptives. Despite arrests and court battles, Sanger successfully challenged the legal system to achieve her goals.[613]

"The Pill," was the common name of an oral contraceptive approved by the Food and Drug Administration in 1960. Its impact on society was profound. For the first time, sexuality and pregnancy were disconnected, allowing women to postpone marriage, pursue higher education and make long-range career goals. College enrollment among women increased sharply. Married women joined the workforce, with no worry that pregnancy would sideline them.[614] According to Planned Parenthood, "Within five years, one out of every four married women in America under the age of 45 has used the pill."[615]

The Sexual Revolution

For some, reproductive freedom included sexual freedom, and many feminists devoted their energies to this cause. For instance, feminist publication *Spare Rib Magazine* (1972–93) declared its purpose was to present alternatives to the traditional female roles of "virgin, wife and mother."[616] The sexual revolution also encompassed the idea of "free love" (sex without marriage or even commitment).[617] Other aspects of the sexual revolution included a growing tolerance of pornography and homosexuality.[618, 619]

Helen Gurley Brown (1922-2012), editor of *Cosmopolitan* magazine, published her highly influential book *Sex and the Single Girl* in 1962. In it, she advised women to pursue financial independence, enjoy sexual relationships before marriage, and possibly forego marriage entirely. She encouraged women to pursue the idea of having it all—"love, sex and money." The book, along with her work at *Cosmopolitan*, was instrumental in starting both the second wave of feminism and the sexual revolution.[620]

Abortion

Although abortion, or its cousin, infanticide, had been practiced for centuries, abortion rates increased to an astounding scale during the Red Horseman era. In the west, second-wave feminists demanded access to safe, legal abortion for all women. In the communist bloc, abortion was seen as a necessary tool to ensure that women remained in the labor force.

Abortion in the Soviet Union

As discussed in the previous chapter, Bolshevik policies on marriage and women meant that women as young as twenty may have had "three or four abortions."[621] In 1922 alone, there were over 20,000 reported abortions in the U.S.S.R. The prevalence of abortion continued to rise so that by 1926 there was an estimated 400,000 abortions. In 1955, the first year we have complete statistical data, there were more than 2.5 million reported abortions in the Soviet Union, which comprised 28 percent of all pregnancies. From 1957 until 1991, the last year for which we have data, over half of all pregnancies in the Soviet Union ended in abortion. In fact, during three of those years (1965, 1967, and 1970), the Soviet abortion rate exceeded an astronomical 70 percent of pregnancies![622]

Abortion in Communist China

China's notorious one-child policy, which went into effect in 1979, had less impact on the abortion rates than might be expected. Before the death of Mao, the Chinese abortion rate was fairly low due to his policy of encouraging large families, which he saw as essential in making China a great nation.[623] During the 1970s, the abortion rate gradually rose from 13 to 23.5 percent. With the implementation of the one-child policy, the rates escalated to slightly more than 30 percent. Barring a couple of spikes in 1983 (40.9 percent) and 1991 (38.2 percent), Chinese abortion rates have consistently remained between 25 and 35 percent. However, the actual number of abortions performed each year has been mind-boggling, with as many as 14 million in a single year (1991).[624]

Abortion in the Western World

Abortion is currently legal in most of the Western world. In the United States, the landmark Supreme Court case *Roe v. Wade* legalized abortion in 1973. Since then, hundreds of thousands of abortions are performed each year, representing between 20 and 30 percent of all pregnancies.[625] In Britain, the abortion rate grew from less than one percent in 1958 until it reached 20 to 22 percent in the 1990s, when the rate stabilized.[626]

Globally, the sheer number of abortions performed over the years is staggering. Before the collapse of the U.S.S.R., more than 282.5 million abortions were reported. In communist China, there were approximately 307.3 million abortions. That's a total of almost 600 million from these two nations alone. As of 2008, reported abortions in the United States totaled 56.7 million. At a minimum, hundreds of millions of abortions have been performed during the time of the Red Horseman.[627] Truly the bear did "devour much flesh."

Conclusion

Everything prophesied about the Red Horseman has been fulfilled in exacting detail. Communism, which is universally associated with the color red, was conceived in 1848, together with social liberalism and feminism. The three movements worked tirelessly to overturn every tradition and institution of the White Horseman. The constantly changing social order combined with the Cold War to absolutely "take peace from the earth." Under the totalitarian regimes spawned by Red Horseman megalomaniac dictators, democide was perfected as a political tool, "that they should kill one another." One of the most nefarious of these dictators, Joseph Stalin, was honored with "a great sword" just as God promised (Rev. 6:4 AV).

This interpretation dovetails perfectly with Daniel's "beast, a second, like to a bear," the symbolic personification of Russia, that "raised up itself on one side," to dominate Eastern Europe. The "three ribs in the mouth of it [the bear] between the teeth of it" are the three phases of feminism, all of which demanded access to abortion, fulfilling the ribs' cry to the bear, "Arise, devour much flesh" (Dan. 7:5 AV).

PART 4:

The Black Horseman

⁵When he had opened the third seal, I heard the third beast say, Come and see. And I beheld, and lo a black horse; and he who sat on him had a pair of balances in his hand. ⁶And I heard a voice in the midst of the four beasts say, A measure of wheat for a penny, and three measures of barley for a penny; and [see] thou hurt not the oil and the wine. (Rev. 6:5–6 KJV)

After this I beheld, and lo another, like a leopard, which had upon the back of it four wings of a fowl; the beast had also four heads, and dominion was given to it. (Dan. 7:6 KJV)

CHAPTER 21:

The Face of a Man

When he had opened the third seal, I heard the third beast say, Come and see. And I beheld, and lo a black horse; (Rev. 6:5a KJV)

Who Was the Black Horseman?

Once again it is time to scan the horizon of human history to match the clues that will identify the Black Horseman. This can be more challenging than it was for the White and Red Horsemen since many of these events happened in our lifetimes. Furthermore, the systems established during the previous seals don't disappear but become part of the backdrop of society.

When the third seal was broken, it began another global movement identified by the color black. The Black Horseman unleashed a constellation of developments, including one represented by an object the English Bible translators generally refer to as "scales" or a "pair of balances." It is accompanied by skyrocketing inflation, particularly of commodities such as wheat and barley. Oil and wine are significant, as are the leopard and the number four (the leopard had four wings and four heads). Finally, the movement follows the explosive growth in communication and transportation technologies that began in the first half of the twentieth century.

Many of these prophecies were fulfilled by the American Civil Rights movement and the African quest for independence from colonial rule, which began in the 1950s. Even vocabulary changed, as the word "negro" was replaced by "black." At the same time, the era experienced galloping inflation, and rapid social and technological reforms. It made the changes of the previous horsemen pale in comparison.

Secular Humanism

The Black Horseman was introduced by the third living creature with the face of a man. Once again, this is a detail that gives insight into the period. The era of the Black Horse was characterized by each person doing what is right in his or her own judgment despite biblical warnings against this (Deut. 12:8); the book of Judges relates the sad consequences of Israel's pursuit of this lifestyle (Judg. 17:6, 21:25).

In modern times, "doing what is right in your own eyes" is called secular humanism, a philosophy that became prominent during the second half of the twentieth century. In fact, the *Secular Humanist Declaration* was published in 1980. Humanism, defined as the admiration of man as the pinnacle of creation and the study of all human activities—art, music, history, philosophy, etc.—had been around since the early modern period. It was adopted during the Renaissance, in response to the newly rediscovered writings of Greek philosophers.

Traditionally, there was no perception that humanism was in conflict with Christianity, at least in the view of the thinkers of the time. There had always been the understanding that God was in the picture somewhere, even if He was only the "great clockmaker" or the "supreme architect," as deists called Him.[628] Secular humanism stepped away from God to embrace the idea that man himself was the god of man and enthroned the idealized human at the center of a system designed to replace traditional religions.[629]

Although secular humanists acknowledged that man was not innately good, they believed that good would result if humanity based its moral decisions on science and the laws of nature. Secular humanists encouraged individuals not to accept or reject anything by faith but to examine ideologies of all kinds—political, social, or religious—to determine what was best for them. The definition given by the Council of Secular Humanism added,

Secular humanism, then, is a philosophy and world view which centers upon human concerns and employs rational and scientific methods to address the wide range of issues important to us all. While secular humanism is at odds with faith-based religious systems on many issues, it is dedicated to the fulfillment of the individual and humankind in general. To accomplish this end, secular humanism encourages a commitment to a set of principles which promote the development of tolerance and compassion and an understanding of the methods of science, critical analysis, and philosophical reflection.[630]

The ideas of modern and secular humanism were laid out in a series of manifestos. The first was published in 1933 and had much in common with the socialist ideals of the time. After World War II, secular humanism stepped out of the ivory towers of academia into the arena of policy makers. When the United Nations was founded in 1946, three prominent humanists were appointed as directors over the major divisions of the organization. Julian Huxley was named director of the United Nations Educational, Scientific and Cultural Organization. A prominent evolutionary biologist, he was a proponent of Planned Parenthood and a member of the British Eugenics Society.[631] Brock Chisholm, who was appointed Director-General of the World Health Organization, was a psychiatrist who advocated that children be "raised in an 'as intellectually free environment' as possible, independent of the prejudices and biases— political, moral and religious—of their parents."[632] John Boyd Orr, a physician and biologist who won a Nobel Peace Prize for his research into nutrition, worked as head of the United Nations Food and Agriculture Organization.[633]

The Black Horse era began with a sense of optimism, the idea that humanity could do anything it could envision, from flying to the moon to conquering poverty. Humanity's achievements became the center of all things, the yardstick by which all else was measured. Relativity became the watchword in morality as well as physics. Men and women of beauty and talent were revered; elite athletes, movie stars, and pop musicians became the idols of the public, worshipped with the same devotion once reserved for the gods. For example, the behavior of Beatle fans (short for "fanatics") in the early 1960s was a frenzied hysteria that could not be attributed solely to the group's musical achievements. Any doubts on this point can be dispelled by watching film footage of Beatle audiences from the time, such as parts of *A Hard Day's Night*.[634]

Although secular humanism urges individuals to investigate issues for themselves, many people sought the opinions of advice goddesses and other pop "experts." While there is wisdom in consulting true experts on the subjects in question—talking to your family doctor about health issues, for example—the cult of the rich and famous led many to seek expert advice from nonexperts. For example, athletes or performing artists may be at the top of their professions, but they have no greater understanding of other issues, such as politics, than anyone else. Yet how many people have voted for someone solely on the recommendation of a favorite celebrity?

Like the communists before them, secular humanists emphasized the importance of public education in achieving their goals. The *Humanist Manifesto II* asserted,

> The battle for humankind's future must be waged and won in the public school classroom by teachers who correctly perceive their role as the proselytizers of a new faith: a religion of humanity that recognizes and respects the spark of what theologians call divinity in every human being … Utilizing a classroom instead of a pulpit to convey humanist values in whatever subject they teach, regardless of the educational level—preschool day care or large state university.[635]

This effort was helped considerably by the banning of prayer in public schools. In 1960, Madalyn Murray O'Hair sued to prevent her son from being forced to participate in prayer at school. With the backing of the American Atheist Organization, her suit went all the way to the U.S. Supreme Court, which ruled in her favor in 1962.[636] God was no longer necessary or welcome in public life.

1952: A Year of Beginnings

The number four is closely associated with the Black Horseman and Daniel's corresponding vision. After all, Daniel's leopard has four heads and four bird wings. The year 1952 was not only a momentous year of "firsts," it was also a year of fours. It was a leap year in the Gregorian calendar, and an American election year, when Dwight D. Eisenhower defeated Adlai Stevenson in a landslide victory. The election was also noteworthy as the first one in which television played a significant role.[637] In 1952, the Olympic Games were held in Helsinki, Finland.[638] All three of these events happen every four years.

The year 1952 marked the beginning of the end of European colonialism on the African continent. On Christmas Eve, 1951, Libya formally gained its independence, and over the next three decades the rest of Africa followed suit.[639] Ironically, Queen Elizabeth II ascended to the throne of the United Kingdom while making an official visit to Kenya in February 1952. Her coronation ceremony the following year was the first to be broadcast on television.[640]

Africa was not the only part of the British Commonwealth to come out from British rule. In 1952, the queen appointed a new governor general of Canada to be her representative. For the first time, the appointee was a Canadian citizen rather than a British aristocrat. This previously unthinkable appointment was achieved because the Canadian prime minister submitted only one name on his list of potential candidates: Canadian Vincent Massey.[641]

In 1952, several "firsts" heralded the start of a new era in technology. Television moved beyond its pioneer phase to become an integral part of American life. Highlights of the 1952 season included the debut of the *Today* show, the first of its genre,[642] and the launch of the Canadian Broadcasting Corporation's television division. "The Marriage License" episode of NBC's *I Love Lucy* set a new viewing audience record, with approximately 10 million tuning in, a record which was broken the following year with "Lucy Goes to the Hospital."[643]

1952 ushered in a new age of medical technological miracles, foreshadowed when C. Walton Lillehei performed the world's first open-heart surgery. He went on to pioneer the use of pacemakers and prosthetic heart valves.[644] Meanwhile, Wernher von Braun and other cosmology experts of the time published a series of articles about the future of space travel. Braun presented ideas for manned flights to the moon, and possibly Mars, in "Man Will Conquer Space Soon!"[645, 646]

The Black Horseman also began a time when nations were joined in continental unions. For example, France, West Germany, Italy, Belgium, Luxembourg, and the Netherlands formed the European Coal and Steel Community that would later become the European Union.[647] It was the first organization to be founded on the principles of supranationalism. It was governed by the "common assembly," which evolved into one of the most powerful legislatures in the world, the European Parliamentary Assembly. It held its first direct democratic elections in 1979, making it the only supranational organization whose members were not appointed.[648]

The postwar era was undoubtedly a pivotal period when the prophecies concerning the Black Horseman came to pass. It held the promise that one day man would triumph over all he saw, from outer space to disease and eventually death. All that was needed was technology and time.

CHAPTER 22:

The Black Horse

> When he had opened the third seal, I heard the third
> beast say, Come and see. And I beheld, and lo a black
> horse; (Rev. 6:5a KJV)

When the unthinkable happens simultaneously and in many
different locations, seemingly without an overarching leadership,
the movement is spiritual in origin. This was true of the Spring of
Revolutions in 1848, which marked the opening of the second seal.
Similarly, in 1952, black peoples around the world began movements
demanding equal rights and independence from the vestiges of white
imperialism. The fact that the American Civil Rights movement and
the push for independence across Africa occurred simultaneously is
the most obvious fulfillment of the Black Horseman prophecies.

Even the Greek wording of the Revelation passage points to a
racial fulfillment. The Greek *melas* (μέλας), "black,"[649] is the root of
the scientific word "melanin," the name of the pigments that gives
skin—as well as eyes and hair—its color. Melanin in the iris protects
the eyes from light damage, such as snow blindness. Similarly, the
higher the level of melanin in the skin, the less likely that skin will
burn with heavy exposure to the sun.[650]

Ethnos against Ethnos: the Commentary of Jesus

[6]And ye shall hear of wars and rumors of wars: see

> that ye be not troubled: for all [these things] must come to pass, but the end is not yet. [7]For nation shall rise against nation... (Matt. 24:6–7a KJV)

Jesus' dissertation about His return in Matthew 24 confirms that racial issues are an integral part of the Black Horseman. After talking about "wars and rumors of wars" in reference to the first two seals, Jesus describes the third seal as "For nation shall rise against nation." At first glance, this seems to be about more war between nation states. However, "nation" is translated by the Greek word *ethnos* (ἔθνος), defined as "a multitude of individuals of the same nature or genus ... a tribe nation or people group."[651] Our English "ethnic" is derived from it. Thus another possible translation might be, "For ethnic group shall rise against ethnic group" (Matt. 24:7a).

Within the American experience, racial discrimination was the focus of the civil rights movement. Although the black civil rights movement received the most attention, other ethnic groups fought for equal opportunities during the same period. For example, the Chicano movement of the 1960s fought to achieve empowerment for Hispanic and Latino Americans. Like black civil rights activists, Chicanos fought against discrimination, racism, and exploitation. They demanded the desegregation of schools and worked to engage Mexican Americans in the political system. In the late 1960s, the Chicano movement was known for organizing high school walkouts to protest various academic issues.[652]

Ethnic conflicts were not limited to tensions between racial groups or even to North America. In Eastern Europe, ongoing tensions between ethnic groups in Czechoslovakia resulted in splitting the nation into a "federation" of Czech and Slovak socialist republics (1969). After the collapse of communism, the country formally split into two completely independent nations.[653] Ethnic issues in the Balkans gave rise to the Yugoslav wars, which some believe to have been the most deadly European conflict since World War II. The combatants' tactics included mass ethnic cleansing.[654]

Not all equal rights movements were centered on ethnic groups; the modern gay rights movement also began during this period. The turbulence of the mid-1960s included a gay march in front of Independence Hall, Philadelphia (1965) and antipolice rioting by transgender street prostitutes (1966). The militant Gay Liberation Movement, which emphasized "gay pride" and "coming out," emerged by the end of the decade. In the mid-1970s, the movement evolved into a reformist gay rights group that portrayed gays and lesbians as a minority group in need of legal protection.[655]

United States: the Civil Rights Movement

The crusade for African-American civil rights, the best known movement of the 1950s and '60s, worked to outlaw racial discrimination against blacks and to ensure their voting rights. By and large, it followed a policy of nonviolent protest and civil disobedience, including boycotts, marches and sit-ins. Later, this approach was abandoned in favor of the more militant tactics used by the Black Power agitators of the late 1960s and early '70s.

Brown v. Board of Education (1954) came before the U.S. Supreme Court in 1952. The case, which concerned school segregation, was one of a series filed by the NAACP (National Association for the Advancement of Colored People) as part of its effort to secure black civil rights through the court system. After almost two years of deliberation, the court made a unanimous ruling to ban segregated schools. It was ruled that "separate but equal" educational systems were inherently not equal but damaged black children by the very nature of segregation. The law went into effect relatively smoothly in some districts, while others complied only under force from the National Guard.[656, 657]

Although the Supreme Court landmark ruling was a major breakthrough in the fight for black civil rights, the brutal murder of Chicago teenager *Emmett Till* made it clear there was still a long way to go. While visiting Mississippi relatives in the summer of 1955, Till was lynched for allegedly flirting with a white saleswoman. The incident might have been harmless in Chicago, but in the highly segregated Deep South, it was a dance with death. Three days later, the boy was abducted by the woman's husband and brother, who then lynched Till and tossed his weighted body into the Tallahatchie River.

Photos of Till's mutilated body were published, bringing the case to national attention. Till's mother

… insisted on an open-casket funeral, so that "all the world [could] see what they did to my son." Over four days, thousands of people saw Emmett's body. Many more blacks across the country who might not have otherwise heard of the case were shocked by pictures that appeared in *Jet* magazine. These pictures moved blacks in a way that nothing else had.[658]

Till's abductors were charged with murder, and more than seventy reporters from across the nation attended the proceedings. The trial lasted less than a week and resulted in acquittal. It was clear to an outraged public that something needed to be done to put an end to Jim Crow laws and racial violence.[659]

Nonviolent Demonstrations

Three months after the Till trial, Rosa Parks spearheaded the Montgomery, Alabama, Bus Boycott. She was arrested after she refused to give up her seat to a white man on a segregated city bus. Originally, the boycott called for the entire black population to avoid the city bus system for one day, but it lasted over a year. Martin Luther King, elected as the movement's spokesperson, went on to organize similar protests throughout the South.[660] The boycott ended only when the issue of segregated buses came to trial; the Supreme Court ruled bus segregation unconstitutional.[661]

Typically, civil rights activists maintained a policy of nonviolent direct action. During the early 1960s, for example, students protested segregated diners by staging sit-ins. Black activists in the South were supported by northern students, black and white, who staged similar sit-ins in the North.[662] Support from the North continued as the Congress of Racial Equality Northern staged Freedom Rides, desegregated bus journeys to destinations in the South. Freedom Rides were designed to incite white racial violence, forcing President Kennedy to take a stand on the issue. Historian Eric Foner writes,

In most parts of the world, a bus journey would hardly have attracted attention. In the Jim Crow South of 1961, the Freedom Riders encountered shocking violence that deeply embarrassed the Kennedy administration.[663]

Even John Seigenthaler, a justice department aide sent as Kennedy's personal representative, was beaten unconscious and left in the street with a fractured skull and several broken ribs. The Freedom Rides were successful in forcing Kennedy to take a stand for civil rights, and segregation was outlawed on interstate buses.[664]

Peaceful marches were an important tool in the fight for civil rights. Demonstrators adhered to a strict code of nonviolence, taking their inspiration from Gandhi. Their conduct stood in stark contrast to the often violent response of police. This was clearly demonstrated at the May 1963 march in Birmingham, Alabama. Since protesters were being routinely arrested and jailed, march organizers used only children aged six to eighteen. By the end of the first day, 959 children had been arrested and charged, filling the jail to capacity. The next day, a second march of more than a thousand children set out for downtown, where they were met by firefighters armed with powerful fire hoses. The nation watched as children were assaulted with enough water pressure to knock them off their feet, roll them down the street, and even break bones.[665]

> During the next few days images of children being blasted by high-pressure fire hoses, clubbed by police officers, and attacked by police dogs appeared on television and in newspapers, triggering international outrage.[666]

After Birmingham, a new civil rights bill was proposed, and most of the nation was ready to accept it. Civil rights groups organized the March on Washington, D.C. to demonstrate the widespread support for the bill. On August 28, 1963, a vast crowd, estimated to be between 200,000[667] and 250,000[668] converged on the nation's capital for the march. The highlight of the day was Martin Luther King's famous speech "I Have a Dream."[669]

The march was generally successful. With the enactment of the Civil Rights Act of 1964 and the Voting Rights Act of 1965, most of the demands of demonstrators had been achieved.[670] Significant legal reform continued. They included the ratification of the Twenty-Fourth Amendment to the American Constitution that specifically banned the use of any tax to prevent citizens from voting in federal elections,[671] and the Civil Rights Act of 1968, which ended legal housing discrimination.[672]

However, some activists, most notably Malcolm X and John Lewis, felt the time for more-militant action had come. Lewis claimed the Civil Rights Act was "too little, too late."[673] In the mid-1960s, the African-American community splinted as various movements rose to prominence, the most notable being Black Power. The new movement was criticized by both the NAACP and Martin Luther King because it worked against integration and the traditional goals of the civil rights movement.[674]

Africa: A Time for Independence

The civil rights movement unfolded against the backdrop of the liberation of Africa from European colonialism, adding to the frustration of many within the African American community. American author and civil rights activist James Baldwin bitterly observed, "All of Africa will be free before we can get a lousy cup of coffee." [675] During the scramble for colonies in Africa, almost every part of the continent had come under the rule of one of the Great Powers of Europe. Then between late December 1951 and April 1980, a period of just twenty-eight years, nation after nation across Africa gained its independence from European government.

There were a few notable exceptions to this extraordinary movement. The first was Liberia, a republic established in 1847. Twenty-five years earlier, the United States had founded it as a settlement for freed slaves who wanted to return to Africa. In that sense, Liberia was a colony of the United States, and certainly the newly settled American Liberians functioned as colonial overlords despite their racial origins, excluding the indigenous population from political and economic power.[676]

Ethiopia, known as Abyssinia to Europeans, had been the only African nation to maintain its freedom in the face of the aggressive colonial expansion of the late nineteenth and early twentieth centuries.[677]

In the 1870s, the Abyssinian army twice defeated invading Turkish and Egyptian forces, along with their European advisors.

Italy's attempts to colonize Abyssinia in 1889 were settled with a treaty that gave Italy a small portion of northern Ethiopia (Eritrea, along the coast of the Red Sea) in exchange for an arms agreement and recognition of Ethiopia's sovereignty. This agreement remained in place until the late 1930s, when the Italians occupied the rest of the country. Since Ethiopia was a member state of the League of Nations, the emperor was able to present an appeal to the international community and was assisted by the British in restoring full sovereignty to the nation.[678] In 1951, the United Nations mandated the federation of Ethiopia and Eritrea. The former Italian colony of Eritrea broke away from Ethiopia in 1993.[679]

The Independence of Africa in the 1950s

The liberation of Africa began with Libya. The post–World War II peace process forced Italy to renounce all claims to its former colony. A few years later, the newly established United Nations passed a resolution calling for Libyan autonomy by January 1, 1952. On December 24, 1951, just days before the deadline, Libya gained its independence.[680]

Egypt had been a protectorate of the United Kingdom since the completion of the Suez Canal in 1869. The canal had been constructed by the Egyptian king with the help of French investors and loans from British banks. When it was clear that Egypt was financially overextended, the Egyptian monarchy was forced to sell its share to British financiers. From that point on, European advisors had a significant voice in Egyptian politics. After World War I, the nation was granted its independence as the Kingdom of Egypt, but continuing unrest kept the British involved in government affairs. In 1952, the Egyptians overthrew the European-backed monarchy to form a fully independent republic.[681]

In 1956, Tunisia and Morocco won autonomy from France. After the French had exiled the Moroccan sultan, the people revolted, and peace was restored only with the return of the sultan and independence.[682,683] At the same time, the French agreed to grant

Tunisia its sovereignty after decades of struggle.[684] That same year, Sudan gained its freedom from the British Empire.[685]

The following year, Ghana became the first sub-Saharan nation to gain its independence from colonial rule.[686] It came after years of boycotts, strikes, and other modes of civil disobedience. Ghana was formed after a United Nations plebiscite merged the former colonies of the Gold Coast and Togoland.[687] Guinea, formerly known as French Guinea and sometimes called Guinea-Conakry today, gained its independence in 1958. Unfortunately, Guinean history included a long, pre-colonial tradition of autocratic rulers, usually from neighboring empires. The country continued this tradition, suffering under a series of violent dictatorships and the poverty that resulted.[688, 689]

The Independence of Africa in the 1960s

1960 was a banner year for liberation in Africa; no fewer than thirteen nations gained their autonomy. With a couple of exceptions, these nations had been colonies of France. Under the leadership of Charles de Gaulle, France worked to shore up its position in the international community by pursuing a policy of decolonization.[690] In rapid succession, much of French Africa petitioned for complete independence: Benin,[691] Burkina Faso,[692] Central African Republic[693] Chad,[694] the Republic of the Congo,[695] Côte d'Ivoire,[696] Gabon,[697] Madagascar,[698] Mali,[699] Mauritania,[700] Niger,[701] Senegal[702] and Togo[703] all gained their independence between April and November.

Belgium's only colony, once known as the Belgian Congo, declared its independence as the Republic of Congo after a nationalist party won the country's elections. The newly formed nation changed its name under successive regimes, first becoming Zaire and, most recently, the Democratic Republic of Congo.[704]

Nigeria also gained its independence from the United Kingdom in October 1960, the culmination of a series of constitutions drafted by the British to gradually ease the nation into self-government.[705] [706] In July, Britain withdrew from the twin colonies of British Somaliland to the north and Italian Somaliland to the south, which had been a British protectorate since World War II. The new nation was called Somalia.[707]

In 1961, three African nations gained their independence from Britain. Portions of British Cameroon voted to merge with neighboring French Cameroon, which had gained self-rule the previous year, to form the Republic of Cameroon.[708] Sierra Leone became an independent member of the British Commonwealth; it was ruled by a parliamentary system of government for several years before military coups and civil wars devastated the nation.[709] In South Africa, British and Dutch settlers (called Boers or Afrikaners) voted to become an independent republic in an all-white referendum held in May 1961.[710]

Tanganyika was granted independence in December 1961. Two years later, revolutionaries on the neighboring island of Zanzibar overthrew the Arab dynastic rulers to form an independent republic. The two nations unified in 1964 to form Tanzania.[711] In 1962, the nations of Burundi[712] and Rwanda[713] were granted independence.

After fighting throughout most of the 1950s against the French colonial government, Algeria finally achieved its long-awaited goal in July 1962, under the leadership of the National Liberation Front.[714] In October of that same year, Uganda, a protectorate of the United Kingdom, became an independent nation within the British Commonwealth.[715, 716]

Throughout much of the 1950s, Kenya was in a state of emergency due to the Mau Mau uprising against the British colonial government. The government defense relied heavily on the Home Guard comprised of loyalist Africans, which helped propel Kenyans into a more active political role. Nationalists formed an independent government in 1963, and the country became a republic a year later.[717]

During the 1960s, the United Kingdom continued its policy of decolonization in Africa. Malawi[718] and neighboring Zambia received their independence in 1964.[719] The British colony of The Gambia consisted of a sliver of land only a few miles wide on either side of the Gambia River, surrounded on three sides by Senegal. Nevertheless, it has maintained its independence since its emancipation from the United Kingdom in early 1965, except for a brief period in the 1980s.[720]

In southern Africa, Botswana was granted independence from

Britain in 1966,[721] as was Lesotho, a tiny kingdom surrounded by South Africa.[722] In 1968, Britain kept its promise to the Swazis, guaranteeing their autonomy from the rest of Africa by granting the tiny Kingdom of Swaziland complete independence.[723] Britain also granted independence to Mauritius, a small island in the Indian Ocean east of Madagascar.[724]

In 1968, Spain withdrew from most of its few remaining African colonies. Some were incorporated into the surrounding nations; for instance, Ifni[725] became part of Morocco.[726] Others—five islands and a tiny territory between Cameroon and Gabon off the Gulf of Guinea—became Equatorial Guinea, one of the smallest nations in Africa.[727]

The Independence of Africa in the 1970s

Portugal's policy on decolonization was **Don't!** The Portuguese constitution was amended to transform the nation's colonial holdings into overseas provinces, and the government publicly announced its policy of keeping the empire intact.[728] As a result, African nationalists in Portuguese colonies were forced into revolution. In Guinea Bissau, armed rebels backed by Cuba, China, and the Soviet Union began a rebellion in 1956 and unilaterally declared independence in 1973. It was begrudgingly recognized by Portugal the following year.[729, 730]

In Angola, the Colonial War was waged between three nationalist guerrilla armies and the full military power of the Portuguese regime. The war ended in 1974 when a coup d'état placed a new regime over Portugal, one that acknowledged the independence of all Portugal's former colonies the following year. Unfortunately, Angola was ill-prepared for this turn of events. The country devolved into twenty-seven years of bitter civil war between the three guerrilla forces.[731] Mozambique wrenched its independence from Portugal in 1975, after a decade of sporadic guerrilla warfare. Following the immediate deportation of all Portuguese, the country sank into violent civil war between anticommunist rebels and the newly installed Marxist regime.[732, 733]

In late 1975, Spain withdrew from the last of its African colonies, Western Sahara. Morocco promptly annexed the northern half of the territory in 1976 and claimed the rest of the country in 1979. These claims were violently contested by a guerrilla liberation front, and the conflict has yet to be fully resolved despite UN involvement. The Sahrawi Arab Democratic Republic, partially recognized by the international community, claims to have liberated only a quarter of the land that rightfully belongs to it. In the meantime, Morocco views much of the disputed land as a buffer zone between itself and the warring factions.[734, 735]

The last nations to gain independence from European colonial powers were Comoros, Djibouti, and Zimbabwe. Comoros voted for independence from France and has since suffered through numerous coups or attempted coups.[736] It should be noted that one of the islands among the Comoros voted against independence and is still administered as a French overseas department.[737] Djibouti, formerly known as French Somaliland, voted to become independent from France in 1977 but the two nations maintained close diplomatic and economic ties.[738]

The Independence of Africa in 1980 and Beyond

Zimbabwe gained independence from Britain in April 1980. The territory, formerly a part of Southern Rhodesia, had unilaterally declared its independence in 1965, but the United Kingdom refused to recognize it until the black African majority was given full voting rights. After years of UN sanctions and guerrilla uprisings, the country finally had free elections in 1979 and became independent the following year.[739]

Since 1980, all Africa has been free of European colonial rule, although there are still nationalist groups struggling to break away from other African nations and achieve their own independence. For example, Namibia, a former German colony, was annexed by South Africa after World War II. Despite years of resistance by Marxist nationalists, South Africa agreed to relinquish control of the area only in accordance with a UN mandate in 1988; independence followed in 1990.[740] As recently as July 2011, South Sudan gained its independence from Sudan after years of civil war; the South Sudanese had voted 98 percent in favor of secession and independence.[741]

It is amazing that an entire continent should be transformed in just twenty-eight years. In less than three decades, the dominion of the White Horseman over the continent of Africa, epitomized by the Scramble for Africa, had been undone. Each European colonial power approached decolonization very differently, from the French plebiscites to the British constitutional approach to the Portuguese absolute refusal to leave until there was no other choice. But none of that really mattered; it was time for Africa to be free. In the same way, nothing really changed the position of blacks in American society until the fullness of time, a time determined by God and the release of the Black Horseman.

CHAPTER 23:

The Yoke of Debt

> When he had opened the third seal, I heard the third
> beast say, Come and see. And I beheld, and lo a black
> horse; and he who sat on it had a pair of balances in
> his hand. (Rev. 6:5 KJV)

The Black Horseman holds an object in his hand that the Authorized
King James Version translates as "a pair of balances," and other versions
call "a pair of scales" (New King James,[742] New International,[743] and
New American Standard Bible[744]). The Greek noun used here is *zygos*
(ζυγός) that comes from a root word meaning to join, especially by a
yoke. In fact, yoke is the most common translation; Thayer's *Lexicon*
lists the primary meaning as "a yoke; a. prop[erly]such as is put on a
drought-cattle. b. metaph[orically] used of any burden or bondage:
as that of slavery."[745] Zygos is used six times in the New Testament
and is translated "yoke" in all but one of them. In fact, those verses
make no sense if "balances" or "scales" is used:

> Take up my yoke upon you, and learn of me, for I am
> meek and lowly in heart: and ye shall find rest unto
> your souls. (Matt. 11:29 KJV)

> For my yoke [is] easy, and my burden is light.
> (Matt. 11:30 KJV)

> Now, therefore why tempt ye God, to put a yoke

upon the neck of the disciples, which neither our
fathers nor we were able to bear? (Acts 15:10 KJV)

Stand fast therefore in the liberty wherewith Christ
hath made us free, and be not entangled again with
the yoke of bondage. (Gal. 5:1 KJV)

Let as many servants as are under the yoke count their
own masters worthy of all honour, that the name of God
and [his] doctrine be not blasphemed. (1 Tim. 6:1 KJV)

It is only in Revelation 6:5 that zygos is not translated "yoke."
Unlike the other references, the context does not entirely rule out
either possibility. Certainly a case might be made that the Black
Horseman was able to give blacks and other ethnic minorities the
justice they deserved, although this was not universally true; the
whole world did not experience justice. The impact of the White
and the Red Horsemen was global, so it makes sense that the Black
Horseman would also be global.

Perhaps Tyndale thought the "scales" might be used to weigh the
wheat and the barley. Or maybe he chose "a pair of balances" based
on reasoning that goes something like this: a yoke is large and heavy
and is probably too big for a rider to hold in his hand; therefore he
must be holding a pair of scales. However, the four horsemen are not
limited by human abilities; they are prophetic pictures of what God is
planning for the last days. If the Black Horseman is actually carrying
a yoke, it implies the whole world would be enslaved or bound to
some heavy burden. This interpretation lines up with our prophecy
in Amos that spoke of the lion and the bear.

The Snake That Bites

[18]Woe to you that desire the day of the LORD! to what
end [is] it for you? the day of the LORD [is] darkness, and
not light. [19]As if a man did flee from a lion, and a bear met
him; or went into the house, and leaned his hand on the
wall, and a serpent bit him. (Amos 5:18–19 KJV)

At first, the man flees from a lion; the word "flee" (*noos:* נוֹס),

literally means "to flee or escape."[746] Certainly men did what they could to escape from the dominion of the princes of the White Horseman. Unfortunately, the man, in his flight from the lion, meets a bear, a symbol of communism. The word *pega* (פגע) is "to encounter" and can imply both hostility and entreaty.[747]

Since Amos describes a man's interaction with the first two beasts foretold by Daniel, it seems logical to conclude that the next encounter correlates to Daniel's third beast and the Black Horseman. Here we have a picture of an unsuspecting man going into his house to relax, leaning against the wall supported by his hand. Suddenly, apparently without warning, a serpent bites him. Generally, snakes prefer hiding to striking, but when they do bite, the effects can be painful and deadly.[748]

Just as the lion and the bear symbolized government by evil rulers, the snake portrays something the government allows to hide in our homes. What is it that hides in a house, striking its owners without warning to inflict a deadly wound? It has risen to the forefront since the early 1950s and has the ability to yoke people to slavery as surely as chains. The text in Amos provides the answer. The verb *nashak* (נשך) has two meanings: 1) to bite, or 2) to pay interest or lend for interest or usury.[749] How many people feel enslaved by their mortgage payments or have been shocked by the interest they are paying each month?

I remember buying my first home and faithfully making the payments of several hundred dollars each month. At the end of the first year, I received a statement showing how those payments had been applied to taxes, insurance, interest and paying off the principal. Although I knew the amount applied to the loan principal was only a fraction of what I sent to the mortgage company, I was still shocked to learn we had paid a grand total of $32 toward reducing our debt. I had been bitten by a serpent called interest in my own house.

I had been enslaved by debt.

The Bite of Debt

Over the past sixty years, Americans have become slaves to debt personally and nationally. Debt comes in a wide variety of packages, but three types of debt have become ubiquitous in American society:

home mortgages, student loans, and credit card debt. Many people are bound to other types of debt such as car loans, but these three clearly illustrate the insidious yoke that has bound our nation more tightly than any foreign enemy could achieve by force. Historian Vincent Cannato writes,

> Finally, the housing crisis suggests a deeper and more complicated problem: the role of debt in American life. One hundred years ago, most Americans frowned upon debt. Credit cards and student loans did not exist, and large mortgages were rare. It wasn't until the latter half of the 20th century that America saw an explosion of increasingly easy and cheap consumer credit, and so also of consumer debt.[750]

Mortgages

After World War II, people began buying homes at a rate never seen before. In 1945, only 40 percent of British households owned homes, but the proportion of homeowners has been steadily increasing to about 50 percent in 1971, 56 percent in 1981, 66 percent in 1991, and 68 percent in the early 2000s. Interestingly, this same study found that half of all homeowners lived below the poverty line. This means that about two-thirds of the British population is experiencing the serpent bite of interest payments on their own homes, and fully one-third of these people live in poverty.[751]

The situation is similar in the United States. The passage of the G.I. Bill gave returning servicemen access to government–insured mortgages, and the ability to deduct home loan interest payments on income taxes, both of which encouraged buying over renting. When these laws were first enacted, Americans responded enthusiastically. Home ownership increased from 44 to 62 percent between 1940 and 1960, helping to drive the postwar economic boom.

Even during this era of sunny optimism, there were some who warned of the dangers of encouraging homeownership. According to historian Vincent Cannato, sociologist John Dean was sounding the alarm as early as 1945.

"The problem of home ownership ... will presumably someday be faced squarely by the United States," Dean wrote. "When that time comes America will no doubt look back on our own time as an era in which society encouraged its families to stride ahead through a field deliberately sown with booby traps." But while default rates for FHA-insured mortgages were higher than those for other loans, the booby traps that Dean worried about—homeowners enticed to enter into loans they could not possibly repay—would not fully materialize for decades.[752]

A homebuyer with a thirty-year mortgage pays a staggering amount of interest over the life of the loan. One analyst computed the interest paid by a homebuyer purchasing a medium-priced house in 2009 ($172,600) with a thirty-year mortgage at 5.85 percent interest. Assuming the buyer made the minimum down payment required by the FDA (3.5 percent, which would be $6,041), and made no early payments, the total interest collected by the bank would be $187,177. This is $14,577 more than the purchase price of the home, meaning the buyer actually paid $359,777 for a home valued at $172,600.[753]

Imagine going to a car lot and seeing a car with a Blue Book value of $10,000. It's in great shape, and you're thinking of buying it. The fast-talking salesman assures you he's giving you a great deal—practically giving it away. The car can be yours for only $21,000. Would any of us fall for such a bargain? Before answering, consider that most of us agree to just such a deal when it comes to homeownership. We accept these loan shark–like terms because most of us have no hope of ever owning a home without a mortgage, and we have to pay for a place to live whether we rent or buy. We might even persuade ourselves that buying a home is a good investment, so we make a deal with the devil and tie ourselves to a mortgage for fifteen or thirty years. We've been bitten by snakes.

Since interest rates play such an important role in housing costs, it is important to consider the historical rates under the Black Horseman.

- 1948–51—prime rates rise from 2 to 3 percent
- 1951–56—prime rates rise from 3 to 4 percent
- 1956–66—prime rates fluctuate between 3.5 and 6 percent
- Nov. 1966–Mar. 1970—prime rates rise from 6 to 8 percent
- Sept. 1970–Dec. 1972—prime rates decrease from 8 to 5 percent
- Mar. 1973–July 1974—prime rates rise from 6 to 12 percent; this combined with the oil embargo resulted in a recession.
- 1974–76—prime rates decrease from 11.75 to 6.25 percent
- 1977–80—prime rates skyrocket from 6.5 to 21.5 percent
- 1981—prime rates decrease from 20.5 to 16. percent
- 1982—prime rates decrease from 16.5 to 11.5. percent
- 1983–90—prime rates fluctuate between 8.5 and 13 percent
- 1991–2001—prime rates fluctuate between 6 to 9.5 percent
- 2002–2007—prime rates fluctuate between 4 to 8.25 percent
- 2008— prime rates decrease from 11.75 to 6.25 percent

Prime interest rates only returned to something comparable to those in the 1950s with the housing crash at the close of 2008, falling from 6.5 percent in January to 3.25 percent by the end of the year.[754]

Homeowners have been bitten by the snake of interest.

Financial Aid and the Debt of Student Loans

Before the 1950s, tuition made higher education the privilege of the well-to-do. From the days of Thomas Jefferson, many presidents desired to make college access based on "merit and ability," but education was a responsibility of the states.[755] Scholarships were funded privately, and loans for education were virtually nonexistent.

The era of higher education for the masses began with the passing of the G.I. Bill (Servicemen's Readjustment Act of 1944), which included provisions for returning military personnel to access further education from colleges and vocational schools in preparation for civilian careers. The goal of the bill was to minimize the social upheaval that might result from trying to integrate the thousands of returning servicemen back into the economy. Millions made use of their G.I. benefits; in the years following the war, 2.5 million veterans went to college, 3.5 million went to some other type of training, and more than 3 million received on-the-job training.[756]

In 1954, the College Board created the College Scholarship Service with a goal of making students' financial needs secondary to their scholastic abilities when considering admissions. This service allowed students to apply for financial assistance in the form of scholarships, institutional loans, and work-study based on the demonstrated needs of themselves and their families'.[757]

The first federally funded student loans began as a response to the Soviet launch of Sputnik. Believing that America was falling behind in the Cold War due to shortcomings in scientific and technical education, the National Defense Education Act sought to remove financial barriers to college. Students could borrow $1,000 annually, to a maximum of $5,000, to be repaid in ten annual installments after leaving school. In its first year, 1959, a reported "1,188 institutions had loaned $9.5 million to 24,831 students." Twenty years later, nearly $5 billion was lent to 874,000 students. To date, nearly $29 billion has been given in federal student loans since its inception in 1958.[758]

In 1965, the Higher Education Act was passed. The program implemented educational grants (now called Pell Grants) and student loans (now the Stafford Loan Program) guaranteed by the federal government. These were issued to students on the basis of financial need rather than scholastic ability. [759, 760]

However, it was the advent of the Higher Education Reauthorization Act of 1992 that completely changed the future debt load on students. For the first time, the federal government authorized unsubsidized loans, which were not guaranteed by the federal government and required interest payments immediately, even while the loan recipient was still in school. The bill also raised loan limits and exempted family homes as assets when calculating need. The changes were supposedly designed to "help middle– and higher–income families regardless of need." [761]

The bill had an immediate impact. According to California's Stanford University,

> Stanford students and their parents took out 1,790 federally guaranteed low-interest loans totaling $9.2 million in the first half of fiscal year 1994–95, close to what they borrowed in all of 1993–94, and $3 million more than they were borrowing five years ago.

In the first half of fiscal 1993–94 alone, Stanford students took out 387 Stafford Unsubsidized Loans for $3.8 million, compared to 136 loans for $417,471 in the first half of 1993–94.

Stanford families also took out 73 unsubsidized Parent Loans for Undergraduate Students for $895,356 in the first half of this fiscal year, and five unsubsidized Supplemental Loans for Students for $19,598.[762]

The amount of debt someone can accrue though the Stafford loan program is truly staggering. The maximum debt for an undergraduate is $57,500, of which only $23,000 must be subsidized, while a graduate student can accrue $138,500 ($65,500 subsidized). In other words, a student loan payment can be as much as a mortgage payment, and these figures do not include other unsubsidized loan sources, which are being taken out for increasingly larger amounts.[763]

In the last decade (2000–01 to 2010–11), subsidized Stafford loans decreased as a percentage of educational borrowing from 41 to 35 percent, while institutional loans and private student loans have been increasing rapidly. Loans issued by for-profit institutions, which tend to give unfavorable interest rates (15 percent or more are not unheard of), rose from $500 million in 2007–08 to $720 million during the 2010–11 academic year.[764] As a result, American college graduates are bound with massive debts before they buy a home, a car, or any of life's necessities. One U.S. senator, who is working to help protect students from the private student lending bonanza, said,

For the first time in history, Americans owe more on their student loans than on their credit cards…. With virtually no risk, loan companies have seen record profits on high interest rate private student loans that have left students with crushing debt upon graduation.[765]

Because students and their parents can access loans to underwrite college educations, schools are able to increase tuition and other expenses while devaluing the final product by making a degree as commonplace as a high school diploma. Traditionally, the cost of college was considered a good investment because it generally paid off in increased earnings. However, over the last decade, the earnings of young college graduates have dropped, with no relief in sight, while tuition rates have been increasing at eleven times the rate of inflation, faster than any other sector in the economy.[766]

In the face of this, you would think people would be skipping college and pursuing other options, but the financial aid data tell a different story.

> According to FinAid.org a site that tracks student financial aid student loan debt is increasing at an alarming rate of $2,853.88 per second. **This is a stunning rate of $171,180 per minute**. (Emphasis in source) At the current rate we will hit $1 trillion in student loan debt in 2012 since we are adding $89,972,208,000 in student loan debt per year.[767]

These statistics show that our young people and our future are being enslaved by debt. Those with student loans in default will be unable to start a business, buy a house, or make investments. Currently, they can't even escape the debt through bankruptcy court, since student loans, even private ones, are nondischargeable and must be paid. There are no time limits on student loan collections, and in order to collect, the Department of Education is authorized to

- tack collection fees of 25 percent and collection agency commission fees of approximately 28 percent onto the principal, interest, and penalties you already owe,
- take your federal income tax refund until all your defaulted student loans are paid,
- garnish up to 15 percent of your wages without suing you first,
- take as much as $750 per month (up to 15 percent of your income) in federal benefits to which you might be entitled, including Social Security retirement and disability income, and apply that amount toward your outstanding defaulted student loan debt, and
- sue you for your outstanding student loan debt and place liens on your property.[768]

The lives of our young people will be spent working to pay interest to financial institutions unrestrained by normal regulations that govern other types of debt.[769] They are indeed being enslaved.

Students have been bitten by the snake of interest.

Credit Card Debt

The epitome of high-interest debt backed by nothing of tangible value is credit card debt. Unlike mortgages, which pay for tangible assets that serve useful purposes and may appreciate over time, or student loans, that are investments with the possible return of higher earnings, most credit card debt was accrued on spending for items that have no intrinsic resale value. During the ride of the Black Horseman, Americans went from zero credit cards (they didn't exist) to 631 million credit cards in circulation—more than two for every man, woman and child.[770] How did we get here?

The idea of credit began with individual stores extending credit to customers deemed worthy and was used mainly as a convenience for the customer. The first bank card, called Charge-It, was issued by the Flatbush National Bank of Brooklyn for use only by its customers. Next, the Diners Club Card (1950) became the first widely accepted credit card and was used mainly for travel and entertainment expenses. Other companies, including gasoline companies and American Express, issued similar cards. These cards were not truly credit cards but charge cards; users had to pay the balance in full every month.[771]

In 1959, MasterCard began allowing customers the option of not paying off the card each month but maintaining revolving balances. This naturally included finance fees, but it allowed customers greater flexibility, especially when making a single large purchase. By 1966, the general-purpose credit card was introduced by Bank of America under the name of Visa. MasterCard soon followed suit with a similar interbank association. These were "open-loop" systems that required cooperation and the transfer of funds between different banks. From this point, any bank that wished to enter the credit card business could join one of these two associations.[772]

However, the credit card use was still a matter of convenience. They were issued only to people with good financial backgrounds and sufficient incomes to pay outstanding balances. Furthermore, most states had usury laws that limited the amount of interest issuers could charge. All this ended in the late 1970s and early 1980s, when the federal government dealt a series of deathblows to state consumer protections.

The first was an obscure U.S. Supreme Court decision interpreting the National Banking Acts of the 1960s known as *Marquette National Bank v. First of Omaha Service Corp.* According to this ruling, a nationally chartered bank was subject only to the laws of the state in which it was chartered and to federal regulations. Therefore, loans issued by that bank, including credit cards, were governed by the state laws where the loan originated, not those of the state where the borrower lived. The effect was to gut the usury laws in every state.[773]

While the Supreme Court's decision attracted little attention at the time, it laid the foundation for what happened next. Runaway inflation in the 1970s made it increasingly difficult to borrow money for any reason. The Federal Reserve was charging banks up to 15 percent for money, but most states had usury laws that banned interest rates anywhere near that. For example, South Dakota had a cap of 8 percent, which was later raised to 10 percent. This, coupled with high inflation, meant banks lost money by lending to customers.[774]

Citibank, for example, had lost more than $1 billion on its credit card business alone. In 1979, the rate of inflation exceeded allowable interest rates under New York law. In desperation, Citibank executives cut a deal with the governor of South Dakota: if it repealed its usury laws quickly, Citibank would relocate its credit card division to Rapid City, bringing with it hundreds of high-paying, white-collar jobs. South Dakota extended an invitation to Citibank and passed an "emergency" bill that was drafted by Citibank executives through the legislature in a single day. The company relocated its credit card division within months and began issuing high-interest cards throughout the country.[775]

Other states soon followed suit; Delaware repealed its usury laws within the year. As a result, credit cards, which were once losing propositions, became lucrative sources of bank income. Elizabeth Warren, Harvard University law professor, commented,

> We effectively engaged in the single biggest policy
> change in the credit area, the whole consumer credit
> area, through an obscure Supreme Court decision
> interpreting some ambiguous language.[776]

The credit card industry continued to rake in record-breaking profits by creating innovative repayment terms. The first was the 1980 introduction of the annual fee, which meant that even customers who routinely paid their balances each month contributed to a bank's bottom line. This cash cow was undermined in 1990, when AT&T launched its credit card with no annual rate; the public response clearly indicated that cards that maintained the annual fee would lose their customer base.

Mathematical wunderkind Andrew Kahr pioneered several practices that would become the industry standard. This included analyzing vast troves of customer financial data to find the most lucrative customers, those who routinely carried high balances but were unlikely to default. Since higher credit limits were useful for attracting customers, Kahr proposed lowering the minimum payment from 5 to 2 percent, allowing the bank to increase the card limit and still maintain the same monthly payment. The practice, which obscured the true cost of the debt, has resulted in the tripling of the average household credit card debt from $2,500 to $7,500.

In 1996, another U.S. Supreme Court decision effectively removed all restraints on the credit card industry's ability to charge fees at will. Late fees escalated from the $5 to $10 range to as high as $39. Other fees, such as penalties for exceeding a card's credit limit, were routinely imposed and could possibly trigger a sharp increase in interest rates—up to fivefold in some cases. One woman testified that she has paid $24,000 in late fees and interest on her credit cards.[777]

Consumers have been bitten by the snake of interest.

The Creation of Debt Serfdom

One financial analyst sums up the American debt situation succinctly: "The credit card is merely your key into the kingdom of serfdom."[778] The use of credit cards has become not merely a convenience but a necessity. Many transactions, such as car rentals, require credit cards.

Insurance companies demand authorization to directly bill monthly installments, and many businesses, including McDonalds, will no longer accept checks but only cash or credit cards.

> "Since the 1970s, there has been growing evidence supporting the frequently heard conjecture that credit cards encourage spending," wrote Duncan Simester, a professor specializing in marketing at M.I.T.'s Sloan School of Management ... research in the 1970s and 1980s showed that people who own more credit cards make larger purchases per department store visit, tip better at restaurants, and are more likely to underestimate or forget the amount spent on recent purchases... [and] "willingness to pay" can be increased up to 100 percent when customers use a credit card rather than cash.[779]

These findings are significant, especially in light of the changing ratio of household income relative to debt. Before 1980, when credit card companies began aggressively seeking new customers, the ratio was fairly stable, so the debt rose in proportion to rising incomes. Everything changed in the 1980s. Between 1985 and 2008, the debt-to-income ratio of the average household rose from 0.55 to 1.15 (55 percent to 115 percent)—the household's debt exceeded its annual income.[780]

Another way of viewing this is to compare total household debt, including mortgages, car loans, educational loans and other types of consumer debt to GDP (gross domestic product) or what the American economy is actually producing. In 1953, households owed a total of $106 billion (as measured in constant 2000 dollars), while the GDP was $379 billion, which meant that debt was just under 28 percent of GDP. By contrast, consider how the 2010 household debt of $13.5 trillion compares to the 2009 GDP of $13.1 trillion; American's personal debt exceeds the GDP.[781] And these figures don't include business debt or government deficits. Put another way, Americans owe approximately $43,000 per person or $120,000 per household at a time when the average household income is $52,000.[782]

We are being strangled by the serpent of debt.

CHAPTER 24:

The Millstone
of Inflation

> [5]When he had opened the third seal, I heard the third
> beast say, Come and see. And I beheld, and lo a black
> horse; and he who sat on it had a pair of balances in
> his hand. [6]And I heard a voice in the midst of the four
> beasts say, A measure of wheat for a penny, and three
> measures of barley for a penny; and [see] thou hurt
> not the oil and the wine. (Rev. 6:5–6 KJV)

After describing the Black Horseman, John relates a prophetic word
spoken from the midst of the four living creatures: "A measure of
wheat for a penny [or denarius], and three measures of barley for a
penny [or denarius]" (Rev. 6:6 KJV). The Greek *choinix* (χοῖνιξ),
"measure," refers to the amount of grain that "would support a man
of moderate appetite for a day."[783] The monetary unit used in this
passage is a denarius—Greek *denarion* (δηνάριον), the most common
coin circulated in the Roman Empire. According to historians, the
denarius was the standard unit of pay for common foot soldiers,[784] and
many Bible scholars believe it was the daily wage for the ordinary
worker (Matt. 20:2–13).[785, 786]

    This passage describes a situation in which a man's wages cover
the basic necessities of life but nothing more. In Roman society,
bread was a staple food enjoyed by everyone. However, different

classes ate bread made of different grains according to income. A fine, white, wheat bread was preferred, but coarse, brown breads made of emmer wheat or barley were the standard fare of the lower classes.[787] Barley, the least popular of the grains, was definitely avoided by those who could afford wheat.[788]

This passage is speaking of a time when a man's daily earnings will supply only his own needs. His wife must also enter the workforce to make ends meet. If they have children, it will be necessary to accept a lower standard of living represented by the measure of barley.

Inflation

The years of the Black Horseman underwent almost constant inflation. From July 1950 until December 2008, the U.S. economy experienced some level of inflation every month except for a short period of recession from mid-1954 to the end of 1955. Inflation rates peaked to double-digit monthly growth during the mid-1970s and again from 1979 to 1981; the only other periods with this rate of inflation were during and immediately following the two world wars.[789]

Inflation from 1950 to 2010 accrued more than 700 percent, so that an item that cost $20 in 1952 would sell for over $162 in 2008. But even this astounding rate of inflation is less than the price increases of certain staple items such as food and gas. For example, a loaf of bread that sold for 16¢ in 1950 would cost $1.30 today according to the average inflation rate. While this amount may purchase an inexpensive sandwich loaf, a healthy multigrain loaf can often exceed $4. Gas prices should have risen from 20¢ per gallon (1950) to $1.62, but gas has not been that inexpensive for years.[790, 791]

We have been yoked to the millstone of inflation.

A Man's Home is His Castle

The cost of buying a house has also been impacted by inflation. While it is obvious that housing prices have increased consistently over the years, it is difficult to tell how much of this is caused by appreciation and how much can be attributed to inflation. Robert J. Schiller, an economist from Yale, created an index of American house prices since 1890, taking inflation and changes in the dollar into account. It showed that housing prices dropped sharply when the construction industry introduced mass-production techniques, and increased during the postwar housing boom in the 1940s and 1950s. Housing prices returned to equilibrium after the booms of the 1970s and 1980s, but we have yet to see prices stabilize after the recent boom of the 2000s. Prices, which increased by 87 percent, are bound to fall, with painful effects on the economy and on those with upside-down mortgages. [792]

Historically, some connection existed between housing prices and income, a connection that has all but disappeared in the last few years as banks abandoned their traditional ratio between income and loan approvals. A comparison of the median price of a house to the median wage shows that people in the 1950s and 1960s needed to work a little over two years to pay the principal on their homes. For example, in 1950, the ratio of the median-priced home ($7,354) to median income ($3,319) was 2.21, or 221 percent. 1960 had a similar ratio: $11,900 for a home with income of $5,620 is 2.11, or 211 percent.[793]

According to Goldman Sachs, quoted in *USA Today*, the long-standing ratio between housing costs and income has been 2.7, but in the 2000s "a typical existing home costs 3.5 times a median family income," which may have been just barely affordable when interest rates were low.[794] Homebuyers relied on dual incomes to pay their mortgages. They and the banks gambled that nothing would go wrong—no illness, no unemployment, and no divorce—for thirty years.

According to Visual Economics, the national ratio between yearly income and housing costs was 2.97 in 1975, rising to 3.5 in 1980. Over the next twenty years, the median house prices continued to skyrocket, but falling interest rates kept the ratio relatively affordable. Although the median housing prices continued to rise compared to income, the percent of income allotted for mortgage payments dropped dramatically, from over 45 percent in the early 1980s to as low as 21 percent in the late 1990s. However, in the early 2000s, when housing prices rose 87 percent, the median house price approached 500 percent of the median income, and houses were no longer affordable for middle-class buyers.[795]

Data analyst Ben Engebreth points out that the home cost–to–income ratio varies widely from place to place. While many parts of the United States have healthy relationships between incomes and housing prices, some urban areas have a downright terrifying ratio. The worst offenders are New York (6.33), Honolulu (7.81), and California, especially Los Angeles (7.99), San Francisco (8.23), and San Diego (9.29). The people who work in these cities can't afford to live in them.[796]

Inflated housing prices are not unique to the United States. Britain has been experiencing a similar phenomenon. House prices are so out of line with incomes that families buying a home generally require two incomes to make the payments, and the Bank of England was forced to lower interest rates to a paltry 0.5 percent to ensure homeowners didn't default on their loans.[797]

During the late 1980s, Japanese housing prices underwent a meteoric rise in urban centers that was completely disconnected to wages and rents. When the bubble burst in 1990, Japanese home prices dropped sharply, wreaking havoc on the economy.

> After reaching peak values, Japanese home prices declined by an average of 40 percent. In the country's largest cities, the declines were worse, averaging 65 percent. Homes in Tokyo lost 80 percent of their value and are still on the downward slide to this day.[798]

Homeowners have been yoked to the millstone of inflation.

Food: The Staff of Life

> A measure of wheat for a penny, and three measures of barley for a penny; (Rev. 6:6 KJV)

Since the Revelation passage mentions wheat and barley, both staple foods, it seems logical that the Black Horse would have a significant impact on food production and affordability. Ironically, the era that coincides with the Black Horseman featured nearly sixty years of low food prices in comparison with hourly wages. This same period also featured several revolutionary changes in farming methods and the food industry, known as the Green Revolution. The supermarket changed how food was delivered to customers, and the advent of genetically modified organisms (GMO) changed the very molecular structure of food itself.

The Price of Food

As someone who spends a lot of time—and money—grocery shopping, I am painfully aware that the price of food goes up regularly. The question is whether this is just my imagination or the result of inflation, or if food actually does cost more. One woman designed a study to answer these questions. She tracked the number of hours working at minimum wage needed to purchase a standard basket of groceries: a loaf of bread, a pound of coffee, a dozen eggs, three pounds of midprice beef, one box of corn flakes or Cheerios, five pounds of potatoes, and a Hershey bar.

In 1938, when minimum wage was first enacted, the basket would have been worth 9.25 hours of minimum-wage labor, so that workers at the bottom of the economic ladder of the time would literally be working to eat and provide shelter. In 1961, during one of the boom times that saw the proliferation of the middle class, this same food basket cost only 3.75 hours. The cost of the basket remained under 4 hours except during the late 1970s, when high rates of inflation outstripped productivity and the food basket peaked at 5.5 hours, before dropping back down to the 4-hour mark. Despite increases in minimum wage in the 2000s, the price of food has been going up even faster; the cost of the grocery basket is higher than any time since the 1950s and is still climbing.[799]

News reports confirm the advancing cost of feeding a family. One article attributes skyrocketing food costs to higher fuel prices and the demand of ethanol (made from corn). The writer cheerfully states that other nations spend a higher percentage of their income on food than Americans and concludes, "But it actually would be good if food cost a great deal more."[800]

Food shoppers have been yoked to the millstone of inflation.

The Green Revolution

Of course food prices are still significantly below those of the Great Depression. Radical changes in all aspects of the food industry, from field to supermarket, have been revolutionized during the Black Horseman era. During the 1940s, Norman Borlaug began experimenting with new disease-resistant, high-yield strains of wheat combined with mechanized farming technologies to improve yields in Mexico. The country was able to dramatically increase its wheat production, transforming Mexico from an importer to an exporter of grain. In the 1950s and 1960s, American farmers used the same methods with similar results. These technologies were soon implemented around the globe, creating a dramatic increase in grain production.[801, 802]

The high-yield seeds greatly outperformed traditional seeds if they received adequate water, fertilizers, and pesticides. Since the seeds were hybrids, farmers had to buy new ones each year rather than practice traditional seed-saving techniques. The new methods also required expensive irrigation and chemical fertilizers. Furthermore, only a handful of varieties were propagated to the exclusion of most others. For example, traditional farmers cultivated over 30,000 varieties of rice, but today only 10 are grown worldwide.[803]

On the other hand, the combination of hybrid seeds and innovative methods doubled farm output between 1950 and 1965 and again between 1965 and 1975. For many countries, such as India and China, implementing Green Revolution technologies removed the constant fear of famine.[804] Record breaking crop yields were not without risks; the reliance on chemicals and the lack of biodiversity increased the risk of crop failure in less than ideal years.

Genetically Modified Foods

The Green Revolution changed the face of agriculture during the first thirty years of the Black Horseman, but the rise of GMO foods dominated the following thirty years. The scientific foundations for GMO research were established by Francis Crick and James D. Watson, when they discovered the double-helix DNA molecule, containing the genetic blueprints for all living things.[805] According to *Time* magazine,

> On Feb. 28, 1953, Francis Crick walked into the Eagle pub in Cambridge, England, and, as James

Watson later recalled, announced that "we had found the secret of life." ... Not until decades later, in the age of genetic engineering, would the Promethean power unleashed that day become vivid.[806]

If the lid on Pandora's Box had been cracked open by Crick and Watson, it was thrown off by a 1980 decision by the U.S. Supreme Court. *Diamond v. Chakrabarty* centered on Chakrabarty's effort to patent his "invention" of a unique strain of oil-eating bacteria. The patent had been rejected on the grounds that microorganisms were "products of nature" and therefore not patentable. However, the argument was made before the Supreme Court that

> this human-made, genetically engineered bacterium is capable of breaking down multiple components of crude oil. Because of this property, which is possessed by no naturally occurring bacteria, Chakrabarty's invention is believed to have significant value for the treatment of oil spills.[807]

The court decided that patent law distinguished between the "products of nature," whether plant or mineral, which could not be patented, and the products of human invention which could. Since genetically altered life forms were not found in nature but were the product of extensive research and development, the court ruled that genetically modified organisms could indeed be patented. As a result, the patent office "drastically expanded the kinds of inventions it was willing to patent, to include plants, animals, some computer technology, and business methods."[808]

The proliferation of genetically engineered crops soon followed. Since 1996, the cultivation of genetically modified organism (GMO) crops by large-scale commercial enterprises spread rapidly around the world. By 2008, 125 million hectares (a hectare is about two and a half acres) of GMO crops were cultivated globally, with 62.5 million hectares grown in the United States alone.[809]

According to the United States Department of Agriculture, 94 percent of soy, 73 percent of cotton, and 65 percent of corn grown in the United States in 2011 were GMO. The most dramatic rise in the use of these crops, most of which are resistant to insects and herbicides, occurred in the first twelve years after their introduction.[810] There has been a corresponding increase of GMO foods on the supermarket shelves; by 2006, 78 percent of processed foods in the supermarket had some genetically modified ingredient.[811]

The Rise of the Supermarket

Over the last sixty years, the food industry has been completely transformed by an unending quest to bring the modern eater convenient and enticing variations of the key flavors we crave: fat, salt, and sweet. Think of a juicy hamburger served with salty chips and washed down with a sweet soda. Award-winning journalist Michael Pollan has stated,

> The way we eat has changed more in the last 50 years than in the previous 10,000 ... The modern American supermarket has on average 47,000 products. There are no seasons in the American supermarket. Now there are tomatoes all year round, grown halfway around the world, picked when it was green, and ripened with ethylene gas.[812]

The supermarket and the superstores that followed have changed the way we shop for food. Technically, the supermarket was invented during the 1930s, but it really didn't become the industry standard until after World War II. Several trends were instrumental in its development. Falling transportation costs and the popularity of the car allowed customers to go to the store rather than relying on home delivery, while refrigerators allowed customers to buy more groceries each trip. National food brands used extensive advertising campaigns to change consumer preferences for specific brands over generic items.

Between 1935 and 1982, there was a dramatic decrease in the number of food stores in the United States, with almost two-thirds of them closing. At the same time, the number of supermarkets multiplied from 386 in 1935, to 10,506 in 1954, and to 26,640 in 1982. Supermarkets had accounted for 41 percent of grocery sales in 1954 and almost three-quarters of all grocery sales by 1982; they were a perfect fit for the burgeoning suburbs that sprang up during the 1950s and 1960s.[813]

The ever-increasing square footage of the supermarket accommodated the growing lineup of new grocery products. These began with convenience foods developed by the military during World War II, including cake mixes, canned soups, and frozen vegetables served with lots of butter or sauce.[814]

By 1970, the typical U.S. grocery store carried about 7,800 different items, including hundreds of brand-name products completely different from traditional foods, such as Tang, diet sodas—in snazzy, new aluminum cans—Pop-Tarts, Shake 'n Bake, Cool Whip, instant coffee, instant oatmeal, instant mashed potatoes, and Carnation Instant Breakfast.[815]

The number of food products on the market continued to grow exponentially, with about 50,000 products on the shelves of the average grocery store today.[816] An estimated 320,000 different products were on the market in the early 2000s; over 11,000 were introduced in 1998 alone. What were all these new food products?

> More than two-thirds of them were condiments, candy and snacks, baked goods, soft drinks, cheese products, and ice cream novelties. Those products are promoted with millions or even billions of dollars in advertising and careful placement on supermarket shelves.[817]

During the time of the Black Horseman, the median wage could buy high quality food for an individual, but not for a family, despite the appearance of an abundance of food. In ancient times, the poor ate poor quality barley. Today most Americans have plenty of food, but it is a low quality diet based on a myriad of products derived from hybrid wheat, and GMO corn and soy. It may be tasty, but it is not optimal for the human body. Organic foods and other chemical free products are expensive. The millstone of inflation has stolen our food choices, and in the process, robbed us of our health, as we shall see.

Chapter 25:

Oil and Wine

> ⁵When he had opened the third seal, I heard the third beast say, Come and see. And I beheld, and lo a black horse; and he who sat on it had a pair of balances in his hand. ⁶And I heard a voice in the midst of the four beasts say, A measure of wheat for a penny, and three measures of barley for a penny; and [see] thou hurt not the oil and the wine. (Rev. 6:5–6 KJV)

The Revelation passage about the Black Horseman concludes with the command, "hurt not the oil and the wine." Both oil and wine have symbolic significance in the church, which will be examined later. However, during the same period, both the oil and the wine industries rose to prominence.

The Oil Industry

Housing and food are essentials everyone must pay for out of their "denarius"; so is fuel. The days of going out to collect wood for cooking and heat are gone for most of us, but we are painfully aware of our reliance on oil and other fuels as we pay our utility bills or fill our gas tanks. The past few decades have clearly demonstrated that our demand for these fuels is not very elastic; we must buy much the same amount regardless of cost.

Americans also rely on fossil fuels for electricity and for our food supply. Michael Pollan points out,

We eat a lot of oil without knowing it. To bring a
steer to slaughter, it's 75 gallons of oil. So what we're
seeing is that this highly-efficient machine does not
have the resilience to deal with shocks such as the
spike in oil prices.[818]

Like food prices and interest rates, the cost of fuel, especially
crude oil, peaked in 1980. From the late 1940s until 1973, the
price of oil per barrel in inflation-adjusted U.S. dollars remained
fairly constant, between $19 and $26 per barrel. Prices jumped in
1974 (from $23 to $43), and again in 1979 (from $52 to $77). The
following year, oil reached a record high of over $102 per barrel.
Although oil costs fell during the 1980s, they never returned to the
previous rates; instead, they fluctuated around $30 until 2005, when
the prices escalated yet again.[819]

Dependence on Oil

The development of the petroleum and auto industries began in
the early twentieth century, and control of oil reserves was a key issue
during both world wars.[820] However, it was not until 1950 that oil
became the lifeblood of Western economies, particularly that of the
United States. The oil embargo of the 1970s clearly demonstrated the
central economic role oil plays in the Western world.

The power to implement an oil embargo began in 1960 with the
formation of the Organization of Petroleum Exporting Countries,
better known as OPEC. All the OPEC nations—Iran, Iraq, Kuwait,
Saudi Arabia, Venezuela, Qatar, Indonesia, Libya, United Arab
Emirates, and Nigeria[821]—had once been colonial holdings and had
had their oil industries developed by Western interests. Between 1950
and 1970, these nations ended their colonial subservience and took
over their national oil operations. For example, the Anglo-Persian
Oil Company, later British Petroleum, developed the oil industry in
Iran, which was nationalized by the Iranian government in 1953.[822]

After the Arab-Israeli War of 1973, OPEC imposed an oil
embargo on the industrialized world during the winter of 1973–74.
As a result, gasoline prices quadrupled, and supply shortages created
long lines at the pumps. Some places imposed gas rationing, and other

stations were forced to close because they ran out of gas. The oil embargo continued until Israel agreed to withdraw from the Golan Heights.[823, 824]

1979: A Pivotal Year

Once the crisis was over, oil prices failed to return to pre-embargo rates; in 1979, already-inflated oil prices doubled overnight and remained high until the latter part of the decade. Even then, oil costs remained volatile, failing to return to the pre-1973 rates that had remained consistent since World War II.[825] Spiking oil prices were the result of energy production setbacks caused by a series of accidents and regime changes in two of the world's top oil producers: Iran and Iraq.

A series of accidents put upward pressure on energy costs by decreasing supply. In 1978, after the supertanker *Amoco Cadiz* ran aground off the coast of France, creating an ecological disaster,[826] Congress passed the Natural Gas Policy Act, which deregulated prices and allowed "market forces to establish the wellhead price of natural gas."[827] The nuclear accident at Three Mile Island,[828] the blowout of an exploratory oil well IXTOC I in the Gulf of Mexico, and the sinking of the oil tanker *Burmah Agate* off the coast of Texas raised further concerns about the cost of energy.[829]

During the Iranian Revolution, the pro-western shah was ousted and replace by the anti-western Ayatollah Khomeini, who was made the Supreme Leader of an Islamic republic.[830] Next door in Iraq, Saddam Hussein seized the presidency after a decade of consolidating his power. He formed a new Iraqi regime that was closely allied with the Soviet Union. Hussein followed socialist economic policies, nationalizing the oil industry and establishing state-owned banks.[831]

New Fears in the Twenty-First Century

Today, there are still concerns about the supply of oil. Some experts in the twenty-first century fear that worldwide oil production has already reached its peak. An article in *Science* magazine claims there has not been an increase in oil output since 2004, and "many of those same experts, as well as some major oil companies, don't see it increasing again—ever."[832] Other experts point out that limiting output to ensure price stability is a far cry from the exhaustion of all fuel reserves. Furthermore, major changes in oil drilling technology "continually makes unconventional oil into conventional."[833]

The oil industry was protected from harm.

The Wine Industry

The wine industry is steeped in traditions dating back to the time of the Romans. Over most of the last millennium, wine has been made according to the methods developed in France, and even today, French wines are the gold standard by which all other wines are measured. The traditional paradigm of winemaking was based on *terrior*, the idea that the complexity and character of a wine had its source in the unique qualities of the land in which the grapes grew. However, new paradigms of winemaking have emerged over the last few decades.[834]

The reason the European wine industry was even open to change can be traced to the great wine blight of the mid–1800s. A North American aphid called the grape phylloxera was inadvertently transported across the Atlantic in the late 1850s; perhaps the shortened transit times made possible by steamships enabled the aphid to survive the journey. Nevertheless, its timing relative to the Red Horseman, with its focus on the common man, cannot be coincidental. In the space of just fifteen years, 40 percent of the French vines were destroyed, and every vineyard in Europe was at risk.[835] The attack was followed with the 1878 arrival of mildew to France, which took advantage of the weakened state of the vines.[836]

Growers tried everything to stem the blight. Large quantities of chemicals were applied in hopes of killing the organism, but to no avail. The most successful technique was grafting the prized French vines onto the roots of American vines that had a native resistance to the grape phylloxera.[837] Wine expert Burke Morton has commented that the phylloxera continues to be a problem: "...interruption of the life cycle at any stage has done nothing to halt its advance. It has proven so resilient that it is likely to stand with the cockroach in surviving a nuclear holocaust."[838]

Growers were looking for solutions to their pest problems, and the Green Revolution held the promise of miracle cures. In the 1950s, the use of chemical fertilizers became common practice, and in the 1960s, herbicides and other chemical treatments came onto the market.[839] Wineries were increasingly dependent on the use of chemicals, including pesticides, herbicides, and fertilizers.[840]

By the 1970s, it was becoming obvious that the use of all these "miracle" products, which had become essential to modern farming methods, had killed off soil microbes and bacteria, critical elements for healthy vineyards.[841] At this point, new methods of winegrowing and winemaking based on scientific research ("viticulture" and "viniculture" respectively) began to be implemented.[842] These included integrated pest management and soil-restoration practices.[843] Vinicultures used temperature-controlled fermenters and higher standards of sanitation that resulted in "significantly better wines with fewer defects, sweeter fruit, riper tannins and generally lower acidity."[844]

Changes in winemaking and the explosion of grape cultivation in countries around the globe have made a vast array of wines available. Wine has become incredibly popular, outranking beer as Americans' favorite beverage; even red wine is outpacing white in sales.[845] The command "hurt not ... the wine." was fulfilled by the efforts that rescued vineyards from blight, mildew and unhealthy soil, and brought wine into the forefront of popular culture.

The wine industry was protected from harm.

The Oil: the Outpouring of the Holy Spirit

"hurt not the oil and the wine" (Rev. 6:6b KJV)

Since the Bible makes extensive use of oil as a symbol of the Holy Spirit, it seems logical that this prophecy would also have a spiritual significance. During the time of the Black Horseman, much of the church underwent the charismatic movement, which focused on the ministry of the Holy Spirit. Whether you agree with this movement theologically or not, the fact remains it had a profound effect, transforming large sections of the church on a global scale.

The Pentecostal Church

The charismatic movement had its roots in the Pentecostal Church, which had begun with the outpouring of the Holy Spirit at the Azusa Street Mission in Los Angeles. Pentecostalism was characterized by speaking in tongues and supernatural healing. It had developed out of the holiness movement, an eighteenth century branch of Methodism, and was decidedly outside mainstream churches.[846] Nevertheless, Pentecostalism spread worldwide and now has over 50 million adherents, forming "...the largest non–Roman Catholic communion in many countries of Europe and Latin America."[847]

The initial Pentecostal movement bucked the mainstream in its racial views, allowing believers from all races to worship together freely. It was said that the "color–lines [were] washed away by the blood" of Jesus.[848] Although Pentecostals eventually succumbed to pressure and divided into black and white branches, interracial worship reemerged after the civil rights movement.[849]

The Charismatic Movement

The Charismatic Movement emerged in the 1960s, as speaking in tongues and other supernatural gifts of the Holy Spirit moved into mainstream Christianity. Ironically, it began in an Episcopal church in Van Nuys, California, a congregation whose high-church tradition put it among the most formal and most impervious to modernization within the Church of England. The parish rector, Fr. Dennis Bennett, announced that he had personally spoken in tongues and that he believed this was the pattern for the church. In the wake of the resulting controversy, clergy from other mainline churches began announcing their own charismatic experiences.[850]

By the mid-1960s, the movement spread onto the campuses of Roman Catholic universities, where it was readily received by laity and clergy alike. Its endorsement by Leo Joseph Cardinal Suenens, a moderator of the Second Vatican Council,[851] resulted in the spread of the charismatic renewal to every continent, so that "by 1983 about 15 million people in 120 countries were being affected by this move of the Spirit."[852]

The charismatic movement was not a program planned by church leaders; it sprang up spontaneously without regard to denominational divides and was evident in both leadership and laypeople. It was worldwide in scope, appearing in the West, in the communist bloc, and in Third World nations, apparently unaffected by culture, politics, or standard of living. It was generally accompanied by an increased desire for God's Word, outreach to nonbelievers and supernatural gifts such as speaking in tongues and divine healing.[853]

The oil of the Holy Spirit was protected from harm.

The Wine: Focusing on Jesus

Just as oil is symbolic of the Holy Spirit, Christianity has traditionally used wine as a symbol of the blood of Jesus. Wine has also played a significant role in Jewish liturgy. Both of these traditions were expressed within the church during the time of the Black Horseman.

The Jesus Movement

The Jesus movement began in 1967 as part of an outreach to the hippie culture of Haight-Ashbury in San Francisco. One of the first street evangelists was Lonnie Frisbee, a hippie who had recommitted his life to Christ and began preaching the gospel on the streets and at a Christian "coffeehouse." Frisbee also helped found a community house designed to get new believers free of drugs and well grounded in their faith. Coffeehouses and community houses served as models for church outreach around the world.[854]

Although the Jesus movement was relatively short-lived, it had a significant influence on much of the Western church. The Jesus Movement faded as the counterculture became irrelevant and hundreds of thousands of young converts joined established churches. Almost all evangelical churches were impacted by the informality of the Jesus movement's music and worship. Jesus Music—a blend of rock and gospel—became a strong influence on worship and spawned the contemporary Christian music industry. [855]

The Jesus movement has been called the biggest revival in modern church history. Interestingly, it received little attention from mainstream Christianity; Fuller Seminary did not consider the 18,000 converts coming out of the hippie counterculture in Costa

Mesa, California, as church growth. By contrast, the movement was reported by the mainstream media, including *Life* and *Look* magazines and on television.[856]

The Jesus movement produced thousands of converts who became leaders in churches and parachurch organizations around the world. For instance, Greg Laurie of Harvest America, whose evangelistic crusades have been attended by more than 4.4 million people in the English-speaking world,[857] came to know Christ through the ministry of Frisbee. In addition, some of the fastest growing church denominations in the United States of the late twentieth century, including Calvary Chapels, Hope Chapel Churches, and the Vineyard Churches, emerged out of the Jesus Movement.[858, 859]

The Messianic Movement

Another leader that emerged from the Jesus Movement was Moishe Rosen, who founded Jews for Jesus to meet the needs of the many Jewish hippies who were coming to faith in Yeshua Messiah. Rosen was known for developing effective evangelistic methods and materials for reaching Jews with the message of the gospel. Since its humble beginnings in 1973, Jews for Jesus has grown to a worldwide organization, ministering in fifty-five cities, each with a Jewish population of more than a quarter of a million.[860]

Jews for Jesus was part of the wider messianic Jewish movement that was developed to meet the needs of young Jewish believers who desired to maintain a Jewish lifestyle. They blended much of the theology of Christianity with the rituals and traditions of Judaism. The movement was initially viewed as anything from a curiosity to a cult.

> ...both Jews and Christians in the United States were surprised to see the rise of a vigorous movement of Jewish Christians or Christian Jews ... such a combination seemed like an oxymoron because they saw the two faiths as completely separate from each other.[861]

However, the movement grew in significance, with about 400 messianic congregations within the United States, and more around the world.[862] The movement has even made inroads into the Orthodox Jewish community. Today, the Global Association of Orthodox Jewish Believers in Messiah Yeshua, based in Jerusalem, defines messianic Judaism as a sect of Judaism whose

> ...adherents, called "Messianic Jews," "Netzarim," or even "Christians" by their detractors who wish to separate them from Judaism, are disciples of Rabbi Yeshua ben Yosef mi'Netzaret, and believe that he is the Moshiach (Messiah, Christ) of Israel.[863]

The oil and the wine of the church were protected from harm.

CHAPTER 26:

Like a Leopard

> After this I beheld, and lo another, like a leopard, which had upon the back of it four wings of a fowl; the beast had also four heads; and dominion was given to it. (Dan. 7:6 KJV)

In Daniel's vision, the beast correlating to the Black Horseman is a leopard. Although the leopard was native to most of Africa and southern Asia, it is now most common in sub-Saharan Africa and is considered to be a near-threatened species. This amazingly adaptable animal is equally at home in the desert and the rainforest. Leopards with a lot of melanin appear black and are known as black panthers.[864]

Lions and leopards have very different hunting styles. The male lion, the "king of the beasts," lazes around while a group of underlings (the females of the pride) coordinate their efforts to bring down the kill. At this point, the kingly male will drive all others away from the carcass until he has gorged himself. Leopards, on the other hand, are solitary, living with others only for mating and parenting. They will eat anything they can hunt down; their technique combines stealth with an amazing burst of speed—up to thirty-six miles per hour—at the final approach to their quarry. Since they are loners, they will generally drag their kill up trees for safekeeping.[865]

The Leopard and Bacchus

The ancient Greeks associated the leopard with Dionysus, the god of wine and ecstasy. He was generally dressed in leopard skin and was often portrayed riding a leopard or in a chariot pulled by leopards. When the Dionysus cult was incorporated into the Roman pantheon, it was equated with the worship of Bacchus, the god of wine and intoxication, and the ancient Italian god of male fertility called Liber, meaning "free one" and his feminine counterpart, Libera. They came to be known as the deities overseeing the making of wine. Bacchanalia, orgies held in honor of Bacchus, became so notorious for their lewd and criminal activities, that they were actually banned by the Roman Senate in 186 BC.[866, 867, 868]

There are several parallels between the mythology associated with the leopard and the time of the Black Horseman. The command to not harm the wine (Rev. 6:6) and the resurging popularity of wine in recent years mesh well with the symbol of the god of winemaking. Furthermore, German scholar Peter Wick draws parallels between the worship of Jesus and Dionysus and argues that the gospel of John, particularly its account of the wedding at Cana (John 2:1–11), was written as an implicit challenge to the Dionysus cult, showing Jesus superior in every way.[869] The Jesus movement did the same thing during the counterculture of the 1960s.

Just as the cult of Dionysus was characterized by drunkenness and orgies, the time of the Black Horseman was characterized by the dramatic erosion of moral standards that had started in the entertainment industry. In 1968, the movie makers abandoned the Motion Picture Production Code, the guidelines that ensured movies did not portray explicit sexual immorality and other questionable behavior. The moral stringency that had been the hallmark of the code began to erode in the early 1950s. Television was providing stiff competition in family entertainment, and movie makers such as Otto Preminger began releasing films that failed to meet the code's standards. After 1968, the industry responded quickly with the release of hundreds of movies that included nudity, sexually explicit content, and graphic violence. One analyst concluded that

> ... the code helped forge the Hollywood vision. That vision was so powerful, ironically, that a remarkable number of the cynical products of the "new" Hollywood—from Bonnie and Clyde to Blazing

Saddles to The Godfather—were reactions more to it than to the world around them.[870]

The era also introduced the notorious *Playboy* magazine, which featured a blend of nude women and serious articles by well-known authors. The first edition was published in December 1953, and in many ways it set the tone for the decades to come.[871] While feminists were promoting *Sex and the Single Girl,* Hollywood promoted the ideal of the bachelor life, with "its emphasis on pleasure, self-indulgence, and public entertainment." The bachelor ideal was not new—it first developed in urban centers during the latter part of the nineteenth century—and it continued to evoke feelings of excitement and freedom, fear and disdain.[872]

Four Wings of a Bird

> After this I beheld, and lo another, like a leopard, which had upon the back of it four wings of a fowl; (Dan. 7:6 KJV)

The leopard in Daniel's vision, like the lion before it, has wings. Wings are symbolic of speed, and the times of both the White and Black Horsemen involved men traveling vast distances around the globe at speeds previously unimagined. In the time of the White Horseman, Europeans had journeyed to virtually every corner of the earth on increasingly faster ships. Under the Black Horseman, men continued to globetrot, but now they traveled on planes.

The New Immigration

There have always been movements of people from one place to another, but the patterns of migration and the sheer scale of it changed over time. From the days of Columbus, there was a steady stream of emigration to colonies around the globe, and the United States had been built on such immigration. Before World War I, the majority of the American population came from Europe, but from 1914 to 1960, almost half of U.S. immigrants arrived from other parts of the Americas such as Mexico, while Europe supplied the rest. Then, in the 1960s, Europeans stopped leaving their homelands, and most immigrants came from Asia and the Americas.[873]

Europe had a similar experience. In the 1960s and 1970s, European nations began to attract immigrants from Africa, Latin America, and Asia, a trend that continues even to today; over 20 million immigrants from non–European sources came in 2010 alone.[874, 875] Like the United States, Europe struggles with illegal immigrants crossing the Mediterranean from Africa despite efforts to monitor traffic on the sea. It is estimated that Europe is now home to more than 7 million Africans.[876]

Europe's strict regulations regarding immigration combined with the proliferation of ethnic conflicts means that "asylum has become one of the principal means of immigration into the EU."[877] However, the vast numbers who apply for asylum, hoping for better opportunities in Western Europe, have resulted in a backlash against immigration in general. For instance, Germany introduced an interesting rule that states that anyone who has passed through a "safe" country before coming to Germany cannot be given asylum. This effectively means that anyone who has not come by plane will be rejected.[878]

Unusual Wings of Daniel

The wings on Daniel's leopard have an additional significance that can be gleaned only by taking a closer look at the language. Both the lion and the leopard in Daniel's vision are described as having wings. These two verses in Daniel are the only instances of the Aramaic word *gaf* (גף); the translation "wing" was inferred from the fact that they are part of an eagle and a bird respectively.[879] Although the Aramaic and Hebrew languages are frequently quite similar, in this case, gaf bears little resemblance to the frequently used Hebrew word for wing, *kanaph* (כנף).[880] However, gaf, which is derived from an unused Hebrew root meaning "to arch" is used in three Hebrew verses.[881] One describes the maidens of wisdom crying out to the simple from the arches (gaf) of the high places of the city (Prov. 9:3). The other two verses are about slavery.[882]

> ²If thou buy an Hebrew servant, six years he shall serve: and in the seventh he shall go out free for nothing. ³If he came in by himself, [gaf] he shall go

out by himself [gaf]; if he were married, then his wife shall go out with him. ⁴If his master have given him a wife, and she have born him sons or daughters; the wife and her children shall be her master's, and he shall go out by himself [gaf]. (Exod. 21:2–4 KJV)

This is more than coincidence when you remember that one of the characteristics of the Black Horseman was the yoke of slavery, particularly the economic slavery of debt. The Scripture promises, "The rich rules over the poor, And the borrower [is] servant to the lender" (Prov. 22:7 KJV).

African Slavery—Forced Migration

From ancient times, slavery has been practiced in Africa in various forms. One historian from Ghana makes a distinction between the internal slave trade, in which slaves were transported across the continent—between North Africa and West Africa, for example—and the external slave trade, in which Africans were transported overseas to be sold in foreign markets—the Americas, for instance.[883]

The external slave trade was dominated by exit points on the four corners of Africa through which millions were carried off into slavery. These include the Slave Coast in western Africa, the Barbary Coast along the western Mediterranean, North Africa across the Red Sea and eastern Mediterranean, and the Swahili ports along the coast of the Indian Ocean. Historian Elikia M'bokolo, speaking of the external African slave trade, writes,

> The African continent was bled of its human resources via all possible routes. Across the Sahara, through the Red Sea, from the Indian Ocean ports and across the Atlantic. At least ten centuries of slavery for the benefit of the Muslim countries (from the ninth to the nineteenth). Then more than four centuries (from the end of the fifteenth to the nineteenth) of a regular slave trade to build the Americas and the prosperity of the Christian states of Europe. The figures, even where hotly disputed, make your head spin.[884]

The Slave Coast of West Africa

Probably the best-known point of exit was the Slave Coast along the shores of West Africa from Senegal to Nigeria and the Congo. Although estimates vary, somewhere between 11 and 20 million people crossed the Atlantic in slaving vessels over the course of four centuries.[885] Ironically, the area was populated by several tribes that developed a culture

> known for its artistic triumphs, extraordinary oral literature, complex pantheon of gods, and urban lifestyle. Yet, it is also a civilization which sent millions of its men, women and children to the Americas as slaves.[886]

At first glance, these two statements seem incongruous, but really they both required the establishment of sophisticated political and economic systems and the seemingly universal desire of the elite to increase their wealth and power.

When Portuguese explorers first arrived in Ghana, they found a "brisk trade in slaves and other goods," a trade that had been thriving from the first century. The Kingdom of Ghana used its abundant supply of gold to purchase slaves that had been raided from other tribes in the surrounding areas. Many of the slaves were used to increase the amount of land that could be cultivated. In addition, slaves could be transported across the Sahara and sold in Egypt and the Middle East at a profit thanks to the steady demand for black slaves in Arabia.[887]

The arrival of Europeans changed the slave market along the Gold Coast. Merchants soon realized they could sell their slave inventories to Europeans at favorable terms rather than travel inland to the trans-Sahara trade route. Slave Coast tribes responded to the increased demand for slaves in various ways. The Oyo used cavalry forces to expand their empire and sold captives to European traders. The Benin prohibited the export of male slaves but was willing to import slaves and resell them to the Asante. The Akan of Ghana purchased slaves to work in the gold mines and to clear the forests for farming. Historian James Giblin has argued that Europeans initially became involved in human trafficking in response to the Akan thirst for slaves.

Akan entrepreneurs used gold to purchase slaves from both African and European traders. Indeed, while Europeans would eventually ship at least twelve million slaves to the Americas, they initially became involved in slave trading by selling African slaves to African purchasers. The Portuguese supplied perhaps 12,000 slaves to Akan country between 1500 and 1535, and continued selling slaves from Sao Tome and Nigeria to the Gold Coast throughout the 16th century.[888]

The transatlantic slave trade has received probably the most attention of all African slave routes partly because it was done on such a large scale, and partly because these slaves lived long enough to have children, whose descendants remind us of their stories. Slaves were integral to the plantation economy of the Americas, providing the labor necessary to cultivate the abundant land in the New World. The number of slaves transported peaked in the 1700s and subsided in the 1780s as Britain and others outlawed the practice.

The exchange of slaves was a business transaction between the elite of Africa and European merchants who were serving the elite of Europe and the Americas. "Between 1450 and the end of the nineteenth century, slaves were obtained from along the west coast of Africa with the full and active co-operation of African kings and merchants."[889]

The Berbers and the Trans-Saharan Slave Caravan

The Berbers, indigenous people of North Africa, had been in the slave business for centuries, striking terror in the hearts of sailors as they plied the western Mediterranean. The Berbers pursued two sources of slaves over the centuries: European slaves, who were mostly male and used for various types of hard labor, and the sub-Saharan slaves, two-thirds of whom were women. In fact, the Portuguese began their colonial activities in Africa by capturing Barbary ports to counter slave raids that were depopulating the Portuguese coastline.[890]

Barbary pirates, or corsairs, made a living capturing ships' crews and raiding the coastal areas of Europe in search of slaves. According to historian Robert Davis, anyone traveling by sea or who lived along the shores of Italy, France, Spain, Portugal, or even England and Iceland were at real risk of enslavement. The number of Europeans taken by slavers was not insignificant; hundreds of ships were captured each year, and hundreds of slaves could be captured in a single raid. For the people living on the north coast of the Mediterranean, the raids were "almost annual events of terror and pillage."[891]

According to Davis, the slave count in Barbary could fluctuate wildly in the short term, but remained quite stable over the long term at approximately 35,000. Since there was virtually no procreation among the slaves—90 percent were males who had no access to women—it is fairly easy to estimate the number of fresh recruits needed to replace slaves who died. [892]

Life for slaves in Barbary was at least as brutal and lethal as that of African slaves in the Americas. They were put to work "in quarries, in heavy construction and rowing the corsair galleys themselves."[893] Those consigned to

> ...rowing the galleys at sea, half-naked and exposed to the sun, they were not infrequently left so desperately of drinking water that they drank sea water or died on their benches; never allowed to lie down to sleep, many of them had fallen into "continuall extasies" before their voyage was over.[894]

It is estimated that approximately 8,500 slaves needed to be captured each year to meet the demand for slave labor just on the Barbary Coast. That implies more than a million slaves must have been captured between 1580 and 1680 alone.[895]

The second major source of slave labor in northern Africa was via trans-Saharan caravan routes. Since the fifth century, gold had been the principal commodity traded on these routes, followed by kola nuts and slaves.[896] The Berbers transported sub-Saharan slaves purchased from Ghana to the Mediterranean coast. Young males were bought to be trained for military service, but the majority of slaves were females used as domestics, entertainers and concubines.[897] It has been estimated that 9 million slaves were transported across the Saharan Desert to the Muslim slave markets in North Africa and the Middle East.[898]

Interestingly, high–resolution mtDNA (mitochondrial DNA) studies have confirmed the extent of the trafficking in sub–Saharan slaves in North Africa. Between 25 and 50 percent of North African women are descended from sub–Saharan lineages. This genetic imprint indicates that

> the Arab slave trade of black slaves was much the same in total to the Atlantic slave trade, and interestingly far longer in the time scale. It began in the middle of the seventh century (650 A.D.) and survives still today in Mauritania and Sudan, summing up 14 centuries rather than four as for the Atlantic slave trade.[899]

Egypt and the Red Sea

Like the trans–Saharan slaving, the Red Sea slave trade existed long before the trans–Atlantic route. In fact, probably the oldest route for exporting slaves from northeast Africa was down the Nile to Egypt and across the Red Sea to Arabia.[900] Slaves were generally brought from areas inland from the Red Sea, such as Sudan, and transported to the Middle East and India.[901]

Just as European slave traders found a ready market for male slaves who could do heavy work on the plantations and sugar mills, North African traders found buyers in the Middle East equally eager for a different kind of slave. As vast territories from Spain and North Africa to Iran and India had fallen to the jihadist armies, Arab society had been flooded with slaves—the standard fate for the conquered. When the conquests ended, so did the flow of manpower; imported slaves filled the gap. Lewis notes that

> the vast majority of unskilled slaved, however, came from immediately north and south of the Islamic world—white from Europe and the Eurasian steppes, blacks from Africa south of the Sahara ... there was no lack of enterprising merchants and middlemen, eager to share in this profitable trade, who were willing to

capture or kidnap their neighbors and deliver them, as slaves, to a ready and expanding market.[902]

It has been estimated that 4 million slaves were exported from Africa via the Red Sea.[903] About a third of those purchased were male, most of whom were castrated boys destined to serve as eunuchs in the harems of wealthy Arabs. The remaining two-thirds were young women who might become concubines or domestic servants. Although the physical living conditions for these slaves were probably better than in the Americas, the journey crossing the burning sands of the Sahara was not, and many died in transit.[904] Some estimate the death toll from disease, malnutrition, and failure to keep up to be as high as 90 percent.[905]

After Egypt came under British control, slavery was outlawed and all slave transport was officially blockaded, but slave trafficking did not end. The Red Sea route to Arabia was exempted from the ban as a concession to African Muslims making pilgrimages to Mecca or Medina. Needless to say, merchant slave traders took full advantage of this legal loophole.

> Thanks to the exemption from the ban on the slave trade, the flow of slaves from Africa into Arabia and through the Gulf into Iran continued for a long time. Apart from commercial channels, the supply was augmented through the practice by which a wealthy pilgrim brought a retinue of slaves from his own country and sold them one by one—as a kind of traveler's check—to pay the expenses of the pilgrimage.[906]

East Africa

An estimated 4 million African slaves left via the fourth exodus route: the Swahili ports along the Indian Ocean.[907] This route was first developed by Arab slave traders and was similar to the Red Sea route; slaves were shipped across the Indian Ocean to the Arabian Peninsula, to Persia (Iran) and India. It was driven by the sultanates of the Middle East. African slaves ended up as sailors in Persia, pearl divers in the gulf, soldiers in the Omani army, and workers on the salt pans of Mesopotamia (modern Iraq). Many people were domestic slaves, working in rich households, while women were taken as sex slaves.[908]

The East African slave trade expanded significantly in the second half of the eighteenth century for several reasons. When Seyyid Said, sultan of Oman, established clove plantations in his newly conquered holdings along the East African coast, including Zanzibar, there was an increased need for slave labor locally. The Sultan organized slave routes into the interior of East Africa, and in the 1840s, the number of slaves sold annually at Zanzibar alone was between 40,000 and 45,000. The sultan was also anxious to engage in trade with Europeans and even sent an envoy to the United States for this purpose. That venture was unsuccessful, but Portuguese and French traders searching for slaves to work plantations in Brazil, India, and islands of the Indian Ocean were happy to do business with the Arab and Swahili middlemen once the British had shut down the Slave Coast. [909, 910, 911]

The Impact of African Slavery

Many historians point out that slavery as practiced in Africa was quite different from the institution of slavery in the United States. Within Africa, female slaves outnumbered male slaves by at least two to one. Since the children born to these slaves had the legal standing of their fathers rather than their mothers, multigenerational slavery was uncommon. By contrast, the slave population exported to the Americas was made up of 56 percent men, 30 percent women, and 14 percent children under the age of fourteen.[912, 913]

Slavery exacted a terrible economic toll. By removing human capital from the economy, it created significant underdevelopment in the continent of Africa. Those areas most impacted by slavery are the most undeveloped in Africa today.[914] Slavery also resulted in a climate of distrust; researchers have found a notable correlation between how far a community was from a slave coast and levels of trust within that community. It is believed that this happened in two ways. First, exposure to slavery made people less trusting. Second, the slave trade resulted in a long-term deterioration of legal and political institutions, which made it easier for citizens to cheat others.[915]

Under the Black Horseman, people around the world have been increasingly separated from the control as well as the rewards of their labor. Small entrepreneurs find it hard to compete with large companies, and the mom-and-pop stores are being replaced by giant box stores, many of which view their workers with the same concern shown by plantation owners for their slaves. In addition, a culture of distrust has become endemic even in places that traditionally placed a premium on honesty and fair business dealings.

In the heyday of African slavery, wealthy plantation owners and sultans chose to use slave labor rather than hire the laboring population living among them. Today, multinational corporations are shifting their operations overseas, where they can benefit from low—many would say extortionist—labor rates, while leaving their own people out of work and buried in debt. For example, during the 2000s, multinational corporations, which employ a fifth of all American workers, laid off about 2.9 million Americans while hiring 2.4 million employees overseas.[916]

CHAPTER 27:

Four Heads

> After this I beheld, and lo another, like a leopard, which had upon the back of it four wings of a fowl; the beast had also four heads; and dominion was given to it. (Dan. 7:6 KJV)

Daniel's leopard had four heads. The head is often used as a symbol of government, and since Daniel goes on to say the beast was given dominion, this seems the most likely interpretation. Since the opening of the third seal, four government ideologies have wrestled for dominance within Africa and among the black people worldwide. They are Islam, as a religious and political system, various forms of communism or socialism, tribalism and Pan-Africanism. As we review each system, it should be noted that often more than one may be influential in a given area. It is also interesting to note that each of these philosophies was expressed within the African-American community, again with a great deal of overlap.

Islam

Islam has been the dominant belief system in northern Africa since the Muslim conquests of the seventh and eighth centuries. Across North Africa there is a swath of nations with populations that are more than 90 percent Muslim. These include Algeria, Djibouti, Egypt, The Gambia, Libya, Mali, Mauritania, Morocco, Niger, Senegal, Somalia, Tunisia and Western Sahara. South of these nations lays a strip of countries that act as a buffer between the almost universally Muslim north and the generally non-Muslim sub-Sahara. These buffer states, in which over half the inhabitants is Muslim, include: Burkina Faso, Chad, Guinea–Conakry, Sierra Leone and Sudan. All of these nations are ruled by Islamic law at some level of their court systems.[917]

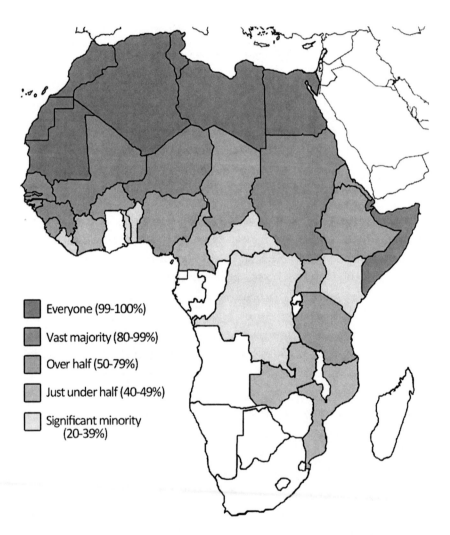

Everyone (99-100%)

Vast majority (80-99%)

Over half (50-79%)

Just under half (40-49%)

Significant minority (20-39%)

Map 12: Muslim majority countries in Africa, 2011.[918]

The Nation of Islam

In the United States, a variation of the Muslim faith has been popularized by the Nation of Islam. The organization was founded in 1930 by Wallace Fard Mohammad, who was proclaimed to be the mahdi or messiah by his followers. Upon his death in 1934, leadership of the Nation of Islam passed to Elijah Mohammad, who held the position until 1975. Currently, the movement is under the leadership of Louis Farrakhan Muhammad, Sr.[919] The stated purpose of the movement was to

> restore and to resurrect His lost and found people, who were identified as the original members of the Tribe of Shabazz from the Lost Nation of Asia. The lost people of the original nation of African descent, were captured, exploited, and dehumanized to serve as servitude slaves of America for over three centuries.... [920]

One of the Nation of Islam's stated goals is to create separation between American blacks and "the children of slave masters." Their vision includes the establishment of separate schools, a separate territory, a separate court system and freedom from all taxation. They hold that African Americans are

> the people of God's choice, as it has been written, that God would choose the rejected and the despised. We can find no other persons fitting this description in these last days more than the so-called Negroes in America.[921]

One of the most promising leaders to emerge from the Nation of Islam was Malcolm X, a rising star within the movement; his inspirational speeches led to an explosive growth in membership from 500 in 1952 to 30,000 in 1963.[922] In 1964, he made a life-changing pilgrimage to Mecca, returning with a desire to build integration between races and a new hope for the future. He resigned from the Nation of Islam and established the Muslim Mosque, Inc. and the Organization of Afro-American Unity, a Pan-African organization.[923]

Although the Nation of Islam teaches the core doctrines of Islam, known as the Five Pillars, the two differ on some key points. Probably the most significant is the fact that while both the Sunni and Shi'a Muslims are still waiting for the advent of the mahdi, the Nation of Islam holds that the Mahdi has already appeared.

> WE BELIEVE that Allah (God) appeared in the Person of Master W. Fard Muhammad, July, 1930; the long-awaited "Messiah" of the Christians and the "Mahdi" of the Muslims.[924]

Communism

Communism was the second political philosophy that has significantly impacted Africa. The Cold War was successfully waged in Africa, with several newly independent nations falling under the sway of either China or the Soviet Union. As a result, many African leaders "professed one form of socialism or another."[925] Prior to the wave of decolonization that swept Africa, many countries viewed communism as the road to independence. An observer from the British Foreign Office wrote,

> Communism has made the least progress where the influence of Islam is strongest. Though in the past year the communist picture has been one of retrogression on some fronts, there are signs of increased interest in anti-colonialism from Moscow.[926]

African nations that have a history of communism are generally sub-Saharan, but there are exceptions, the most notable being Libya. Almost two decades after independence, al-Qaddafi staged a military coup and began to implement his unique blend of socialism and Islam.[927]

After gaining its independence in 1960, Benin was ruled by a series of military governments before a Marxist-Leninist regime was established in 1972. In 1989, the nation moved toward representative government, making it "the first successful transfer of power in Africa from a dictatorship to a democracy."[928] Likewise, the Republic of Congo embarked on a "quarter century of experimentation with

Marxism" shortly after it gained its sovereignty in 1960.[929] In Somalia, a 1969 military coup

> ushered in an authoritarian socialist rule characterized by the persecution, jailing and torture of political opponents and dissidents. After the regime's collapse early in 1991, Somalia descended into turmoil, factional fighting, and anarchy. [930]

The nation still has not successfully established a permanent national government.[931]

In the 1970s, the Soviet play for control of southern Africa continued as Angola, Mozambique, and Ethiopia succumbed to the Iron Curtain. The Soviet Union systematically targeted newly independent African nations, testing the waters to measure the West's response. French journalist Jean-François Revel, documents the remarks of a high ranking Soviet official to a French cabinet minister,

> We took Angola and you did not protest. We even saw that you could have beaten us in Angola … Then we took Mozambique. Forget it, you don't even know where it is. Then we took Ethiopia, a key move. There again we noted that you could have replied via Somalia or Eritrea or both. No reply. We noted that and put it into our analyses. Then we took **Aden** and set up a powerful Soviet base there. Aden! On the Arabian Peninsula! In the heart of your supply center! No response. So we noted: we can take Aden. [932]

After its independence from Portugal, Angola suffered a twenty-seven-year civil war (1975–2002) at a cost of 1.5 million killed and another 4 million displaced.[933] Likewise, Mozambique embraced Marxism for several years after independence; that, coupled with "large-scale emigration, economic dependence on South Africa, a severe drought, and a prolonged civil war hindered the country's development until the mid-1990s."[934] In Ethiopia, a military junta deposed Emperor Haile Selassie and established a socialist state (1974–91).[935]

Map 13: Communist nations of Africa, 1979–1983.[936]

The Black Panthers

The Black Panther Party for Self-Defense was an African-American, leftist revolutionary group that Marxists considered the front line of guerrilla warfare in the United States. Founded by Huey Newton and Bobby Seale in 1966, the party

practiced militant self-defense of minority communities

274

against the U.S. government, and fought to establish revolutionary socialism through mass organizing and community based programs.[937]

Just as Malcolm X did in his later years, the Black Panthers embraced the idea of international workers' solidarity without regard to racial distinctions and were committed to the ideals of socialism and Mao's version of communism. In fact, in 1968, Mao's *Red Book* was required reading for all party members, which put the group at loggerheads with the FBI. By the early 1980s, the party's leadership was completely smashed, and the organization fell apart.[938]

Ethnic Tribalism

Tribalism is defined as the organization, culture, or beliefs of a tribe, or a strong feeling of identity with and loyalty to one's tribe or group.[939] It should not surprise us that ethnicity shaped political development in much of Africa, since Jesus prophesied that ethnicity would be the defining global conflict during the Black Horseman (see chapter 26). Indeed, some scholars object to the use of the word "tribalism" in reference to Africa, charging that "tribe" is merely a way of simplifying the "complexity of the non-Western societies of Africa."[940] David Wiley, a specialist in African studies, argues that what is often referred to as tribalism is really ethnicity and plays a similar role in both Africa and the United States.

> Being an ethnic Irish-American and the wearing of the green in New York became more important that being an Irishman in the old country before immigrating. Similarly in Africa, persons who never identified as Shona in the rural areas but as members of a particular village or lineage or family suddenly find Shona identities in the rough and tumble of urban politics. In New York, we term it ethnicity, but in Africa it becomes tribalism.[941]

Whatever you call the phenomenon—tribalism or ethnicity—it plays an important role in many parts of Africa. In fact, it is arguably the dominant political force in much of the sub-Sahara. Not only are political parties arranged around ethnic allegiances,[942] but self-identification by ethnicity is most pronounced during times of political competition, such as during an election. In fact, Bannon, et al., found that shortly after an election, those from the losing tribe were more likely to use some type of subtribal term to identify themselves out of fear of repercussions from the newly elected tribe.[943] Wittman concludes,

> African democracies are not an outgrowth of western experience ... Born primarily of historical tribal alliances and antipathies, the African political party is defined by its own interests ... It has yet to be proven whether such a formula really can produce a type of representative government that does not simply metamorphose conveniently into yet another form of totalitarianism.[944]

One reason that tribalism is so detrimental to African economic and political development is that resources are always distributed according to ethnic or tribal affiliation. What is viewed as corruption and bribery in the West is seen as the normal "system of reward" within the context of "tribal sociology."[945] Tom O'Connor sums it up this way: "Ethnic group politics in Africa is 'pork barrel' politics with an African twist."

> When philanthropic or international aid goes missing, the disappearance of the money can often be traced to the presumably "honorable" tradition that the tribal headman distribute gifts to those below.[946]

However, tribalism is not some "backward" phenomenon that will disappear as Africans become more "modernized." On the contrary, the Bannon, et al. study found that "modernity" was one of two factors that were strong predictors of self-identification according to ethnicity.

> Education, working in non-traditional occupations that expose people to competition for employment, and exposure to political mobilization all increase the

likelihood that an individual will see him or herself primarily in ethnic rather than non-ethnic terms. Strikingly, we find that the closer a country is to a national election and the greater the degree of political rights the people in a country enjoy, the greater the likelihood that respondents from that country will say that they identify themselves ethnically first and foremost.[947]

In other words, the more educated and urbanized a person is, the more likely he or she will cling to ethnic heritage for the same reason being Irish is ordinary in Ireland but significant in New York.

Tribalism has the greatest impact in nations dominated by two or three tribes; the more ethnically diverse the population, the less importance tribal affiliation holds.[948] Not coincidentally, many of the civil wars that have plagued Africa have occurred in countries in which there are two or three overwhelmingly dominant tribes.[949]

Black Power

Ethnic tribalism was embraced by both the Nation of Islam and the Black Panthers. It was also the underlying idea of Black Power, an African-American political philosophy based on a phrase from a speech given by Stokely Carmichael in 1966. The exact meaning of the slogan "Black Power" was unclear from the start and held different meanings for various people.[950] Some defined it as the emergence of the political voice of African Americans, a call for blacks to elevate themselves within American society, assuming positions of power. Others argued that Black Power should entail the complete separation of blacks from whites, with blacks providing for all the needs of the black community, political and economic. However, many saw it as a black version of a Marxist workers' revolution, an interpretation favored by the Black Panthers.[951]

Ironically, while the civil rights movement had worked to integrate blacks into American society, ending segregation and Jim Crow laws, black power supporters focused on creating a self-sufficient black community separated from white America. It was this dichotomy within the black community that ended the united front presented by the civil rights movement. On one hand, you had the increasingly radical agenda of Carmichael and others, who believed that whites were untrustworthy. They envisioned a "purely black society in which white people were not allowed to trespass."[952] Carmichael left no illusions that in his view, black power included using violence and separatism to achieve its goals.

> When you talk about black power you talk about bringing this country to its knees any time it messes with the black man ... any white man in this country knows about power. He knows what white power is and he ought to know what black power is.[953]

On the other hand, the more conservative leaders of the civil rights movement condemned the black power agenda. King expressed concern that it would evolve into "black supremacy," while the NAACP called it a "menace to peace and prosperity ... no negro who is fighting for civil rights can support black power, which is opposed to civil rights and integration."[954]

A more positive aspect of the black power movement was its new emphasis on racial pride. Carmichael called for "black people in this country to unite, to recognize their heritage, and to build a sense of community." Black Pride included the adoption of a distinctly "Black is Beautiful" perspective on fashion, rejecting white standards of beauty. There was resurgence in the appreciation of African and African-American culture such as soul music and soul food. The black arts movement published the work of dozens of African-American writers. As author Ishmael Reed explained,

> I think what Black Arts did was inspire a whole lot of Black people to write. Moreover, there would be no multiculturalism movement without Black Arts. Latinos, Asian-Americans and others all say they began writing as a result of the example of the 1960s. Blacks gave the example that you don't have to assimilate. You could do your own thing, get into your own background, your own history, your own tradition and your own culture. I think the challenge

is for cultural sovereignty and Black Arts struck a blow for that.[955]

Some church leaders in the black community also embraced the idea of black power, creating black liberation theology. The denomination began in 1966, when fifty-one pastors bought a full-page ad in *The New York Times* and "demanded a more aggressive approach to eradicating racism. They echoed the demands of the Black Power movement, but the new crusade found its source of inspiration in the Bible." Specifically, black liberation theology understood the gospel message in terms of slavery: a brown-skinned Jesus who was member of a race oppressed by the white-skinned Romans had come to "eradicate poverty and to bring about freedom and liberation for the oppressed."[956]

Jonathan L. Walton, an expert on African-American religion, argues that black liberation theology has its roots in the First Great Awakening, when Christianity was introduced to black slaves. The stories of the exodus and salvation merged with their experiences as slaves and the hope that Jesus would one day liberate them soul and body. Articulating this worldview, theologian James Cone laid the theological groundwork in a series of books, beginning with *Black Theology and Black Power*. In it, Cone wrote,

> the Gospel message of Jesus in relationship to the black community's need for power ... It's not simply about deliverance. It's also about acquiring political and socioeconomic power for African-Americans ... Cone argued that Jesus reveals himself as black in order to disrupt and dismantle white oppression.[957]

Black liberation theology maintains that African Americans must be liberated from multiple forms of bondage—political, social, economic and religious. Cone even looked to Marxists as potential partners in achieving these goals.

> Perhaps what we need today is to return to that "good old-time religion" of our grandparents and combine with it a Marxist critique of society. Together black religion and Marxist philosophy may show us the

way to build a completely new society. With that combination, we may be able to realize in the society the freedom of which we sing and pray for in the black church.[958]

Pan-Africanism

The fourth governmental philosophy that held sway in Africa was Pan-Africanism. As mentioned earlier, the Black Horseman was characterized by the desire to unify continents. For example, a Pan-European vision led to the inception of the European Union in 1952.[959] Similarly, Pan-Africanism worked to unify the continent of Africa into a community united economically and politically. On another level, the movement sought to unify native Africans and those of African descent into a "global African community."[960]

In 1958, Kwame Nkrumah, a leader within the movement, called for a United States of Africa.[961] Similarly, Motsoko Phoko of the South African Parliament published this definition of the movement in 1999.

> Following the dark cloud of slavery and colonialism in Africa, visionary African leaders realised [sic] that it was imperative that all Africans—wherever they might be—should unite to end their holocaust which began with the 'European Renaissance' in Italy in 1400.... Pan-Africanism includes the intellectual, political and economic cooperation that should lead to the political unity of Africa. The Pan-African alternative provides a framework for African unity.[962]

The idea of Pan-Africanism was first conceived by Edward Wilmot Blyden, a Christian minister and politician in Liberia. His controversial book, *Christianity, Islam and the Negro Race* (1887), promoted the idea that practicing Islam was more unifying and fulfilling for Africans than Christianity.[963]

Marcus Garvey, a contemporary of Blyden, was a key leader in the Pan-African movement in the United States. He argued for the necessity of a "Race First" philosophy to spearhead the emancipation of all those of African descent around the globe.

For Garvey, the black man was oppressed globally on the basis of race and no other grounds, and thus any program of emancipation would have to be built around the question of "race first." Whites, he contended, had built an unconscious and conscious ideology of race preservation and advancement. Wherever whites existed, the prevailing ideology and social structure benefited whites first as a result of their economic and political domination. Thus Africans, in order to survive racist programs of black decimation through white domination had to develop a single minded race first ideology, "In a world of wolves, one should go armed, and one of the most defensive weapons within in [sic] reach of the Negro is the practice of 'Race First' in all parts of the world."[964]

Garvey's ideas, although highly controversial even within the black community, inspired a flourishing artistic expression of black self-love known as the Harlem Renaissance of the 1920s, and Garvey himself designed the pan-African flag, also known as "the Red, Black, and Green." This flag, which symbolizes the struggle for the unification and liberation of African people, has been used as the basis of the Australian Aboriginal flag[965] and the national flags of Malawi,[966] Kenya,[967] and Saint Kitts and Nevis.[968]

In the United States, the Organization Us has been a key proponent of Pan-Africanism. One of its founders, Maulana Karenga, created Kwanzaa, the first specifically African-American holiday, for the purpose of celebrating family, community and the seven values of African culture. While lighting seven candles in the colors of the Pan-African flag, Kwanzaa recites these key principles in "Swahili, a Pan-African language which is the most widely spoken African language." Kwanzaa is not a religious celebration but a cultural celebration of Africanness and a tool for meeting "the indispensable need to preserve, continually revitalize and promote African-American culture."[969]

The World Impact of the Black Horseman

The time of the Black Horseman was a time of unparalleled changes that transformed the globe into an increasingly unified place. It introduced the possibility of a one-world government connected by a web of mass communication and high-speed intercontinental transport. At the same time, the world became increasingly fragmented as ethnic groups rose up against one another. Nowhere was this more evident than the rapid independence of Africa and the corresponding activism in the African-American community.

It was a time of unparalleled prosperity coupled with an unparalleled, ever-tightening yoke of debt worsened by galloping inflation. The Green Revolution divorced food production from traditional agriculture, and even the seeds used had been transformed beyond recognition by hybrid and GMO science. Revolutionary change and a rejection of the established way of doing things were everywhere, within the church and in society at large. The generation gap had become a chasm in the life span of one generation: the baby boomers. The world stage was set for the rise of the final system foretold by the prophets: the time of the Green Horseman and Daniel's forth beast.

PART 5:

The Green Horseman

⁷And when he had opened the fourth seal, I heard the voice of the fourth beast say, Come and see. ⁸And I looked, and behold a pale horse: and his name that sat on him was Death, and Hell followed with him. And power was given unto them over the fourth part of the earth, to kill with sword, and with hunger, and with death, and with the beasts of the earth. (Rev. 6:7–8 KJV)

⁷After this I saw in the night visions, and behold a fourth beast, dreadful and terrible, and strong exceedingly; and it had great iron teeth: it devoured and brake in pieces, and stamped the residue with the feet of it: and it [was] diverse from all the beasts that [were] before it; and it had ten horns. ⁸I considered the horns, and, behold, there came up among them another little horn, before whom there were three of the first horns plucked up by the roots: and, behold, in this horn [were] eyes like the eyes of man, and a mouth speaking great things. ⁹I beheld till the thrones were cast down, and the Ancient of days did sit, whose garment [was] white as snow, and the hair of his head like the pure wool: his throne [was like] the fiery flame, [and] his wheels [as] burning fire.

[10]A fiery stream issued and came forth from before him: thousand thousands ministered unto him, and ten thousand times ten thousand stood before him: the judgment was set, and the books were opened. [11]I beheld then because of the voice of the great words which the horn spake: I beheld [even] till the beast was slain, and his body destroyed, and given to the burning flame. [12]As concerning the rest of the beasts, they had their dominion taken away: yet their lives were prolonged for a season and time. [13]I saw in the night visions, and, behold, [one] like the Son of man came with the clouds of heaven, and came to the Ancient of days, and they brought him near before him. [14]And there was given him dominion, and glory, and a kingdom, that all people, nations, and languages, should serve him: his dominion [is] an everlasting dominion, which shall not pass away, and his kingdom [that] which shall not be destroyed. (Dan. 7:7–14 KJV)

CHAPTER 28:

The Fourth Horse

> ⁷And when he had opened the fourth seal, I heard
> the voice of the fourth beast say, Come and see. ⁸And
> I looked, and behold a pale horse: and his name that
> sat on him was Death, and Hell followed with him.
> And power was given unto them over the fourth part
> of the earth, to kill with sword, and with hunger,
> and with death, and with the beasts of the earth.
> (Rev. 6:7–8 KJV)

We come finally to the fourth horseman, the one ridden by Death
and followed by Hades, the Greek god of the underworld and ruler of
the dead.[970] Truly, death seems to be the hallmark of this horseman,
although we have seen that death was definitely part of the reign
of the previous horsemen, particularly the Red one. The list of
means of death—sword, famine, beasts, and the seemingly redundant
"Death"—is interesting, but all these things have been part of human
existence for centuries. Somehow, this is different.

This is the last of the four horsemen although not the last of
the seals—there are three more to come. The corresponding beast
described by Daniel has dominion over the earth until the Ancient
of Days is seated, the books are opened, and judgment begins. (Dan.
7:9–14) In other words, the world system ushered in by the fourth
horseman will be in place until the return of the Messiah.

The Face of an Eagle

> And when he had opened the fourth seal, I heard the voice
> of the fourth beast say, Come and see. (Rev. 6:7 KJV)

The fourth horseman is introduced by the living creature with an eagle's face; and the characteristics of the eagle perfectly portray this time. Unlike the other predators associated with the horsemen, the eagle does not hunt from the ground. Instead, it hunts from high in the sky, soaring on air thermals at speeds of up to twenty miles an hour. Its telescopic vision allows it to spot prey such as a rabbit from up to a mile overhead, giving the victim no warning of its impending doom. Once the target is sighted, the eagle swoops down, drop its feet armed with hook-like, razor-sharp claws, snatches up its prey, and returns to the air. The deep wounds inflicted by the eagle's talons and the rough surface of the eagle's toes ensure that nothing can wriggle out of its grasp.[971]

Eyes in the Sky: Satellites

For the first time in recorded history, the world is under constant surveillance from high in the sky. If you don't believe it, just check out Google maps—the satellite image of my home is detailed enough to identify cars and make out specific plants. No doubt government and military surveillance images are even more specific.

When the Russians launched Sputnik into orbit, it raised doubts about the American ability to win the Cold War in the international community[972] and produced near-panic in the United States.

> The *Chicago Daily News* declared that if the Soviets "could deliver a 184-pound 'moon' into a predetermined pattern 560 miles out into space, the day is not far distant when they could deliver a death-dealing warhead onto a predetermined target almost anywhere on the earth's surface." *Newsweek* magazine dolefully predicted that several dozen Sputniks equipped with nuclear bombs could "spew their lethal fallout over the U.S. and Europe."[973]

As was discussed in chapter 4, hundreds of satellites and thousands of aircraft crisscross the globe at such high altitudes we are generally unaware of them. We are like rabbits, blissfully minding our own business, living in the illusion of an eagle-free world. If our neighbor should mysteriously disappear, that has nothing to do with us—or birds. Anything flying overhead is friendly, right?

Military Reconnaissance

In reality, we live in a world of amazing reconnaissance capabilities, including high-resolution aerial photography (from planes or satellites), available for military as well as commercial use. With a high enough resolution, it is possible to read a license plate.[974] The military have developed stealth aircraft with the capability of confusing RADAR devices and entering a nation's airspace unnoticed: "Planes capable of dropping nuclear bombs can now fly invisibly into enemy airspace, drop a payload, and fly back out without even being detected."[975] In addition, the U.S. Air Force is increasingly using unmanned drones, such as the Predator system, which are able to do real-time reconnaissance and hit small targets with pinpoint accuracy.[976]

Interestingly, many of these aircraft are named for birds of prey. For example, a stealth fighter made by Lockheed, which has the RADAR cross section of a seagull and can accurately hit a target one square yard, is called Nighthawk.[977] Drone fighters used by the U.S. military include the air force's Global Hawk, the marine's ScanEagle, and the army's Gray Eagle.[978]

Symbol of Arab Nations

The eagle is used as a national symbol by many nations, including the United States. We saw that the eagle was widely used in the heraldry of countries in central and eastern Europe, but it was also a favorite symbol of countries in the Middle East. Iraq uses the golden eagle of Saladin,[979] as does Egypt,[980 981] and several other Arab nations.[982] A similar bird known as the hawk of Quraish, the native tribe of Muhammad, is also widely used as a national emblem in the Middle East.[983]

What Color Was the Fourth Horseman?

> [7]And when he had opened the fourth seal, I heard the voice of the fourth beast say, Come and see. [8]And I looked, and behold a pale horse: (Rev. 6:7–8a KJV)

The color of the fourth horse has been translated many different ways. Most versions, including the Authorized King James, the New International Version, and the English Standard Version, refer to a "pale" horse, while the New American Standard refers to an "ashen" horse with a footnote calling it "sickly pale." The New Living Translation is a little closer to the Greek with "pale green." None of these translations convey a clear picture in the reader's mind the way the White, Red and Black Horsemen did. Exactly what color is this horse?

The remarkable thing about this translation is that the Greek word is not obscure, nor does it mean pale. *Chloros* (χλωρός) is the common, everyday word for green.[984] It is the root of the word "chlorophyll," the green pigment found in almost all plants that gives them their green color.[985] In other words, chloros is as green as grass. This is an important detail to keep in mind as we look for the fulfillment of this prophecy. Pale could mean anything—a sickly ashen shade, a putrid shade like vomit, like pus, like death? But bright green is very specific and easily identified.

As with the three previous horsemen, the Green Horseman will be fulfilled by a pair of vast movements with global impact characterized by the color green. It is possible that the impact of these movements may be emerging and therefore not as obvious as European imperialism or communism. However, just as green is usually associated with spring and new life, these movements will appear to bring the promise of good and hope for the future. Because this is our time and the world we live in, it is very possible we may view one or both of these movements as harmless or even beneficial. Whether you are offended or shouting in agreement, we must keep in mind what the Word of God says: at some point, the hope assured by these movements will be shattered as the promised solutions enslave us not merely to debt, but to the Lord of Death.

There are two global influences associated with the color green. The first is the Green Political movement, which began as environmentalism and has become what some have called a global revolution. The second is the rise of Islam to a position of influence on the world stage. We will look at both of these movements in detail, but first we will look at the timing of the opening of the fourth seal.

The Timing of the Opening of the Seal

[7]And when he had opened the fourth seal...
(Rev. 6:7a KJV)

The impact of the fourth horseman is more difficult to observe than the others because it is unfolding as we go about our daily lives. Although we are without the benefit of hindsight, most of us sense something is up but have trouble pinpointing the time frame. Nevertheless, the fourth seal seems to have opened some time in the late 1970s, probably in 1979. The opening of the fourth seal was preceded by revolutionary improvements in technology that allowed men to go "to and fro" around the globe and even into space in ever-increasing numbers and at ever-increasing speeds. It also gave access to an avalanche of information from all around the globe in seconds; "knowledge [was] increased," just as Daniel had foretold (Dan. 12:4 KJV).

An Ever-Shrinking World

The late 1970s witnessed several significant developments in space technology and global transportation. Transcontinental flights crisscrossed the globe and the Concorde supersonic jet began regular flights between Europe and New York, shortening the transatlantic journey to a mere three and a half hours. Not content with soaring through the skies, NASA began testing the *Enterprise* space shuttle, which mated a reusable shuttle with disposable propellant containers. The design made it economically feasible to launch satellites for a variety of purposes, including surveillance, GPS, telecommunications, and exploration. The most famous was the Hubble telescope. [986] [987]

Aerospace technology made circumnavigating the globe almost routine. The world came to be viewed as a global village, in which travelers could hop from continent to continent the way people used to jaunt across town.[988] Federal Express, which was founded in 1973, offered air-freight service that guaranteed next-day delivery, changing the way businesses operated. For example, many companies no longer kept a large store of supplies on hand, preferring instead to order items on demand.[989]

The Aerospace Age transformed science fiction into reality, and men travelled "to and fro" farther and faster than ever before.

The Information Age

The opening of the fourth seal was proceeded by the launch of the computer age, which made personalized media possible. Now messages, including news, advertising and entertainment could be customized to the interests of individual users, replacing mass media such as newspapers, television and radio as the primary sources of information. In a single year, 1977, three companies released versions of the personal computer.

January 1977 marked the launch of the Commodore PET personal computer. Commodore, known for its typewriters and calculators, demonstrated the PET, the first all-in-one personal computer, at electronics shows in Chicago and on the West Coast. Known for its gaming capabilities, Commodore was considered Apple's greatest rival and was used by "tens of millions of people that grew up with Commodore machines."[990] Later that year, Tandy's Radio Shack stores sold the TRS-80 by the hundreds of thousands, introducing shoppers to the computer and making Radio Shack the world's leading computer retailer of the time.[991]

In 1977, Microsoft licensed its BASIC software to both Apple and Radio Shack for use in their computers. By the close of 1978, the software behemoth had $1 million in revenue and was the leading distributor of microcomputer languages. The following year, 1979, the company relocated to Seattle, and the rest, as they say, is history.[992]

The other computing giant, Apple Computer, was incorporated in January 1977, after having begun in Steve Jobs' garage the previous year; by June, its sales figures had reached $1 million. The company continued to set the pace for the personal computing industry with the launch of Apple II (1979), which stored data on floppy discs instead of cassette tapes.[993]

The current line of Apple products illustrates the impact that the computer revolution had on information access. The lineup of products includes Mac PCs, laptops and the tiny mini-Mac. The iPod has become the definitive line of "portable media players," sending the transistor radio the way of the dinosaur. The company also manufactures a line of smart iPhones, which function as cell phones but are also handheld computers with Internet capabilities, still and video cameras, and media players. Apple can even store data remotely with iCloud. In other words, Apple and its competitors have changed the very fabric of knowledge dissemination.[994, 995]

Computers are only part of the equation in the information revolution. The other piece is the Internet, or information highway, which allows knowledge to flow in seconds around the globe. High-speed Internet has traditionally run on fiber optic cable, flexible fibers made of pure glass about the diameter of a human hair. Optical fibers made possible long distance transmission of communication signals with minimal information loss and electromagnetic interference.[996]

Fiber optics were first used for telephone lines in 1977, laying down the infrastructure for the Internet.[997] That same year, AT&T and Bell Labs launched a prototype of a cell phone system in Chicago with 2,000 users but were unable to get approval from the FCC to implement the technology nationwide. As a result, Tokyo was the first to launch a commercial cell phone system in 1979.[998]

The Information Age was born, and knowledge multiplied and flowed at an astounding pace.

Time to Go Green

The upheavals of the late 1970s culminated in 1979, a transformative year for all things green. Several events merged to change the localized environmentalist movement into the Green Political movement with an international agenda. That same year, events in the Middle East moved Islam, particularly radical Islam, from third world obscurity to the center of international attention.

Environmentalism was not new in 1979; it had been an influence since 1962 when Rachel Carson published her seminal work *Silent Spring*. Activists pushed environmental issues into the public spotlight and policy makers responded to public outcry by passing legislation designed to clean up and protect the environment. One of these, the Endangered Species Act, was actually challenged before the U.S. Supreme Court, which ruled that the "plain intent" of the law was to save all species "whatever the cost." Although the battle was far from over, it sent a message that the safety of the environment trumped profit interests.[999]

While many resented laws such as the Endangered Species Act or simply were indifferent to it, a series of highly visible environmental disasters underscored the importance of environmentalism in the public eye. One of the most dramatic events happened at Three Mile Island. In 1979, the Three Mile Island nuclear power plant experienced a cooling malfunction that led to a meltdown. Although government officials called the long-term impact of the accident "minimal," others called it the worst nuclear accident in U.S. history. Nevertheless, it was notable for what did not happen: "There was no 'China Syndrome.' There were no injuries or detectable health impacts from the accident, beyond the initial stress."[1000] However, the event triggered widespread fear about the safety of nuclear energy, curtailing public support of nuclear power plant construction.[1001]

At the same time, the world was introduced to the specter of global warming and climate change, a key issue for the Green Movement. In 1979, the first World Climate Conference was held in Geneva. This event was attended by scientific experts from a wide range of disciplines, who laid the foundations for climate change research and policy development. Traditionally, environmentalists directed their efforts on issues such as clean water or endangered species, which could be dealt with by local or national governments. Global warming, on the other hand, involves the whole planet, so it must be dealt with on a global level.[1002]

The globe was being primed for a Green One-World government.

The Rise of Islam onto the World Stage

Events in the Middle East thrust Islam onto the center of the international stage. Generally, Western society had viewed Islam as a major world religion that dominated Middle Eastern and North African societies in much the same way Christianity once dominated Europe. It was an interesting aspect of Eastern culture, but had nothing to do with modern society or global events. All this changed in 1979.

The events of 1979 that had caused spiking oil prices also changed the world's understanding of security and war. First, the Islamic Revolution in Iran pushed the nation to the brink of civil war and enabled the Ayatollah to declare Iran an Islamic republic with himself as supreme spiritual leader. A new constitution based on Shiite law soon followed.[1003] That same year, Saddam Hussein became president and de facto dictator of Iraq. A week later, Saddam consolidated his power by executing more than sixty party leaders as "traitors."[1004]

In November 1979, the political upheavals in Iran galvanized Americans after the U.S. embassy in Tehran was attacked and fifty-two American citizens were taken hostage. U.S. President Jimmy Carter made every effort to secure the hostages' safe release, including a complete oil embargo and other economic sanctions, the severing of diplomatic relations, and an attempted rescue operation by the military. Despite this, the hostages were not released until after the inauguration of Ronald Reagan in 1981, 144 days later.

The world had seen the flexed arm of radical Islam.[1005]

CHAPTER 29:

Death and Hades

> [7]And when he had opened the fourth seal, I heard the voice of the fourth beast say, Come and see. [8]And I looked, and behold a pale horse: and his name that sat on him was Death, and Hell followed with him. And power was given unto them over the fourth part of the earth, to kill with sword, and with hunger, and with death, and with the beasts of the earth. (Rev. 6:7–8 KJV)

The Green Horseman has two riders: Death and Hades, the Lord of the Dead. While it might be debatable who is Death and who is Hades, it is clear that the Green Political Movement is one and the Islam is the other. It is important to keep in mind that many of the key players in these movements are sincere and well meaning, but they have eaten from the tree of the knowledge of good and evil. They are doing what seems right without a full understanding of all the consequences of their ideas.

For example, Rachel Carson, founder of the environmental movement, wrote *Silent Spring* (1962), in which she "challenged the practices of agricultural scientists and the government, and called for a change in the way humankind viewed the natural world."[1006] The book specifically argued for the banning of the insecticide DDT, calling it a dangerous "agent of death." However, J. Gordon Edwards, a well-known entomologist, writes,

The World Health Organization stated that DDT had "killed more insects and saved more people than any other substance." A leading British scientist pointed out that "If the pressure groups *had* succeeded, if there *had* been a world ban on DDT, then Rachel Carson and *Silent Spring* would now be killing more people in a single year than Hitler killed in his whole holocaust."[1007]

The Four Pillars of Green Politics

Everybody has heard of the Green Movement on some level. We are constantly being encouraged to "Go Green," to conserve natural resources such as water and energy, to "Reduce, Reuse, Recycle." Billboards shout "Green is the New Black." Reduced carbon footprint, sustainability, and "Save the Planet" have become marketing buzz-words. While there is nothing wrong with encouraging responsible behavior towards our environment, there is something sinister about the Green Political agenda. It is the distinction between encouraging the responsible use of alcohol—don't drink and drive, for instance—and Prohibition.

The goal of Green Politics is to create an environmentally stable society through political means. Although several Green political parties were formed during the 1970s, the German Green Party was the first to successfully run for office in 1979. Their four pillars of Green Politics, which serve as the unifying platform for green political parties around the world, are Ecological Wisdom, Social Justice, Grassroots Democracy and Nonviolence.[1008] [1009]

Ecological Wisdom

Ecological Wisdom holds that humans are "part of nature, not separate from nature"[1010] and that we must "respect the specific values of all forms of life, including nonhuman species."[1011] The "light green" approach to ecological wisdom is a matter of personal responsibility, such as taking care not to dump pollutants into the environment, minimizing our wastes and conserving natural resources.[1012]

At the other extreme, "dark green" environmentalists dismiss such actions as too little too late, embracing a more radical approach. Some, like Greenpeace and Sea Shepherd, achieve their goals through confrontation, such as deliberately ramming ships suspected of whaling.[1013] For many "dark green" environmentalists, human needs are of secondary importance to the needs of nature. National Park Service ecologist David M. Graber wrote,

> Human happiness and certainly human fecundity, are not as important as a wild and healthy planet … We have become a plague upon ourselves and upon the Earth … Until such time as Homo sapiens should decide to rejoin nature, some of us can only hope for the **right virus to come along** [emphasis mine].[1014]

Similarly, the Club of Rome, a global advisory think tank to the United Nations, stated in their report, *The First Global Revolution*, that

> in **searching for a new enemy to unite us** [emphasis mine], we came up with the idea that pollution, the threat of global warming, water shortages, famine and the like would fit the bill. In their totality and their interactions these phenomena do constitute a common threat which must be confronted by everyone together. But in designating these dangers as the enemy, we fall into the trap, which we have already warned readers about, namely mistaking symptoms for causes. All these dangers are caused by *human* intervention, and it is only through changed attitudes and behavior that they can be overcome. **The real enemy then, is humanity itself** [emphasis mine].[1015]

Social Justice

Social Justice, the second pillar of Green politics, is defined as

> the equitable distribution of social and natural resources, both locally and globally, to meet basic human needs

unconditionally, and to ensure that all citizens have full opportunities for personal and social development."[1016]

Green politics espouses a "third way," in which economic and political power are decentralized and accessible to all; it seeks to use technology to create a "Win-win, synergistic, post-scarcity ... orientation."[1017]

Social justice has long been used as a rallying cry by the left calling for the redistribution of wealth from the elite to the working classes. Under the Green agenda, social justice also encompasses the redistribution of wealth from "have" nations to "have not" nations with the goal of creating a new economic order in which the needs of all are met. Ramon Tamames, economics professor and European Union authority, expressed this as a necessary goal for the United Nations.

> It is increasingly evident that globalization must be accompanied by measures designed to combat not only unequal development, but also the creation of social outcasts and other scars that continue to come to light.
>
> Specifically, regarding aid in favor of less developed countries, it is clear that bigger allocations by the advanced nations to the developing countries is necessary ... [to] achieve more equitable international burden-sharing in reducing and preventing global environmental damage and in reducing global poverty.[1018]

Similarly, this new ideal of social justice was called for by Dr. Ida Urso in a talk entitled *The New World Order and the Work of the United Nations.*

> The NWO to which we refer must recognize that the resources of the earth must be set free to be used justly and fairly by all of the world's people. Ended must be the sorry spectacle of those nations and those people who suffer from overabundance and the often corollary sense of meaninglessness, and alienation and the opposite experience of nations

and people who suffer from want and destitution.

This unhealthy imbalance is succinctly summarized in the 1994 *Human Development Report* which states that "Our world cannot survive one-fourth rich and three-fourths poor, half democratic and half authoritarian, with oases of human development surrounded by deserts of human deprivation."

Many claimed at the recent United Nations Social Summit that this discrepancy between the haves and have-nots is indecent and immoral and it cannot continue. Poverty, it was stated, is a blight in our world society and must be abolished just as surely as colonialism and slavery were abolished.[1019]

Grassroots Democracy

Since the Green Party began as a minority movement that used Western democratic structures to gain a political voice, it is not surprising that its third pillar is Grassroots Democracy. It encompasses the ideals of holding elected officials accountable to those who elected them and developing "new types of political organizations which expand the process of participatory democracy by directly including citizens in the decision-making process."[1020]

However, the Green political agenda is also embraced by individuals with significant wealth and power who view democracy as a tool to further their own agenda, not as something of intrinsic worth. A report to the U.N. entitled *The First Global Revolution* states

> But freedom alone cannot … build a new social structure. It is a necessary and noble inspirational force, but it is far from being an operating manual for a new government. This is why the concept of human rights simply initiates but cannot implement the process of democratization.
>
> This is where the question must be raised—what sort of democracy is required today and for what purpose?
>
> The old democracies have functioned reasonably well over the last 200 years, but they appear now to be in a phase of complacent stagnation

with little evidence of real leadership and innovation.

Democracy is not a panacea. It cannot organize everything and it is unaware of its own limits. These facts must be faced squarely, sacrilegious though this may sound. In its present form, democracy is no longer well suited for the tasks ahead. The complexity and the technical nature of many of today's problems do not always allow elected representatives to make competent decisions at the right time.[1021]

Nonviolence

Nonviolence is the fourth pillar advocated by Green political groups, although how this value actually works is up for debate. The Green Party of Canada declares it is a "commitment to strive for a culture of peace and cooperation between states, inside societies and between individuals, as the basis of global security."[1022]

Many look to the Schuman Declaration as a blueprint for world peace. After World War II, Robert Schuman proposed his declaration to as a way to make war not only "unthinkable but materially impossible." [1023] By intertwining the economic and military destinies of nations with the creation of a common market in coal and steel (European Coal and Steel Community), he sought to eliminate any chance of a third pan-European war. Thanks to the Schuman Declaration, Western Europeans recently celebrated more than sixty straight years of peace, the longest stretch of continuous peace since the opening of the first seal in 1492. Some experts point to the results of Schuman's brainchild, advocating that its application in volatile situations such as Sudan as the key to building world peace.[1024]

Agenda 21 is a blueprint for sustainable global development in the twenty-first century, a sort of international Schuman Declaration. It was agreed to by 179 nations at a UN conference in 1992 and has been confirmed in the UN (1997) and the World Summit on Sustainable Development (2002).[1025] Just as the Schuman Declaration was the idea that birthed the European Union, Agenda 21 is the foundation for a one-world government. The Club of Rome outlined a similar strategy to create a unified, interdependent world system in its report *Mankind at the Turning Point*. They advocated a worldwide restructuring of resources and societal values as the only means to ensure the world's problems do not destroy us.

> An analysis of problems and crises as reported in subsequent chapters indicate that (1) a "horizontal" restructuring of the world system is needed, i.e., a change in relationships among nations and regions and (2) as far as the "vertical" structure of the world system is concerned, drastic changes in the norm stratum—that is, in the value system and the goals of man—are necessary in order to solve energy, food, and other crises, i.e., social changes and changes in individual attitudes are needed if the transition to organic growth is to take place.[1026]

The attitudes and values specified in the report—membership in a global rather than national community, conservation rather than consumption, living in harmony with nature rather than in dominion over it, and the sacrifice of personal desires for the benefit of future generations—are the attitudes and values most suited to living under a global, totalitarian regime. It advocates the use of fear of global catastrophe to transform mankind into a "living global system" under a world government.[1027] As we saw earlier, threats of overpopulation, global warming, massive famine, and water shortages are tools being used to unite us into a collective whole.

An economic analysis of *Mankind at a Turning Point* highlights the report's focus on the equitable distribution of resources and the rejection of the machine age as key policies for saving the world. Global redistribution of wealth should be achieved through vast, unprecedented quantities of foreign aid. Solar energy should replace the use of both fossil fuels and nuclear energy, and people should refrain from economic and technological advancement. The analysis sums up the report as a great example of neo–Malthusian thinking.

> It greatly reinforces the arguments of the trendy environmental lobby in the developed world. In spite of the complicated and sophisticated mathematical modeling the results and interpretations cannot claim immunity from value-judgements [sic] of the authors

… I cannot but fail to describe the Mesarovid–Pestel model as the latest and most numerate addition to the growing family of models of eco-doom.[1028]

The Leading Proponents of Green Politics

It is important to keep in mind that the agenda of Green politics is not the ranting of a lunatic fringe but a carefully constructed argument of the global elite. Several of the above quotes come from reports published by The Club of Rome, a nongovernmental think tank organization comprising

> independent leading personalities from politics, business and science, men and women who are long-term thinkers interested in contributing in a systemic interdisciplinary and holistic manner to a better world.[1029]

Reading the membership lists of the Club of Rome and its affiliate organizations, the Club of Budapest, the Club of Madrid, and its thirty-three national associations is like reading a who's who of the world's rich and powerful. The Club of Rome acts as a consultant for the United Nations; several senior United Nations officials are among its past and present members:

- Maurice Strong, former head of the UN Environment Program, chief policy advisor to Kofi Annan, secretary general of the Rio Earth Summit, and Petro Canada president[1030]
- Robert Muller, former assistant secretary general of the United Nations[1031]
- Kofi Annan[1032] and Javier Perez de Cuellar,[1033] both former secretaries general of the United Nations

Other former or current members include:

- Bill Clinton, former president of the United States[1034]
- Mikhail Gorbachev, former president of the U.S.S.R.[1035]
- Pierre Trudeau, former prime minister of Canada[1036]
- Juan Carlos I of Spain

- Queen Beatrix of the Netherlands[1037]
- David Rockefeller, Sr., former CEO of Chase Manhattan Bank and founder of the Trilateral Commission[1038]
- Al Gore, former vice–president of the United States[1039]
- Bill Gates, CEO of Microsoft[1040]
- Jimmy Carter, former president of the United States [1041]
- Katherine Graham, former publisher of the *Washington Post*[1042]

Green Religion

Like so many other advocates of the Green political agenda, James Lovelock is not a quack. He is a highly respected scientist who worked on NASA's Viking Project, invented the electron capture detector, and was awarded a Nobel Prize in chemistry for his work on CFCs and ozone depletion.[1043] He is also a leading proponent of the Gaia Theory, which proposes that "the Earth is a self-regulating system able to keep the climate and chemical composition comfortable for organisms." Although the Gaia hypothesis was initially rejected by much of the scientific community, it has been increasingly accepted as part of conventional thinking under the name of Earth System Science, especially among climatologists. Lovelock asserts, "Following the Amsterdam Declaration in 2001, most scientists around the world now accept that the Earth does indeed self-regulate."[1044]

However, Gaia Theory is more than an interpretation of scientific data; it is an embracing of the ancient cult of the Gaia, the Greek earth goddess. In *A New Look at Life*, Lovelock writes,

> Still more important is the implication that the evolution of *homo sapiens,* with his technological inventiveness and his increasingly subtle communications network, has vastly increased Gaia's range of perception. She is now through us awake and aware of herself. She has seen the reflection of her fair face through the eyes of astronauts and the television cameras of orbiting spacecraft. Our sensations of wonder and pleasure, our capacity for conscious thought and speculation, our restless curiosity and drive are hers to share. This new

interrelationship of Gaia with man is by no means fully established; we are not yet a truly collective species, corralled and tamed as an integral part of the biosphere, as we are as individual creatures. It may be that the destiny of mankind is to become tamed, so that the fierce, destructive, and greedy forces of tribalism and nationalism are fused into a compulsive urge to belong to the commonwealth of all creatures which constitutes Gaia.[1045]

In other words, Gaia worship is a formative influence on the Green political agenda. This explains why the Club of Rome includes leading New Age advocates such as the fourteenth Dalai Lama[1046] and Barbara Marx Hubbard, fellow of the Club of Budapest and founder of the Foundation for Conscious Evolution.[1047]

Green: the Color of Islam

The other movement associated with the color green and the Green Horseman is Islam. Green was the favorite color of Muhammad; it is the traditional color of Islam and used extensively among his followers. Khalil Green, an imam in the United States, writes,

> The color green as the color of Islam was first used by the prophet himself. The color of the Islamic flag was green. To Muslims, green represents the freshness of Islam and how it is meant to bring the mind of the Muslim from ignorance into light.[1048]

Followers of Islam will often wear a green wristband, thread, or bracelet to indicate they are Muslim.[1049] The flags of several Muslim nations, including Mauritania,[1050] Nigeria,[1051] Pakistan[1052] and Saudi Arabia[1053] are predominantly green. In fact, under the al-Qaddafi regime, the Libyan flag was solid green.[1054]

Obviously, the Muslim faith is not new, but its global prominence is. Several factors have propelled Islam to international attention. As mentioned, the Middle East, with its incredible oil wealth, played a vital role in the Western economy. By the early 1970s, 40 percent of the world's energy came from oil. At the same time, the Middle East was producing 30 percent of the world's oil supply.[1055] This has put the leadership of OPEC nations in the position to exact a stranglehold on the economies of the industrial world; the 1980 war between the newly established regimes of Iran and Iraq underscored how tenuous the oil supply could be.[1056]

Additionally, the spread of Islamic fundamentalism sometimes referred to as Islamic activism or radical Islam, raised growing concerns about global security, especially since 9/11. On a personal level, the movement emphasized faithful adherence to religious observances prescribed by the five pillars of Islam, including praying five times daily, giving alms, and ritual fasting during Ramadan.[1057] In addition, Islamic activism played an increasingly prominent role in the public life and the politics of the Middle East. In fact, Islamic activist groups frequently received support from conservative regimes such as Saudi Arabia that were concerned about the growth of nationalism in neighboring states.[1058] John Esposito, an authority on religion and international affairs, cites many examples of Muslim nationalism.

> Libyan leader Col. Muammar al-Qaddafi's *Green Book* of Islamic socialism and use of Islam internationally; Gen. Zia ul-Haq's 1977 coup d'état in Pakistan and his call for the establishment of an Islamic system of government; Ayatollah Khomeini's Iranian revolution of 1978–79; the seizure of the Grand Mosque in Mecca by militants in 1979; Pres. Anwar as-Sadat's appeal to Islam in Egyptian politics, his legitimation [sic] of the 1973 war with Israel as a jihad, and his assassination in 1981 by religious extremists; the Afghan resistance (by mujahideen, or holy warriors) to the Soviet invasion and occupation throughout the 1980s—all were instances of Islam reasserting itself.[1059]

The activities of Islamic fundamentalists have not been limited to the Middle East; Islamic terrorism has been used as a political tool at least since radical Palestinian groups began targeting civilians, especially in crowded urban locations, in the 1960s and '70s. The Iranian Revolution and the Soviet invasion of Afghanistan in 1979 marked a turning point in international terrorism ... Indeed, the growth of a post-jihad pool of well-trained, battle-hardened militants is a key trend in contemporary international terrorism and insurgency-related violence. Volunteers from various parts of the Islamic world fought in Afghanistan, supported by conservative countries such as Saudi Arabia. In Yemen, for instance, the Riyadh–backed Islamic Front was established to provide financial, logistical, and training support for Yemeni volunteers. So called "Arab–Afghans" have—and are—using their experience to support local insurgencies in North Africa, Kashmir, Chechnya, China, Bosnia, and the Philippines.[1060]

Many militant Muslims, with the backing of Islamic nations, see themselves as combatants in a global jihadist army and have been willing to strike targets in the West as part of that war. Targets included the attacks on the World Trade Center in 1993 and again in 2001. Terrorists have clearly aimed at killing large numbers of innocent citizens, as demonstrated by bombings targeting morning commuters in London (2005) and Madrid (2004), and the Beslan school hostage situation in Russia (2004).[1061]

Finally, there is concern about the growing number of Muslims in Western society. The United States has seen a rapid increase in Muslims, particularly among incarcerated African Americans, where an estimated 20 percent of inmates are Muslim.[1062] In Europe, the agents of change come from large numbers of Middle Eastern immigrants who, rather than adopting the ways of their chosen homelands, live in Muslim enclaves, where the authority of local and national courts are subservient to Sharia law. As a result, Europe is rapidly becoming an extension of the Muslim world. In 2006, German author Henryk M. Broder claimed, "Europe as we know it will no longer exist 20 years from now." He described how Europe is turning Muslim and reverting backward in time. "We are watching the world of yesterday."[1063]

The Merging of the Greens

At first glance, these two Green movements seem to have little in common other than the desire to transform the world around them according to their visions. However, there has been a growing effort to link the two, and environmentalism is creating the common bond. The Islamic Foundation for Ecology and Environmental Sciences has "worked particularly hard to highlight the Islamic teachings on nature."[1064] Muslims are being exhorted to become "green like Mohammad," following his example of care for the environment.

> As trustees, the children of Adam are expected to rise above greedy impulses and turn the earth into a manifestation of the Garden of Eden in anticipation of the promised Gardens of Paradise.[1065]

What could be greener than environmentally green Islam?

CHAPTER 30:

Power to Kill— Sword and Hunger

> [7]And when he had opened the fourth seal, I heard the voice of the fourth beast say, Come and see. [8]And I looked, and behold a pale horse: and his name that sat on him was Death, and Hell followed with him. And power was given unto them over the fourth part of the earth, to kill with sword, and with hunger, and with death, and with the beasts of the earth. (Rev. 6:7–8 KJV)

In John's vision, the Green Horseman, ridden by Death and followed by Hades, were given power over a fourth of the earth to kill in four specific ways: with sword, with famine, with death, and with beasts. The question is, of course, whether a movement dedicated to saving the planet and/or the "religion of peace" can be capable of such mass carnage. This chapter will look at these Green Horse movements' capacity of killing with sword and hunger.

But first, a disclaimer: this is far from an exhaustive listing of all the events happening that could be fulfillments of the Green Horseman. That would consume reams of paper and is beyond the scope of this book. Instead, the following examples are evidence that support John's specific predictions concerning the Green Horseman that have already occurred and involved widespread issues.

A Fourth of the Earth

> And power was given unto them over the fourth part of
> the earth... (Rev. 6:8b KJV)

As any math student knows, the key to setting up the correct equation when solving word problems is to determine the numerical value of each word. In this case, we must first decide whether "the earth" refers to land, people, or wealth. The word translated "earth" is the Greek word *ge* (γη), which refers to the actual ground, and could mean arable land or a county with fixed boundaries.[1066] "Power," the Greek word *exousia* (ἐξουσια), can mean strength but usually refers to permission or authority.[1067] Thus, the Green Horseman is permitted by God to take authority over one-quarter of the earth's land mass.

The Authority of Green Environmentalism

It is difficult to assess the area of land under the authority of the Green political agenda. However, a possible measurement might be the area of nations that have ratified the Kyoto Protocol, an international agreement sponsored by the United Nations Framework Convention of Climate Change. The United Nations calls the protocol

> an important first step towards a truly global emission
> reduction regime that will stabilize GHG emissions,
> and provides the essential architecture for any future
> international agreement on climate change.[1068]

In keeping with Social Justice, one of the pillars espoused by Green political groups, Kyoto aims to redistribute wealth on a global scale. The economic activities of the Western world are to be penalized by placing "a heavier burden on developed nations under the principle of 'common but differentiated responsibilities.'"[1069]

Note that the United Nations openly refers to the Kyoto Protocol as the start of a global regime, like the one-world government called for in Agenda 21 and various Club of Rome reports. The 191 countries that ratified the protocol have tacitly agreed to submit to the Green political agenda knowingly or unknowingly. Map 14 shows the countries that have ratified the protocol. The United States and Israel have made it clear they have no intention of ratifying the treaty. Canada initially ratified it but renounced the plan in 2011. There are a handful of nations, including Afghanistan, Andorra, Vatican City, Taiwan, and Western Sahara, that have neither ratified the treaty nor indicated whether they will ever do so.

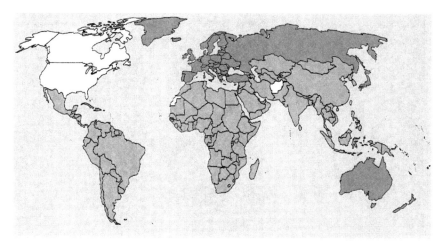

Map 14: Nations that have ratified the Kyoto Protocol.[1070]

The proportion of land held by Kyoto-ratifying nations relative to the total surface area of the globe is compelling. In round figures, the surface of the earth is 510 million square kilometers, of which 148 million square kilometers is land (about 29 percent). The area held by nations not participating in the Kyoto Protocol (drawn from the CIA World Factbook) was subtracted from the earth's total land mass to calculate the area in compliance with the agreement. These figures were used to calculate a percentage of the earth's surface under the authority of the Kyoto Protocol:

Percent = $\dfrac{100 \times 127{,}213{,}206 \text{ square km of land under Kyoto}}{510{,}000{,}000 \text{ square km of earth's total surface area}}$

When the answer rounded to the nearest whole number, Kyoto participants control exactly 25 percent of the globe's surface.

The Authority of Green Islam

The land mass under the authority of Islam is easier to compute. Map 15 shows the approximately fifty Muslim-majority countries, an area covering 28.5 million kilometers. [1071] When this is calculated as a proportion of the world's total land mass (148 million kilometers[1072]), it constitutes about 20 percent. Given the number of Muslim enclaves in predominantly non-Muslim nations such as France, the United States, and Great Britain and the rapid growth rate of Muslim populations, it is not had to conceive a time when Muslims do control a quarter of the earth's land.

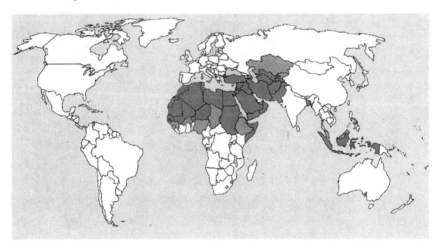

Map 15: Nations with Muslim majorities.[1073]

To Kill with Sword

> And power was given unto them over the fourth part
> of the earth, to kill with sword... (Rev. 6:8b KJV)

It always seems like an oxymoron when a last-days prophesy mentions a pre-modern weapon such as a sword. While this prophesy may one day be fulfilled with the use of a literal sword, it seems more likely to have an allegorical or symbolic meaning. When John describes the sword wielded by the Green Horseman, he does not use the common Greek word *machaira* (μάχαιρα).[1074] Instead, he reports that the riders kill with a *rhomphaia* (ρομφαια), a large sword or a long javelin associated with the Thracians.[1075]

Of the seven times rhomphaia is used in the New Testament, five are in reference to Jesus as the One who has a two-edged sword coming out of His mouth (Rev. 1:6, 2:12, 2:16, 19:15 and 19:21).[1076] The writer of Hebrews tells us that "the word of God [is] quick, and powerful, and sharper than any twoedged sword" (Heb. 4:12a KJV). This verse in Revelation 6 is the **only** time the word is used without specific reference to the words of Jesus. Thus, it is not a stretch to interpret the *rhomphaia* in Revelation 6:8 as a word or edict that kills.

Edicts of Death: Green Politics

Since many "dark green" proponents view the human race as a cancer that threatens the long-term survival of the planet, there has been much speculation about the ideal population size to ensure sustainability. The figures range between 500 million and 3 billion, all well below the current population of the world (over 6 billion and growing). Ecologist David Pimental sums up our choice as

> a planet with 2 billion people thriving in harmony with the environment; or, at the other extreme, 12 billion miserable humans suffering a difficult life with limited resources and widespread famine.[1077]

Bill Gates, founder and head of Microsoft and of the Gates Foundation, the world's largest philanthropic organization, announced that his most important priority is to develop the means of reducing CO^2 emissions to zero. This, he believes, is the most valuable thing he can do to help the most vulnerable people on the planet. In a speech he made at TED in February 2010, he outlined his plan based on a simple equation: $CO^2 = P \times S \times E \times C$. Total carbon dioxide emissions is the product of the number of people (P) times the number of services each person uses (S) times the amount of energy each service uses (E) times the quantity of CO^2 emitted per unit of energy (C).[1078]

Gates points out that mathematically, "Probably one of these numbers has to get pretty close to zero." He suggests that population growth could be slowed by using vaccines and reproductive services (think birth control and abortion). The need for services, which include everything from food to TVs to heat to cars, are guaranteed to continue rising sharply as we work to eliminate poverty and increase living standards in Third World nations. Gates predicts the services per person will more than double over the coming years. The amount of energy used per service is being reduced through energy-efficient technology, but there are limits to how much we can reduce emissions this way. Therefore, Gates argues we need "Energy Miracles," and our best hope for achieving these is to develop and use "climate neutral" energy, or energy that emits no greenhouse gases.[1079]

So what if we don't achieve an energy miracle in time? There is one other number in the equation that can be quickly reduced in a crisis—population. Gates mentioned family planning as a key tool in reducing population, and environmentalists rank overpopulation as the most significant threat to the planet. In fact, one ecologist calls overpopulation the only problem, saying, "If we had 100 million people on Earth—or better, 10 million—no others would be a problem."[1080]

These figures require that the earth's population be reduced by at least two-thirds and as much as 90 percent. Population reduction can be achieved in two ways: reducing birth rates or increasing death rates. China's one-child policy demonstrates that government edicts can impact birth rates. Couples everywhere have responded to the pressure to have fewer children, and not just in the industrialized West. Current data indicates that birthrates all over the world except in sub-Saharan Africa are approaching replacement levels. Even in Muslim countries, which have traditionally had high birthrates, women are having fewer children, and birth rates are only slightly above replacement levels.

Unfortunately, there is an unexpected outcome from the push to lower fertility: gender imbalances. In many cultures where there is a preference for sons over daughters, couples have used sonograms to practice gender-specific abortions. An estimated 90 million women are "missing" in Asia.

> The official Chinese figures suggest that 118 boys are now being born in China for every 100 girls. As a result, millions of Chinese males may never find a mate

with whom to raise a conventional family ... Gender imbalances are not limited to China. They are apparent in South Korea, Taiwan, Pakistan, Bangladesh, and increasingly in India, particularly among the Sikhs.

In a recent paper Hudson and den Boer asked, "Will it matter to India and China that by the year 2020, 12 to 15 percent of their young adult males will not be able to 'settle down' because the girls that would have grown up to be their wives were disposed of by their societies instead?" They answered, "The rate of criminal behavior of unmarried men is many times higher than that of married men; marriage is a reliable predictor of a downturn in reckless, antisocial, illegal, and violent behavior by young adult males."[1081]

In the West, voluntary abortion has had a similar impact on fertility rates, especially in Europe. As shown in the chart below, European fertility rates have been below replacement levels for some time, accelerating the aging of Europe's population. While researchers have found that government policies can impact fertility rates, they are slow to take effect and not politically popular, since it takes at least twenty years before children enter the workforce and the ranks of voters. [1082]

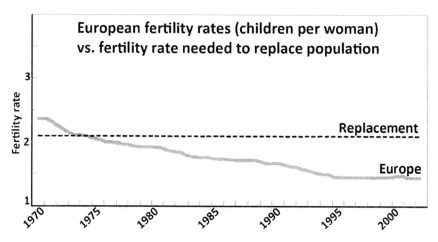

Chart 2: Trends in fertility rates in the European Union, 1970–2002[1083]

Lower birth rates alone have been unable to reduce global population to "optimum" levels. To achieve this, there needs to be a significant death toll as well. Conveniently, the failure to replace the population by having two children per couple has created a large aging population with insufficient young people to support them.[1084] By failing to replace themselves, baby boomers have becoming an inviting target for edicts of death. As they retire, collect pensions and need expensive medical treatment for the chronic health problems associated with aging, they will become an overwhelming burden on limited government resources. The money seniors paid into social security systems has been spent. There will be a strong temptation to euthanize the elderly as a first step in democidal population reduction.

Edicts of Death: Islam

Within Islam, edicts, or *fatwas*, are generally issued by religious authorities who may or may not be speaking with the backing of civil authorities. The Huffington Post observes that "scholars who operate solely in academic institutions ... have just as much (if not more) authority than those scholars who are appointed to religious authority positions within the state."[1085]

Although fatwas issued by theological leaders generally deal with religious questions such as fasting requirements during Ramadan, they can and do address political issues with potentially huge repercussions. For example, it is believed that Sheikh Omar Abdel Rahman, a leading religious authority in Egypt, issued a fatwa authorizing Islamic militants to assassinate Anwar al-Sadat, Egypt's president at the time. Another declared that in light of Serbian "ethnic cleansing" efforts, Muslims had the right to enslave Serbian prisoners and force their wives and daughters to engage in sex.[1086]

The tenor of most of these edicts is best illustrated by the exception: a 600-page fatwa issued by Muhammad Tahir-ul-Qadri, a former Pakistani lawmaker and a leading scholar of Islam. The fatwa, described as "a rare religious edict condemning terrorism and denouncing suicide bombers as 'heroes of hellfire'," was eagerly received by both the British and American authorities.[1087] The fact that this is a lone statement in a sea of jihadist fatwas is pause for consideration.

While "to kill by the sword," may refer to edicts for execution, it is not the only possibility. Islam is known for its use of a literal sword; the tradition of execution by beheading with the sword is still practiced today. Most men sentenced to be executed in this manner have been found guilty of murder or drug trafficking. These executions are done in the full view of the public, and the families of both the condemned and the victim. Medical, religious, and judicial authorities are also present.[1088]

The practice of beheading is associated with terrorists and therefore often dismissed by Westerners as the actions of a lunatic fringe. However, the beheading of infidels was commanded by Muhammad himself.

> [33]Indeed, the penalty for those who wage war against Allah and His Messenger and strive upon earth [to cause] corruption is none but that they be killed or crucified or that their hands and feet be cut off from opposite sides or that they be exiled from the land. That is for them a disgrace in this world; and for them in the Hereafter is a great punishment, [34]Except for those who return [repenting] before you apprehend them. And know that Allah is Forgiving and Merciful. (Qur'an 5:33–34)[1089]
>
> [12][Remember] when your Lord inspired to the angels, "I am with you, so strengthen those who have believed. I will cast terror into the hearts of those who disbelieved, so strike [them] upon the necks and strike from them every fingertip." [13]That is because they opposed Allah and His Messenger. And whoever opposes Allah and His Messenger—indeed, Allah is severe in penalty. (Qur'an 8:12–13)[1090]
>
> [4]So when you meet those who disbelieve [in battle], strike [their] necks until, when you have inflicted slaughter upon them, then secure their bonds, and either [confer] favor afterwards or ransom [them]

until the war lays down its burdens. That [is the command]. And if Allah had willed, He could have taken vengeance upon them [Himself], but [He ordered armed struggle] to test some of you by means of others. And those who are killed in the cause of Allah—never will He waste their deeds. (Qur'an 47:4)[1091]

Many terrorists prefer the sword over the gun as a tool of execution because of its endorsement in the Qur'an. For example, *Wall Street Journal* reporter Daniel Pearl, who was abducted by a militant Pakistani group, was later beheaded, and graphic video footage of his execution was included in the jihadist recruiting film *The Slaughter of the Spy-Journalist, the Jew Daniel Pearl.*[1092]

While it may be easy to dismiss Pearl's beheading as the warped, misguided expression of legitimate political grievances as a *New York Times* editorial did, other examples of Muslim beheadings are not.[1093] For instance, in 2005, three Christian high school girls were beheaded in Indonesia as a Ramadan "trophy," an offering planned to coincide with Labaran, the festival that ends the month of Ramadan. The heads of the victims were later dumped in their village with a note reading: "Wanted: 100 more Christian heads, teenaged or adult, male or female; blood shall be answered with blood, soul with soul, head with head."[1094]

Both of these incidents are ritual-style executions done to those who are "infidels" who are unlikely to convert to Islam, done by people who are deadly serious about obeying the Qur'an and the tenants of Islam. Contrary to Western political correctness, radical Muslims have not hijacked Islam but believe in a strict adherence to the Qur'an and the five pillars of their faith.

Perhaps the observance of the Day of Ashura best illustrates the difference between Western and Muslim views of the sword. The tenth of the month of Muharram commemorates both the death of Al-Imam Al-Hussein, the grandson of Muhammad who was "martyred" in battle in 680 AD, and the crossing of the Red Sea led by the prophet Moses. The Sunnis celebrate the day as one of great victory, while the Shiites observe it as a time of intense mourning.

The mourning may take many forms, including wailing, weeping, and the pounding of the head and chest to express grief.

One highly controversial display of mourning is the practice of "whipping themselves with chains and cutting their heads with swords to recall the suffering of Al-Imam Al-Hussein." Although officially condemned by many Muslim leaders, each year thousands "of mourners slit open their heads with swords, big knives and razor blades, causing their blood to stream."[1095] The practice is required of men, but mothers stand on the sidelines, encouraging their sons to follow the men's example. For instance, the Associated Press published a photo with the caption,

> A Shiite woman beats her four-year-old son with a sword in the southern Lebanese town of Nabatiyeh Saturday, May 17, 1997. For the second day, thousands of Shiite Muslim commemorated Ashoura, the seventh century martyrdom of their most revered saint....[1096]

If Islam tolerates and possibly condones a mother hitting her four-year-old with a sword as part of a religious ritual, why would anyone assume all Muslims would be so westernized that they would refrain from executing "infidels" with swords?

To Kill with Hunger

> And power was given unto them over the fourth part of the earth, to kill with sword, and with hunger, (Rev. 6:8b KJV)

A second method of Green-Horse killing is hunger or famine. The Greek word *limos* (λιμός), literally "a scarcity of harvest," is also used by Jesus in Matthew 24:7 as a feature of the time when the kingdom of darkness will battle against the kingdom of God.[1097] The good news is that God assures us He will take care of us even in times of famine!

> [35]Who shall separate us from the love of Christ? [shall] tribulation, or distress, or persecution, or famine [*limos,* λιμός], or nakedness, or peril, or sword? [36]As

it is written, For thy sake we are killed all the day long; we are accounted as sheep for the slaughter. [37]Nay, in all these things we are more than conquerors through him that loved us. [38]For I am persuaded, that neither death, nor life, nor angels, nor principalities, nor powers, nor things present, nor things to come, [39]Nor height, nor depth, nor any other creature, shall be able to separate us from the love of God, which is in Christ Jesus our Lord. (Rom. 8:35–39 AV)

It seems difficult for those of us living in the Western world to take the prospect of famine seriously. I have heard people argue that the "time of the end" cannot be happening because they have not yet experienced famine. However, widespread famine is raging in many parts of the world, and "global food security" is of ongoing concern to the United Nations.

The Club of Rome has worried that agricultural production was vulnerable to global warming-induced droughts and the Green Revolution farming methods that made food production and distribution so dependent on petroleum. It reported that the world food supply was sufficient to provide approximately 19 percent more calories than necessary to adequately feed every man, woman, and child on the planet. Nevertheless, they observed,

> hunger and malnutrition persist in vast areas, worsened by drought, famine and warfare. It seems, therefore, that the production of enough food has little relevance to the persistence of hunger in the world ... The hungry are the poor, unable to buy the food that exists, so that hunger in large areas of the world is but a symptom of the basic problem of poverty. It is true that more people are being fed adequately [but] ... in absolute terms, hunger continues to grow.[1098]

Hunger and Poverty

Hunger and poverty go hand in hand. The international poverty line, near a dollar a day, is scarcely enough to meet even the most basic of needs, including adequate food. The World Bank estimates the effect of the one-two punch of skyrocketing global food prices in 2008 followed by a worldwide recession in 2009 and 2010 pushed between 100 and 150 million people below the poverty line. Millions of people suffer from hunger and severe malnutrition. Each day, thousands of children die of starvation, an average of one every five seconds.[1099] Many more suffer from malnutrition, the state of not getting enough nutrients to support normal growth and development.

> Half of all children under five years of age in South Asia and one third of those in sub-Saharan Africa are malnourished ... Malnutrition is implicated in more than half of all child deaths worldwide—a proportion unmatched by any infectious disease since the Black Death.[1100]

It is tempting to dismiss hunger as a problem of Third World nations such as those in East Africa. However, the United States, one of the wealthiest countries on the globe, is not immune to food insecurity. Approximately one out of every eight American children under the age of twelve goes to bed hungry each night.[1101] The U.S. Department of Agriculture estimates that almost 15 percent of American households struggle to put food on the table and that 20 percent of all children are at risk of hunger. The figures are even more daunting for minority children. Ironically, poverty and food insecurity are key predictors of obesity, particularly in children. Thanks to government food subsidies, poor Americans eat a diet of cheap processed foods that are high in calories but lack adequate nutrition.[1102]

Hunger and Parasitic Weeds

Noxious and parasitic weeds are a growing contributor to famine. Witchweed (*striga*) is considered by many to be "among the most destructive and difficult to control weeds in agriculture," the king of noxious weeds. The seeds, which can remain dormant in the ground for up to a decade, grow in the roots of many staple grain and legume crops, including corn, sugarcane, and sorghum, and are virtually undetectable until the crop damage has been done. Witchweed is particularly devastating in Africa, where about two-thirds of cropland is affected and yield losses can be as high as 100 percent.[1103]

Another parasitic weed is broomrape (*orobanche*), which attacks a wide range of crops including tomatoes, potatoes, eggplant, pepper, and legumes as well as tobacco. The Food and Agriculture Organization of the United Nations reports that

> both complexes of parasitic weeds cause huge crop yield losses annually, and in severe cases when the infestation is very high farmers have no other option than to abandon their fields. The situation is aggravated by the fact that pressure for land has increased at the same time as demographic growth in several countries affected by the parasitic weeds. In the past long fallow was practised largely for the control of *Striga* or *Orobanche* ... but nowadays this method of rotation is not possible due to the shortage of land—particularly non-infested—and the accelerated degradation and impoverishment of soils.[1104]

Hunger and Drought

Drought, a classic cause of famine, has been a key factor in food scarcity in Africa. The Sahel is a swath of land running from Senegal on the Atlantic seaboard across Africa to the Red Sea. The name means "shore," and it functions much like a shoreline between the savannah grasslands to the south and the Sahara Desert to the north. During the rainy season, which varies from one to three months, it is lush and green, but afterward, during the dry season, the grasses die and many trees lose their leaves, making it very challenging to survive.

Over the last forty years, the area has been wracked with severe droughts that are pushing the Sahara south and destroying farmland. Between 1968 and 1973, as many as 250,000 people died in the drought, and famine continues to threaten the area.[1105] The UN estimates that more than 16 million people in the region are at risk of famine. Drought has caused declines in crop yields of up to 50 percent, forcing food prices up to unaffordable levels. The resulting desertification of the Sahel has triggered mass migration of thousands to the south.[1106]

Meanwhile, the Horn of Africa struggles with famine (in 2011) after two years without rain. More than 10 million people are suffering from the impact of the drought, and more than a thousand arrive at the Dadaab refugee camp in east Kenya daily. Livestock, often the sum total of a family's wealth, drop like flies. Mounds mark the graves of those who have fallen victim to famine and dehydration. Mothers frequently allow weaker children to die so they can pour their resources into the strongest. No wonder the BBC described the Horn of Africa as a "vision of hell."[1107]

To grasp the desperateness of the situation, envision the arrival of 21,000 refugees to a camp in the middle of the Somali war zone in just ten days in July 2011. Since the camp is only 400 meters from the frontline, it is often hit by cross fire. Still, the availability of food and water makes conditions in the camp better than those at home.[1108]

Ironically, the impact of the drought has been exacerbated by the policies of the al-Shabab, an al-Qaeda–affiliated Islamic group that controls large areas of Somalia. This Green Horse organization generally refuses to allow Western groups, including the United Nations, to enter the area, and those who are permitted are charged significant fees to operate. As a result, the famine is "far worse in areas under its control than other parts of the country...."[1109]

Hunger and Natural Disasters

Floods and other natural disasters also contribute to famine. For example, the monsoon of 2010 brought a deluge of water that caused widespread, devastating flooding to Pakistan. "A torrent of freezing cold water, which eventually went roof-high, had come in the dead of night and by the next afternoon, almost everything was washed away." [1110] When the waters receded, what was left was a quagmire littered with the corpses of drowned livestock and stagnant pools. Approximately 20 million people, living in an area the size of England, lost everything.[1111] United Nations officials reported that 6 million were without drinking water or adequate food and estimated it would take three years for the area to recover from the disaster.[1112]

Ironically, the most insidious threat of famine is the agricultural methods developed as part of the Green Revolution. The GMO crops that dominate much of modern food production yield an abundance of food only under ideal conditions. However, their operational yields from actual farms have been found to be no better than traditional crops, but a lot more expensive to grow. Not only must GMO soybeans and corn be purchase anew each year—saving GMO seeds is considered a copyright violation and is illegal—but it requires liberal applications of expensive chemicals, representing a huge investment on the part of farmers. For many, a bad year equals ruin, with no option but suicide.[1113]

When ancient Egypt experienced a severe seven year famine under Joseph, the food collected in Pharaoh's storehouses fed the people but at the cost of their livestock, their homes, and their liberty. By the end of the famine, Pharaoh owned all of Egypt and his subjects were his slaves. The new high-tech seeds ensure that even a year or two of crop failures will cause men to cut a deal with the devil in desperation. Stalin and others have clearly demonstrated how food can be used as a political tool.

The Green Revolution has set in place the potential of "killing by famine."

CHAPTER 31:

Power to Kill— Death and Beasts

To Kill With Death

> And power was given unto them over the fourth part of the earth, to kill with sword, and with hunger, and with death, and with the beasts of the earth (Rev. 6:8b KJV).

"Killing with death." This seems like the ultimate in redundancy, except for the fact there are no superfluous words in Scripture. However, in Hebrew word repetition is commonly used for emphasis. The best-known example is the partitioning of the temple into the Holy Place and the Holy of Holies, literally the Holy Holy Place. Since John was a Hebrew, it should not surprise us to find Hebraic idioms within his writing.

Killing is the translation of the Greek *apokteino* (ἀποκτείνω), meaning to **kill in any way whatever**, to destroy, to allow to perish, to inflict mortal death (emphasis mine). Killing in any way possible is a key theme in Revelation; 20 percent of the biblical uses of apokteino appear in John's vision.[1114] The Greek word *thanatos* (θάνατος), translated "death," can refer to the death of the body but implies the miseries of sin and the darkness of the "nether world, the abode of the dead," or "the misery of the soul arising from sin, which begins on earth but lasts and increases after the death of the body in hell."[1115]

In other words, killing by death is the process of doing whatever it takes to either kill people physically or to sear their souls to such an extent that nothing can move them to repent and turn back to God. This explains the human reactions to the plagues as they were being poured out of the bowls onto the earth.

> [9]And men were scorched with great heat, and blasphemed the name of God, which hath power over these plagues: and they repented not to give him glory. [10]And the fifth angel poured out his vial upon the seat of the beast; and his kingdom was full of darkness; and they gnawed their tongues for pain, [11]And blasphemed the God of heaven because of their pains and their sores, and repented not of their deeds. (Rev. 16:9–11 KJV)

It would appear that nothing God does, whether blessings or disasters, can penetrate the hearts of those whose souls have been hardened by this form of death.

Killing by Death the Modern Way

The traditional causes of death and the leading causes of death today are different. Yes, there are some similarities. People died of apoplexy (probably heart attacks) and long-lingering illnesses such as consumption (tuberculosis or possibly cancer) in the "good old days." However, the top killers of the past were infectious diseases and malnutrition, both of which are most likely to strike at the very young and the elderly.

The Mortality Bill for London in 1665 gives us a good picture of the traditional causes of death. Looking through the statistics, we see a few people died from the killers most familiar to us: apoplexy (probably heart attack or stroke—116), cancer and gangrene (56), and old age (1,545). Remarkably, only 9 people were murdered in the entire city of London that year. [1116]

By comparison, infectious diseases were the top cause of

death. They included plague (68,596), fever (5,257), consumption (tuberculosis—4,808), dropsy (1,478), smallpox (655), "griping in the guts" (1,288), colic and wind (134), "spotted fever and purples" (1,929), surfeit (1,251), and "teeth and worms" (these victims presumably died from dental abscesses—2,614). [1117]

Afflictions caused by malnutrition also ravaged Londoners. These included rickets (557), scurvy (105), starvation (45) and convulsion—most cases where probably related to the use of lead drinking vessels (2036). In other words, 90 percent of the population died of disease and malnutrition.[1118]

When we look at the leading causes of death today, there are significant differences based on income levels. The World Health Organization lists the top ten killers both globally and according to income ranking. Interestingly, the death rates associated with childbearing are similar in the low-income nations of today and seventeenth-century London (2.9 compared to 2.7 percent). Infectious diseases, which ravaged old London, still account for six of the ten leading killers in today's low-income nations. In high-income nations, the only infectious disease to make the top ten list is "lower respiratory infections," generally an opportunist condition such as pneumonia that strikes those who are elderly or have compromised health. Although HIV/AIDS does not even make the list in developed countries, it is taking a devastating toll in low-income nations, especially among younger adults in the most productive years of their lives.

In high-income nations, the top killers are cardiovascular diseases and cancers. Almost a third of deaths worldwide can be attributed to these two causes, compared to 16 percent from all infectious diseases, including HIV/AIDS. In addition to heart disease and cancer, diabetes and Alzheimer's appear to be diseases of the modern age, as came be seen in Table 2.[1119]

Causes of Death	Low Income	Middle Income	High Income	World	London 1665
Infectious Disease	31.60%	12.20%	3.80%	12.80%	19.95%
HIV/AIDS/Plague	7.80%	2.70%	0.00%	3.10%	70.50%
Infectious Subtotal	*39.40%*	*14.90%*	*3.80%*	*15.90%*	*90.45%*
Malnutrition	3.20%	0.00%	0.00%	0.00%	0.73%
Birth Difficulties	2.90%	0.00%	0.00%	0.00%	2.73%
Alzheimer's	0.00%	0.00%	4.10%	0.00%	0.00%
Cardiopulmonary diseases	11.00%	35.90%	30.10%	29.40%	0.12%
Cancers	0.00%	0.00%	11.10%	2.40%	0.06%
Car Accidents	0.00%	2.40%	0.00%	2.10%	0.00%
Diabetes	0.00%	2.30%	2.60%	2.20%	0.00%
Total	*56.50%*	*55.50%*	*51.70%*	*52.00%*	*94.09%*

*Table 2: Causes of death as listed by WHO[1120]
and the City of London 1665[1121]*

*Note: the WHO percentages add up to less than 100 percent since they include the
top ten causes of death only.*

Killing by Death: Syndrome X

Most of us can recite the killers that plague modern society,
things such as AIDS, illegal drugs, and violence. However, the data
show that several of the top ten killers in high-income nations are
cardiovascular diseases such as heart disease, high blood pressure,
and stroke. This cluster of illnesses, sometimes called syndrome X or
metabolic syndrome,[1122] are interlinked. For instance, the syndrome
is link with obesity and high blood pressure; the latter is the most
common risk factor for heart disease and often leads to stroke.[1123]

Obesity has been implicated in the rise of these killers as well as
type 2 diabetes and certain cancers, which are other leading causes

of death in high-income nations. It is no coincidence that the United States is experiencing an "epidemic" of obesity at the same time. In 2009, the Centers for Disease Control and Prevention reported that at least 20 percent of American adults are obese, and in some parts of the country the rate is more than 30 percent.[1124]

High rates of obesity among adults are concerning enough. However, recent studies found that half of American children already have risk factors for heart attacks. A third of school children are overweight, with 20 percent classified as obese; the study also found that 20 percent of children have high cholesterol levels. These statistics virtually guarantee that the number of deaths from heart attacks and related diseases will skyrocket in the future.[1125] Alarming rates of obesity are not limited to the West. Since 1980, global obesity rates have doubled.[1126]

Many blame the surge in obesity rates on the standard American diet, which is full of highly refined, calorie-dense foods loaded with fat, salt, and sugar. Experts dutifully warn us this sort of diet is bad for us and to eat a healthy diet. Obesity, they say, is a matter of self-control and making good choices. What most experts fail to mention is that Americans are bombarded with foods that are cheap (read "government subsidized crops" such as corn[1127]), convenient (think "fast"), and carefully designed to trigger our innate cravings.

> The industry blames obesity on a crisis of personal responsibility. But when you're engineering foods you are pressing our evolutionary buttons. The fact is we're hardwired to go for three tastes—salt, fat and sugar. These things are very rare in nature. Now sugar is available 24/7 in tremendous quantities. We're eating hundreds of pounds of the stuff a year.[1128]

The food industry's advertising bombardment begins in early childhood. In 2009, Neilsen reported that preschoolers watch an average of thirty-two hours of TV a week, while school-aged children watch about twenty-eight hours a week. Researchers noted that "increased television watching is linked to delayed language skills and obesity."[1129] As anyone who has watched Saturday morning cartoons knows, children's television shows are laced with slick advertising for fast-food outlets and processed foods. This advertising is incredibly effective, and when kids have the opportunity to buy these products, they do.

For example, a study of millions of schoolchildren found that ninth graders who attend schools near fast-food outlets are more likely to be obese than their peers whose schools are at least a quarter-mile from one. Another study of weight gain during pregnancy revealed a similar pattern. The data are compelling enough to make one specialist in food policy and obesity to state, "Zoning laws that prohibit fast-food restaurants near schools are absolutely indicated, and neighborhoods that choose to zone out fast-food restaurants are probably taking a step to protect the future health of their children."[1130]

Killing by Death: High-Tech Foods

Highly processed foods bear little resemblance to their raw ingredients and are loaded with strange new ingredients unheard of by our forefathers. Our food supply has been permeated with hybrid crops, genetically modified crops, substances derived from them such as high-fructose corn syrup and a host of chemicals additives. Many experts are implicating these laboratory-created foods in the modern epidemic of obesity and its companion diseases.

Genetically modified crops, especially corn and soybeans, have come to dominate the American food supply both as fodder for livestock and as key ingredients for thousands of grocery products from soft drinks to baked goods. Approximately 70 percent of what we eat is based on corn and soy. Corn is used in obvious products like corn chips, and in highly refined corn products such as corn oil and the ubiquitous high-fructose corn syrup found in ketchup and other condiments, beverages, and baked goods. Americans eat so much corn that much of their hair is made up of a form of carbon unique to corn. In addition, it is estimated that soybean oil alone accounts "for an astonishing 10 percent of our total calories in the United States."[1131]

In addition to the health implications of a diet that relies so heavily on just two crops is the fact that most of the corn and soy produced are GMO. The most common GMO crops have pesticides and herbicides biogenetically engineered into them. We are forced to ingest these toxins since they are impossible to wash off. Furthermore, the widespread cultivation of these GMO crops washed in gallons of Roundup is creating super-weeds that are impervious to even the strongest weed killers. How do these chemicals affect the human body? There is a growing body of evidence that GMO foods are linked to shorter life spans and infertility.

> Offspring of rats fed GM soy showed a five-fold increase in mortality, lower birth weights, and the inability to reproduce; male mice fed GM soy had damaged young sperm cells; the embryo offspring of GM soy-fed mice had altered DNA functioning; many US farmers report sterility or fertility problems among pigs and cows fed GM corn; investigators in India have documented fertility problems, abortions, premature births, and other serious health issues, including deaths, among buffaloes fed GM cottonseed products. Additionally Data [sic] from 19 animal studies has linked GM foods to organ disruption. A Purdue University researcher has found a new organism related to GM corn and soy appears to be responsible for plant death, and infertility and abortion in animals given GM feed.[1132]

Another "frankenfood" is high-fructose corn syrup (HFCS), sometimes referred to as corn sugar, which is the main sweetener in soft drinks, juice-like products, and many commercial baked goods. Like sucrose (table sugar), it is clearly implicated in both obesity and Type 2 diabetes when eaten in "pharmacologic doses" of 140 pounds per person per year. Natural sugars, such as the kind found in fruit, come packaged with fiber and nutrients, drastically slowing their absorption into the blood stream. Even table sugar, a two-sugar molecule made of glucose and fructose tightly bonded together, requires digestive enzymes to split apart before it can be absorbed.

In contrast, high-fructose corn syrup, which is extracted from corn stalks through a top-secret, industrial chemical process, consists of 55 percent fructose to 45 percent glucose in an "unbounded" form. This means that there is nothing to hinder the absorption of these sugars directly into the blood stream. The dump of glucose triggers a spike of insulin, leading to insulin resistance and all the diseases that accompany syndrome X.[1133]

The impact of glucose is benign compared to that of fructose. Like alcohol, fructose can be metabolized only by the liver, where it is converted into new fatty acids (triglycerides and cholesterol), which get stored in adipose tissue (fat cells). Not only does fructose metabolism divert the liver from its many essential functions, but it is also the leading cause of liver disease. In fact, from the liver's perspective, there is no difference between fructose and alcohol. According to Dr. Lustig, fructose is ethanol without the buzz. He points out, "You wouldn't think twice about not giving your kid a beer, but you don't think twice about giving your kid a can of Coke."[1134] Finally, Lustig and others found that fructose fails to trigger hormones that regulate appetite and metabolism. By making the brain feel that the body is starving, it results in increased appetite and weight gain. "In short, the more HFCS you consume, the more HFCS you may want to eat."[1135]

Hybrid strains of wheat and other grains have also been implicated in the obesity epidemic. The ubiquitous wheat that forms the staple of the modern diet is not an heirloom plant but a hybrid dwarf plant designed to produce high yields quickly. This is the backbone of the Green Revolution of fifty years ago. While saving hundreds of thousands from starvation, it also contains proteins not found in nature that have negative consequences on our bodies. Dr. William Davis found that modern hybrid wheat raised his blood sugar more than three times higher compared with an ancient strain of wheat. In fact, Dr. William Davis states, "Wheat products elevate blood sugar levels more than virtually any other carbohydrate, from beans to candy bars."[1136] Given the epidemic of type 2 diabetes, especially among teens, this is cause for concern. Davis makes a strong case that our consumption of modern wheat is a cofactor in a range of other health problems, including obesity.

> While much of the Wheat Belly story is about overweight, it is also about the complex and not fully understood range of diseases that have resulted from

it—from celiac disease, the devastating intestinal disease that develops from exposure to wheat gluten, to an assortment of neurological disorders, curious rashes, and the paralyzing effects of schizophrenia. Documented peculiar effects of wheat on humans include appetite stimulation, exposure to brain-active exorphins (the counterpart of internally derived endorphins), exaggerated blood-sugar surges that trigger cycles of satiety alternating with increased appetite, the process of glycation that underlies diseases and aging, inflammatory and pH effects that erode cartilage and damage bone, and activation of disordered immune response.[1137]

Excitotoxins: MSG and Aspartame

Another suspect in the obesity epidemic is MSG (monosodium glutamate), a flavor enhancer found in a myriad of food products from soups to hamburger to baby formula. Yes, even baby formula contains MSG, also known as L-glutamic acid, despite the fact that a FDA sponsored study stated that "it is prudent to avoid the use of dietary supplements of L-glutamic acid by pregnant women, infants, and children ... [and] by women of childbearing age and individuals with affective disorders."[1138]

Putting aside safety concerns about babies ingesting food additives, the fact remains that MSG causes obesity in laboratory mice, and its introduction into the food supply corresponds with the surge in obesity rates. Furthermore, MSG and the ubiquitous sweetener aspartame (brand name NutraSweet) are excitotoxins that both stimulate and poison the brain. It has been linked to sudden cardiac arrest, especially in young people with no previous history of heart disease.[1139]

Neurologists have found that some excitotoxins, including those routinely added to many commercial foods, have been found to "freely penetrate certain brain regions and rapidly destroy neurons" This can cause brain damage in vulnerable populations such as the young and the elderly.

Thus, the human food supply is a source of excitotoxins that can damage the brain by one type of mechanism to which immature consumers are hypervulnerable, or by other mechanisms to which adult and elderly consumers are peculiarly sensitive.[1140]

Carcinogenics and Modern Times

Cancer is the other great killer of modern times. The very mention of a diagnosis of cancer is enough to send shivers of fear through most people. As we noted earlier, cancer was very rare in earlier times, but now three of the top ten killers in high-income nations are cancers: lung cancer (number 3), colon cancer (number 7), and breast cancer (number 10).[1141] The rise in cancer rates is not surprising since we live in an environment awash in cancer-causing agents.

The U.S. government lists many commonplace items as carcinogens, including asbestos, a popular building material for years;[1142] formaldehyde, which is used in a wide variety of household products including fabrics, adhesives, building supplies, and nail polish;[1143] and even some hair dyes.[1144] Sunlight[1145] and smoking[1146] are also risk factors. This doesn't take into account items that are possible carcinogens, including various food additives, molecules found in plastic bottles, and the electromagnetic fields emitted by cell phones and other electronics.

As if introducing a vast array of chemicals into our environment was not sufficient cause for alarm, our world has been bombarded with the effects of hundreds of nuclear explosions. Since 1945, there have been 522 atmospheric detonations, 1,892 underground detonations, and 8 underwater detonations. That's a total of 2,422 nuclear detonations over the last sixty-five years. All were test detonations, with the exception of the bombs dropped on Nagasaki and Hiroshima. Although these two clearly had devastating impact, they were small blips compared with some of the explosions that followed. Given the impact of nuclear fallout on the human body and the environment, it's a wonder we don't all suffer from cancer of one form or another.[1147]

To Kill with the Beasts of the Earth

> And power was given unto them over the fourth part
> of the earth, to kill with sword, and with hunger,
> and with death, and with the beasts of the earth.
> (Rev. 6:8b KJV)

The fourth mode of killing that will be associated with the Green Horseman seems something of an enigma. Our ancestors had far more reason to fear being mauled by a wild animal than we do. However, two trends may provide insight into the fulfillment of this prophesy: the animal rights movement and role of animals in the spread of disease.

Animals have enjoyed more protection and a higher prestige than any time in recorded history unless the particular animal had the good fortune to be the object of worship. Until modern times, animals were valued for their usefulness to humans. Horses were the major means of transportation. Dogs were used for guarding property, to assist with hunting or in agriculture, as was the case with sheepdogs. Cats were used for killing vermin; sheep were valued for their wool. Cattle, sheep, pigs, and poultry were raised for food and various byproducts such as leather. Animals were certainly kept as pets, but practical needs ensured affection played a secondary role.

Practicality also ensured that livestock lived in fairly natural surroundings. Flocks and herds grazed in pastures, poultry scratched for bugs on the ground, and pigs were corralled in barnyard sties or even let loose to forage in the woods. There were cruel and selfish men who mistreated their animals, but the vital role animals played in the lives of their owners gave strong incentive to keep livestock alive and in decent health until the moment of slaughter.

Under the Green Horseman, the status of animals has been completely transformed. On one hand, agribusiness has ensured that those who care for livestock no longer make decisions about their treatment or well-being. Instead, livestock are kept in crowded feedlots and poultry houses to be fattened up on corn and soy-based feeds. The feed is laced with hormones to ensure rapid growth and antibiotics to prevent infections caused by overcrowding.[1148]

At the same time, many in the animal rights movement have progressed beyond pushing for the humane treatment of animals to advocating that animals be treated as persons. They consider it morally wrong to use animals, whom they consider to be nonhuman persons, for food, clothing (think "leather"), research, or entertainment.[1149]

Environmentalism has involved campaigns to artificially reestablish animal populations into areas where they once existed before being settled by humans. The most famous is the reintroduction of wolves in wilderness areas including Yellowstone National Park. Wolves were deemed helpful to the environment by checking growth in coyote and elk populations that had boomed in the absence of a larger preditor.[1150]

However, wolves also prey on livestock. Wolves are opportunistic hunters, meaning they go after the easiest prey, including livestock. The reason wolves were hunted out of much of North America and Europe in the first place is because they have been a direct threat to human survival by killing the animals we depend on. Generally, wolves prey on the young in a herd, meaning the most likely livestock victims are calves and lambs. Although Defenders of Wildlife have a program to compensate ranchers for their losses, it is estimated only 10 percent of kills can actually be proven, since wolves and the scavengers that follow, leave no evidence uneaten.

Growing wolf populations have a devastating impact on herd wildlife such as elk, deer and moose. While it was true there were reports of overpopulation of these animals in national parks, the excess population can easily be thinned by hunting. Hunting licenses can ensure that the young are not taken but remain to continue a healthy herd. Thinning by wolves is not so careful; in fact, wolves are specifically most likely to kill the young preventing the herds from reproducing and endangering their existence. Under these conditions, hunting will not be permitted.[1151]

Killing with Animals: Carriers of Disease

Animals have long been associated with the spread of disease. Without rats carrying fleas infected with the plague bacillus, the Black Death that devastated late medieval Europe would never have happened. In fact, the bubonic plague is still killing today; the World

Health Organization reports up to 3,000 cases each year. Fortunately, early treatment with antibiotics has proven effective against the disease.[1152] Since the start of the Green Horseman's ride, the news has been sprinkled with reports of looming pandemics, including swine flu, bird flu, West Nile virus, mad cow disease and Ebola, all of which have been transferred from animal to human populations.

The H1N1 virus, or swine flu, was declared a pandemic by the World Health Organization in 2009.[1153] The swine flu virus, so named because it shares genes with a virus that is commonly found in pigs, rarely passes to humans. However, the H1N1 strain was able to pass between humans in a manner similar to the strain that caused the flu epidemic of 1918.[1154]

Avian flu, or bird flu, is caused by a virus usually found in birds. A particularly pathological strain of avian flu caused a pandemic that killed millions of birds and has been passing from birds to humans since 1987, resulting in "clinically severe and fatal human infections."[1155]

West Nile virus, frequently passed from birds to humans through mosquitoes, has one of three outcomes. It can be asymptomatic, it may produce a mild fever, or it may result in meningitis or encephalitis, both of which are life-threatening.[1156]

Hoof and mouth disease once instilled terror into the hearts of farmers, but now it is mad cow disease. Also known as bovine spongiform encephalopathy, the disease is a progressive neurological disorder caused by the mutation of normal prion proteins. Researchers suspect it resulted from feeding cattle meat and bone meal containing beef or sheep material infected with the diseases. Creutzfeldt-Jacob disease, a similar illness found in humans, is "thought to be caused by eating beef products from BSE-infected cattle."[1157]

Ebola, a viral infection most commonly found in Africa, usually causes flu-like symptoms. Unfortunately, about 10 percent of its victims experience bleeding from the mucus membranes. The disease is often transmitted from animal to human hosts.

> Outbreaks of EVD among human populations generally result from handling infected wild animal carcasses. Declines in animal populations generally precede outbreaks among human populations.[1158]

Conclusion

In high school, I read a poem by Edwin Brock entitled, "Five Ways to Kill a Man." After describing a Roman crucifixion, knightly jousts, the trench warfare of World War I, and the dropping of a nuclear bomb, it concludes,

> These are, as I began, cumbersome ways
> to kill a man. Simpler, direct and much more neat
> is to see that he is living somewhere in the middle
> of the twentieth century, and leave him there.[1159]

We have reviewed only a handful of lethal methods available today. Ironically, humans of the late twentieth century were living longer than any others in recorded history (with the exception of Adam and his pre-flood descendants). However, warnings that today's children are likely to die younger than their parents are being announced by the media in Canada,[1160] the United States,[1161] and Britain.[1162] It is easy to get caught up in feelings of fear and impending doom when you start to listen to the news pundits broadcasting the latest political or economic development. We are pummeled with reports of wars, violent crimes, revolutions, floods, famines, natural disasters, and the latest cancer risk or threat to our well-being. Evil reports come at us with the relentless intensity of labor contractions. And that is the good news!

Don't panic! We are in labor. We are preparing to give birth. When I was in labor with my first child, an experienced mother coached me to focus on my breathing, to focus on something on the wall, to focus on anything but the labor contractions. It worked. In the same way, we must focus on Jesus, on His Word, and on breathing in the sweet presence of the Holy Spirit. This is what will enable us to endure the labor pains and push through the pressure to the end.

CHAPTER 32:

A Fourth Beast

⁷After this I saw in the night visions, and behold a fourth beast, dreadful and terrible, and strong exceedingly; and it had great iron teeth: it devoured and brake in pieces, and stamped the residue with the feet of it: and it [was] diverse from all the beasts that [were] before it; and it had ten horns. ⁸ I considered the horns, and, behold, there came up among them another little horn, before whom there were three of the first horns plucked up by the roots: and, behold, in this horn [were] eyes like the eyes of man, and a mouth speaking great things. ⁹ I beheld till the thrones were cast down, and the Ancient of days did sit...

¹¹ I beheld then because of the voice of the great words which the horn spake: I beheld [even] till the beast was slain, and his body destroyed, and given to the burning flame. ¹²As concerning the rest of the beasts, they had their dominion taken away: yet their lives were prolonged for a season and time. (Dan. 7:7–9c, 11–12 KJV)

The Green Horseman described in Revelation corresponds to a fourth beast in Daniel's vision. While Daniel paints a clear picture of the first three beasts, his description of the fourth is more like a teaser for a horror film—you're not sure what it is, but you know it's really scary! According to Daniel, this beast is "dreadful and terrible" with incredible strength—this from a man who just saw a lion, a bear, and a leopard! This creature was different from its predecessors, and it terrified Daniel. All he could see was "great iron teeth" that "devoured and brake in pieces," and stomping feet with brass claws that destroyed everything in its wake. Nothing escapes this thing until the Ancient of Days returns (Dan 7:9).

> After this I saw in the night visions, and behold a fourth beast, dreadful and terrible, and strong exceedingly; and it had great iron teeth: it devoured and brake in pieces, and stamped the residue with the feet of it …
> (Dan. 7:7a KJV)

Daniel describes this beast as "dreadful, terrible and exceedingly strong." The Aramaic word *dechal* (דחל), translated "dreadful," is actually a verb, and implies the kind of fear that makes one creep along as quietly as possible so as not to attract attention.[1163] It is too powerful to fight, and its reach is too long to risk fleeing openly. Suddenly, the actions of "preppers" who practice survival and self-sufficiency seem less like paranoia and more like a rational response to what was prophesied in Scripture.

This beast is also "terrible"; the Aramaic word *emtaniy* (אמתני)[1164] comes from a Hebrew word meaning "loins" and the strength bound up in them.[1165] This was the part of the body covered with what Paul referred to as the "belt of truth" (Eph. 6:14), the place where a soldier would hang his weapons and other equipment in readiness.[1166] The beast has the power and ability to do whatever it desires. It can see its prey and nothing can stop it. Today, we see businessmen hanging cell phones on their belts unaware they are two-way radio tracking devices that enable government agents to monitor the user's whereabouts and conversations at all times.[1167]

The Green Horseman is given the power "over the fourth part of the earth, to kill" (Rev. 6:8). Daniel uses three verbs to describe the way this fourth beast/horseman kills with its teeth and feet. First, the beast is devouring; the tense of the Aramaic verb to eat (*akal*, אכל) "represents an action or condition in its unbroken continuity."[1168] In other words, the fourth beast is constantly devouring people with an appetite never satiated. Think "Hitler" on an international scale.

Second, it causes everything to be smashed into pieces. The verb *deqaq* (דְּקַק) is a participle in the causative tense. Not satisfied with devouring everything it sees and leaving a few crumbs behind, the beast will not stop until everything in its wake is smashed into dust. Daniel is the only biblical author to use this word, and he uses it three times in reference to the fourth beast (Dan. 7:7, 19, 23). He uses it twice to describe how the lions treated those who had accused Daniel after they were thrown into the lion's den (Dan. 6:24). The word is used seven times in the account of King Nebuchadnezzar's dream of the statue that is broken to pieces by the "stone ... cut out without hands" (Dan. 2:34, 35, 40, 44, 45). The stone, which represents Jesus and His kingdom, smashes the statue so completely that the remains are like chaff carried off in the wind. In the same way, the fourth beast will use his mouth to reduce everything not under his power to the level of insignificance.[1169]

Finally, the beast tramples—*rephas* (רְפַס) in Aramaic—whatever is left under his feet.[1170] The corresponding Hebrew word, *raphas* (רָפַס), is associated with the idea of lying prostrate under the feet of someone in humility or submission.[1171] Islam, which literally means submission, has a long history of forcing those who surrender to jihadist armies to submit to *dhimmitude*. This is a state of protection from the penalties for infidels—death and slavery—along with limited religious freedom and autonomy. The institution of dhimmitude is the perfect example of a vanquished people being forced into humiliating submission under the feet of the conquerors.

> These rights are subject to two conditions: the payment of a poll tax (the *jizya*) and submission to the provisions of Islamic law. The concept of toleration is linked to a number of discriminatory obligations in the economic, religious and social fields, imposed by the *shari'a* on the *dhimmis*. The transgression by the *dhimmis* of some of these obligations, abolished their protection, and threaten them with death or slavery. *Dhimmis* suffered many legal disabilities intended to reduce them to a condition of humiliation, segregation and discrimination.[1172]

Thus, Daniel's fourth beast has two components, the mouth and the feet, which correspond to the two riders of the Green Horse; whatever survives the devouring, devastating edicts from the mouth of the Green political agenda will be trampled into absolute submission by the feet of jihadist Islam.

No wonder Daniel observes that this beast is different from all that came before it: "It [was] diverse from all the beasts that [were] before it, and it had ten horns" (Dan. 7:7b KJV). The Aramaic word *shena* (שְׁנָה) is translated "different" or sometimes "diverse," but that omits an important inference; the word literally means changing or altering something, "especially for the worse." Daniel uses this word six times to describe the fourth beast and its kingdom. He also uses it to describe the succession of the four beasts that he envisions coming out of the sea, implying that the impact of each successive beast is worse than the previous one.[1173]

Daniel's final beast has ten horns, but he is not the only prophet to envision a ten-horned beast rising out of the sea. In Revelation, John records,

> [1]And I stood upon the sand of the sea, and saw a beast rise up out of the sea, having seven heads and ten horns, and upon his horns ten crowns, and upon his heads the name of blasphemy. [2]And the beast which I saw was like unto a leopard, and his feet were as [the feet] of a bear, and his mouth as the mouth of a lion: and the dragon gave him his power, and his seat, and great authority. (Rev. 13:1–2 KJV)

Daniel's fourth beast is the dreaded beast in Revelation, the one that rules the earth until Jesus comes back, the beast whose power and authority are given to him by the dragon, Satan himself. John's description reveals that the fourth beast is actually a composite of the three previous ones. It will have a familiar appearance "like unto a leopard," the Black Horseman system that has enslaved the world with debt, inflation, and globalism. As a result, this final beast's arrival will be barely perceptible since it will look so much like what has gone before it. In fact, people around the globe will worship those who personify the beast, believing they hold the solutions to the world's problems.

The beast of Revelation does not have leopard's feet; its "feet were as [the feet] of a bear" (Rev. 13:2 KJV). Daniel's description of trampling feet with claws of brass (Dan. 7:19) correspond to the Red Horseman and its penchant for ruthless, democidal killing, especially of "useless eaters" such as the elderly, the infirmed, unborn babies, and anyone who disagrees. Think of a blend of Adolf Hitler and Joseph Stalin with twenty-first century technology at their disposal.

The beast has the "mouth of a lion," a mouth that speaks like the royal elites of the White Horseman, an elite that does not care what hurt may result from its self-serving edicts but cares only that every vestige of wealth goes to feed its insatiable appetite. This is an elite that receives from the dragon "his power, his throne, and his authority." In other words, the world will be ruled by Satan-worshipping, self-serving elitists. This is not as farfetched as it sounds. Remember the Gaia hypothesis?

Finally, both John and Daniel record that the beast has ten horns. In 1973, the Club of Rome published a report that recommended dividing the globe into ten administrative regions, as shown in Map 16, to facilitate the global governance.[1174]

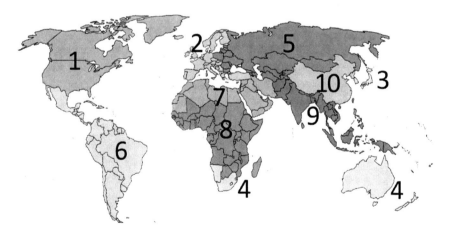

Map 16: Ten regions of the world from Club of Rome report.[1175]

Conclusion

Over the last thirty years, we have seen the dual movements of the Green political agenda and Green radical Islam rise to global significance. Everywhere we see trends that will hold the promise of killing by "death" unless they are reversed, and most of us are powerless to halt them. Those who have the power seem determined to push them forward. The leaders of both Green movements have two things in common: the desire to kill vast numbers of the human population, although with different criteria, and a hatred of the God of the Bible and His Anointed Messiah, and those who belong to Him.

Take heart, for the Scripture has already foretold of these days:

> [1]Why do the heathen rage, and the people imagine a vain thing? [2]The kings of the earth set themselves, and the rulers take counsel together, against the LORD, and against his anointed, [saying], [3]Let us break their bands asunder, and cast away their cords from us. [4]He that sitteth in the heavens shall laugh: the Lord shall have them in derision. [5]Then shall he speak unto them in his wrath, and vex them in his sore displeasure. [6]Yet have I set my king upon my holy hill of Zion. (Ps. 2:1–6 KJV)

Be strong and of good courage, for the day is fast approaching when we will yet see the triumph of God over all those who have aligned themselves against Him!

PART 6:

Seals, Trumpets, and Bowls

¹And there appeared a great wonder in heaven; a woman clothed with the sun, and the moon under her feet, and upon her head a crown of twelve stars. ²And she being with child cried, travailing in birth, and pained to be delivered. ³And there appeared another wonder in heaven; and behold a great red dragon, having seven heads and ten horns, and seven crowns upon his heads. ⁴And his tail drew the third part of the stars of heaven, and did cast them to the earth: and the dragon stood before the woman which was ready to be delivered, for to devour her child as soon as it was born. ⁵And she brought forth a man child, who was to rule all nations with a rod of iron: and her child was caught up unto God, and [to] his throne. ⁶And the woman fled into the wilderness, where she hath a place prepared of God, that they should feed her there a thousand two hundred [and] threescore days. (Rev. 12:1–6 KJV)

Daniel's terrifying final beast, the one corresponding to the Green Horseman, is The Beast described in Revelation 13 whose rule is ended by the return of the Messiah. The remaining seals and prophesies recorded in Revelation are additional details about the reign of the Fourth Beast, details that Daniel saw and recorded in the scroll that was sealed until the "time of the end" (Dan. 12:5).

It is not really in the scope of this book to prognosticate about what will happen in the future but simply to demonstrate how far we have come on the last-days timeline. Isaac Newton, author of the Universal Theory of Gravity and inventor of calculus, is thought by many to have been "the greatest and most influential scientist who ever lived."[1176] He was also a dedicated student of the Bible, writing more than a million words of notes on Scripture.[1177] In his posthumously published book *Observations Upon the Prophecies of Daniel and the Apocalypse of St. John*, Newton proposed why God gave men prophesies.

> The folly of Interpreters has been, to foretel [sic] times and things by this Prophecy, as if God designed to make them Prophets. By this rashness they have not only exposed themselves, but brought the Prophecy also into contempt. The design of God was much otherwise. He gave this and the Prophecies of the Old Testament, not to gratify men's curiosities by enabling them to foreknow things, but that after they were fulfilled they might be interpreted by the event, and His own Providence, not the Interpreters, be then manifested thereby to the world. For the event of things predicted many ages before, will then be a convincing argument that the world is governed by providence. [1178]

Prophesy is best understood from the perspective of hindsight, when history and Scripture can be compared. Up until now, we have looked at past events; the accuracy and detail of prophesy is astonishing and causes us to glorify God. Nevertheless, the metaphor of birth used by Jesus allows me to respond to the question people constantly ask: what's next?

The Fifth Seal

> ⁹And when he had opened the fifth seal, I saw under the altar the souls of them that were slain for the word of God, and for the testimony which they held: ¹⁰And they cried with a loud voice, saying, How long, O Lord, holy and true, dost thou not judge and avenge our blood on them that dwell on the earth? ¹¹And white robes were given unto every one of them; and it was said unto them, that they should rest yet for a little season, until their fellowservants also and their brethren, that should be killed as they [were], should be fulfilled. (Rev. 6:9–11 KJV)

The fifth seal gives a heavenly perspective of conditions under the Green Horseman. Martyrdom was nothing new to John. Many of his fellow believers were killed for their faith by the Roman authorities. Except for the miraculous intervention of God, John himself would have been among them. It is likely that John had spent hours interceding for those in the church who might face the test of martyrdom.

The fifth seal, however, is different. John sees the vast number of martyred souls and hears their cries for justice. Then he sees God's answer: He would act in His perfect time. Justice would be satisfied. It is a heavenly parallel to the children of Israel, who cried out for deliverance when they were enslaved in Egypt. Although their pleas seemed to be of no avail, God would intervene spectacularly but only at His appointed moment. Once again, the **end is soon, but not yet**.

In the meantime, the opening of the fifth seal triggered a marked increase in the number of martyred Christians. Furthermore, God assures John that the number of martyred believers was not yet complete and more will die as the time of Jesus' return approaches. According to Revelation, a time will come when the dragon, Satan, will be thrown out of heaven "into the earth" (Rev. 12:9–10 KJV) and no longer be permitted access to the Heavenlies or to be the "prince of the power of the air" (Eph. 2:2 KJV). John goes on to say,

> [11]And they overcame him by the blood of the Lamb, and by the word of their testimony; and they loved not their lives unto the death. [12]Therefore rejoice, [ye] heavens, and ye that dwell in them. Woe to the inhabiters of the earth and of the sea! for the devil is come down unto you, having great wrath, because he knoweth that he hath but a short time. (Rev. 12:11–12 KJV)

It is illuminating to look at the phrase "word of their testimony" in the original language. The Greek word for testimony is *martyrias* (μαρτυρίας) *from which we get the English word* martyrdom.[1179] This is not a recipe for happiness: take the blood of Jesus, add your testimony of what He has done for you, and all will be sweetness and light. It reads more like a great chemistry experiment in which alkaline and acid are combined to generate explosive power.

Remember pouring baking soda and vinegar in a bottle, corking it, and watching the reaction that forced the cork high into the air, almost beyond sight? This Scripture describes a similar reaction and holds the key to the kind of power that will carry believers through to the end: take the blood of Jesus, add martyrdom for your faith, the most vehement of demonic attacks possible, and dynamite power in the spirit realm will be unleashed. This power is stronger than anything you can imagine. This is overcoming power, the kind that raised Christ from the dead!

We are on a high-speed trajectory hurtling toward the end, the time when Jesus returns and overcomes all His enemies, when God judges the whole earth, and Satan is bound for a thousand years (Rev. 20:2). Once the Green Horseman goes forth and the fifth seal is opened, Satan knows the time until his judgment day is short, and he is working to take down as many people with him as possible.

Martyrdom seems very far away to most believers in the Western world. However, in many parts of the globe, martyrdom and violent persecution such as abduction and rape are daily threats. One journalist writes,

> A silent holocaust of Christian martyrs is taking place around the world. While individual instances

of murder and mayhem are sometimes reported, the general pattern of violence is ignored by the media, the United Nations, and most national governments. The perpetrators belong primarily to one of two groups: fundamentalist Islamists or Communist-controlled governments.[1180]

The number of martyrs is shockingly high.

The twentieth century saw more Christian martyrs, 45 million, than all the previous centuries combined. In his book, *The New Persecuted: Inquiries into Anti-Christian Intolerance in the New Century of Martyrs,* Italian journalist Antonio Socci, writes that an average of 160,000 Christians have been killed each year since 1990 in places like Algeria, Nigeria, Sudan, and Pakistan.[1181]

The rate of martyrdom appears to be on the rise; a 2006 report estimated the toll of Christian martyrs at 171,000 each year.[1182] Massimo Introvigne, an Italian sociologist, calculated one Christian was killed for no other reason than for his or her faith in Christ about every five minutes. He called the "slaughter" and persecution of Christians "the first worldwide emergency in the matter of violence and religious discrimination."[1183]

One of the most shocking things about the holocaust of Christians is the silence that surrounds it. Journalists, who are usually quick to ferret out the slightest hint of human-rights abuses, have ignored the international plight of Christians while working to marginalize Christians within Western democracies. Although a few church leaders have spoken out, the Western church has by and large been silent. Perhaps one reason John sees the souls of the martyrs crying to God for justice is because no one else is.

However, statistics about the growth of Christianity do support the brilliance of God's plan: His chemical formula of the blood of Jesus combined with edicts of martyrdom is resulting in powerful growth in the church worldwide. The 2011 Global Mission Report shows there were about 270 martyrs every day for the past decade:

"the number of martyrs [in the period 2000–2010] was approximately 1 million." At the same time, it found that about a third of the earth's population, 2.3 billion, are Christians, and the church is growing at the rate of about 80,000 new Christians daily. And most of that growth is occurring in areas where Christians are under the greatest persecution.[1184] The numbers point to one conclusion—the seal of the martyrs has been opened.

The Sixth Seal

> [12]And I beheld when he had opened the sixth seal, and, lo, there was a great earthquake; and the sun became black as sackcloth of hair, and the moon became as blood; [13]And the stars of heaven fell unto the earth, even as a fig tree casteth her untimely figs, when she is shaken of a mighty wind. [14]And the heaven departed as a scroll when it is rolled together; and every mountain and island were moved out of their places. [15]And the kings of the earth, and the great men, and the rich men, and the chief captains, and the mighty men, and every bondman, and every free man, hid themselves in the dens and in the rocks of the mountains; [16]And said to the mountains and rocks, Fall on us, and hide us from the face of him that sitteth on the throne, and from the wrath of the Lamb: [17]For the great day of his wrath is come; and who shall be able to stand? (Rev. 6:12–17 KJV)

I believe we are waiting for the opening of the sixth seal. The events depicted in this passage are not subtle; they do not unfold over a period of years, as did the previous ones. Instead, they will induce widespread panic in everyone: from top-ranking leaders in government to the union rank and file, from millionaires to the destitute, from Hollywood movie moguls to couch potatoes, from five-star generals to army grunts, and from industrial giants to ordinary Joes just trying to get by.

Everyone will try to hide. Everyone will pray prayers birthed in fear. It will be like 9/11 all over again but on a much larger scale.

No doubt, CNN and other news outlets will prattle on, trying to explain the unexplainable. Whatever this is, it will shock even the most jaded of reporters. Everyone will agree: "For the great day of his wrath is come; and who shall be able to stand?"

Who shall be able to stand? The ones who can stand are those who know the Most High, who are walking in His covenant sealed by the blood of the Lamb. Paul exhorts us to put on the tools that will give us the strength to stand.

> [11]Put on the whole armour of God, that ye may be able to stand against the wiles of the devil. [12]For we wrestle not against flesh and blood, but against principalities, against powers, against the rulers of the darkness of this world, against spiritual wickedness in high [places]. [13]Wherefore take unto you the whole armour of God, that ye may be able to withstand in the evil day, and having done all, to stand.
>
> [18]Praying always with all prayer and supplication in the Spirit, and watching thereunto with all perseverance and supplication for all saints. (Eph. 6:11–13, 18 KJV)

So whether the sixth seal is a nuclear war, a terrorist attack, an asteroid plummeting into the earth's atmosphere, or some other cataclysmic event we have yet to imagine, God has given His people the key to withstanding the storm by faith.

However, we must remember that frightening as this may be, **the end is still not yet**. Scripture consistently says that the cosmic phenomena accompanying the sixth seal—the blackened sun, the bloody moon, and the stars falling from the sky like late figs— immediately **precede** the "Day of the Lord."

> [9]Behold, the day of the LORD cometh, cruel both with wrath and fierce anger, to lay the land desolate: and he shall destroy the sinners thereof out of it. [10]For the stars of heaven and the constellations thereof shall not give their light: the sun shall be darkened in his going forth, and the moon shall not cause her light to shine. (Isa. 13:9–10 KJV)

The sun shall be turned into darkness, and the moon into blood, before the great and the terrible day of the LORD come. (Joel 3:31 KJV)

[19]And I will shew wonders in heaven above, and signs in the earth beneath; blood, and fire, and vapour of smoke: [20]The sun shall be turned into darkness, and the moon into blood, before that great and notable day of the Lord come: [21]And it shall come to pass, [that] whosoever shall call on the name of the Lord shall be saved. (Acts 2:19–21 KJV)

In his inaugural speech of 1933, President F. D. Roosevelt stated,

the only thing we have to fear is fear itself—nameless, unreasoning, unjustified terror which paralyzes needed efforts to convert retreat into advance.[1185]

The same principle applies to the people of God as we face the coming of the great and dreadful day of the Lord. God does not give us the spirit of fear (Rom. 8:15). That always comes from Satan, our enemy. The only fear appropriate for the believer is the fear of God, which perfects us in holiness (2 Cor. 7:1). The fear of the Lord gives us the Godly wisdom we need to navigate the last days (Job 28:28, Prov. 14:26-27). The fear of the Lord brings us to repentance: "By the fear of the LORD [men] depart from evil" (Prov. 16:6). Even as the Day of Judgment arrives, God exhorts all the earth to fear Him (Rev. 14:7 KJV).

The Sixth Seal: Transition in Labor

The church is entering into labor. Jesus characterized the events of the four horsemen as birth pangs, or Braxton-Hicks contractions, those that help thin the cervix and prepare the body for real labor. At some point it will be clear we are no longer experiencing Braxton-Hicks contractions but the first stage of active labor. Although every birth is different, they all progress through three distinct stages. The Mayo Clinic writes,

In some cases, labor is over in a matter of hours—or less. In other cases, labor tests a mother's physical and emotional stamina. You won't know how your labor will unfold until it happens. You can prepare, however, by understanding the typical sequence of events.[1186]

This is good advice. Knowing that her pain is a normal part of the birthing process helps a mother cope with her labor. Imagine having excruciating abdominal pain and not knowing the cause; the natural reaction would be fear and panic, the kind described at the opening of the sixth seal. But I say to the church, "Do Not Panic! Do not be alarmed! What you are experiencing is normal when you are in labor!"

Early labor can be unpredictable; sometimes it is difficult to know if contractions are the start of real labor or strong Braxton-Hicks contractions, also called false labor. But at some point, as the contractions get longer and stronger and closer together, it will become clear that active labor is underway.

The purpose of active labor is to fully open the cervix. Progress can seem painfully slow—or it can happen so fast you can feel the cervix dilate with each contraction. When the cervix is almost ready, transition, the final step in the first stage of labor, begins. The pain will be particularly intense. It will feel like the end is **now** and it is time to give birth. The urge to try to push the baby out will be strong. Like a woman in transition, those who live during the time of the sixth seal will feel as if "the great day of his wrath is come." **But the end is not yet**.

Trying to force the birth process by pushing during transition is not only futile but damaging. According to the Mayo Clinic, "Pushing too soon could cause your cervix to tear or swell, which might delay delivery or cause troublesome bleeding. Pant or blow your way through the contractions."[1187]

John reports that the world interprets the events of the sixth seal as the second coming, but Jesus does not return. When things don't happen as the experts predicted, they will demand of believers, "Where is your God?" Secular leaders may dismiss all Christianity as a myth, and the hearts of many will be hardened at this time. Remember the spiritual implications of killing by Death?

For those of us who are believers, the medical advice to "pant or blow your way through the contractions" is good. Those whose hearts pant after the Living God and His Holy Spirit will have the spiritual fortitude to endure transition. The psalmist describes this beautifully.

> [1]As the hart panteth after the water brooks, so panteth my soul after thee, O God. [2]My soul thirsteth for God, for the living God: when shall I come and appear before God? [3]My tears have been my meat day and night, while they continually say unto me, Where [is] thy God? [4]When I remember these [things], I pour out my soul in me: for I had gone with the multitude, I went with them to the house of God, with the voice of joy and praise, with a multitude that kept holyday. [5]Why art thou cast down, O my soul? and [why] art thou disquieted in me? hope thou in God: for I shall yet praise him [for] the help of his countenance. (Ps. 41:1–5 KJV)

Interestingly, the psalmist is constantly being taunted with the question, "Where is your God?" (Ps. 41:2). When the sixth seal opens, the whole world braces for the "day of the Lord's wrath" and prepares for an international emergency. *Except the end is not yet.* Rather than admit their mistake, the people of the world embark on a campaign of discrediting faith in God. Since Jesus did not appear at the hour *they* said He would, they conclude that there must be no God and that the Christian faith is foolishness or a harmful delusion.

Men and women of faith who seek the approval of God alone with no concern for the opinions of others will be able to get through this time. We must pant after God, to derive our life breath from Him. We must know how to coach our souls: "Why art thou cast down, O my soul? and [why] art thou disquieted in me? hope thou in God: for I shall yet praise him [for] the help of his countenance." (Ps. 41:5) This is the oil that will carry us through the second stage of labor.

The Seventh Seal: Sounding the Trumpets

> [1]And when he had opened the seventh seal, there was

> silence in heaven about the space of half an hour. [2]And I saw the seven angels which stood before God; and to them were given seven trumpets. (Rev. 8:1–2 KJV)

When the seventh seal opens, everything changes. An amazing thing happens: silence in heaven. Think about this for a moment. The "thunderings and voices" emitted out of the throne of God pause. The four living creatures, the twenty-four elders, and the angels stop articulating their worship of God. The souls of the martyrs under the throne cease to cry out. Even on earth, the wind ceases to blow. All wait in hushed awe (Rev. 4–8).

Remarkably, a pause is expected at the conclusion of the first stage of labor. Transition itself can be grueling and overwhelming as wave after wave of contractions spasm the body, often with a new one beginning before the previous one ends. Transition signals that the end is near and concludes with a pause of about 30 minutes. The Baby Center Medical Advisory Board reports: "Thankfully, there's often a lull at the end of transition when the contractions pause and you and your baby can rest."[1188]

When the cervix is fully dilated, transition and the first stage of labor are complete. We then enter into the second stage of labor; pushing the baby out. The child that was conceived 2,000 years ago with the coming of the Holy Spirit and all the events triggered by the seals over the last 600 years have been directed toward this moment, when the woman gives birth to a "man child" (Rev. 12:6 KJV). The time of the birth process will be marked by the seven trumpets blown in succession by angels.

Labor is not easy. The Mayo Clinic points out, "It can take from a few minutes up to several hours or more to push your baby into the world." It can be painful, exhausting and push you past the point you think is possible to bear. When I was giving birth to my oldest son, I remember telling the nurse, after twenty-two hours of active labor and what seemed like endless pushing, that I was going to push once more and then I was going home. I felt as if I had used all my reserves of strength and just wanted to go to sleep. I learned an irrevocable truth that day: once the baby starts its journey through the birth canal, there is no way out except to give birth. There is a point when even a Caesarian is not possible. The only other option is death.

The time of the trumpets is one we would all like to escape, but we cannot. We cannot be like the five virgins who were unprepared for a long haul. We cannot hop up from the delivery table to make a quick trip to the market. Once we enter the second stage of labor, we have what we have; we are what we are. We must persevere to the end or forfeit.

Twice, John exhorts the saints—us—to patiently endure and be faithful. The first is in Revelation 13:10. The scene is set with a description of the beast and the dragon that gives it power. During their reign, which lasts forty-two months, the people of the world will fall into two groups, those who worship the beast, drinking in his blasphemes as truth, and the saints, whom the beast will apparently overcome: "And it was given unto him to make war with the saints, and to overcome them ..." (Rev. 13:7 KJV).

John concludes his account with an interesting encouragement. "He that leadeth into captivity shall go into captivity: he that killeth with the sword must be killed with the sword. Here is the patience and the faith of the saints" (Rev. 13:10 KJV).

We are presented with the previously explained triple choice given by traditional jihadists: convert, go into *dhimmitude*, or be executed by the sword. John encourages the saints not to worry— God will deliver justice in due time. Meanwhile, they are exhorted to demonstrate patient endurance and faith.

John continues his narrative by describing the mark of the beast, the economic consequences of not receiving it, and the angelic warnings about the spiritual consequences of taking it. After crying out about the eternal torment that awaits those who receive the mark of the beast, John repeats, "Here is the patience of the saints: here [are] they that keep the commandments of God, and the faith of Jesus" (Rev. 14:12 KJV).

Thayer's *Lexicon* defines patient endurance—Greek *hypomone* (ὑπομονη)—as "the characteristic man who is unswerved from his deliberate purpose and his loyalty to faith and piety by even the greatest trials and sufferings."[1189] This quality, combined with our faith, the absolute conviction that God is whom He said He is and can be trusted to do as He said He would do, give us the reserves to endure until the end.

The third and final stage of labor is represented by the bowls filled with the wrath of God poured out on the earth. The baby has been born. All that remains is to remove the placenta. During pregnancy, the placenta was an essential lifeline, providing all the baby needed as it grew. In the same way, even though we are believers, we live in the world system and work to make a living within that system. Without contact with the world, it is almost impossible to survive. As the current age comes to a close, God pours out His wrath, destroying the world system. All that made the earth unclean is removed, and the bride goes into the marriage supper of the Lamb.

Jesus promises,

> [7]Behold, I come quickly: blessed [is] he that keepeth the sayings of the prophecy of this book.
>
> [17]And the Spirit and the bride say, Come. And let him that heareth say, Come. And let him that is athirst come. And whosoever will, let him take the water of life freely.
>
> [18]For I testify unto every man that heareth the words of the prophecy of this book, If any man shall add unto these things, God shall add unto him the plagues that are written in this book: [19]And if any man shall take away from the words of the book of this prophecy, God shall take away his part out of the book of life, and out of the holy city, and [from] the things which are written in this book. [20]He which testifieth these things saith, Surely I come quickly. Amen. (Rev. 22:7, 17–20a KJV)

> To which we reply, "Even so, come, Lord Jesus." (Rev. 22:20b KJV)

APPENDIX A: EARLY JUBILEES

Adam—Created 1; Died 930*; most recent Jubilee—18 (year 900)

Seth—Born 130; Died 1042; most recent Jubilee—20 (year 1000)

Enos—Born 235; Died 1140; most recent Jubilee—22 (year 1100)

Cainan—Born 325; Died 1165; most recent Jubilee—23 (year 1150)

Mahlalaleel—Born 395; Died 1290; most recent Jubilee—25 (year 1250)

Jared—Born 460; Died 1422; most recent Jubilee—28 (year 1400)

Enoch—Born 622; Taken up 938; most recent Jubilee—18 (year 900)

Methuselah—Born 687; Died 1656; most recent Jubilee—33 (year 1650)

Lemach—Born 874; Died 1651; most recent Jubilee—33 (year 1650)

Noah—Born 1056; Died 2006; most recent Jubilee—40 (year 2000)

Shem—Born 1556; Died 2156; most recent Jubilee—43 (year 2150)

Arphaxad—Born 1658; Died 2096; most recent Jubilee—41 (year 2050)

Salah—Born 1693; Died 2126; most recent Jubilee—42 (year 2100)

Eber—Born 1723; Died 2187; most recent Jubilee—43 (year 2150)

Peleg—Born 1757; Died 1996; most recent Jubilee—39 (year 1950)

Reu—Born 1787; Died 2026; most recent Jubilee—40 (year 2000)

Serug—Born 1819; Died 2049; most recent Jubilee—40 (year 2000)

Nahor—Born 1849; Died 1997; most recent Jubilee—39 (year 1950)

Terah—Born 1878; Died 2153; most recent Jubilee—43 (year 2150)

Abraham—Born 1948; Died 2123; most recent Jubilee—42 (year 2100)

Isaac—Born 2048; Died 2228; most recent Jubilee—44 (year 2200)

Jacob—Born 2108; Died 2255; most recent Jubilee—45 (year 2250)

*Dates are calculated from the creation of Adam according to Genesis.

Dates are incomplete from this point on. However, Abraham was promised that his seed would receive the land in 400 years (Gen. 15:14-16). 400 + 2100 (year of most recent Jubilee at Jacob's birth, and before Abraham died) = 2500 or Jubilee 50. At the same time, he was promised that the fourth generation would come out of Egypt. Moses is the fourth generation from Levi, who fathered Kohath, who fathered Amram, father of Moses and Aaron (Exod. 6:16–20).

NOTES

These references are, in effect, a running bibliography, making a list of sources unnecessary. References are given in full when first cited and abbreviated thereafter. For space considerations, URLs are not given for pages that can be accessed by searching the title and site name. If two dates are given, the first refers to the last site update; the second is the date the information was accessed.

1. Mordechai Pinchas, "The Formation of the Letters," *Mordechai Pinchas Sofer Stam,* 2011, 2 9, 2011, *www.sofer.co.uk/html/aleph_bet.*

2. "800-Year-Old Torah," *Rhodes Jewish Museum,* 2010. 7 30, 2012, *www. rhodesjewishmuseum.org/history/the-800-year-old-torah.*

3. Mordechai Pinchas, "Diary of a Sofer—part 5," *Mordechai Pinchas Sofer Stam,* 2011, 2 9, 2011, *www.sofer.co.uk/html/diary_5.*

4. "Translation Problems," *Translation Schools,* 2005–2011, 2 9, 2012, *www. translationschools.org/translation/process/problems.*

5. George V. Wigram, *The Englishman's Hebrew Concordance of the Old Testament* (Peabody, MA: Hendrickson, 2001), 362–66.

6. James Strong, *The New Strong's Exhaustive Concordance of the Bible* (Nashville: Thomas Nelson, 1884), 405–09, 834.

7. Blue Letter Bible, Lexical Definitions—Hiphil, Blue Letter Bible, 1996–2011, 5 28, 2011, *www.blueletterbible.org/help/lexicalDefinitions. cfm?lang=H&num=8818.*

8. Blue Letter Bible, Parsing Information, *Blue Letter Bible,* 1996–2011, 5 28, 2011, *www.blueletterbible.org/Bible.cfm?t=KJV&x=0&y=0&b=Rev& c=6&v=1#conc/2.*

9. "Saint Jerome," *Encyclopædia Britannica,* 2012, web, 7 29, 2012.

10. "John Wycliffe," *Encyclopædia Britannica,* 2012, web, 7 29, 2012.

11. "Jan Hus: Beliefs and writings," *Encyclopædia Britannica,* 2012, web, 7 29, 2012.

12. Joseph Henry Thayer, *A Greek-English Lexicon of the New Testament* (New York: Harper and Brothers, 1886), 481.

13. Thayer, 313.

14. Thayer, 122.

15. Thayer, 622.

16. Thayer, 334.

17. Thayer, 517–18.

18. Tracey R. Rich, "Marriage," *Judaism 101*, 1996–2011, 7 25, 2011, *www. jewfaq.org/marriage*.

19. Francis Brown, S. R. Driver, and Charles A. Briggs, *The Brown-Driver-Briggs Hebrew and English Lexicon* (Peabody, MA: Henrickson, 2001), 416.

20. Albert Vanhoye, "The Jubilee Year in the Gospel of Luke," *Vatican Theological-Historical Commission*, 2000, 6 2, 2012, *www.vatican.va/ jubilee_2000/ magazine/documents/ju_mag_01031997_p-22_en*.

21. Robin Elise Weiss, "When will my baby be born? Pregancy Due Date Calculator," *About.com Pregancy and Childbirth*, 2012, web, 6 3, 2012.

22. "Aramaic language," *Encyclopædia Britannica*, 2012. Web, 7 29, 2012.

23. Thayer, 679.

24. Robin Elise Weiss, "Braxton-Hicks Contractions—Are they practise contractions or the real thing?" *About.com Pregancy and Childbirth*, 2012, web, 6 3, 2012.

25. "European Exploration: Age of Discovery," *Encyclopædia Britannica*, 2012, web, 7 29, 2012.

26. "Spice trade," *Encyclopædia Britannica*, 2012, web, 7 29, 2012.

27. *The History of Gold* (Washington, D.C.: National Mining Association, 2004), 2 15, 2011, *www.nma.org/pdf/gold/gold_history*, 3.

28. Peter N. Stearns, Michael Adas, Stuart B. Schwartz, and Marc Jason Gilbert,"The West and the Changing World Balance," from *World Civilizations: the Global Experience* (New York: Longman Publishing Group, 2004), 338–40.

29. *The History of Gold*, 3.

30. "Prince Henry the Navigator," *Encyclopædia Britannica*, 2012, web, 7 29, 2012.

31. "Compass," *Encyclopædia Britannica*, 2012, web, 7 29, 2012.

32. "Zacuto, Abraham Ben Samuel," *Jewish Encyclopedia*, 1906, 7 29, 2012, *www.jewishencyclopedia.com*.

33. "Portolan Chart," *Encyclopædia Britannica*, 2012, web, 7 29, 2012.

34. Matt Rosenberg, "Prince Henry the Navigator," *About.com: Geography*, 2012, web, 7 7, 2012.

35. "Caravel," *Encyclopædia Britannica*, 2012, web, 7 29, 2012.

36. "Bartolomeu Dias," *Encyclopædia Britannica*, 2012, web, 7 29, 2012.

37. "Vasco da Gama," *Encyclopædia Britannica*, 2012, web, 7 29, 2012.

38. "Brazil: Exploration and Initial Settlement," *Encyclopædia Britannica*, 2012, web, 7 29, 2012.

39. "Ferdinand Magellan," *Encyclopædia Britannica*, 2012, web, 7 29, 2012.

40. Brown, Driver, and Briggs, 915–16.

41. "Renaissance man," *Encyclopædia Britannica*, 2012, web, 7 29, 2012.

42. "The Printing Revolution," *Encyclopædia Britannica* 26 (2005), 73–75.

43. Lisa Jardine, "Britain and the Rise of Science," *BBC History*, 2 17, 2011, 7 25, 2012, *www.bbc.co.uk/history/british/empire_seapower/jardineih_01*.

44. "Renaissance," *Encyclopædia Britannica*, 2012, web, 7 29, 2012.

45. "Aldus Manutius the Elder," *Encyclopædia Britannica*, 2012, web, 7 29, 2012.

46. Niccolo Machiavelli, *The Prince* (Florence: Antonio Blado d'Asola, 1532).

47. "Humanism," *Encyclopædia Britannica*, 2012, web, 7 29, 2012.

48. "Gutenberg Bible," *Encyclopædia Britannica*, 2012, web, 7 29, 2012.

49. "Desiderius Erasmus," *Encyclopædia Britannica*, 2012, web, 7 29, 2012.

50. "Protestant Reformation," *Encyclopædia Britannica* 26 (2005), 213–14.

51. "The Printing Revolution," *Encyclopædia Britannica* 26 (2005), 73–75.

52. "Martin Luther." *Encyclopædia Britannica*, 2012, web, 7 29, 2012.

53. "William Tyndale," *Encyclopædia Britannica*, 2012, web, 7 29, 2012.

54. "Nicolaus Copernicus," *Encyclopædia Britannica*, 2012, web, 7 29, 2012.

55. "Andreas Vesalius," *Encyclopædia Britannica*, 2012, web, 7 29, 2012.

56. "The Printing Revolution," *Encyclopædia Britannica* 26 (2005), 73–75.

57. Ibid.

58. Chris Butler, "The rise of the nation state during the Renaissance," *The Flow of History*, 2007, 10 23, 2011, *www.flowofhistory.com/units/ west/11/ FC79*.

59. Shawn Greenwell, "STS-113 Space Shuttle Processing Q & A," *NASA*, 11 15, 2002, web, 2 10, 2011.

60. "How many commercial airline flights are there per day in the world?" *Answerbag*, 2006, web, 2 10, 2011.

61. Jay Spenser, "Connecting the Dots," *Boeing Frontiers*, 7 2007, 2 10, 2011, *www.boeing.com/news/frontiers/archive/2007/july/i_ca01*.

62. "Five billion people to use mobile phones in 2010: UN," 2 15, 2010, 6 4, 2012, *phys.org/news185467439*.

63. "Usage and Population Statistics," *Internet World Stats*, 2001–2012, 6 4, 2012, *www.internetworldstats.com/stats*.

64. "Facebook Statistics, Stats and Facts For 2011," *Digital Buzz*, 1 18, 2011, 6 4, 2012, *www.digitalbuzzblog.com/facebook-statistics-stats-facts-2011*.

65. "Books published per country per year, *Wikipedia*, 5 24, 2012, web, 6 4, 2012.

66. James Burke, "Thunder in the Skies," *Connnections: An Alternative View of Change* 6, documentary, directed by Mick Jackson, produced by James Burke (New York: Ambrose Video, 1978).

67. Chris Butler, "Railroads and Their Impact (c. 1825–1900)," *The Flow of History*, 2007, 2 27, 2011, *www.flowofhistory.com/units/eme/17/FC112*.

68. Reuben Goossens, "Trans Atlantic Record Breakers and Blue Riband Holders," *ssMaritime*, 2010–2012, 8 23, 2012, *www.ssmaritime.com/Blue-Riband*.

69. Burke, "Thunder in the Skies."

70. Victor Bailey, "The Rise of Popular Literacy in Victorian England," *History of Education Quarterly*, 34:1 (Spring, 1994), 89–91.

71. Kathryn Gundlach, "Serialized Fiction in the Victorian Era," *School of Information and Library Science, UNC-CH*, 4 18, 2001, 2 27, 2011, *www. unc.edu/~gundlach/pathfinder.*

72. Laurel Braker and Marysa Demoor, *Dictionary of nineteenth-century journalism in Great Britain and Ireland* (Belgium: Academia Press, 2009), 10 17, 2011, *books.google.com,* 567.

73. Gundlach, "Serialized Fiction in the Victorian Era."

74. "Newspaper," *Encyclopædia Britannica,* 2012, web, 7 29, 2012.

75. "History of newspapers and magazines," *Encyclopædia Britannica* 9 (2005), 781.

76. Catherine J. Golden, "The Victorian Revolution in Letter Writing," The Victorian Web, 7 22, 2010, 10 17, 2011, *www.victorianweb.org/technology/ letters/intro.*

77. "Telegraph," *Encyclopædia Britannica,* 2012, web, 7 29, 2012.

78. John Casale, "The telegraph," *Telegraph History,* 2011, 8 23, 2012, *www. telegraph-history.org/edison/appletons/index* l.

79. "Telephone," *Encyclopædia Britannica,* 2012, web. 8 23, 2012.

80. "Guglielmo Marconi," *Encyclopædia Britannica,* 2012, web, 7 29, 2012.

81. "Nellie Bly," *Encyclopædia Britannica,* 2012, web, 7 29, 2012.

82. Paul Skellett, *Around the world in 80 hours—Maxim Naviede,* updated 7 30, 2008, film 3 3, 2011, *www.youtube.com/watch?v=3qDONGVkcj4.*

83. "History of Aviation," GlobalAircraft.org, 2008, 8 23, 2012, *http://www. globalaircraft.org.*

84. Josh Brancheau, Abi Wharton, and Firuz Kamalov, " The History of the Automobile," *The Impact of the Automobile on the 20ᵗʰ Century,* 3 3, 2011, 3 3, 2011, *l3d.cs.colorado.edu/systems/agentsheets/New-Vista/automobile.*

85. "'Goldin' Age of Radio Blog promotes collection highlights," on Shafferg's Blog, 3 4, 2010, 8 23, 2012, *library.umkc.edu/blog/news-blog/ node/2060.*

86. "Golden Age of American radio," *Encyclopædia Britannica,* 2012, web, 8 23, 2012.

87. Jesse Walker, "Radio Goes to War: The Cultural Politics of Propaganda during World War II," *The Independent Review: A Journal of Political Economy,* 2011, 3 3, 2011, *www.independent.org/publications/tir/article. asp?a=63.*

88. "Newsreel," *Encyclopædia Britannica,* 2012, web, 8 23, 2012.

89. Carole D. Hicks, "Television's Impact on Society," *Soul Food,* 3 28, 2008, 3 3, 2011, *carolehicks.wordpress.com/2008/03/28/televisions-impact-on-society.*

90. "Concorde," *Encyclopædia Britannica,* 2012, web, 8 4, 2012.

91. "Earth satellite," *Encyclopædia Britannica,* 2012, web, 8 4, 2012.

92. "GPS," *Encyclopædia Britannica,* 2012, web, 8 4, 2012.

93. "Timeline of Computer History," *Computer History Museum,* 2006, 8 4, 2012, *www.computerhistory.org/timeline/?category=cmptr.*

94. "Internet," *Encyclopædia Britannica,* 2012, web, 8 4, 2012.

95. "Mobile phone," *Wikipedia,* 3 6, 2011, web, 3 6, 2011.

96. "European Lion," *Of Cats: Resource of everything feline*, 11 20, 2008, 8 4, 2012, *www.ofcats.com/2008/11/european-lion*.

97. "Bow and arrow," *Encyclopædia Britannica*, 2 (2010), 435–36.

98. Ron Leadbetter, "Apollo," *Encyclopedia Mythica*, 3 3, 2009, 8 23, 2012, *www.pantheon.org/articles/a/apollo*.

99. Ron Leadbetter, "Artemis," *Encyclopedia Mythica*, 8 10, 2005, 8 23, 2012, *www.pantheon.org/areas/mythology/europe/greek/articles*.

100. Charles Gabriel Seligman, "Bow and Arrow Symbolism," *Asian Traditonal Archery Research Network*, 8 19, 2000, 4 5, 2011, *www.atarn.org/chinese/seligman/seligman*.

101. "Bow and arrow," *Encyclopædia Britannica*.

102. Ibid.

103. Ibid.

104. Dave Grossman, "Evolution of Weaponry," *Killology Research Group; Warrior Science Group* (Academic Press, 2000), 4 5, 2011, *www.killology.com/print/print_weaponry*.

105. "Battle of Crécy," *Encyclopædia Britannica* 3 (2010), 721.

106. "Battle of Agincourt," *Encyclopædia Britannica* 1 (2010), 148.

107. Clifford J. Rogers, "The Military Revolutions of the Hundred Years' War," *The Journal of Military History* 57 (1993), 11 21, 2010, *www.deremilitari.org/resources/articles/rogers*.

108. "Battle of the Golden Spurs," *Encyclopædia Britannica*, 2012, web, 8 4, 2012.

109. Joris de Sutter, The Goedendag, *De Liebaart*, 12 25, 2001, 4 10, 2011, *www.liebaart.org/goeden_e*.

110. "Pike," *Encyclopædia Britannica*, 2012, web, 8 4, 2012.

111. "Battle of Laupen," *Absolute Astronomy*, 2011, web, 8 4, 2012.

112. "Battle of Morat," *Encyclopædia Britannica*, 2012, web, 8 4, 2012.

113. "Battle of Nancy," *Encyclopædia Britannica*, 2012, web, 8 4, 2012.

114. "Pike," *Encyclopædia Britannica*.

115. Rogers, "The Military Revolutions of the Hundred Years' War," 8

116. Ibid.

117. Geoffrey Parker, ed., *Cambridge Illustrated History of Warfare: The Triumph of the West* (Cambridge: Cambridge University Press, 1995), 5.

118. Geoffrey Parker, *The Military Revolution: Military Innovation and the Rise of the West* (Cambridge: Cambridge University Press, 1988), 3.

119. Rogers, "The Military Revolutions of the Hundred Years' War," 7.

120. Thayer, 587.

121. Blue Letter Bible. "Parsing Information," Blue Letter Bible, 1996–2011, 12 11, 2011, *www.blueletterbible.org/Bible.cfm?b=Rev&c=6&v=1&t=KJV#conc/2*.

122. Brenda Ralph Lewis, "Princess Louise," *Britannia Biography*, 2012, 8 4, 2012, *www.britannia.com/history/biographies/louise*.

123. "Morganatic marriage," *Encyclopædia Britannica*, 2012, web, 8 4, 2012.

124. "Charles V," *Encyclopædia Britannica*, 2012, web, 8 4, 2012.

125. "Maria Theresa, *Encyclopædia Britannica*, 2012, web, 8 4, 2012.

126. "Victoria," *Encyclopædia Britannica*, 2012, web, 8 4, 2012.

127.   *Portugal: A Country Study* (Federal Research Division, Library of Congress, 7 27, 2010), 7 31, 2012, *lcweb2.loc.gov/frd/cs/pttoc.*

128.   "1383–1385 Crisis," *Wikipedia*, 11 15, 2011, web, 12 11, 2011.

129.   "John I," *Encyclopædia Britannica*, 2012, web, 8 4, 2012.

130.   "United Spain Under Catholic Monarchs," *Encyclopædia Britannica* 28 (2005), 37–38.

131.   "Treaty of Tordesillas," *Encyclopædia Britannica*, 2012, web, 8 4, 2012.

132.   "Henry III," *Encyclopædia Britannica*, 2012, web, 8 4, 2012.

133.   "Henry IV," *Encyclopædia Britannica*, 2012, web, 8 4, 2012.

134.   "Isabella I," *Encyclopædia Britannica*, 2012, web, 8 4, 2012.

135.   "Sir Francis Drake," *Encyclopædia Britannica*, 2012, web, 8 4, 2012.

136.   "Elizabeth I," *Encyclopædia Britannica*, 2012, web, 8 4, 2012.

137.   "British Empire," *Encyclopædia Britannica* 2 (2005), 528–29.

138.   "James I," *Encyclopædia Britannica*, 2012, web, 8 4, 2012.

139.   "British Empire," *Encyclopædia Britannica*.

140.   "John Beaufort, 1st Earl of Somerset," *Wikipedia*, 12 4, 2011, web, 12 11, 2011.

141.   "Margaret Tudor," *Encyclopædia Britannica*, 2012, web, 8 4, 2012.

142.   "Henry VIII," *Encyclopædia Britannica*, 2012, web, 8 4, 2012.

143.   "Union of the Crowns 1603," Scotland's History (Education Scotland Foghlam Alba, 2012), 8 23, 2012, *www.educationscotland.gov.uk/scotlandshistory/unioncrownsparliaments/unionofthecrowns/index.*

144.   "James I," *Encyclopædia Britannica*, 2012, web, 8 4, 2012.

145.   "Jacques Cartier," *Encyclopædia Britannica*, 2012, web, 8 4, 2012.

146.   "French colonial empire," *Wikipedia*, 12 11, 2012, web, 12 11, 2012.

147.   "Henry II," *Encyclopædia Britannica*, 2012, web, 8 4, 2012.

148.   "Francis II" *Encyclopædia Britannica*, 2012, web, 8 4, 2012.

149.   "Charles IX," *Encyclopædia Britannica*, 2012, web, 8 4, 2012.

150.   "Francis, Duke of Anjou," *Wikipedia*, 12 7, 2011, web, 12 11, 2011.

151.   "Henry IV," *Encyclopædia Britannica*, 2012, web, 8 4, 2012.

152.   "Henry III," *Encyclopædia Britannica*, 2012, web, 8 4, 2012.

153.   "Henry IV," *Encyclopædia Britannica*.

154.   "History of the Low Countries," *Encyclopædia Britannica*, 2012, web, 8 4, 2012.

155.   "Mary of Burgundy," *Encyclopædia Britannica*, 2012, web, 8 4, 2012.

156.   "Charles V," *Encyclopædia Britannica*.

157.   "William I," *Encyclopædia Britannica*, 2012, web, 8 4, 2012.

158.   "Henry Hudson," *Encyclopædia Britannica*, 2012, web, 8 4, 2012.

159.   "Willem Barents," *Encyclopædia Britannica*, 2012, web, 8 4, 2012.

160.   "Abel Janszoon Tasman," *Encyclopædia Britannica*, 2012, web, 8 4, 2012.

161.   "Indonesia: Growth and Impact of the Dutch East India Company," *Encyclopædia Britannica*, 2012, web, 8 4, 2012.

162.   "William I," *Encyclopædia Britannica*.

163.   Blue Letter Bible. "Parsing Information," *Blue Letter Bible*, 1996–2011, 12 11, 2011, *www.blueletterbible.org/Bible.cfm?b=Rev&c=6&v=1&t=KJV#conc/2.*

164. "Crusades," *Encyclopædia Britannica*, 2012, web, 8 4, 2012.

165. "Reconquista," *Encyclopædia Britannica*, 2012, web, 8 4, 2012.

166. Bamber Gascoigne, "Fall of Constantinople: AD 1453," History World, 2001, 8 23, 2012, *www.historyworld.net/wrldhis/ plaintexthistories. asp?historyid=ab37*.

167. "Norman conquest," *Encyclopædia Britannica*, 2012, web, 8 4, 2012.

168. "Hundred Years' War," *Encyclopædia Britannica*, 2012, web, 8 4, 2012.

169. "Wars of the Roses," *Encyclopædia Britannica*, 2012, web, 8 4, 2012.

170. "List of wars 1000–1499," *Wikipedia*, 10 12, 2011, web, 10 30, 2011.

171. "List of wars 1500–1799," *Wikipedia*, 10 23, 2011,web, 10 30, 2011.

172. "List of wars 1800–1899," *Wikipedia*, 10 19, 2011, web, 10 30, 2011.

173. "Ivan III," *Encyclopædia Britannica*, 2012, web, 8 4, 2012.

174. "Russo-Swedish War (1495–1497)," *Wikipedia,* 7 20, 2011, web, 10 31, 2012.

175. "Vasili III," *Encyclopædia Britannica*, 2012, web, 8 25, 2012.

176. "Margaret I," *Encyclopædia Britannica*, 2012, web, 8 4, 2012.

177. "Russo-Swedish War (1495–1497)," *Wikipedia*.

178. "House of Habsburg," *Encyclopædia Britannica*, 2012, web, 8 4, 2012.

179. "Europe 1430, 1492–1522 (Map Game)," *Althistory Wikia*, 2011, 10 31, 2011, *althistory.wikia.com/wiki/Europe_1430,_1492–1522_(Map_Game)*.

180. "Mary of Burgundy," *Encyclopædia Britannica*.

181. "Anne of Brittany," *Encyclopædia Britannica*, 2012, web, 8 4, 2012.

182. Johnathan Bousfield and Rob Humphreys, *The Rough Guide to Austria* (U.S.A.: Penguin, 2088), 560.

183. "Ludovico Sforza," *Encyclopædia Britannica*, 2012, web, 8 4, 2012.

184. "Italian War of 1494–1498," *Encyclopædia Britannica* 18 (2005), 637–38.

185. "Louis XII," *Encyclopædia Britannica*, 2012, web, 8 4, 2012.

186. Machiavelli, *The Prince*, 77.

187. William Gilbert, "Chapter 4: The Invasions of Italy 1494–1527, Machiavelli and Guicciardini," *Renaissance and Reformation* (Lawrence, KS: Carrie, 1998), 8 25, 2012, *vlib.iue.it/carrie/texts/carrie_books/gilbert/04*.

188. "Italian Wars," *Encyclopædia Britannica*, 2012, web, 8 4, 2012.

189. Andrew C. Hess, "The Mediterranean and Shakespeare's Geopolitical Imagination," 'The Tempest' and Its Travels, Peter Hulme and William H. Sherman, ed. (U.K.: Reaktion Books, 2006), 122.

190. "Mamlūk," *Encyclopædia Britannica*, 2012, web, 8 4, 2012.

191. "Ottoman Empire: Selim I," *Encyclopædia Britannica*, 2012, web, 8 4, 2012.

192. "Ottoman Empire: Süleyman I," *Encyclopædia Britannica*, 2012, web, 8 4, 2012.

193. "Battle of Mohács," *Encyclopædia Britannica*, 2012, web, 8 4, 2012.

194. "Ottoman Empire: Süleyman I," *Encyclopædia Britannica*.

195. "Ethiopian–Adal War," *Encyclopædia Britannica* 1 (2005), 75–76.

196. "Ṭahmāsp I," *Encyclopædia Britannica*, 2012, web, 8 19, 2012.

197. "Ivan the Terrible," *Encyclopædia Britannica* 6 (2005), 439.

198. "Lithuanian and Polish rule," *Encyclopædia Britannica*, 2012, web, 8 25, 2012.

199. "Russo-Swedish War (1554–1557)," *Encyclopædia Britannica* 28 (2005), 333.

200. "Italian War of 1521–1526," *Encyclopædia Britannica* 18 (2005), 637–38.

201. "Germany: Lutheran church organization and confessionalization," *Encyclopædia Britannica*, 2012, web, 8 25, 2012.

202. "Italian War of 1551–1559," *Encyclopædia Britannica* 18 (2005), 637–38.

203. "Teutonic Order," *Encyclopædia Britannica*, 2012, web, 8 19, 2012.

204. "Albert," *Encyclopædia Britannica*, 2012, web, 8 19, 2012.

205. "Gustav I Vasa," *Encyclopædia Britannica* 5 (1995), 577.

206. Robert I. Frost, *The Northern Wars: War, State, and Society in Northeastern Europe, 1558–1721, Modern wars in perspective* (Upper Saddle River, NJ: Pearson Education, 2000).

207. "Livonian War," *Encyclopædia Britannica*, 2012, web, 8 15, 2012.

208. "Northern Seven Years' War," *Wikipedia*, 10 14, 2011, web, 11 17, 2011.

209. Nikolay Andreyev, "Ivan IV," *Encyclopædia Britannica*, 2012, web, 8 25, 2012.

210. "Royal Hungary and the Rise of Transylvania," *Encyclopædia Britannica*, 2012, web, 8 25, 2012.

211. "Moldavia," *Encyclopædia Britannica*, 2012, web, 8 25, 2012.

212. "Abbās I," *Encyclopædia Britannica*, 2012, web, 8 25, 2012.

213. "Eighty Years' War," *Encyclopædia Britannica* 4 (2005), 104.

214. "Portuguese Restoration War," *Wikipedia*, 10 5, 2011, web, 11 21, 2011.

215. "Desmond Rebellions, *Wikipedia*, 11 20, 2011, web, 11 21, 2011.

216. "Nine Years' War (Ireland)," *Wikipedia*, 8 27, 2011, web, 11 21, 2011.

217. "Religious war and the peace of Augsburg," *Encyclopædia Britannica*, 2012, web, 8 25, 2012.

218. John Hearsey McMillan Salmon, "The Wars of Religion," *Encyclopædia Britannica*, 2012, web, 8 25, 2012.

219. "French Wars of Religion," *Encyclopædia Britannica*, 19 (2005), 479–80.

220. Chris Butler, "An overview of the Thirty Years War (1618–48)," *Flow of History*, 2007, 8 25, 2012, *www.flowofhistory.com/units/west/13/FC88*.

221. "Thirty Years' War," *Wikipedia*.

222. "What was the population of Europe in the 1600's?," Yahoo Answers, 2010, 11 22, 2011, *answers.yahoo.com/question/index?qid=20100926013613AA7Tyb8*.

223. Vaughn Aubuchon, "World Population Growth History Chart," *Vaughn's Summaries*, 10 30, 2011, 11 22, 2011, *www.vaughns-1-pagers.com/history/world-population-growth.htm#topofpage*.

224. "Thirty Years' War," *Wikipedia*, 11 22, 2011, web, 11 22, 2011.

225. "World War I," *Wikipedia*, 11 22, 2011, web, 11 22, 2011.

226. "English Civil Wars," *Encyclopædia Britannica*, 2012, web, 8 25, 2012.

227. "Restoration," *Encyclopædia Britannica*, 2012, web, 8 25, 2012.

228.   "Glorious Revolution," *Encyclopædia Britannica*, 2012, web, 8 25, 2012.
229.   "English Civil Wars," *Encyclopædia Britannica*, 2012, web, 8 25, 2012.
230.   "The Fronde," *Encyclopædia Britannica*, 2012, web, 8 25, 2012.
231.   "Louis XIV," *Encyclopædia Britannica*, 2012, web, 8 25, 2012.
232.   George T. Thompson and Laural Elizabeth Hicks, *World History and Cultures* (Pensacola, FL: A Beka Book Publications, 1985), 253–55.
233.   "War of Devolution," *Encyclopædia Britannica*, 2012, web, 8 25, 2012.
234.   "William III," *Encyclopædia Britannica*, 2012, web, 8 25, 2012.
235.   "Dutch War," *Encyclopædia Britannica*, 2012,web, 8 25, 2012.
236.   "Golden Libert," *Wikipedia*, 11 18, 2011, web, 12 11, 2011.
237.   "Poland: the Commonwealth," *Encyclopædia Britannica*, 2012, web, 8 25, 2012.
238.   "The Khmelnytsky Insurrection," *Encyclopædia Britannica*, 2012, web, 8 25, 2012.
239.   "John II Casimir Vasa," *Encyclopædia Britannica*, 2012, web, 8 25, 2012.
240.   "Second Northern War," *Encyclopædia Britannica*, 2012, web, 8 25, 2012.
241.   "Anglo-Dutch Wars," *Encyclopædia Britannica*, 2012, web, 8 25, 2012.
242.   "Russo-Turkish Wars," *Encyclopædia Britannica* 10 (2005), 260.
243.   "Peace of Westphalia," *Encyclopædia Britannica*, 2012, web, 8 25, 2012.
244.   "Second Northern War," *Encyclopædia Britannica*, 2012, web, 8 25, 2012.
245.   "War of the Spanish Succession," *Encyclopædia Britannica*, 2012, web, 8 25, 2012.
246.   "War of the Spanish Succession," *Wikipedia*, 11 11, 2011, web, 11 27, 2011.
247.   Gabagool, "Locator map of the competing sides of the War of the Spanish Succession," *Wikipedia*, 6 14, 2009, 11 30, 2011, *en.wikipedia.org/wiki/File: WaroftheSpanishSuccession.png.*
248.   Gabagool, "Locator map of the competing sides of the War of the Austrian Succession before outset of the war (1740)," *Wikipedia*, updated 6 25, 2009, 11 30, 2011, *en.wikipedia.org/wiki/File:WaroftheAustrianSuccession.png.*
249.   "Peter I: The Persian campaign," *Encyclopædia Britannica*, 2012, web, 8 25, 2012.
250.   "Treaty of the Three Black Eagles," *Wikipedia*, 4 26, 2011, web, 11 27, 2011.
251.   "War of the Polish Succession," *Encyclopædia Britannica*, 2012, web, 8 25, 2012.
252.   "Russo-Turkish Wars," *Encyclopædia Britannica*.
253.   "Chickasaw," *Encyclopædia Britannica*, 2012, web, 8 25, 2012.
254.   "Dummer's War," *Wikipedia*, 11 10, 2011, web, 11 27, 2011.
255.   "Charles VI," *Encyclopædia Britannica*, 2012, web, 8 25, 2012.
256.   "War of the Austrian Succession," *Encyclopædia Britannica*, 2012, web, 8 25, 2012.
257.   "Carnatic Wars," *Encyclopædia Britannica*, 2012, web, 8 25, 2012.
258.   "King George's War," *Encyclopædia Britannica*, 2012, web, 8 25, 2012.

259. "War of Jenkins' Ear," *Encyclopædia Britannica*, 2012, web, 8 25, 2012.

260. "Seven Years' War," *Wikipedia*, 11 27, 2011, web, 11 29, 2011.

261. "Seven Years' War," *Encyclopædia Britannica*, 2012, web, 8 25, 2012.

262. Gabagool," Locator map of the competing sides of the Seven Years War before outset of the war (mid-1750s)," *Wikipedia*, 6 7, 2009, 11 30, 2011, *en.wikipedia.org/wiki/File:SevenYearsWar.png*.

263. Gabagool," Locator map of the competing sides of the Napoleonic Wars before outset of the war (early 1800s)," *Wikipedia*, 6 8, 2009, 11 30, 2011, *en.wikipedia.org/wiki/File:NapoleonicWars.png*.

264. "Pontiac," *Encyclopædia Britannica*, 2012, web, 8 25, 2012.

265. "Mysore Wars," *Encyclopædia Britannica*, 2012, web (8 25, 2012).

266. "Russo-Turkish Wars," *Encyclopædia Britannica*.

267. "Maratha Wars," *Encyclopædia Britannica*, 2012, web, 8 25, 2012.

268. "Mysore Wars," *Encyclopædia Britannica*.

269. "Cape Frontier Wars," *Encyclopædia Britannica*, 2012, web. 8 25, 2012.

270. "Australian Aborigine: the Europeans," *Encyclopædia Britannica*, 2012, web, 8 25, 2012.

271. "Viceroyalty of New Granada," *Encyclopædia Britannica*, 2012, web, 8 25, 2012.

272. "Battle of Fallen Timbers," *Encyclopædia Britannica*, 2012, web, 8 25, 2012.

273. "American Revolution," *Encyclopædia Britannica*, 2012, web, 8 25, 2012.

274. "Partitions of Poland," *Encyclopædia Britannica*, 2012, web, 8 25, 2012.

275. "Declaration of the Rights of Man and of the Citizen," *Encyclopædia Britannica*, 2012, web, 8 25, 2012.

276. "Alexis de Tocqueville," *Encyclopædia Britannica*, 2012, web, 8 25, 2012.

277. Alexis de Tocqueville, "Chapter XVII: Principal Causes Maintaining The Democratic Republic—Part II," *Democracy In America, Volume 1 (of 2)*, (Project Gutenberg, 1 21, 2006), 12 1, 2011, *www.gutenberg.org/files/815/815-h/815-h.htm#2HCH0041*.

278. "The Reign of Terror," *Encyclopædia Britannica*, 2012, web, 8 26, 2012.

279. "French revolutionary and Napoleonic wars," *Encyclopædia Britannica*, 2012, web, 8 26, 2012.

280. James Burke, "Eat, Drink and Be Merry," *Connnections: An Alternative View of Change* 6, documentary, directed by Mick Jackson, produced by James Burke (New York: Ambrose Video Publishing, 1978).

281. John A. Lynn, "Nation in Arms 1763–1815," in *Cambridge Illustrated History of Warfare: Triumph of the West*, Geoffrey Parker, ed., 186–213 (Cambridge: Cambridge University Press, 1995), 194.

282. Ibid., 187.

283. Ibid., 199.

284. "French revolutionary and Napoleonic wars," *Encyclopædia Britannica*.

285. Bamber Gascoigne, "History of Germany," *History World*, 2001, 8 26,

2012, *www.historyworld.net/wrldhis/PlainTextHistories.asp?groupid=2803& HistoryID=ac62&gtrack=pthc*, 8.

286. Bamber Gascoigne, "History of Italy," *History World*, 2001, 8 26, 2012, *www.historyworld.net/wrldhis/PlainTextHistories.asp?groupid =2699&History ID=ac52&gtrack=pthc*, 4.

287. Bamber Gascoigne, "History of Italy," 8.

288. Jluisrs, "Colonial empires in 1800," *Wikipedia*, 3 1, 2008, 12 11, 2011, *en.wikipedia.org/wiki/File:Colonisation_1800.png*.

289. Andrew0921, "World empires and colonies in 1914, just before the First World War," *Wikipedia*, 7 27, 2010, 12 11, 2011, *en.wikipedia.org/wiki/File:World_1914_empires_colonies_territory.PNG*.

290. "The Great Game," *Wikipedia*, 11 13, 2011, web, 12 1, 2011.

291. "Crimean War," *Encyclopædia Britannica*, 2012, web, 8 26, 2012.

292. "Ottoman Empire: The 1875–78 crisis," *Encyclopædia Britannica*, 2012, web, 8 26, 2012.

293. John Tenniel, "Great Game Cartoon Published in Punch magazine, Nov. 30 1878," *Wikipedia*, 11 27, 2005, 12 1, 2011, *en.wikipedia.org/wiki/File:Great_Game_cartoon_from_1878.jpg*.

294. Henri Meyer," "China—the cake of kings ... and emperors"; An illustration from supplement to "Le Petit Journal," 16th January 1898," *Wikipedia*, 8 8, 2011, 12 1, 2011, *en.wikipedia.org/wiki/File:China_imperialism_cartoon.jpg*.

295. Edward Linley Sambourne, "'The Rhodes Colossus' from Punch Dec. 10, 1892," *Wikipedia*, 10 10, 2007, 12 4, 2011, *en.wikipedia.org/wiki/File:Punch_Rhodes_Colossus.png*.

296. Patrick N. Allitt, "No. 15: China and the Opium War," *Victorian Britain*, course 8490 (The Great Courses, 2008).

297. "Imperialism in Asia," *Wikipedia*, 12 1, 2011, web 12 1, 2011.

298. "Scramble for Africa," *Wikipedia*, 12 2, 2011, web,12 4, 2011.

299. "World War I," *Encyclopædia Britannica*, 2012, web, 8 26, 2012.

300. Williamson A. Murray, "The Industrialization of War 1815–17," in *Cambridge Illustrated History of Warfare: Triumph of the West*, Geoffrey Parker, ed., 116–242 (Cambridge: Cambridge University Press, 1995), 223–241.

301. Williamson A. Murray, "The West at War 1914–1918," in *Cambridge Illustrated History of Warfare: Triumph of the West*, Geoffrey Parker, ed., 266–297 (Cambridge: Cambridge University Press, 1995), 266.

302. Thomashwang, "Map of the World showing the Participants in World War I," *Wikipedia*, 5 6, 2006, 12 4 2011, *en.wikipedia.org/wiki/File:WWI-re.png*.

303. Vittore Carpaccio, "1516, The Lion of St Mark (detail) Tempera on canvas, Palazzo Ducale, Venice," *Wikipedia*, 8 19, 2006, 12 4, 2011, *en.wikipedia.org/wiki/File:1516_Vittore_Carpacci,_The_Lion_of_St_Mark_(detail)_Tempera_on_canvas,_Palazzo_Ducale,_Venice.jpg*.

304.   Flanker, "Flag of Most Serene Republic of Venice," *Wikipedia*, 3 27, 2007, 12 11, 2011, *en.wikipedia.org/wiki/File:Flag_of_Most_Serene_ Republic_of_Venice.svg.*

305.   "Jesuit," *Encyclopædia Britannica*, 2012, web, 8 26, 2012.

306.   "Mission," *Encyclopædia Britannica*, 2012, web, 8 26, 2012.

307.   "Aldus Manutius the Elder," *Encyclopædia Britannica*.

308.   "Lion (heraldry)," *Wikipedia*, 12 1, 2011, web, 12 7, 2011.

309.   "Coat of arms of Sweden," *Wikipedia*, 10 2, 2011, web 12 8, 2011.

310.   "Picardy," *Wikipedia*, 8 16, 2011, web, 12 8, 2011.

311.   "Coat of arms of Castile and León," *Wikipedia*, 8 14, 2011, web, 12 8, 2011.

312.   "Duchy of Burgundy," *Wikipedia*, 10 7, 2011, web, 12 8, 2011.

313.   "Royal coat of arms of Scotland," *Wikipedia*, 11 21, 2011, web, 12 7, 2011.

314.   "Coat of arms of the Netherlands" *Wikipedia*, 12 2, 2011, web 12 7, 2011.

315.   "Coat of arms of Belgium," *Wikipedia*, 11 24, 2011, web 12 7, 2011.

316.   "Coat of arms of Finland," *Wikipedia*, 11 19, 2011, web, 12 7, 2011.

317.   "National symbols of Luxembourg," *Wikipedia*, 10 8, 2010, web, 12 7, 2011.

318.   "Coat of arms of Norway," *Wikipedia*, 12 24, 2011, web, 12 7, 2011.

319.   "Coat of arms of Flanders," *Wikipedia*, 11 21, 2011, web 12 8, 2011.

320.   "Lyon," *Wikipedia*, 12 4, 2011, web, 12 8, 2011.

321.   "Lion (heraldry)," *Wikipedia*.

322.   "Aquitaine," *Wikipedia*, 12 7, 2011, web, 12 8, 2011.

323.   "Normandy," *Wikipedia*, 12 4, 2011, web 12 8, 2011.

324.   "Royal Arms of England," *Wikipedia*, 12 7, 2011, web, 12 7, 2011.

325.   "Coat of arms of Denmark," *Wikipedia*, 11 15, 2011, web, 12 7, 2011.

326.   "Eagle (heraldry)," *Wikipedia*, 12 5, 2011, web, 12 8, 2011.

327.   "Russia," *Wikipedia*, 12 8, 2011, web, 12 7, 2011.

328.   "Romania," *Wikipedia*, 12 8, 2011, web, 12 8, 2011.

329.   "Reichsadler," *Wikipedia*, 11 22, 2011, web, 12 8, 2011.

330.   "Brandenburg-Prussia," *Wikipedia*, 12 7, 2011, web, 12 8, 2011.

331.   "German Empire," *Wikipedia*, 12 8, 2011, web, 12 8, 2011.

332.   "Poland," *Wikipedia*, 12 5, 2011, web, 12 8, 2011.

333.   "Austrian_Empire," *Wikipedia*, 12 3, 2011, web, 12 8, 2011.

334.   "Holy Roman Empire," *Wikipedia*, 12 8, 2011, web, 12 8, 2012.

335.   Created by Jane Cody—shields from sources cited in text.

336.   "European states by head of state," *Wikipedia*, 9 11, 2011, 12 7, 2011, *en.wikipedia.org/wiki/File:European_states_by_head_of_state.png.*

337.   "Vatican City," *Encyclopædia Britannica*, 2012, web, 8 26, 2012.

338.   "Andorra," *Encyclopædia Britannica*, 2012, web, 8 26, 2012.

339.   "Liechtenstein," *Encyclopædia Britannica*, 2012, web, 8 26, 2012.

340.   "Monaco," *Encyclopædia Britannica*, 2012, web, 8 26, 2012.

341.   "Monarchies in Europe," *Wikipedia*, 11 20, 2011, web, 12 7, 2011.

342.   "Partitions of Poland," *Encyclopædia Britannica*.

343.   "Russia: War and the Fall of the Monarchy," *Encyclopædia Britannica*, 2012, web, 8 26, 2012.

344. "Austria: End of the Habsburg Empire," *Encyclopædia Britannica*, 2012, web, 8 26, 2012.

345. "Germany: History" *Encyclopædia Britannica*, 2012, web, 8 26, 2012.

346. "Her Majesty: Her Children," *Queen Victoria's Empire* (PBS, 2012), web, 8 26, 2012, *www.pbs.org/empires/victoria/majesty/children.html*.

347. "Mary of Teck," *The Guide to Life, the Universe and Everything*, 5 2, 2009, 8 26, 2012, *www.h2g2.com/approved_entry/A404038*.

348. "Philip, duke of Edinburgh," *Encyclopædia Britannica*, 2012, web, 8 26, 2012.

349. Jone Johnson Lewis, "Queen Elizabeth—Elizabeth Bowes-Lyon—Queen Mum," *About.com Women's History*, 2012, 12 10, 2012, *womenshistory.about.com/od/queenmothers/p/elizabeth_queen.htm*

350. "Diana, Princess of Wales," *Wikipedia*, 12 11, 2012, web, 12 11, 2012.

351. "Catherine, Duchess of Cambridge," *Encyclopædia Britannica*, 2012, web, 8 26, 2012.

352. "Francis Ferdinand, archduke of Austria-Este," *Encyclopædia Britannica*, 2012, web, 8 26, 2012.

353. Thayer, 29.

354. Thayer, 559.

355. "Quintuple Alliance as related to Quadruple Alliance," *Encyclopædia Britannica* 9 (2010), 837.

356. "Ferdinand VII, 1814–1833," *Encyclopædia Britannica* 28 (2010), 54.

357. "Greek War of Independence," *Encyclopædia Britannica*, 2012, web, 8 26, 2012.

358. "France History: July Revolution," *Encyclopædia Britannica* 19 (2010), 510–11.

359. "Belgiam History: Kingdom of the Netherlands," *Encyclopædia Britannica* 14 (2010), 867.

360. "Poland History: Early Russian rule," *Encyclopædia Britannica* 25 (2010), 949.

361. "Revolutions of 1848," *Wikipedia*, 10 12, 2011, web 12 12, 2011.

362. Shane White, *The French Worker and the Revolution of 1848* (University of Kentucky, 2002), 6 14, 2012, *www.uky.edu/~popkin/frenchworker/white.htm*.

363. "Ireland History: Modern Ireland Under British rule," *Encyclopædia Britannica* 21 (2010), 1013.

364. "Italy History: the revolution of 1848," *Encyclopædia Britannica* 22 (2010), 229–30.

365. "France History: the revolution of 1848, the second republic," *Encyclopædia Britannica* 19 (2010), 510–12.

366. "Revolutions of 1848," *Encyclopædia Britannica*, 2012, web, 8 26, 2012.

367. "Germany History: the Revolutions of 1848–49," *Encyclopædia Britannica*, 2012, web, 8 26, 2012.

368. "Denmark History: the liberal movement," *Encyclopædia Britannica* 17 (2010), 239–40.

369. "Denmark History: The National Liberals and the Schleswig-Holstein question," *Encyclopædia Britannica* 17 (2010), 240.

370. Austria History: Revolution and counterrevolution, 1848–49," *Encyclopædia Britannica* 14 (2010), 523–25.

371. "Hungary History: Revolution, reaction and 'compromise'," *Encyclopædia Britannica* 20 (2010), 706.

372. "Switzerland History: The Liberal Triumph," *Encyclopædia Britannica*, 2012, web, 8 26, 2012.

373. Poland History: Emigration and Revolt," *Encyclopædia Britannica* 25 (2010), 949.

374. "Romania History: Nation building," *Encyclopædia Britannica*, 2012, web, 8 26, 2012.

375. United Kingdom History: Chartism and the Anti-Corn Law League," *Encyclopædia Britannica*, 2012, web, 8 26, 2012.

376. "Communism," *Encyclopædia Britannica*, 2012, web, 8 26, 2012.

377. "Liberalism," *Encyclopædia Britannica*, 2012, web, 8 26, 2012.

378. "Hegelians," *Encyclopædia Britannica*, 2012, web, 8 26, 2012.

379. "Karl Marx," *Encyclopædia Britannica*, 2012, web, 8 26, 2012.

380. "Marxism," *Encyclopædia Britannica*, 2012, web, 8 26, 2012.

381. Cyril Smith, "The Communist Manifesto After 150 Years," *Cyril Smith Internet Archive* (Marxist Internet Archive, 1998) 12 14, 2011, *www.marxists.org/reference/archive/smith-cyril/works/articles/cyril_02.htm*

382. Karl Marx and Richard Engels, "Manifesto of the Communist Party," *Marx/Engels Selected Works,* 1 (Moscow: Progress Publishers, 1969), 98–137, Samuel Moore, trans. On Marx/Engels Internet Archive, 2000, 12 15, 2011, *www.marxists.org/archive/marx/works/1848/communist-manifesto/index.htm.*

383. "Fabian Society," *Encyclopædia Britannica*, 2012, web, 8 26, 2012.

384. "Leninism," *Encyclopædia Britannica*, 2012, web, 8 26, 2012.

385. Paul Brians, *Karl Marx and Friedrich Engels: The Communist Manifesto (1848)* (Washington State University, 12 23, 1998) 12 15, 2011, *public. wsu.edu/~wldciv/world_civ_reader/world_civ_reader_2/marx.html*

386. Nicole Smith, "Analysis and Chapter Summaries of Das Kapital by Karl Marx" (Article Myriad, 2011) 12 19, 2011, *www.articlemyriad.com/marx_kapital_chapter_summary_analysis.htm.*

387. "Karl Marx: Analysis of the economy," *Encyclopædia Britannica*, 2012, web, 8 26, 2012, 3.

388. "Liberalism," *Encyclopædia Britannica*, 2012, web, 8 26, 2012.

389. "John Locke," *Encyclopædia Britannica*, 2012, web, 8 26, 2012.

390. "Liberalism: Classical liberalism," *Encyclopædia Britannica*.

391. "Laissez-faire," Liberalism," *Encyclopædia Britannica*, 2012, web, 8 26, 2012.

392. "Corn Laws," *Encyclopædia Britannica*, 2012, web, 8 26, 2012.

393. "Liberalism," *Encyclopædia Britannica*.

394. John Stuart Mill, *On Liberty* (London: Longman, Roberts & Green, 1869, Bartleby.com, 1999), 11 11, 2012, *www.bartleby.com/130.*

395. John Stuart Mill, *Principles of political economy, with some of their applications to social philosophy in two volumes* (Google Books, 1848), web, 6 18, 2012, 239–40.

396. Fred Wilson, "John Stuart Mill," *The Stanford Encyclopedia of Philosophy* (Fall 2011), 12 17, 2011, *plato.stanford.edu/archives/fall2011/entries/mill.*

397. "Monarchies in Europe," *Wikipedia*, 11 20, 2011, web, 12 7, 2011.

398. "France History 1815–1940," *Encyclopædia Britannica*, 2012, web, 8 26, 2012.

399. "Switzerland, the Liberal Triumph," *Encyclopædia Britannica*, 2012, web, 8 26, 2012, 23.

400. "San Marino History," *Encyclopædia Britannica*, 2012, web, 8 26, 2012, 2.

401. "bull market," *Encyclopædia Britannica*, 2012, web, 8 26, 2012.

402. "bear market," *Encyclopædia Britannica*, 2012, web, 8 26, 2012.

403. "Stock Market History," *Stock Market Investing Guide* (2004), 12 18, 2011, *www.stockmarketinvestinginfo.com/smi_history.html*.

404. Jason Chavis, 1800s History of the Stock Market," eHow (1999–2011), 12 15, 2011, *www.ehow.com/facts_5032867_history-stock-market.html*.

405. Leonard "Craven Hill" Raven-Hill, As Between Friends from Punch, or The London Charivari 141:429, 12 13, 2011 7 28, 2012, *commons.wikimedia.org/wiki/File:As_Between_Friends_(Punch_magazine,_13_December_1911).jpg*.

406. "Misha," *Wikipedia*, 12 5, 2011, web 12 19, 2011.

407. "Russia History: The October(November) Revolution)," *Encyclopædia Britannica*, 2012, web, 8 26, 2012, 69.

408. Thompson and Hicks, *World History*, 360.

409. R. G. Price, "The Russian Revolution," The War is About So Much More, March and April, 2003, 12 20, 2011, *rationalrevolution.net/war/russian_revolution.htm*.

410. Karl Marx, *Critique of the Gotha Programme*, Marxists Internet Archive: 130 Karl Marx Quotes & 30 Frederick Engels Quotes, 1875, 12 20, 2011, *www.marxists.org/archive/marx/works/subject/quotes/index.htm*.

411. John Simkin, Communist Secret Police: Cheka, Spartacus Educational, 1979, 12 20, 2011, *www.spartacus.schoolnet.co.uk/RUScheka.htm*.

412. Hephaestos, John Bull, World War I recruiting poster, c. 1915, *Wikipedia*, 8 1, 2005, 8 15, 2012, *en.wikipedia.org/wiki/File:John_Bull_-_World_War_I_recruiting_poster.jpeg*.

413. "Did You Know ... Where the Name 'John Bull' Comes From?" Historic UK: The Heritage Accommodation Guide, 2011, 12 20, 2011, *www.historic-uk.com/CultureUK/JohnBull.htm*.

414. "Social liberalism, *Wikipedia*, 12 21, 2011, web, 12 21, 2011.

415. "Labour Party (UK)," *Wikipedia*, 12 19, 2011, web, 12 21, 2011.

416. "Liberalism: The modern liberal program," *Encyclopædia Britannica*, 2012, web, 8 26, 2012, 6.

417. Sheri Berman, Understanding Social Democracy, Georgetown University, 2011, 12 21, 2011, *www8.georgetown.edu/centers/cdacs/bermanpaper.pdf*.

418. "Georges Sorel," *Encyclopædia Britannica*, 2012, web, 8 26, 2012.

419. "Socialism: Syndicalism," *Encyclopædia Britannica*, 2012, web, 8 26, 2012.

420. John Simkin, "Eduard Bernstein," Sparticus Educastional, 1997, 12 21, 2011, *www.spartacus.schoolnet.co.uk/GERbernstein.htm*.

421. Eduard Bernstein, *Evolutionary Socialism*, Edith C. Harvey, trans., Marxist Internet Archives, 3 16, 2003, web, 12 21, 2011.

422. Berman, *Understanding Social Democracy.*

423. "Georges Sorel," *Encyclopædia Britannica.*

424. "Georges Sorel," Friends of Oswald Mosley, 2005–2011, 12 21, 2011, *www.oswaldmosley.com/georges-sorel.htm.*

425. fascism (definition), *Merriam-Webster*, 2011, web 12 21, 2011.

426. "Fascism," *Wikipedia*, 12 22, 2011, web, 12 22, 2011.

427. Jon Jay Ray, *Hitler Was a Socialist* (Jon Jay Ray Tripod, 5 2012), 8 20, 2012, *jonjayray.tripod.com/hitler.html*

428. Ray, *Hitler Was a Socialist.*

429. Otto Rühle, "The Struggle Against Fascism Begins with the Struggle Against Bolshevism," (Marxist Internet Archive, 1939), web 12 22, 2011

430. Daniel D. Moseley, "What is Libertarianism?" Social Science Research Network, *Basic Income Studies*, 6:2. 2011, *papers.ssrn.com/sol3/papers.cfm?abstract_id=1872578.*

431. "Introduction to World War-1," *Worldwar-1*, 2006, 12 14, 2011, *www.worldwar-1.net.*

432. "Total War," History Learning Site, 2000–2012, 6 19, 2012, *www.historylearningsite.co.uk/total_war.htm.*

433. "The Blitz," *Wikipedia*, 12 24, 2011, web, 12 24, 2011.

434. "rumor (definition)," *Merriam-Webster*, 2011, web, 12 14, 2011.

435. "Rumor," *Wikipedia*, 12 2, 2011, web, 12 24, 2011.

436. Paul Jonathan Meller, "The Development of Modern Propaganda in Britain, 1854–1902," Phd diss., Durham University, 2010, 12 24, 2011, *etheses.dur.ac.uk/246*, 57–58.

437. "The Times," *Wikipedia*, 12 23, 2011, web, 12 24, 2011.

438. "Crimean War," *Wikipedia*, 12 1, 2011, web, 12 1, 2011.

439. Meller, "The Development of Modern Propaganda," 87–92.

440. "Propaganda and World War One," History Learning Site, 2000–2011, 12 24, 2011, *www.historylearningsite.co.uk/propaganda_and_world_war_one.htm.*

441. "American propaganda during World War II," *Wikipedia*, 12 20, web, 2011, 12 24, 2011.

442. "Fireside chats," *Wikipedia*, 2 24, 2011, web, 3 3, 2011.

443. "King George VI Addresses the Nation," BBC Archive— WWII: Outbreak | Britain on the brink of World War II, 1939, 12 24, 2011, *www.bbc.co.uk/archive/ww2outbreak/7918.shtml.*

444. "George VI," *Encyclopædia Britannica*, 2012, web, 8 26, 2012.

445. "Nazi propaganda," *Wikipedia*, 12 6, 2011, web, 12 24, 2011.

446. "Tokyo Rose," *Wikipedia*, 11 23, 2011, web, 12 24, 2011.

447. "Mildred Gillars," *Encyclopædia Britannica*, 2012, web, 8 26, 2012.

448. "Rita Zucca," *Wikipedia*, 12 13, 2011, web, 12 24, 2011.

449. "William Joyce," *Encyclopædia Britannica*, 2012, web, 8 26, 2012.

450. "Leni Riefenstahl," *Encyclopædia Britannica*, 2012, web, 8 26, 2012.

451. Fritz Hippler, "Campaign in Poland (Felzug in Poland)," film (St. Clare Vision, 1940).

452. "Frank Capra," *Encyclopædia Britannica*, 2012, web, 8 26, 2012.

453. Jennifer Rosenberg, "Hiroshima and Nagasaki," *About.com 20th Century History*, 2011, 12 25, 2011, *history1900s.about.com/od/worldwarii/a/hiroshima.htm*.

454. John Pike, "Cold War—Rollback," Global Security, 2000–2012, 6 19, 2012, *www.globalsecurity.org/military/ops/cold-war-rollback.htm*.

455. "File:Soviet empire 1960," *Wikipedia*, 8 9, 2010, 6 20 2012, *en.wikipedia.org/wiki/File:Soviet_empire_1960.png*.

456. "Korean War," *Encyclopædia Britannica*, 2012, web, accessed 8 26, 2012.

457. "Vietnam War," *Encyclopædia Britannica*, 2012, web, 8 26, 2012.

458. "Communist revolution," *Wikipedia*, 11 26, 2011, web, 12 25, 2011.

459. "Cold War," *Wikipedia*, 12 25, 2011, web, 12 25, 2011.

460. "Shakhty Trial," *Wikipedia*, 12 10, 2011, web, 12 25, 2011.

461. "Red Scare," *Wikipedia*, 12 15, 2011, web, 12 25, 2011.

462. Thayer, 182.

463. "The Holmes and Rahe Stress Scale," Mind Tools, 1996–2012, 8 27, 2012, *www.mindtools.com/pages/article/newTCS_82.htm*.

464. "Great Chain of Being," *Encyclopædia Britannica*, 2012, web, 8 27, 2012.

465. "Russian Revolution of 1917," *Encyclopædia Britannica*, 2012, web, 8 27, 2012.

466. "China History: War Between Nationalists and Communists," *Encyclopædia Britannica*, 2012, web, 8 27, 2012, 143.

467. John Simkin, "Robert Raikes," Spartacus Educational, 1997–2012, 8 27, 2012, *www.spartacus.schoolnet.co.uk/EDraikes.htm*.

468. "History of education in England," *Wikipedia*, 12 14, 2011, web, 12 26, 2011.

469. "History of education in the United States," *Wikipedia*, 12 15, 2011, web, 12 26, 2011.

470. "History of education in the United States."

471. Dennis O'Neil, Socialization, Palomar College, 12 8, 2011, 8 27, 2012, *anthro.palomar.edu/social/soc_1.htm*.

472. Vladimir Lenin, "Vladimir Lenin Quotes," Brainiy Quotes, 2001–2011, 12 26, 2011, *www.brainyquote.com/quotes/quotes/v/vladimirle153238.html*.

473. Theodore Caplow, Louis Hicks and Ben Wattenberg, *The First Measured Century: An Illustrated Guide to Trends in America, 1900-2000* (Washington, DC: American Enterprise Institute for Public Policy Research, 2001), 53.

474. "Kindergarten," *Wikipedia*, 12 14, 2012, web, 12 17, 2012.

475. Caplow, et. al., 58.

476. "Home-Schooling: Socialization not a problem," *Washington Times*, 12 13, 2009, 12 25, 2011, *www.washingtontimes.com/news/2009/dec/13/home-schooling-socialization-not-problem*.

477. Sheldon Harrick, "Tevye's Monologue," from Fiddler on the Roof, St Lyrics, 2002–2011, 12 26, 2011, *www.stlyrics.com/lyrics/fiddlerontheroof/tevyesmonologue.htm*.

478. John P. McKay, Bennett D. Hill, and John Buckler, "Chapter 24: Life in the Emerging Urban Society," *A History of Western Society* (Cengage Learning: Online Study Center, 2010), ed. 7, 12 26, 2011, *college.cengage.com/history/west/mckay/western_society/7e/students/glossary/ch24.html#i, 805*.

479. William M. Reddy, "The History of Romantic Love" (Duke University, 2008), 12 26, 2011, *www.duke.edu/~wmr/romantic%20love.htm*

480. "Anthony Giddens, Baron Giddens," *Wikipedia*, 12 3, 2011, web, 12 26, 2011.

481. "The Hollywood Romantic Love Myth," Pickup Artist Porai Koshitz: Your awesome Tagline, 8 24, 2010, 12 26, 2011, *porai747.tumblr.com/post/2924143735/the-hollywood-romantic-love-myth*.

482. Eban Harrell, "Are Romantic Movies Bad For You? *Time* magazine, 12 23, 2008, 12 26, 2011, *www.time.com/time/health/article/0,8599,1868389,00.html*.

483. Steven Halpern, "Quotations about Stress," The Quote Garden, 1998–2011, 12 26, 2011, *www.quotegarden.com/stress.html*.

484. "Demographics of the United States," *Wikipedia*, 12 30, 2011, web, 12 30, 2011.

485. "Urbanization," *Wikipedia*, 12 21, 2011, web, 12 28, 2011.

486. "Victorian Cities and Towns." The Victorian Web, 6 29,2011, 12 28, 2011, *www.victorianweb.org/places/cities/cities.html*.

487. Patrick N. Allitt, "No. 10: Work and Working-Class Life," *Victorian Britain*, course 8490 (The Great Courses, 2008).

488. "History of Europe: the 'Second Industrial Revolution.'" *Encyclopædia Britannica*, 2012, web, 8 27, 2012, 125.

489. "Scientific management," *Wikipedia*, 12 9, 2012, web, 12 18, 2012.

490. "Frank Bunker Gilbreth, Sr.," *Wikipedia*, 12 18, 2012, web, 12 18, 2012.

491. "Joseph Lister, 1st Baron Lister," *Encyclopædia Britannica*, 2012, web, 8 27, 2012.

492. "Florence Nightingale," *Encyclopædia Britannica*, 2012, web, 8 27, 2012.

493. "Charles Darwin," *Encyclopædia Britannica*, 2012, web, 8 27, 2012.

494. "Alfred Russel Wallace," *Wikipedia*, 12 18, 2011, web, 12 27, 2011.

495. "Herbert Spencer," *Encyclopædia Britannica*, 2012, web, 8 27, 2012.

496. Richard W. Macomber, "Sir Charles Lyell, Baronet," *Encyclopædia Britannica*, 2012, web, 8 27, 2012.

497. Adrian J. Desmond, "T. H. Huxley," *Encyclopædia Britannica*, 2012, web, 8 27, 2012.

498. Adrian J. Desmond, "Charles Darwin: The private man and the public debate," *Encyclopædia Britannica*, 7.

499. Adrian J. Desmond, "T. H. Huxley," *Encyclopædia Britannica*.

500. "Alfred Russel Wallace," *Encyclopædia Britannica*.

501. "Herbert Spencer," *Encyclopædia Britannica*.

502. "Charles Lyell," *Wikipedia*, 11 20, 2011, web, 12 27, 2011.

503. V. I. Lenin, "On the Significance of Militant Materialism," Marxist Internet Archive, 2002, 12 27, 2011, *www.marxists.org/archive/lenin/works/1922/mar/12.htm*.

504. "Laissez-faire," Liberalism," *Encyclopædia Britannica*.

505. "Gregor Mendel," *Encyclopædia Britannica*, 2012, web, 8 27, 2012.

506. Geoffrey H. Beale, Jr., "August Weismann," *Encyclopædia Britannica*, 2012, web, 8 27, 2012.

507. Jon Jay Ray, "Eugenics and the Left," *Front Page* magazine, 9 25, 2003, 12 28, 2011, *archive.frontpagemag.com/readArticle.aspx?ARTID=16217*.

508. Ibid.

509. "Eugenics," *Encyclopædia Britannica*, 2012, web, 8 27, 2012.

510. Sophie J. Evans, *Public Policy Issues Research Trends* (New York: Nova Science Publishers, 2008) 126.

511. "Scientific racism," *Wikipedia*, 12 28, 2012, web, 12 28, 2012.

512. Ibid.

513. "Phrenology," *Encyclopædia Britannica*, 2012, web, 8 27, 2012.

514. "Turning race into 'species,'" *Encyclopædia Britannica*, 2012, web, 8 27, 2012.

515. "The White Man's Burden," *Wikipedia*, 12 28, 2011, web, 12 28, 2011.

516. Mark P. Mostert, "Useless Eaters: Disability as Genocidal Marker in Nazi Germany," *The Journal of Special Education* 36:3 (2002), 155–168, 12 28, 2011.

517. Jennifer Rosenberg, "Holocaust Facts: What You Need to Know About the Holocaust," About.com 20th Century History, 2011, web, 12 29, 2011.

518. John K. Roth, "Theodicy of Protest," *Encountering Evil: Live Options in Theodicy*, Steven T. Davis, ed. (Louisville KY, Westminster John Knox Press, 2001), 2.

519. "Ukraine Famine," United Human Rights Council, 2012, 6 21, 2012, *www.unitedhumanrights.org/genocide/ukraine_famine.htm*.

520. "Ukrainian Famine," Library of Congress: Revelations from the Russian Archives, 7 22, 2010, 12 29, 2011, www.*loc.gov/exhibits/archives/ukra.html*.

521. R. J. Rummel, "Power, Genocide and Mass Murder," *Journal of Peace Research* 31: 1 (1994) 1–10, 12 30, 1211, *hawaii.edu/powerkills/POWER.ART.HTM*.

522. "Khmer Rouge," *Encyclopædia Britannica*, 2012, web, 8 27, 2012.

523. R. J. Rummel, "Democide: Nazi Genocide and Mass Murder." *Power Kills*, 1993, 12 30, 2011, *hawaii.edu/powerkills/NAZIS.CHAP1.HTM*.

524. R. J. Rummel, "How Many Did Communist Regimes Murder?" *Power Kills*, 1993, 12 30, 2011, *www.hawaii.edu/powerkills/COM.ART.HTM*.

525. Rummel, "Power, Genocide and Mass Murder."

526. "Totalitarianism (definition), Merriam-Webster, 2012, web, 8 25, 2012.

527. Thayer, 393.

528. Strong, 1028–30.

529. "U.S. Civil War Weapons," *Real Armor of God*, 2005–2011, 11 30, 2011, *www.realarmorofgod.com/civil-war-weapons.html*.

530. "List of infantry weapons of World War I," *Wikipedia*, 12 15, 2011, web, 12 30, 2011.

531. "List of common World War II infantry weapons," *Wikipedia*, 12 29, 2012, web, 12 30, 2012.

532. "U.S. Civil War Weapons."

533. Donald N. Moran "George Washington's Swords," *Revolutionary War Archives* (Liberty Tree Newsletter, 6 2004), 12 30, 2011, *www.revolutionarywararchives.org/washsword.html*.

534. Howard G. Lanham, "Presentation Swords and Scabbards," *Union Army Uniforms and Insignia of the American Civil War 1861–1865*, 1998, 12 30, 2011, *howardlanham.tripod.com/link11e.htm*.

535. "Sword," *Wikipedia*, 12 24, 2011, web, 12 30, 2011.

536. Lanham.

537. Richard Swain, "Reflection on an Ethic of Officership," U.S. Army War College, 2007, 12 30, 2011, *www.carlisle.army.mil/usawc/parameters/Articles/07spring/swain.pdf*.

538. "Surrender at Appokmattox, 1865," Eye Witness to History (1997) 8 27, 2012, *www.eyewitnesstohistory.com*.

539. "The Presentation of a Samurai Sword," The Millicent Library, Fairhaven, MA, 1918, 1926, 12 30, 2011, *manjiro1.tripod.com/sword1918.htm*.

540. "The Presentation of a Samurai Sword."

541. "Invasion of the Soviet Union, 1941," *Encyclopædia Britannica*, 2012, web, 8 27, 2012.

542. "Volgograd," *Wikipedia*, 12 29, 2011, web, 1 1, 2012.

543. U.S. Signal Corps Photo, "Teheran conference—1943," *Wikipedia*, 11 28 to 12 1, 1943, 1 1, 2012, *en.wikipedia.org/wiki/File:Teheran_conference-1943.jpg*.

544. Eduard Levin, "Sword of Stalingrad," *Wikipedia*, 6 11, 2009, 1 1, 2012, *en.wikipedia.org/wiki/File:Sword_of_Stalingrad.jpg*.

545. Simon Sebag Montefiore, *Stalin: the Court of the Red Tsar* (New York: Vintage Books, 2005), 468.

546. Montefiore, xix.

547. Piers Brendon, "Sir Winston Churchill: Biographical History," Churchill College Cambridge, 3 6, 2009, 1 1, 2012. *www.chu.cam.ac.uk/archives/collections/churchill_papers/biography/*.

548. "Franklin D. Roosevelt," *Encyclopædia Britannica*, 2012, web, 8 27, 2012.

549. Charles G. Stefan, "Roosevelt and the Wartime Summit Conferences with Stalin," *American Diplomacy*, 1997, 1 1, 2012, *www.unc.edu/depts/diplomat/AD_Issues/amdipl_6/stefan.html#intro*.

550. "Tehrn Conference," *Encyclopædia Britannica*, 2012, web, 8 27, 2012.

551. "Joseph Stalin," *Encyclopædia Britannica*, 2012, web, 8 27, 2012, 3.

552. Joanne Hubbs, *Mother Russia: the feminine myth in Russian culture* (USA: Indiana University Press, 1993) 26.

553. Hubbs, 43.

554. Hubbs, 253.

555. Hubbs, 31.

556. Brown, Driver, and Briggs, 803.

557. Brown, Driver, and Briggs, 803.

558. "Russia: Land," *Encyclopædia Britannica*, 2012, web, 8 27, 2012, 1.

559. Laural Brown, "Topographical Map of Russia"; Painting based on information from U.S. Visa to Russia—Russia Information—Maps of Russia, 6 22, 2012, *www.usvisatorussia.com/russiamaps.htm*.

560. Pauline Weston Thomas, "Rational Dress Reform," Fashion-Era.com, 2001–2012, 8 27, 2012, *www.fashion-era.com/rational_dress.htm*.

561. Patricia A. Cunningham, Reforming Woman's Fashion, 1850–1920: Politics, Health, and Art (Kent, Ohio: The Kent State University Press, 2003), 171.

562. Tom Gross, "Communist Underwear is the Latest Art," *Art Around the World*, 7 31, 2001, 1 2, 2012, *www.tomgrossmedia.com/art/archives/000325.html*.

563. Sue Best, "Foundations of femininity: Berlei corsets and the (un)making of the modern body," *Murdoch University School of Media Communication and Culture, Australia*, 1991, 1 2, 2012, *wwwmcc.murdoch.edu.au/ReadingRoom/5.1/Best.html*.

564. "History of brassieres," *Wikipedia*, 1 2, 2012, web, 1 2, 2012.

565. Karl Marx, "130 Karl Marx Quotes & 30 Frederick Engels Quotes," *Marxists Internet Archive*, 1868, 1 2, 2012, *www.marxists.org/archive/marx/works/subject/quotes/index.htm*.

566. John Stuart Mill, "The Subjection of Women," *Constitution Society*, 11 4, 2011, 1 2, 2012, *www.constitution.org/jsm/women.htm*.

567. "Declaration of Sentiments and Resolutions," The Elizabeth Cady Stanton & Susan B. Anthony Papers Project (Rutgers: The State University of New Jersey, 1997), 8 27, 2012, *ecssba.rutgers.edu/docs/seneca.html*.

568. "Elizabeth Cady Stanton," *Encyclopædia Britannica*, 2012, web, accessed 8 28, 2012.

569. "Says Suffragettes Lean to Socialism" *The New York Times*, 4 1,1908, 1 2, 2012, *query.nytimes.com/mem/archive-free/pdf?res=FB0A11FF3F5A177 38DDDA80894DC405B888CF1D3*.

570. Elizabeth Cady Stanton, "'Elizabeth Cady Stanton on Socialism' published in Progressive Women," *Pittsburgh: University of Pittsburgh, Digital Research Library*, 3 3, 2008, 1 2,2012, *digital.library.pitt.edu/cgi-bin/t/text/pageviewer-idx?c=amlefttxt;cc=amlefttxt;q1=Socialist%20Party%20of%20the%20 United%20States%20of%20America;rgn1=subject;idno=rjo0117;rgn=works; didno=rjo0117;view=image;seq=4;page=root;size=s;frm=frameset;*.

571. "Biography of Susan B. Anthony," *Susan B. Anthony House*, 2009, 1 3, 2012, *susanbanthonyhouse.org/her-story/biography.php*.

572. Gary Daily "Woman's Rights: Debs and Women's Rights—A Lifetime Commitment," *Eugene V. Debs Foundation*, 2011, 1 3, 2012, *debsfoundation. org/womensrights.html*.

573. "Ella Reeve Bloor," *Wikipedia*, 12 17, 2012, web, 1 3, 2012.

574. Margaret Sanger, "Woman and the New Race: XII. Will Birth Control Help The Cause Of Labor?," *Marxist Internet Archive*, 1920, 1 3, 2012 *www.marxists.org/subject/women/authors/sanger/labor.html*.

575. Tim Davenport, "Intercollegiate Socialist Society (1905–1921)," *Marxist History*, 2011, 1 3, 2012, *www.marxisthistory.org/subject/usa/eam/iss.html*.

576. "NAACP History: Mary White Ovington," *National Association for the Advancement of Colored People*, 2009–2011, 1 3, 2012, *www.naacp.org/pages/naacp-history-Mary-White-Ovington*.

577. Helen Keller, Her Socialist Years: Writings and Speeches, Phillip S. Agnew, ed. (New York: International Publishers, 1967), 120, 123.

578. "Helen Keller," *Encyclopædia Britannica*, 2012, web, 8 28, 2012.

579. John Simkin, "Helen Keller," *Spartacus Educational*, 1997, 1 3, 2012, *www.spartacus.schoolnet.co.uk/USAkeller.htm*.

580. John Simkin, "Emmeline Pankhurst," *Spartacus Educational*, 1997, 1 4, 2012, *www.spartacus.schoolnet.co.uk/WpankhurstE.htm*.

581. V. I. Lenin, "Soviet Power and the Status of Women," *Marxists Internet Archive*, 11 6, 1919, 1 2, 2012, *www.marxists.org/archive/lenin/works/1919/nov/06.htm*.

582. Mao Tse Tung, "Quotations from Mao Tse Tung," *Marxists Internet Archive*, 1955, 1 2, 2012, *www.marxists.org/reference/archive/mao/works/red-book/ch31.htm*.

583. Karl Marx, "Manifesto of the Communist Party," *Marxists Internet Archive*, 1947, 6 24, 2012, *www.marxists.org/archive/marx/works/1848/communist-manifesto/ch01.htm*.

584. Fulton J. Sheen, "Communism and Woman," *Catholic Apologetics Information*, 1947, 1 4, 2012, *www.catholicapologetics.info/morality/general/cwoman.htm*

585. "The Russian Effort To Abolish Marriage," *Equal Justice Foundation*, 2001, 1 4, 2012, *www.ejfi.org/Civilization/Civilization-5.htm*.

586. Jennifer Rosenberg, "Flappers in the Roaring Twenties," *About.com Guide*, 2001, web, 1 4, 2012.

587. "United States: New Social Trends," *Encyclopædia Britannica*, 2012, web, 8 28, 2012.

588. "Flapper," *Wikipedia*, 1 8, 2012, web, 1 10, 2012.

589. Teresa R. Wagner and Leslie Carbone, *Fifty Years After the Declaration: The United Nations' Record on Human Rights* (Lantham, Maryland: University Press of America, 2001), 111.

590. Zoe Williams, "Marie Stopes: a turbo-Darwinist ranter, but right about birth control," *The Guardian*, 9 2, 2011, 8 28, 2012, *www.guardian.co.uk/theguardian/2011/sep/02/marie-stopes-right-birth-control*.

591. "Married Love," *Wikipedia*, 11 4, 2011, web, 1 10, 2012.

592. "woman's movement," *Encyclopædia Britannica*, 2012, web, accessed 8 28, 2012.

593. Henry Makow, "American Communism and the Making of Women's Liberation," *Jesus is Savior*, 7 12, 2003, 1 11, 2012, *www.jesus-is savior.com/Evils%20in%20America/Feminism/american_communism_and_feminism.htm*.

594. Kate Weigand, *Red Feminism: Communism and the Making of Women's Liberation* (Baltimore, MD: The Johns Hopkins University Press, 2001), 154.

595. Weigand, 149–50.

596. Margalit Fox, "Betty Friedan, Who Ignited Cause in 'Feminine Mystique,' Dies at 85," *The New York Times*, 2 5, 2006, 1 11, 2012, *www.nytimes.com/2006/02/05/national/05friedan.html?pagewanted=all*.

597. David Horowitz, " Betty Friedan's Secret Communist Past," *Salon*, 1 18, 1999, 1 11, 2012, *writing.upenn.edu/~afilreis/50s/friedan-per-horowitz.html*.

598. Daniel Horowitz, *Betty Friedan and the Making of The Feminine Mystique: The American Left, the Cold War and Modern Feminism* (USA: Sheridan Books, Inc., 1998), 90–93.

599. Carey Roberts, "The Untold Story of Betty Friedan," *ifeminists*, 11 25, 2003, 1 11, 2012, *www.ifeminists.net/introduction/editorials/2003/1125roberts. html*.

600. Marianne Schnall, "Interview with Gloria Steinem," *Feminist.com*, 3 3, 1995, 6 24, 2012, *www.feminist.com/resources/artspeech/interviews/gloria.htm/*.

601. Gloria Steinem, "Women Are Never Front-Runners," *The New York TImes*, 1 8, 2008, 8 28, 2012, *www.nytimes.com/2008/01/08/opinion/08steinem.html*.

602. "Democratic Socialists of America," *Wikipedia*, 12 27, 2011, web, 1 12, 2012.

603. "Democratic Socialists of America."

604. Barbara Ehrenreich, "What is Socialist Feminism?" *Marxist Internet Archive*, 1976, 6 24, 2012, *www.marxists.org/subject/women/authors/ehrenreich-barbara/socialist-feminism.htm*.

605. Germaine Greer, "Germaine Greer. 1970. The Female Eunuch. Summary," *Marxist Internet Archive*, 1971, 6 24, 2012, *www.marxists.org/subject/women/authors/greer-germaine/female-eunuch.htm*.

606. "Peter Alekseyevich Kropotkin: Philosopher of revolution," *Encyclopædia Britannica*, 2012, web, 8 28, 2012, 2.

607. Christine Wallace, *Germaine Greer, Untamed Shrew*, cited in "Germaine Greer," *Wikipedia*, 1 5, 2012, 1 14, 2012, *en.wikipedia.org/wiki/Germaine_Greer*.

608. "Red Rag: A Magazine of Women's Liberation (1973?–1980?)," *Grassroots Feminism*, 11 12, 2009, 1 12,2012, *www.grassrootsfeminism.net/cms/node/521*.

609. "Redstockings," *Wikipedia*, 12 26, 2011, web, 1 14, 2012.

610. "S.C.U.M. Manifesto," *Wikipedia*, 1 14, 2012, web 1 14, 2012.

611. "Andy Warhol," *Encyclopædia Britannica*, 2012, web, 8 28, 2012.

612. "American Experience: The Pill: People & Events: Margaret Sanger (1879–1966)," *PBS Online*, 1999–2001, 1 15, 2012, *www.pbs.org/wgbh/amex/pill/peopleevents/p_sanger.html*.

613. "Planned Parenthood History & Successes," *Planned Parenthood*, 2012, 1 15, 2012, *www.plannedparenthood.org/about-us/who-we-are/history-and-successes.htm*.

614. "Combined oral contraceptive pill," *Wikipedia*, 1 13, 2012, web, 1 14, 2012.

615. "Planned Parenthood History & Successes," *Planned Parenthood, 2012, 1 15, 2012, www.plannedparenthood.org/about-us/who-we-are/history-and-successes.htm*.

616. "Spare Rib (Magazine, 1972–1993)," *Grassroots Feminism*, 7 7,2009, 1 12, 2012, *www.grassrootsfeminism.net/cms/node/234*.

617. Victoria Woodhull, *Encyclopædia Britannica*, 2012, web, 8 28, 2012.

618. "Sexual revolution," *Wikipedia*, 1 12, 2012, web, 1 15, 2012.

619. "Same-Sex Marriage is a Feminist Issue," National Organization for Women, 5 17, 2004, 8 28, 2012, *www.now.org/issues/lgbi/marr-rep.html*.

620. "Helen Gurley Brown," *Encyclopædia Britannica*, 2012, web, accessed 8 28, 2012.

621. "The Russian Effort To Abolish Marriage," *Equal Justice Foundation*, 2001, 1 4, 2012, *www.ejfi.org/Civilization/Civilization-5.htm*.

622. William Robert Johnston, "Historical abortion statistics, U.S.S.R.," *Johnston's Archive*, 11 21, 2010, 1 15, 2012, *www.johnstonsarchive.net/policy/abortion/ab-ussr.html*.

623. Weiliang Nie, "China's one-child policy—success or failure?" *BBC Chinese Service*, 8 24, 2012, 1 15, 2012, *www.bbc.co.uk/news/world-asia-pacific-11404623*.

624. William Robert Johnston, "Historical abortion statistics, PR China," *Johnston's Archive*, 11 21, 2010, 1 15, 2012, *www.johnstonsarchive.net/policy/abortion/ab-prchina.html*.

625. William Robert Johnston, "Historical abortion statistics, United States," *Johnston's Archive*, 1 17, 2011, 1 15, 2012, *www.johnstonsarchive.net/policy/abortion/ab-unitedstates.html*.

626. William Robert Johnston, "Historical abortion statistics, United Kingdom," *Johnston's Archive*, 11 21, 2010, 1 15, 2012, *www.johnstonsarchive.net/policy/abortion/ab-unitedkingdom.html*.

627. William Robert Johnston, "Abortion statistics and other data," *Johnston's Archive*, 11 11, 2011, 1 17, 2012, w*ww.johnstonsarchive.net/policy/abortion/index.html*.

628. "Deists," *Wikipedia*, 1 12, 2012, web, 1 22, 2012.

629. "Humanist Manifesto," *Wikipedia*, 1 2, 2012, web, 1 22, 2012.

630. Fritz Stevens, Edward Tabash, Tom Hill, Mary Ellen Sikes, and Tom Flyn," What Is Secular Humanism?," *Council for Secular Humanism, 2011*, 1 22, 2012, *www.secularhumanism.org/index.php?page=what&section=main*.

631. "Julian Huxley," *Wikipedia*, 1 20, 2012, web, 1 22, 2012.

632. "Brock Chisholm," *Wikipedia*, 3 8, 2011, web, 1 22, 2012.

633. "John Boyd-Orr," *Wikipedia*, 12 27, 2011, web. 1 22, 2012.

634. "The Beatles," *Encyclopædia Britannica*, 2012, web, 8 28, 2012.

635. John J. Dunphy, "My View—The Book that Started It All," *Council for Secular Humanism,* Winter 2005–2006, 1 22, 2012, *www.secularhumanism.org/index.php?section=library&page=dunphy_21_4*.

636. "Prayer In Public School—A Brief History," *All About History*, 2002–2012, 1 22, 2012, *www.allabouthistory.org/prayer-in-public-school.htm*.

637. "United States presidential election of 1952," *Encyclopædia Britannica*, 2012, web, 8 28, 2012.

638. "Olympic Dates and History," *World Atlas: Explore Your World*, 2012, 1 22 2012, *www.worldatlas.com/aatlas/infopage/olympic.htm*.

639. "Africa: Libya," *CIA—The World Factbook*, 12 22, 2012, 1 29, 2012, *www.cia.gov/library/publications/the-world-factbook/geos/ly.html*.

640. "Elizabeth II," *Encyclopædia Britannica*, 2012, web, 8 28, 2012.

641. "Former Governors General," *The Governor General of Canada*, 2012, 1 22, 2012, *www.gg.ca/document.aspx?id=55*.

642. "Today (NBC program)," *Wikipedia*, 1 21, 2012, web,1 22, 2012.

643. "I Love Lucy," *Wikipedia*, 1 22, 2012, web, 1 22, 2012.

644.   "C. Walton Lillehei," *Encyclopædia Britannica*, 2012, web, 8 28, 2012.

645.   "Man Will Conquer Space Soon!" *Wikipedia*, 8 12, 2011, web, 1 22, 2012.

646.   "Wernher von Braun," *Encyclopædia Britannica*, 2012, web, 8 28, 2012.

647.   "European Coal and Steel Community," *Encyclopædia Britannica*, 2012, web, 8 28, 2012.

648.   "European Parliament," *Encyclopædia Britannica*, 2012, web, 8 28, 2012.

649.   Thayer, 386.

650.   Michael Douma, "The color of our eyes, hair and skin," *In Causes of Color*, 2008, 1 23, 2012, *www.webexhibits.org/causesofcolor/7F.html*.

651.   Thayer, 168.

652.   "Chicano Movement," *Wikipedia*, 12 11, 2011, web, 1 23, 2012.

653.   "Czechoslovakia," *Wikipedia*, 1 21, 2012, web, 1 23, 2012.

654.   "Yugoslav Wars," *Wikipedia*, 1 22, 2012, web, 1 23, 2012.

655.   "LGBT social movements," *Wikipedia*, 1 21, 2012, web, 1 24, 2012.

656.   Brian Duignan, "Brown v. Board of Education of Topeka," *Encyclopædia Britannica*, 2012, web, 8 28, 2012.

657.   "Brown v. Board of Education, 347 U.S. 483 (1954) (USSC+)," *The National Center for Public Policy Research*, 2012, 1 24, 2012, *www.nationalcenter.org/brown.html*.

658.   Lisa Cozzens, "The Murder of Emmett Till," *African American History*, 1997, 1 24, 2012, *www.watson.org/~lisa/blackhistory/early-civilrights/emmett.html*.

659.   Chris Crowe, "The Lynching of Emmett Till," *The History of Jim Crow*, 2012, 1 26, 2012, *www.jimcrowhistory.org/resources/lessonplans/hs_es_emmett_till.htm*.

660.   "Rosa Louise Parks Biography," *Parks Institute for Self Development, 2012*, 1 24, 2012, *www.rosaparks.org/index.php?option=com_content&view=article&id=118&Itemid=60*.

661.   Lisa Cozzens, "The Montgomery Bus Boycott," *African American History*, 1997, 1 26, 2012, *www.watson.org/~lisa/blackhistory/citing.html*.

662.   Lisa Cozzens, "Sit-Ins," *African American History*, 1997, 1 26, 2012, *www.watson.org/~lisa/blackhistory/civilrights-55-65/sit-ins.html*.

663.   Eric Foner, "Bound for Glory," *The New York Times*, 2 19, 2006, 1 26, 2012, *www.nytimes.com/2006/03/19/books/review/19foner.html*.

664.   Lisa Cozzens, "Freedom Rides," *African American History*, 1997, 1 26, 2012, *www.watson.org/~lisa/blackhistory/civilrights-55-65/freeride.html*.

665.   Lisa Cozzens, "Birmingham," *African American History*, 1997, 1 26, 2012, *www.watson.org/~lisa/blackhistory/civilrights-55-65/birming.html*.

666.   "Birmingham Campaign (1963)," Martin Luther King, Jr. and the Global Freedom Struggle, 2012, 1 27, 2012, *www.kinginstitute.info/*.

667.   "March on Washington for Jobs and Freedom," Martin Luther King, Jr. and the Global Freedom Struggle, 2012, 1 27, 2012, *www.kinginstitute.info/*.

668.   Lisa Cozzens, "The March on Washington," *African American History*, 1997, 1 27, 2012, *www.watson.org/~lisa/blackhistory/civilrights-55-65/marchwas.html*.

669.   Cozzens, "The March on Washington."

670. "March on Washington for Jobs and Freedom."

671. Steve Mount, "Amendment 24—Poll Tax Barred," *US Constitution.net*, 1 24, 2010, 1 27, 2012, *www.usconstitution.net/xconst_Am24.html*.

672. "The Civil Rights Act of 1968," My Library of Congress, 2012, 1 29, 2012, *myloc.gov/Exhibitions/naacp/civilrightsera/ExhibitObjects/ CivilRightsAct1968*.

673. "March on Washington for Jobs and Freedom."

674. Chris Trueman, "Black Power," History Learning Site, 2000–2012, 1 29, 2012, *www.historylearningsite.co.uk/black_power.htm*.

675. Michael W. Jones, "Famous Humanists—Baldwin, James," 7 15, 2012, 7 30, 2012, *www.eloquentatheist.com/2012/07/famous-humanists-baldwin-james/*.

676. "Africa: Liberia," *CIA—The World Factbook*, 11 17, 2011, 1 29, 2012, *www.cia.gov/library/publications/the-world-factbook/geos/li.html*.

677. "Africa: Ethiopia," *CIA—The World Factbook*, 1 11, 2012, 1 30, 2012, *www.cia.gov/library/publications/the-world-factbook/geos/et.html*.

678. Thomas P. Ofcansky and LaVerle Berry, ed., *Ethiopia: A Country Study*, Federal Research Division, Library of Congress DT373 .E83 1993, 3 22, 2011, 7 31, 2012, *lcweb2.loc.gov/frd/cs/ettoc.html*.

679. "Africa: Eritrea," *CIA—The World Factbook*, 1 11, 2012, 1 29, 2012, *www. cia.gov/library/publications/the-world-factbook/geos/er.html*.

680. "Africa: Libya," *CIA*.

681. "Africa: Egypt," *CIA—The World Factbook*, 1 11, 2012, 1 30, 2012, *www. cia.gov/library/publications/the-world-factbook/geos/eg.html*.

682. "People in the News: Moroccan Sultan Returns From Exile," (United Kingdom: Pathe News, 1955), 7 31, 2012, *www.britishpathe.com/video/ moroccan-sultan-returns-from-exile*.

683. "Africa: Morocco," *CIA—The World Factbook*, 1 11, 2012, 1 30, 2012, *www.cia.gov/library/publications/the-world-factbook/geos/mo.html*.

684. "Africa: Tunisia," *CIA—The World Factbook*, 1 10, 2012, 1 30, 2012, *www.cia.gov/library/publications/the-world-factbook/geos/ts.html*.

685. "Africa: Sudan," *CIA—The World Factbook*, 1 17, 2012, 1 30, 2012, *www. cia.gov/library/publications/the-world-factbook/geos/su.html*.

686. "Africa: Ghana," *CIA—The World Factbook*, 1 17, 2012, 1 30, 2012, *www. cia.gov/library/publications/the-world-factbook/geos/gh.html*.

687. La Verle Berry, ed., *Ghana: A Country Study*, Federal Research Division, Library of Congress DT510 .G44 1995, 7 27, 2010, 7 31, 2012, *lcweb2. loc.gov/frd/cs/ghtoc.html*.

688. "Guinea—History, *Encyclopedia of the Nations*, 2012, 7 31, 2012, *www. nationsencyclopedia.com/Africa/Guinea-HISTORY.html#b*.

689. "Africa: Guinea," *CIA—The World Factbook*, 11 15, 2011, 1 30, 2012, *www.cia.gov/library/publications/the-world-factbook/geos/gv.html*.

690. Danielle Costa, "Decolonization and French Society," *University of London: History of Europe Since 1945*, 5 1999, accessed 7 31, 2012, *www. indyflicks.com/danielle/papers/paper06.htm*.

691. "Africa: Benin," *CIA—The World Factbook*, 1 19, 2012, 1 31, 2012, *www. cia.gov/library/publications/the-world-factbook/geos/bn.html*.

692. "Africa: Burkina Faso," *CIA—The World Factbook*, 12 22, 2012, 1 31, 2012, *www.cia.gov/library/publications/the-world-factbook/geos/uv.html*.

693. "Africa: Central African Republic," *CIA—The World Factbook*, 1 19, 2012, 2 1, 2012, *www.cia.gov/library/publications/the-world-factbook/geos/ct.html*.

694. "Africa: Chad," *CIA—The World Factbook*, 1 11, 2012, 1 31, 2012, *www. cia.gov/library/publications/the-world-factbook/geos/cd.html*.

695. "Africa: Republic of the Congo," *CIA—The World Factbook*, 1 11, 2012, 1 31, 2012, *www.cia.gov/library/publications/the-world-factbook/geos/cf.html*.

696. "Africa: Côte d'Ivoire," *CIA—The World Factbook*, 1 19, 2012, 1 31, 2012, *www.cia.gov/library/publications/the-world-factbook/geos/iv.html*.

697. "Africa: Gabon," *CIA—The World Factbook*, 1 19, 2012, 1 31, 2012, *www. cia.gov/library/publications/the-world-factbook/geos/gb.html*.

698. "Africa: Madagascar," *CIA—The World Factbook*, 1 17, 2012, 1 31, 2012, *www.cia.gov/library/publications/the-world-factbook/geos/ma.html*.

699. "Africa: Mali." *CIA—The World Factbook*, 12 21, 2011, 1 31, 2012, *www. cia.gov/library/publications/the-world-factbook/geos/ml.html*.

700. "Africa: Mauritania," *CIA—The World Factbook*, 1 5, 2012, 1 31, 2012, *www.cia.gov/library/publications/the-world-factbook/geos/mr.html*.

701. "Africa: Niger." *CIA—The World Factbook*, 12 17, 2011, 1 31, 2012, *www. cia.gov/library/publications/the-world-factbook/geos/ng.html*.

702. "Africa: Senegal," *CIA—The World Factbook*, 11 17, 2011, 1 31, 2012, *www.cia.gov/library/publications/the-world-factbook/geos/sg.html*.

703. "Africa: Togo," *CIA—The World Factbook*, 1 4, 2012, 1 31, 2012, *www. cia.gov/library/publications/the-world-factbook/geos/to.html*.

704. "Africa: Congo, Democratic Republic of the," *CIA—The World Factbook*, 1 19, 2012, 2 1, 2012, *www.cia.gov/library/publications/the-world-factbook/geos/cg.html*.

705. "Africa: Nigeria," *CIA—The World Factbook*, 1 4, 2012, 1 31, 2012, *www. cia.gov/library/publications/the-world-factbook/geos/ni.html*.

706. "Nigeria—History," *Encyclopedia of the Nations*, 2012, 7 31, 2012, *www. nationsencyclopedia.com/Africa/Nigeria-HISTORY.html*.

707. "Africa: Somalia," *CIA—The World Factbook*, 11 23, 2011, 1 31, 2012, *www.cia.gov/library/publications/the-world-factbook/geos/so.html*.

708. "Africa: Cameroon," *CIA—The World Factbook*, 1 17, 2012, 2 1, 2012, *www.cia.gov/library/publications/the-world-factbook/geos/cm.html*.

709. "Sierra Leone—History," *Encyclopedia of the Nations*, 2012, 7 31, 2012, *www.nationsencyclopedia.com/Africa/Sierra-Leone-HISTORY.html*.

710. "Africa: South Africa," *CIA—The World Factbook*, 1 19, 2012, 2 1, 2012, *www.cia.gov/library/publications/the-world-factbook/geos/sf.html*.

711. "Tanzania—History," *Encyclopedia of the Nations*, 2012, 7 31, 2012, *www. nationsencyclopedia.com/Africa/Tanzania-HISTORY.html*.

712. "Africa: Burundi," *CIA—The World Factbook*, 1 19, 2012, 2 1, 2012, *www.cia.gov/library/publications/the-world-factbook/geos/by.html*.

713. "Africa: Rwanda," *CIA—The World Factbook*, 1 19, 2012, 2 1, 2012, *www. cia.gov/library/publications/the-world-factbook/geos/rw.html*.

714. "Africa: Algeria," *CIA—The World Factbook*, 1 15, 2012, 2 1, 2012, *www. cia.gov/library/publications/the-world-factbook/geos/ag.html*.

715. "Uganda—History," *Encyclopedia of the Nations*, 2012, 7 31, 2012, *www. nationsencyclopedia.com/Africa/Uganda-HISTORY.html*.

716. (Africa: Uganda) *CIA—The World Factbook*, 1 19, 2012, 2 1, 2012, *www. cia.gov/library/publications/the-world-factbook/geos/ug.html*.

717. "Kenya—History," *Encyclopedia of the Nations*, 2012, 7 31, 2012, *www. nationsencyclopedia.com/Africa/Kenya-HISTORY.html*.

718. "Africa: Malawi," *CIA—The World Factbook*, 1 19, 2012, 2 2, 2012, *www. cia.gov/library/publications/the-world-factbook/geos/mi.html*.

719. "Africa: Zambia," *CIA—The World Factbook*, 1 17, 2012, 2 2, 2012, *www. cia.gov/library/publications/the-world-factbook/geos/za.html*.

720. "Africa: Gambia, The," *CIA—The World Factbook*, 1 18, 2012, 2 2, 2012, *www.cia.gov/library/publications/the-world-factbook/geos/ga.html*.

721. "Africa: Botswana," *CIA—The World Factbook*, 1 19, 2012, 2 2, 2012, *www.cia.gov/library/publications/the-world-factbook/geos/bc.html*.

722. "Africa: Lesotho" *CIA—The World Factbook*, 1 24, 2012, 2 2, 2012, *www. cia.gov/library/publications/the-world-factbook/geos/lt.html*.

723. "Africa: Swaziland," *CIA—The World Factbook*, 1 19, 2012, 2 2, 2012, *www.cia.gov/library/publications/the-world-factbook/geos/wz.html*.

724. "Africa: Mauritius," *CIA—The World Factbook*, 1 17, 2012, 2 2, 2012, *www.cia.gov/library/publications/the-world-factbook/geos/mp.html*.

725. "Ifni," Merriam-Webster, 2012, web, 7 31, 2012.

726. Eric Solsten and Sandra Meditz, ed., *Spain: A Country Study*, Federal Research Division, Library of Congress DP17 .S67 1990, 7 27, 2010, 7 31, 2012, *lcweb2.loc.gov/frd/cs/estoc.html*.

727. "Africa: Equitorial Guinea," *CIA—The World Factbook*, 1 19, 2012, 2 2, 2012, *www.cia.gov/library/publications/the-world-factbook/geos/ek.html*.

728. Eric Solsten, ed., *Portugal: A Country Study*, Federal Research Division, Library of Congress DP517 .P626 1993, 7 27, 2010, 7 31, 2012, *lcweb2. loc.gov/frd/cs/pttoc.html*.

729. "Guinea-Bissau—History" *Encyclopedia of the Nations*, 2012, 7 31, 2012, *www.nationsencyclopedia.com/Africa/Guinea-Bissau-HISTORY.html*.

730. "Africa: Guinea-Bissau," *CIA—The World Factbook*, 1 18, 2012, 2 2, 2012, *www.cia.gov/library/publications/the-world-factbook/geos/pu.html*.

731. "Angola—History," *Encyclopedia of the Nations*, 2012, 7 31, 2012, *www. nationsencyclopedia.com/Africa/Angola-HISTORY.html*.

732. "Mozambique—History," *Encyclopedia of the Nations*, 2012, 7 31, 2012, *www.nationsencyclopedia.com/Africa/Mozambique-HISTORY.html*.

733. "Africa: Mozambique," *CIA—The World Factbook*, 1 17, 2012, 2 2, 2012, *www.cia.gov/library/publications/the-world-factbook/geos/mz.html*.

734. "Africa: Western Sahara," *CIA—The World Factbook*, 11 17, 2011, 2 2, 2012, *www.cia.gov/library/publications/the-world-factbook/geos/wi.html*.

735. Solsten and Meditz, *Spain.*

736. "Africa: Comoros," *CIA—The World Factbook,* 1 19, 2012, 2 2, 2012, *www.cia.gov/library/publications/the-world-factbook/geos/cn.html.*

737. "French African Dependencies—Mayotte," *Encyclopedia of the Nations,* 2012, 7 31, 2012, *www.nationsencyclopedia.com/Africa/French-African-Dependencies-MAYOTTE.html.*

738. "Africa: Djibouti," *CIA—The World Factbook,* 12 21, 2011, 2 2, 2012, *www.cia.gov/library/publications/the-world-factbook/geos/dj.html.*

739. "Africa: Zimbabwe," *CIA—The World Factbook,* 1 19, 2012, 2 2, 2012, *www.cia.gov/library/publications/the-world-factbook/geos/zi.html.*

740. "Africa: Nambia," *CIA—The World Factbook,* 1 17, 2012, 2 2, 2012, *www.cia.gov/library/publications/the-world-factbook/geos/wa.html.*

741. "Africa: South Sudan," *CIA—The World Factbook,* 1 11, 2012, 2 2, 2012, *www.cia.gov/library/publications/the-world-factbook/geos/od.html.*

742. Blue Letter Bible, "Revelation of Jesus Christ 6—(NKJV—New King James Version)," Blue Letter Bible, 1996–2012, 2 2, 2012, *www.blueletterbible.org/Bible.cfm?b=Rev&c=6&t=NKJV.*

743. Blue Letter Bible, "Revelation of Jesus Christ 6—(NIV—New International Version)," Blue Letter Bible, 1996–2012, 2 2, 2012, *www.blueletterbible.org/Bible.cfm?b=Rev&c=6&t=NIV.*

744. Blue Letter Bible, "Revelation of Jesus Christ 6—(NASB—New American Standard Bible)," Blue Letter Bible, 1996–2012, 2 2, 2012, *www.blueletterbible.org/Bible.cfm?b=Rev&c=6&t=NASB.*

745. Thayer, 272–73.

746. Brown, Driver, and Briggs, 630–31.

747. Brown, Driver, and Briggs, 803.

748. "Snake bites," Midiline Plus, National Institutes of Health, 9 1, 2011, 2 2, 2012, *www.nlm.nih.gov/medlineplus/ency/article/000031.htm.*

749. Brown, Driver, and Briggs, 675.

750. Vincent J. Cannato, "A Home of One's Own," *National Affairs* 3, Spring 2010, 2 2, 2012, *www.nationalaffairs.com/publications/detail/a-home-of-ones-own.*

751. Roger Burrows, "Home-Ownership and Poverty in Britain," Joseph Rondtree Foundation, 1 8, 2010, 2 2, 2012, http://www.jrf.org.uk/publications/home-ownership-and-poverty-britain.

752. Cannato, "A Home of One's Own."

753. "Buying a Home in America today is Expensive Thanks to the Banking Sector: Examining Income and Home Prices from 1950 to the Present. Can Home Prices Fall Another 38 Percent?" *My Budget 360,* 1 5, 2010, web, 2 3, 2012.

754. "Prime Rate: Historical Data," Mortgage (ARM) Indexes, 1998–2012, 2 3, 2012, *mortgage-x.com/general/indexes/prime.asp.*

755. "Not Just for the Elite: A History of College Student Loans in America," *Random History and Word Origins for the Curious Mind,* 3 15, 2008, 2 5, 2012, *www.randomhistory.com/1-50/032loan.html.*

756. "Servicemen's Readjustment Act (G.I. Bill)," *NOLO Legal Encyclopedia*, 2012, 2 5, 2012, *www.nolo.com/legal-encyclopedia/content/gi-bill-act.html*.

757. "Principles and Practices of Financial Aid Administration," *College Board*, 2012, 2 5, 2012, *www.collegeboard.com/prod_downloads/prof/principlesandpracticesofFA.pdf*.

758. "History of the Perkins Loan," eHow Money, 2 28, 2011, 2 5, 2012, *www.ehow.com/info_7984782_history-perkins-loan.html*.

759. "History: Timeline of Important Events," The New Hampshire Higher Education Assistance Foundation Network, 2012, 2 5, 2012, *www.gsmr.org/index.asp?page=abt_timeline*.

760. "Direct Stafford Loans," Federal Student Aid, 6 30, 2011, 2 5, 2012, *studentaid.ed.gov/PORTALSWebApp/students/english/studentloans.jsp?tab=funding*.

761. "Federal changes lead to a record year for student loans," Stanford University News Service, 3 23, 1993, 2 5, 2012, *news.stanford.edu/pr/95/950323Arc5311.html*.

762. Ibid.

763. "Direct Stafford Loans."

764. "Trends in Student Aid 2011: Overview of Loans," *College Board*, 2011, 5 5, 2012, *trends.collegeboard.org/student_aid/report_findings/indicator/accessible/Overview_of_Loans*.

765. "Durbin Applauds Subcommittee Passage of Legislation to Restore Fairness in Student Lending," Dick Durbin: US Senator for Illinois, Assistant Majority Leader, 12 10, 2009, 2 5, 2012, *durbin.senate.gov/public/index.cfm/pressreleases?ID=885de006-f6a8-4197-9c1e-6a86fd95cf8b*.

766. "Is college worth the money and debt? The cost of college has increased by 11x since 1980 while inflation overall has increased by 3x. Diluting education with for-profits, and saddling millions with debt," *My Budget 360*, 1 5, 2012, web, 2 5, 2012.

767. "The $1 trillion student loan market begins to implode – Department of Education shows two-year default rate at for-profit colleges up to 15 percent. Student loan debt increasing at a rate of $170,000 per minute," *My Budget 360*, 9 13, 2011, web, 2 5, 2012.

768. "Student Loans in Bankruptcy," Lawyers.com, 2011, 2 6, 2012, *bankruptcy.lawyers.com/consumer-bankruptcy/Student-Loans-In-Bankruptcy.html*.

769. "Durbin Applauds ..."

770. "Credit Cards the Opiate of the American Middle Class—The Withdrawal is in And the Wall Street Dealers are Raking in Trillions of Dollars. 2 Credit Cards for Every Man, Woman, and Child in the U.S." My Budget 360, 4 1, 2010, web, 2 6, 2012.

771. Mary Bellis, "Who Invented Credit Cards?" About.com Inventors—The New York Times, 2012, 2 6, 2012, *inventors.about.com/od/cstartinventions/a/credit_cards.htm*.

772. Ben Woolsey and Emily Starbuck Gerson, "The history of credit cards," Credit Cards.com, 2012, 2 6, 2012, *www.creditcards.com/credit-card-news/credit-cards-history-1264.php*.

773. Leslie McFadden, "Credit cards trump state usury law," Bankrate.com, 2012, 2 6, 2012, *www.bankrate.com/finance/credit-cards/credit-cards-trump-state-usury-law.aspx.*

774. Terry Woster, "Slight shift in law changed trajectory of state's history," Argus Leader.com, 2012, 2 7, 2012, *www.argusleader.com/apps/pbcs.dll/article?AID=/20070813/NEWS/708130308/1186/COSTOFCREDIT.*

775. Robin Stein, "The Ascendancy of the Credit Card Industry," *PBS Frontline: Secret history of the Credit Card,* 11 23, 2004, web, 2 7, 2012.

776. Woster, "Slight shift in law changed trajectory of state's history."

777. Stein, "The Ascendancy of the Credit Card Industry."

778. "FICA and the Credit Card Financial Prison: How a Three Digit Credit Score Reflects Consumerism and not Financial Independence," *My Budget 360,* 12 3, 2009, web, 2 7, 2012.

779. Marlena Telvick, "Charge It!" *PBS Frontline: Secret History of the Credit Card,* 11 23, 2004, web, 2 7, 2012.

780. "The systematic financial pillaging of the middle class—Millionaires don't feel rich unless they have $7.5 million while 45 million Americans live on food stamps. Another 50 percent cannot come up with $2,000 in the next 30 days," *My Budget 360,* 6 11, 2011, web, 2 7, 2012.

781. "How the Middle Class Slowly Evaporated in the Last 40 Years—Loss of Manufacturing, Bank Deregulation, Hyper Consumption, and Short-term Profit Seeking from Wall Street," *My Budget 360,* 3 24, 2010, web, 2 7, 2012.

782. "The great American debt purge ..."

783. Thayer, 669.

784. Susan Headley, "What is a Denarius?" *About.com Coins,* 2012, 2 8, 2012, *coins.about.com/od/coinsglossary/g/denarius_define.htm.*

785. Thayer, 132.

786. "Coins: Denarius/Penny/Talent/Farthing/Mite," Historic Jesus, 2012, 2 8, 2012, *www.historicjesus.com/glossary/coins.html.*

787. Kimberly B. Flint-Hamilton, "Legumes in Ancient Greece and Rome: Food, Medicine or Poison?" *Hesperia: The Journal of the American School of Classical Studies at Athens* 68:3 (Jul.–Sep., 1999), 371–385, 2 8, 2012, *www.jstor.org/pss/148493.*

788. Fuiltigherne ni Ruadh O'Finn, "Roman Foods," *Early Period: Roman Life,* 8 14, 2007, 2 8, 2012, *housebarra.com/EP/ep01/02romanfood.html.*

789. "Historical Inflation Rates: 1914–2012," US Inflation Calculator, 2012, 2 8, 2012, *www.usinflationcalculator.com/inflation/historical-inflation-rates/.*

790. "What Things Cost: Prices for 1952," Fifties Web, 2012, 2 8, 2012, *www.fiftiesweb.com/pop/prices-1952.htm.*

791. "Find US Dollar's Value from 1913–2011," Inflation Calculator, 2012, 2 8, 2012, *www.usinflationcalculator.com/.*

792. Bill Marsh, "A History of Home Values," *The New York Times,* 8 26, 2006, 2 8, 2009, *www.nytimes.com/imagepages/2006/08/26/weekinreview/27leon_graph2.html.*

793. "Buying a Home in America today is Expensive Thanks to the Banking Sector: Examining Income and Home Prices from 1950 to the Present. Can Home Prices Fall Another 38 Percent?" *My Budget 360*, 1 5, 2010, web, 2 8, 2012.

794. Sue Kirchhoff, "Bubble or not, high home prices can hurt," *USA Today*, 5 13, 2005, 2 8, 2012, *www.usatoday.com/money/perfi/housing/2005-05-10-housing-cover_x.htm*.

795. "Cost of Home Ownership," Visual Economics, 2010, 2 9, 2012, *visualeconomics.creditloan.com/the-cost-of-home-ownership/*.

796. Ben Engebreth, "Housing Price-to-Income Ratio as a Way to Measure Maximum Local Affordability," Ben Engebreth.org, 6 2, 2005, 2 9, 2012, *www.benengebreth.org/2005/06/housing_priceto*.

797. "House prices vs average earnings: What next?" Mail online: This is Money, 4 29, 2010, 2 9, 2012, *blogs.thisismoney.co.uk/2010/04/house-prices-vs-average-earnings.html*.

798. Ben W., "The Dangerous Disconnect Between Home Prices and Fundamentals," eFinance Directory, 7 9, 2007, 2 9, 2012, *efinancedirectory. com/articles/The_Dangerous_Disconnect_Between_Home_Prices_and_Fundamentals.html*.

799. Lynn Carpenter, "The Real Basket of Goods," Inflation Data, 8 17, 2011, 2 10, 2012, *inflationdata.com/articles/2011/08/17/the-real-basket-of-goods/*.

800. John Cloud, "The Rising Costs of Food," *Time* magazine, 6 21, 2007, 2 10, 2012, *www.time.com/time/magazine/article/0,9171,1635836,00. html#ixzz1m3RgOBls*.

801. Henry I. Miller, "Norman Borlaug: The Genius Behind The Green Revolution," *Forbes* magazine, 1 18, 2012, 2 10, 2012, *www.forbes.com/sites/ henrymiller/2012/01/18/norman-borlaug-the-genius-behind-the-green-revolution/*.

802. Brian0918, "Wheat yields in developing countries 1951–2004," *Wikipedia*, 7 2, 2005, 2 10, 2012, *en.wikipedia.org/wiki/File:Wheat_yields_ in_developing_countries_1951-2004.png*.

803. Amanda Briney, "Green Revolution," *About.com*, 5 5, 2010, 2 10, 2012, *geography.about.com/od/globalproblemsandissues/a/greenrevolution.htm*.

804. "History of agriculture," *New World Encyclopedia*, 4 2, 2008, 2 10, 2012, *www.newworldencyclopedia.org/entry/History_of_agriculture*.

805. "The Francis Crick Papers: The Discovery of the Double Helix, 1951–1953," National Library of Medicine: Profiles in Science, 2012, 8 11, 2012, *profiles.nlm.nih.gov/ps/retrieve/Narrative/SC/p-nid/143*.

806. Robert Wright, "Molecular Biologists WATSON & CRICK," *Time* magazine, 2012, 2 11, 2012, *www.time.com/time/magazine/ article/0,9171,990626,00.html#ixzz1m6BTyoi0*.

807. "Diamond, Commisioner of Patents and Trademarks v. Chakrabarty," Supreme Court of the United States, 2012, 2 11, 2012, *scholar.google.com/scholar_c ase?case=3095713882675765791&hl=en&as_sdt=2&as_vis=1&oi=scholarr*.

808. Rebecca S. Eisenberg, "Story of Diamond v. Chakrabarty, The: Technological Change and the Subject Matter Boundaries of the Patent System," Microsoft: Technology Policy, 2012, 2 11, 2012, *www.techpolicy.com/Articles/Story-of-Diamond-v--Chakrabarty,-The--Technologica.aspx*.

809. Clive James, "Global Status of Commercialized Biotech/GM Crops: 2008," *International Service for the Acquisition of Agri-biotech Applications*, 2008, 2 11, 2012, *www.isaaa.org/resources/publications/briefs/39/executivesummary/pdf/Brief%2039%20-%20Executive%20Summary%20-%20English.pdf*.

810. "Adoption of Genetically Engineered Crops in the U.S.," *United States Department of Agriculture Economic Research Service*, 7 1, 2011, 2 11, 2012, *www.ers.usda.gov/Data/BiotechCrops/*.

811. Robert Kenner, *Food, Inc.* (USA: Participant Media; Dogwoof Films; River Road Entertainment and Magnolia Pictures, 2008).

812. Kenner, *Food, Inc.*

813. Paul B. Ellickson, "The Evolution of the Supermarket Industry From A&P to Wal-Mart," University of Rochester, 4 2011, 2 12, 2012, *web.me.com/pellickson/SMEvolution.pdf*.

814. Lynne Olver, "1950s Food," *The Food Timeline*, 9 22, 2011, 2 12, 2012, *www.foodtimeline.org/fooddecades.html#1900snew*.

815. Lynne Olver, "1960s Foods: New Products," *The Food Timeline*, 9 22, 2011, 2 12, 2012, *www.foodtimeline.org/fooddecades.html#60snewproducts*.

816. Stanley Sacharow, "Educate the consumer to become a better customer," Paper, Film and Foil Converter, 7 1, 1995, 2 12, 2012, *pffc-online.com/mag/799-paper-educate-consumer-become*.

817. Nestle, "The soft sell: how the food industry shapes our diets," CBS Life and Health Library, 9 2002, 2 12, 2012, *www.findarticles.com/p/articles/mi_m0813/is_7_29/ai_90980246*.

818. Kenner, *Food, Inc.*

819. "Historical Crude Oil Prices (Table)," Inflation Data 1 19, 2012, 2 13, 2012, *inflationdata.com/inflation/inflation_rate/Historical_Oil_Prices_Table.asp*.

820. "History of the World Petroleum Industry (Key Dates)," Geo-Help, Inc., 2012, 2 14, 2012, *www.geohelp.net/world.html*.

821. "Oil Embargo," University of Michigan: Auto Life, 2004, 2 14, 2012, *www.autolife.umd.umich.edu/Design/Gartman/D_Casestudy/Oil_Embargo.htm*.

822. "History of Iran: Oil Nationalization," Iran Chamber Society, 2 14, 2012, 2 14, 2012, *www.iranchamber.com/history/oil_nationalization/oil_nationalization.php*.

823. "Oil Embargo."

824. "OPEC Oil Embargo, 1973–1974," U.S. Department of State Office of the Historian, 2012, 2 14, 2012, *history.state.gov/milestones/1969–1976/OPEC*.

825. "Historical Oil Prices Chart," Inflation Data, 1 19, 2012, 2 14, 2012, *inflationdata.com/inflation/inflation_rate/historical_oil_prices_chart.asp*.

826. "1978: Tanker Amoco Cadiz splits in two," BBC: On This Day, 2012, 2 16, 2012, *news.bbc.co.uk/onthisday/hi/dates/stories/march/24/newsid_2531000/2531211.stm*.

827. "The History of Regulation," Natural Gas.org, 2004–2011, 2 16, 2012, *www.naturalgas.org/regulation/history.asp#gasact1978*.

828. "Backgrounder on the Three Mile Island Accident," U.S. Nuclear Regulatory Commission, 3 15 2011, 2 16, 2012, *www.nrc.gov/reading-rm/doc-collections/fact-sheets/3mile-isle.html*.

829. "Economic Impact of Oil Spills on the Texas Coast, FY 1980," Bureau of Ocean Energy Management, 4 1982, 2 16, 2012, *www.data.boem.gov/PI/PDFImages/ESPIS/3/3931.pdf*.

830. "History of Iran: Islamic Revolution of 1979," Iran Chamber Society, 2 12, 2012, 8 3, 2012, *www.iranchamber.com/history/islamic_revolution/islamic_revolution.php/*.

831. Jessica Moore, "The Iraq War: Saddam Hussein's Rise to Power," PBS: Online News Hour, 1996–2012, 8 3, 2012, *www.pbs.org/newshour/bb/middle_east/iraq/war/player1.html*.

832. Richard A. Kerr, "Peak Oil Production May Already Be Here," *Science Magazine*, 3 2011, 2 13, 2012, *www.sciencemag.org/content/331/6024/1510.short*.

833. Robin Mills, Flawed views on peak oil rear their ugly heads again," *The National*, 2 14, 2011, 2 14, 2012, *www.thenational.ae/thenationalconversation/industry-insights/energy/flawed-views-on-peak-oil-rear-their-ugly-heads-again*.

834. Tynan Szvetecz, "What Revolution?" *Savor Each Glass*, 2012, 2 25, 2012, *www.savoreachglass.com/articles/what-revolution*.

835. Pat Montague, "The Great French Wine Blight," *Wine Tidings* 96, 7–8 2012, 2 25, 2012, *www.wampumkeeper.com/wineblight.html*.

836. "Landmark dates in the history of French wine," Wine Tourism in France, 2012, 2 26, 2012, *www.winetourisminfrance.com/an/grandesdates.htm*.

837. Montague, "The Great French Wine Blight."

838. Burke Morton, "The Vine's Enemy: Phylloxera Vastatrix," *Wine Think*, 11 4, 2009, 2 25, 2012, *winethink.net/blog/2009/11/phylloxera/*.

839. "Landmark dates in the history of French wine."

840. Otis Rubottom, "Organic Wine Comes Alive," *Imbibe Magazine*, 5–6, 2006, 2 25, 2012 *imbibemagazine.com/Organic-Wine-Comes-Alive*.

841. "What is Organic?" Henry Wine Group Learning Center, 2012, 2 25, 2012, *www.henrywinegroup.com/henrywinegroup/action?do=learn&catid=25*.

842. Szvetecz, "What Revolution?"

843. "What Is Sustainable Viticulture?" Lodi Wine, 2012, 2 25, 2012, *www.lodiwine.com/what-is-sustainable-viticulture*.

844. Robert M. Parker, Jr., "Robert Parker on Wine Trends: The New Philosophy of Winemaking," *Food and Wine*, 9 2008, 2 25, 2012, *www.foodandwine.com/articles/robert-parker-on-wine-trends-the-new-philosophy-of-winemaking*.

845. Robert M. Parker, Jr., "Robert Parker on Wine Trends: Wine Is Now Number One," *Food and Wine*, 9 2008, 2 25, 2012, *www.foodandwine.com/articles/robert-parker-on-wine-trends-wine-is-now-number-one*.

846. "The Pentecostal group of denominations," Ontario Consultants on Religious Tolerance: Christian meta-groups, 4 11, 2000, 2 23, 2012, *www.religioustolerance.org/chr_pent.htm*.

847. Charles Hummel, "Worldwide renewal: the charismatic movement," *Christianity Today* 9 (1986), 2 23, 2012, *www.christianitytoday.com/ch/1986/issue9/9105.html?start=2.*

848. "The Azusa Street Outpouring's 100-Year Birthday Celebration," *Breaking Christian News*, 2 28, 2006, 2 16, 2012, *www.breakingchristiannews. com/articles/display_art.html?ID=2187.*

849. "Pentecostalism," *Wikipedia*, 2 10, 2012, web, 2 16, 2012.

850. "Charismatic Movement," *Wikipedia*, 2 15, 2012, web, 2 23, 2012.

851. "Catholic Charismatic Renewal," *Wikipedia*, 2 20, 2012, web, 2 23, 2012.

852. Hummel, "Worldwide renewal."

853. Ibid.

854. "Lonnie Frisbee and the Jesus People Revival," Jesus Movement by Grace World Mission, 2 26, 2012, 2 26, 2012, *wn.com/Jesus_Movement.*

855. David Di Sabatino, "History of the Jesus Movement," One Way, 11 1997, 2 26, 2012, *www.one-way.org/jesusmovement/.*

856. "Lonnie Frisbee and the Jesus People Revival."

857. "About Harvest: Greg Laurie," Harvest: Greg Laurie, 2012, 2 26, 2012, *www.harvest.org/crusades/general-information/about.html.*

858. "Jesus Movement," *Wikipedia*, 2 20, 2012, web, 2 26, 2012.

859. "Lonnie Frisbee and the Jesus People Revival."

860. "Jews For Jesus Timeline," Jews For Jesus, 2012, 2 26, 2012, *www. jewsforjesus.org/about/timeline.*

861. Ariel, "Judaism and Christianity Unite!: The Unique Culture of Messianic Judaism," *Introduction to New and Alternative Religions in America*, Eugene V. Gallagher and Michael W. Ashcraft, ed. (Westport, CT: Greenwood Press, 2006), 191.

862. "Messianic Judaism," *Wikipedia*, 2 20, 2012, web, 2 26, 2012.

863. "Entries for the 'FAQs' Catagory: What is HaDerech (Messianic Judaism)?" *The Jerusalem Council*, 2 10, 2012, 2 26, 2012, *jerusalemcouncil. org/category/articles/faqs/.*

864. "Leopard," *Encyclopædia Britannica*, 2012, web, 8 29, 2012.

865. Paul Gross, "Serengeti Cats," 2001, 2 26, 2012, *paulgross.com/tanzania/ serengeticats.htm.*

866. Micha F. Lindemans, "Bacchus," *Encyclopedia Mythica*, 9 2, 2003, 2 27, 2012, *www.pantheon.org/articles/b/bacchus.html.*

867. Micha F. Lindemans, "Liber," *Encyclopedia Mythica*, 3 17, 2003, 2 27, 2012, *www.pantheon.org/articles/l/liber.html.*

868. "Dionysus," *Encyclopædia Britannica*, 2012, web, 8 29, 2012.

869. Peter Wick, "Jesus gegen Dionysos? Ein Beitrag zur Kontextualisierung des Johannesevangeliums," Vol. 85 (2004) 179–198, *Biblical Studies on the Web*, 2012, 2 27, 2012, *www.bsw.org/?l=71851&a=Comm06.html.*

870. Ben Yagoda, "Hollywood Cleans Up Its Act: the curious career of the Hays Office," *American Heritage* 31:2 (2–3 1980), 2 27, 2012, *www. americanheritage.com/content/hollywood-cleans-its-act.*

871. "Playboy," *Encyclopædia Britannica*, 2012, web, 8 29, 2012.

872. Howard P. Chudacoff, *The Age of the Bachelor: Creating an American Subculture*," (Princeton, NJ: Princeton University Press, 1999), 68–74.

873. Raymond L. Cohn, "Immigration to the United States," Economic History Association, 2 1, 2012, 2 27, 2012, *eh.net/encyclopedia/article/cohn.immigration.us.*

874. "Total population and resident non-national population by group of citizenship, 2010," Eurostat, 11 25, 2011, 2 28, 2012, *en.wikipedia.org/wiki/Immigration_to_Europe#cite_note-1.*

875. "Immigration to Europe," *Wikipedia*, 2 19, 2012, web 2 28, 2012.

876. "Emigration from Africa," *Wikipedia*, 1 4, 2012, web, 2 28, 2012.

877. Ben Hall, "Immigration in the European Union: problem or solution?" *The Observer*, 2 6, 2000, 2 28, 2012, *www.oecdobserver.org/news/fullstory.php/aid/337/.*

878. Ibid.

879. Wigram, *The Englishman's Hebrew Concordance*, 314.

880. Strong, 1221.

881. Brown, Driver, and Briggs, 172.

882. Wigram, *The Englishman's Hebrew Concordance*, 314.

883. Akosua Perbi, "Slavery and the Slave Trade in Pre-Colonial Africa," *Latin American Studies*, 4 5, 2001, 2 28, 2012, *www.latinamericanstudies. org/slavery/perbi.pdf.*

884. Elikia M'bokolo, "The impact of the slave trade on Africa," *Le Monde doplomatique*, English Ed., 4 1998, 2 28, 2012, *mondediplo. com/1998/04/02africa.*

885. Ibid.

886. James Giblin, "Introduction: Diffusion and other Problems in the History of African States," The University of Iowa, 3 7, 1999, 2 29, 2012, *www. uiowa.edu/~africart/toc/history/giblinstate.html.*

887. Perbi, "Slavery and the Slave Trade in Pre-Colonial Africa."

888. Giblin, "Introduction: Diffusion and other Problems."

889. Alistair Boddy-Evans, "The Trans-Atlantic Slave Trade," *About.com African History*, 2012, 3 2, 2012, *africanhistory.about.com/od/slavery/tp/ TransAtlantic001.htm.*

890. "Henry the Navigator," *Wikipedia*, 2 24, 2012, web, 3 1, 2012.

891. Robert C. Davis, *Christian Slaves, Muslim Masters: White Slavery in the Mediterranean, the Barbary Coast, and Italy 1500–1800*, Rab Houston and Edward Muir (Basingstoke: Palgrave MacMillan, 2003), 6.

892. Davis, *Christian Slaves, Muslim Masters*, 6–12.

893. Jeff Grabmeier, "When Europeans Were Slaves: Research Suggests White Slavery Was Much More Common Than Previously Believed," Ohio State University, 2012, 3 2, 2012, *researchnews.osu.edu/archive/ whtslav.htm.*

894. Davis, *Christian Slaves, Muslim Masters*, 16.

895. Grabmeier, "When Europeans Were Slaves."

896.   "The Trans-Saharan Gold Trade (7th–14th century)" In Heilbrunn Timeline of Art History, Department of Arts of Africa, Oceania, and the Americas (New York: The Metropolitan Museum of Art, 10 2000), 3 1, 2012, *www.metmuseum.org/toah/hd/gold/hd_gold.htm (October 2000)*.

897.   Nourdin Harich, Marta D. Costa, Veronica Fernades, et al., "The trans-Saharan slave trade—clues from interpolation analyses and high-resolution characterization of mitochondrial DNA lineages," *Bio Medical Central Evolutionary Biology*, 2010, 3 1, 2012, *www.biomedcentral.com/content/pdf/1471-2148-10-138.pdf*, 2-3.

898.   M'bokolo, "The impact of the slave trade on Africa."

899.   Harich, Costa and Fernades, 2.

900.   Bernard Lewis, Race and Slavery in the Middle East (New York: Oxford University Press, 1990), 73.

901.   Nathan Nunn and Leonard Wantchekon, "The Slave Trade and the Origins of Mistrust in Africa," New York University, 12 2008, 3 2, 2012, *as.nyu.edu/docs/IO/2807/Trust.pdf*.

902.   Lewis, 11.

903.   M'bokolo, "The impact of the slave trade on Africa."

904.   Richard R. Bailey, "Who is the Real Slave Master?" *Answering Islam*, 2012, 3 2, 2012, *www.answering-islam.org/Bailey/real_slave_master.html*.

905.   "The Scourge of Slavery," *Christian Action*, 2004, 3 3, 2012, *www.christianaction.org.za/articles_ca/2004-4-thescourgeofslavery.htm*.

906.   Lewis, 51.

907.   M'bokolo, "The impact of the slave trade on Africa."

908.   "The East African Slave Trade," BBC: The Story of Africa—Slavery, 2012, 3 4, 2012, *www.bbc.co.uk/worldservice/africa/features/storyofafrica/9chapter3.shtml*.

909.   "Said bin Sultan, Sultan of Muscat and Oman," *Wikipedia*, 1 12, 2012, web, 3 4, 2012.

910.   "The East African Slave Trade," BBC.

911.   "The Slave Trade in East Africa," E-Learning and Teacher Education, 2012, 3 4, 2012, *www.elateafrica.org/elate/history/slavery/slaveryintro.html*.

912.   "Slavery Fact Sheets," Digital History, 3 3, 2012, 3 3, 2012, *www.digitalhistory.uh.edu/historyonline/slav_fact.cfm*.

913.   "Alik Shahadah, The History of Arab Slavery in Africa", Arab Slave Trade 2001–2005, 3 4, 2012, *www.arabslavetrade.com/*.

914.   Nathan Nunn, "The Historical Origins of Africa's Underdevelopment," *VOX*, 12 8, 2007, 3 2, 2012, *www.voxeu.org/index.php?q=node/779*.

915.   Nunn and Wantchekon, "The Slave Trade and the Origins of Mistrust in Africa."

916.   David Wessel and Scott L. Greenberg, "Big U.S. Firms Shift Hiring Abroad," *Wall Street Journal*, 4 19, 2011, 3 4, 2012, *online.wsj.com/article/SB10001424052748704821704576270783611823972.html*.

917.   "The Future of the Global Muslim Population," The Pew Forum on Religion and Public Life, 1 2000, 3 5 2012, *features.pewforum.org/muslim-population/?sort=Country&order=ASC*.

918. "Muslim majority countries," *Wikipedia*, 12 1, 2011, web, 3 5, 2012, *en.wikipedia.org/wiki/File:Muslim_majority_countries2.png.*

919. "Nation of Islam," *Encyclopædia Britannica*, 2012, web, 8 29, 2012.

920. Tynetta Muhammad, "A Brief History on the Origins of the Nation of Islam in America," Nation of Islam 3 28, 1996, 3 5, 2012, *www.noi.org/about.shtml.*

921. "What The Muslims Want," Nation of Islam 2012, 3 5, 2012, *noi.org/muslim_program.htm.*

922. "Biography—A Born Leader," Malcolm X, 2012, 2 5, 2012, *www.malcolmx.com/about/bio2.html.*

923. "Malcolm X," *Encyclopædia Britannica*, 2012, web, 8 29, 2012.

924. "What The Muslims Want."

925. Tongkeh Joseph Fowale, A Discourse on African Socialism, African History suite 101 5 30, 2009, 3 5, 2012, *tongkeh-joseph-fowale.suite101.com/a-discourse-on-african-socialism-a121555.*

926. "The Story of Africa: Independence." BBC World Service, 2012, 3 5, 2012, *www.bbc.co.uk/worldservice/africa/features/storyofafrica/14chapter1.shtml.*

927. "Africa: Libya," *CIA.*

928. "Africa: Benin," *CIA.*

929. "Africa: Congo," *CIA.*

930. "Africa: Somalia," *CIA.*

931. Ibid.

932. Jean-Francois Revel, *How Democracies Perish* (Garden City, NY: Doubleday, 1984), 340-41.

933. "Africa: Angola," *CIA—The World Factbook*, 1 19, 2012, 2 2, 2012, *www.cia.gov/library/publications/the-world-factbook/geos/ao.html.*

934. "Africa: Mozambique," *CIA.*

935. "Africa: Ethiopia," *CIA.*

936. "Communist countries 1979–1983," *Wikipedia*, 8 18, 2011, 3 6, 2012, *en.wikipedia.org/wiki/File:Communist_countries_1979-1983.png.*

937. Brian Baggins, History of the Black Panther Party, Marxist Internet Archive, 2002, 3 6, 2012, *www.marxists.org/history/usa/workers/black-panthers/.*

938. Ibid.

939. "Tribalism," *Merriam-Webster Dictionary*, 2012, web, 8 3, 2012.

940. David Wiley, "Using 'Tribe' and 'Tribalism'—Categories to Misunderstand African Societies," University of Pennsylvania—African Studies Center, 1981, 3 6, 2012, *www.africa.upenn.edu/K-12/Tribe.html.*

941. Wiley, "Using 'Tribe' and 'Tribalism'."

942. George H. Wittman, "Tribalism cripples Africa," Ghana web, 12 24, 2005, 3 6, 2012, *www.ghanaweb.com/GhanaHomePage/features/artikel.php?ID=96612.*

943. Alicia Bannon, Edward Miguel, and Daniel N. Posner, "Sources of Ethnic Identification in Africa." *Afro Barometer Working Papers* 44, 8 2004, 3 6, 2012, *www.sscnet.ucla.edu/polisci/wgape/papers/5_Bannon.pdf.*

944. Wittman, "Tribalism cripples Africa."

945. Ibid.

946. Tom O'Connor, "African Tribalism," MegaLinks in Criminal Justice, 12 24, 2005, 3 6, 2012, *www.drtomoconnor.com/3160/3160lect04.htm.*

947. Bannon, Miguel, and Posner.

948. Bannon, Miguel, and Posner.

949. O'Connor.

950. "Martin Luther King, Jr. and the Global Freedom Struggle," Stanford Encyclopedia, 2012, 3 8, 2012, *mlk-kpp01.stanford.edu/index.php/encyclopedia/encyclopedia/enc_black_power/.*

951. George Breitman, "In Defense of Black Power," Encyclopedia of Trotskyism On-Line—Marxists Archives Online, 1–2, 1967, 2 8, 2012, *www.marxists.org/history/etol/document/swp-us/bpower.htm.*

952. Chris Trueman, "Black Power," History Learning Site, 2000–2012, 1 29. 2012, *www.historylearningsite.co.uk/black_power.htm.*

953. "Martin Luther King, Jr. and the Global Freedom Struggle."

954. Trueman, "Black Power."

955. "The Black Power Movement," Events in Black History, 1 29, 2008, 3 8, 2012, *www.blackhistory.com/cgi-bin/blog.cgi?blog_id=62378&cid=54.*

956. Barbara Bradley Hagerty, "A Closer Look at Black Liberation Theology," National Public Radio, 3 18, 2008, 3 10, 2012, *www.npr.org/templates/story/story.php?storyId=88552254&ft=1&f=1001.*

957. Sarah Posner, "Wright's theology not 'new or radical'," Salon, 3 5, 2008, 3 10, 2012, *www.salon.com/2008/05/03/black_church/.*

958. James H. Cone, "The Black Church and Marxism: What Do They Have To Say To Each Other?" Archive.org, 4 1980, 3 10, 2012, *www.archive.org/stream/TheBlackChurchAndMarxismWhatDoTheyHaveToSayToEachOther/BCM#page/n0/mode/1up.*

959. "History: 1952," European Union, 2012, 3 10, 2012, *europa.eu/about-eu/eu-history/1945-1959/1952/index_en.htm.*

960. "Pan-African movement," *Encyclopædia Britannica*, 2012, web, 8 29, 2012.

961. Kwame Nkrumah, "The United States of Africa, Kwame Nkrumah Speaks!" You Tube, 1958, 3 10, 2012, *www.youtube.com/watch?v=foDlCCudcsE&feature=player_embedded.*

962. Motsoko Pheko, "Road to Pan-Africanism," Pan-African Perspective, 11 15, 1999, 3 9, 2012, *www.panafricanperspective.com/pheko.htm.*

963. "Pan-Africanism," *Wikipedia*, 3 3, 2012, web, 3 9, 2012.

964. Ayanna Gillian, "Garvey's Legacy in Context: Colourism, Black Movements and African Nationalism," Race and History, 8 17, 2005, 3 8, 2012, *www.raceandhistory.com/historicalviews/2005/1708.html.*

965. "Australian Aboriginal Flag," *Wikipedia*, 3 8, 2012, web, 3 10, 2012.

966. "Africa: Malawi," *CIA.*

967. "Africa: Kenya," *CIA.*

968. "Central America and Caribbean: Saint Kitts and Nevis," *CIA—The World Factbook*, 7 5, 2012, 8 3, 2012, *www.cia.gov/library/publications/the-world-factbook/geos/sc.html.*

969. "Kwanzaa: Roots and Branches," Official Kwanzaa website, 1999–2012, 3 3, 2012, *www.officialkwanzaawebsite.org/origins1.shtml*.

970. Micha F. Lindemans, "Hades," *Encyclopedia Mythica*, 3 5, 2004, 3 13, 2012, *www.pantheon.org/articles/h/hades.html*.

971. "Eagle Facts: Feeding," Eagle Virtual Field Trip, 2012, 3 15, 2012, *webhost.bridgew.edu/jhayesboh/trips/eagles/feeding_facts.htm*.

972. Roger D. Launius, "Sputnik and the Origins of the Space Age," NASA, 2 2, 2005, 3 17, 2012, *history.nasa.gov/sputnik/sputorig.html#american*.

973. Roger Guillemette, "Sputnik and the Crisis That Followed," U.S. Centennial of Flight Commission, 2003, 3 17, 2012, *www.centennialofflight.gov/essay/SPACEFLIGHT/Sputnik/SP16.htm*.

974. "Introduction to Imagery Intelligence," *Global Security*, 2000–2012, 3 17, 2012, *www.globalsecurity.org/intell/library/imint/imint_101.htm*.

975. "Stealth Aircraft," Ohio University, 2012, 3 17, 2012, *www.seorf.ohiou.edu/~af641/*.

976. Gino Guzzardo, "Predator Drones," Kidz Online Media—You Tube, 7 26, 2006, 3 19, 2012, *www.youtube.com/watch?v=nMh8Cjnzen8*.

977. "Stealth Aircraft."

978. "Unmanned aerial vehicle," *Wikipedia*, 3 13, 2012, web, 3 19, 2012.

979. Ralf Hartemink, "Civic Heraldry of Iraq," Heraldry of the World, 7 20, 2010, 3 19, 2012, *www.ngw.nl/int/asia/iq-nat.htm*.

980. "Egypt," Heraldry of the World, 3 6, 2012, web, 3 19, 2012.

981. "Yemen," Heraldry of the World, 3 6, 2012, 3 19, 2012, *www.ngw.nl/heraldrywiki/index.php?title=Yemen*.

982. "Category:Eagle of Saladin," *Wikipedia*, 1 29, 2010, web, 3 19, 2012.

983. "Category:Hawk of Quraish," *Wikipedia*, 8 27, 2009, web, 3 19, 2012.

984. Thayer, 669.

985. "chlorophyll," *Merriam-Webster Dictionary*, 2012, web, 8 5, 2012.

986. "Space Shuttle Enterprise," *Wikipedia*, 3 19, 2012, web, 3 20, 2012.

987. "List of space shuttle missions," *Wikipedia*, 2 28, 2012, web, 3 20, 2012.

988. "Concorde Aircraft Facts," Flight Level 350, 2004–2012, 3 20, 2012, *www.flightlevel350.com/Concorde_aircraft_facts.html*.

989. Asif Siddiqi, "A History of Commercial Air Freight," U.S. Centennial of Flight Commission, 2012, 3 21, 2012, *www.centennialofflight.gov/essay/Commercial_Aviation/AirFreight/Tran10.htm*.

990. "About Commodore," Commodore USA, 2012, 3 20, 2012, *www.commodoreusa.net/CUSA_AboutCommodore.aspx*.

991. Harry McCracken, The Most Collectible PCs of All Time," *PC World*, 8 27, 2007, 3 20, 2012, *www.pcworld.com/article/136242/the_most_collectible_pcs_of_all_time.html*.

992. "Microsoft Corporation Company History," Funding Universe, 2012, 3 20, 2012, *www.fundinguniverse.com/company-histories/Microsoft-Corporation-Company-History.html*.

993.   "Apple Computer, Inc.," Funding Universe, 2012, 3 20, 2012, *www. fundinguniverse.com/company-histories/Apple-Computer-Inc-Company-History.html.*

994.   "Apple, Inc.," *Encyclopædia Britannica*, 2012, web, 8 29, 2012.

995.   "Apple home page," apple.com, 2012, 3 20, 2012, *www.apple.com/.*

996.   "Telephone," *Encyclopædia Britannica*, 2012, web, 8 26, 2012.

997.   "Telephone," *Encyclopædia Britannica*.

998.   Mary Bellis, "Selling The Cell Phone," *About.com Inventors*, 2012, 5 3, 2012, *inventors.about.com/library/weekly/aa070899.htm.*

999.   Randal O'Toole, "The History of the Endangered Species Act," *Different Drummer*, Winter 1996, 3 20, 2012, *www.ti.org/ESAHistory.html.*

1000.   "Three Mile Island Accident," World Nuclear Association, 3 2001, 3 21, 2012, *www.world-nuclear.org/info/inf36.html.*

1001.   "Timeline of Nuclear Tehcnology," PBS: American Experience, 1996–2012, 3 21, 2012, *www.pbs.org/wgbh/amex/three/timeline/index_2.html.*

1002.   "World Climate Conferences," World Meteorological Organization, 2012, 8 28, 2012, *www.wmo.int/pages/themes/climate/international_wcc.php.*

1003.   "Islamic Revolution of 1979," Iran Chamber Society, 3 25, 2012, 2 25, 2012, *www.iranchamber.com/history/islamic_revolution/islamic_revolution.php.*

1004.   Bay Fang, "When Saddam ruled the day," *U.S. News & World Report*, 7 11, 2004, 3 25, 2012, *www.usnews.com/usnews/news/articles/040719/19iraq.htm.*

1005.   "Terrorist Attacks on Americans, 1979–1988," PBS: Frontline, 1995–2012, 3 25, 2012, *www.pbs.org/wgbh/pages/frontline/shows/target/etc/cron.html.*

1006.   Linda Lear, "Rachel Carson's Biography," Rachel Carson, 1998, 3 25, 2012, *www.rachelcarson.org/.*

1007.   J. Gordon Edwards, "The Lies of Rachel Carson," *21st Century Science & Technology Magazine*, Summer 1992, 3 25, 2012, *www.21stcenturysciencetech. com/articles/summ02/Carson.html.*

1008.   "the Greens," *Encyclopædia Britannica*, 2012, web, 8 29, 2012.

1009.   George McGuire, "The Four Pillars of the Green Party," Vote Cheryl Wolfe, 9 2002, 8 26, 2012, *cosmiccpa.com/votecherylwolfe/the-four-pillars-of-the-green-party/.*

1010.   "Ten Key Values of the Green Party," Green Party of the United States, 6 2000, 3 27, 2012, *www.gp.org/tenkey.shtml.*

1011.   "Ecological Wisdom," Green Party of Canada, 2012, 3 27, 2012, *www. greenparty.ca/party/values/ecological-wisdom.*

1012.   "Environmentalist Colors: Light Green vs Dark Green," Solve Your Problem Article Series: Global Warming, 2007, 3 27, 2012, *globalwarming. solveyourproblem.com/environmentalist-light-dark-green.shtml.*

1013.   "Greenpeace Rams Japanese Vessel," The Institute of Cetacean Research, 1 8, 2006, 3 27, 2012, *www.icrwhale.org/eng/060108Release.pdf.*

1014.   Michael W. Lynch, "Wild idea—interview with National Park Service ecologist David M. Graber—Interview," CBS Interactive Business Network Resource Library, 2 1999, 3 27, 2012, *findarticles.com/p/articles/ mi_m1568/is_9_30/ai_53747403/.*

1015.   Alexander King and Bertrand Schneider, *The First Global Revolution: A Report by the Council of the Club of Rome* (India, Orient Longman, 1993), 75.

1016.   "Social Justice," Green Party of Canada, 2012, 3 29, 2012, *www.greenparty.ca/party/values/social-justice.*

1017.   "The Just Third Way," Global Justice Movement, 2012, 3 29, 2012, *www.globaljusticemovement.org/thirdway.htm.*

1018.   Ramon Tamames, "World Economic and Environmental Order," EUMED.net Virtual Encyclopedia (United Nations, UNESCO, 11 2000), 3 30, 2012, *www.eumed.net/cursecon/textos/Tamames-Env_Order.pdf*, 11, 44.

1019.   Ida Urso, "The New World Order and the Word of the United Nations," The New World Order and the Word of the United Nations, 10, 28, 1995, 3 30, 2012, *www.aquaac.org/un/nwo.html.*

1020.   "Ten Key Values of the Green Party."

1021.   King and Schneider, *The First Global Revolution*, 71.

1022.   "Non-Violence," Green Party of Canada, 2012, 4 2, 2012, *www.greenparty.ca/party/values/non-violence.*

1023.   Maxime Larive, "Why can European integration offer the tools for success to Sudan?" Foreign Policy Association, 1 13, 2011, 4 10, 2012, *foreignpolicyblogs.com/2011/01/13/why-can-european-integration-offer-the-tools-for-success-to-sudan.*

1024.   Larive, "Why can European integration."

1025.   "Agenda 21: The United Nations Programme of Action from Rio," United Nations Department of Economic and Social Affairs, 2009, 4 10, 2012, *www.un.org/esa/dsd/agenda21/.*

1026.   Mihajlo Mesarovic and Eduard Pestel, *Mankind at a Turning Point: The Second Report to The Club of Rome* (New York: E. P. Dutton, 1974).

1027.   Brent Jessop, "The Transition to a Totalitarian World Government: 'Mankind at the Turning Point,'" Global Research, 3 18, 2008, *www.globalresearch.ca/index.php?context=va&aid=8357.*

1028.   N. D. Karunaratne, "Mankind at the Turning Point—The Second Report of The Club of Rome," Economic Analysis and Policy, Manuela Torgler, ed., 3 1976, 4 10, 2012, *ideas.repec.org/a/eap/artid/v6y1976i3p69-73.html, 69–73.*

1029.   "About the Club of Rome," The Club of Rome, 2012, 4 10, 2012, *www.clubofrome.org/?p=324.*

1030.   "Maurice Strong," NNDB tracking the entire world, 2012, 4 10, 2012, *www.nndb.com/people/665/000207044/.*

1031.   "Robert Muller," The Club of Budapest—Membership, 2012, 4 11, 2012, *www.clubofbudapest.org/p-amb-muller.php.*

1032.   "Annan, Kofi," Club de Madrid, 2012 4 11, 2012, *www.clubmadrid.org/en/miembro/kofi_annan.*

1033.   "Javier Pérez de Cuellar," Club de Madrid, 2012, 4 11, 2012, *www.clubmadrid.org/en/miembro/javier_perez_de_cuellar.*

1034.   "Bill Clinton," Club de Madrid, 2012, 4 11, 2012, *www.clubmadrid.org/en/miembro/bill_clinton.*

1035. "Mikhail Gorbachev," NNDB tracking the entire world, 2012, 4 11, 2012, *www.nndb.com/people/416/000023347/*.

1036. "Pierre Elliott Trudeau," *Wikipedia*, 4 8, 2012, web, 4 10, 2012.

1037. "Membership of the Club of Rome," The Club of Rome, 2012, 4 10, 2012, *www.clubofrome.org/cms/Index.php?cat=52&paged=3*.

1038. "David Rockefeller," NNDB tracking the entire world, 2012, 4 11, 2012, *www.nndb.com/people/728/000022662/*.

1039. "'Club of Rome' member warns against council amalgamations," ABC News, 5 6, 2007, 4 10, 2012, *www.abc.net.au/news/2007-06-05/club-of-rome-member-warns-against-council/58734*.

1040. Ibid.

1041. Ibid,

1042. "Katherine Graham," NNDB tracking the entire world, 2012, 4 11, 2012, *www.nndb.com/people/533/000051380/*.

1043. "James Lovelock," The Green Interview, 2010, 8 28, 2012, *www.thegreeninterview.com/james-lovelock-bio*.

1044. James Lovelock, "Significant scientific contributions," Jame Lovelock, 1965–2011, 4 15, 2012, *www.jameslovelock.org/page3.html*.

1045. James Lovelock, *Gaia: A new look at life on Earth* (Oxford: Oxford University Press, 1979).

1046. "H.H. The XIVth Dalai Lama," Club of Budapest, 2012, 3 12, 2012, *www.clubofbudapest.org/p-amb-dalailama.php*.

1047. "Bio of Barbara Marx Hubbard," Foundation for Conscious Evolution, 2012, 4 12, 2012, *www.barbaramarxhubbard.com/site/bio*.

1048. Khalil Green, "The Color of Islam is Green," Suite 101, 4 29, 2009, 4 12, 2012, http://khalil-green.suite101.com/the-color-of-islam-is-green-a113707.

1049. "Green in Islam," *Wikipedia*, 1 14, 2012, web, 2 12, 2012.

1050. "Africa: Mauritania," *CIA*.

1051. "Africa: Nigeria," *CIA*.

1052. "South Asia: Pakistan," *CIA: The World Factbook*, 3 29, 2012, 4 12, 2012, *www.cia.gov/library/publications/the-world-factbook/geos/pk.html*.

1053. "Middle East: Saudi Arabia," *CIA: The World Factbook*, 3 6 2012, 4 12, 2012, *www.cia.gov/library/publications/the-world-factbook/geos/sa.html*.

1054. "Islamic flags," *Wikipedia*, 4 7, 2012, web, 4 12, 2012.

1055. E. Roger Owen, "One Hundred Years of Middle Eastern Oil," *Brandeis University and Crown Center for Middle East Studies* 24 (1 2008), 4 12, 2012, *www.brandeis.edu/crown/publications/meb/MEB24.pdf*, 1, 5.

1056. "The Mideast Oil Crisis," Oracle Education Foundation Think Quest, 2012, 4 12, 2012, *library.thinkquest.org/20331/history/mideast.htm*.

1057. "The Five Pillars of Islam," Islami City.com, 1995–2012, 4 15, 2012, *www.islamicity.com/mosque/pillars.shtml*.

1058. John Moore, "The Evolution of Islamic Terrorism: an Overview," PBS Frontline, 1995–2012, 4 15, 2012, *www.pbs.org/wgbh/pages/frontline/shows/target/etc/modern.html*.

1059. John L. Esposito, "Islamic Fundamentalism," Afghanistan Research Group, 1996, 4 15, 2012, *www.ag-afghanistan.de/funda.htm*.

1060. Moore, "The Evolution of Islamic Terrorism."

1061. "Terror Threat," Radical Islam, 2009, 4 15, 2012, *www.radicalislam.org/threat/global-threat/terror*.

1062. "U.S. Prisons," Radical Islam, 2009, 4 15, 2012, *www.radicalislam.org/threat/homegrown-threat/us-prisons*.

1063. "Eurabia," Radical Islam, 2009, 4 15, 2012, *www.radicalislam.org/threat/global-threat/eurabia*.

1064. Arwa Aburawa, "Islamic Foundation for Ecology and Environmental Sciences," Green Prophet, 11 14, 2011, 4 15, 2012, *www.greenprophet.com/2011/11/interview-ifees-green-islamic-org/*.

1065. Sadia Dehlvi, "Islam and Environment: Leaders Must Act 'Green' Like Prophet Muhammad," *The Times of India*, 6 7, 2011, 4 15, 2012, *timesofindia.indiatimes.com/life-style/spirituality/faith-and-ritual/Islam-and-environment/articleshow/7053540.cms*.

1066. Thayer, 114.

1067. Thayer, 225.

1068. "Kyoto Protocol," United Nations Framework Convention on Climate Change, 2012, 4 17, 2012, *unfccc.int/kyoto_protocol/items/2830.php*.

1069. Ibid.

1070. "Kyoto Protocol participation map 2010," *Wikipedia*, 10 20, 2011, 4 17, 2012, *en.wikipedia.org/wiki/File:Kyoto_Protocol_participation_map_2010.png*.

1071. "List of Muslim-majority countries," Da'wah Skills, 2012, 8 28, 2012, *www.dawahskills.com/skills-tools/list-of-countries-by-muslim-population/*.

1072. "How many square kilometers of land mass are there in the world?" WikiAnswers, 2012 4 16, 2012, *wiki.answers.com/Q/How_many_square_kilometers_of_land_mass_are_there_in_the_world*.

1073. "File: Muslim majority countries2," *Wikipedia*, 11 23, 2009, 4 16, 2012, *en.wikipedia.org/wiki/File:Muslim_majority_countries2.png*.

1074. Thayer, 393.

1075. Thayer, 564.

1076. Strong, 1030.

1077. "Ecologist Says Unchecked Population Growth Could Bring Misery," Utne Reader: The Best of the Alternative Press, 2012, 4 19, 2012, *www.utne.com/archives/EcologistSaysUncheckedPopulationGrowthCouldBringMisery.aspx*.

1078. Alex Steffen, "Bill Gates: the Most Important Climate Speech of the Year," UCT Center of Criminology, 2 18, 2010, 4 29, 2012, *uctcriminology.wordpress.com/2010/02/18/bill-gates-co2-p-x-s-x-e-x-c/*.

1079. Bill Gates, "Bill Gates on energy: Innovating to zero!" TED Ideas worth spreading, 2 2010, *www.ted.com/talks/bill_gates.html*.

1080. "Worst Environmental Problem? Overpopulation, Experts Say," *Science Daily*, 4 18, 2009, 4 29, 2012, *www.sciencedaily.com/releases/2009/04/090418075752.htm*.

1081. Martin Walker, "The World's New Numbers," The Wilson Quarterly, Spring 2009, 5 3, 2012, *www.wilsonquarterly.com/article.cfm?aid=1408*.

1082. Jonathan Grant, Stijn Hoorens, Suja Sivadasan, et al., "Population Implosion? Low Fertility and Policy Responses in the European Union," Rand Europe, 2005, 4 22, 2012, *www.rand.org/pubs/research_briefs/RB9126/index1.html.*

1083. Grant, Hoorens, and Sivadasan, "Population Implosion?"

1084. John McCarthy, "Human Population and its Limits," Stanford University, 1998, 4 29, 2012, *www-formal.stanford.edu/jmc/progress/population.html.*

1085. H. A. Hellyer, "Religious Authority, Islam and Revolution," Huffington Post, 6 12, 2011, 4 24, 2012, *www.huffingtonpost.com/ha-hellyer/religious-authority-islam_b_875517.html.*

1086. Youssef M. Ibrahim, "Muslim Edicts Take on New Force," *The New York Times*, 2 12, 1995, 4 24, 2012, *www.nytimes.com/1995/02/12/world/muslim-edicts-take-on-new-force.html?pagewanted=all&src=pm.*

1087. Nicholas Kralev, "Muslim leader's edict decries terrorism," *Washington Times*, 3 3, 2010, 4 19, 2012, *www.washingtontimes.com/news/2010/mar/03/muslim-leaders-edict-decries-terrorism/?page=all.*

1088. Mahmood Ahmad, "Moments Before the Execution," Arab News, 2 8, 2003, 4 22, 2012, *archive.arabnews.com/?page=1&section=0&article=23428&d=8&m=3&y=2003.*

1089. Surat Al-Ma'idah, *Qur'an*, 2012, 4 24, 2012, *quran.com/5.*

1090. Surat Al-'Anfal, *Qur'an*, 2012, 4 24, 2012, *quran.com/8.*

1091. Surat Muhammad, *Qur'an*, 2012, 4 24, 2012, *quran.com/47.*

1092. Joel Roberts, "Terror, Lies And Videotape," CBS News, 2 11, 2009, 4 24, 2012, *www.cbsnews.com/2100-500164_162-509059.html.*

1093. Bruce Thornton, "The Unlearned Lessons of Daniel Pearl's Murder," Frontpage Magazine, 1 24, 2012, 4 24, 2012, *frontpagemag.com/2012/01/24/the-unlearned-lessons-of-daniel-pearl%E2%80%99s-murder/.*

1094. Stephen Fitzpatrick, "Beheaded Girls were Ramadan 'trophies,'" The Australian, 11 9, 2006, 4 24, 2012, *www.theaustralian.com.au/news/world/beheaded-girls-were-ramadan-trophies/story-e6frg6so-1111112492769.*

1095. Ismail Zabeeh, "Ashura observed with blood streams to mark Karbala tragedy," Jafariya News—Largest Shia News Website, 2 20, 2005, 4 24, 2012, *www.jafariyanews.com/2k5_news/feb/20ashur.htm.*

1096. Associated Press, "Ashoura Day in Nabatiyeh, Lebanon" World News, 5 17, 1997, 4 19, 2012, *cdn8.wn.com/pd/ba/03/134fae842d20e95611355e97fbce_grande.jpg.*

1097. Thayer, 378.

1098. King and Schneider, *The First Global Revolution*, 38–41.

1099. "Global Hunger," Bread for the World, 2012, 4 26, 2012, *www.bread.org/hunger/global/.*

1100. "The world hunger problem: Facts, figures and statistics," Oracle Think Quest, 2012, 4 26, 2012, *library.thinkquest.org/C002291/high/present/stats.htm.*

1101. Ibid.

1102. "Hunger and Poverty Facts," Bread for the World, 2012, 4 26, 2012, *www.bread.org/hunger/us/facts.htm.*

1103.   Annie Johnson, "Weed Alert: Witchweed," New South Wales, 4 2008, 4 24, 2012, *www.dpi.nsw.gov.au/agriculture/pests-weeds/weeds/profiles/witchweed.*

1104.   "Progress on farmer training in parasitic weed management," Ricardo Labrada, ed., 2008, 4 24, 2012, *ftp.fao.org/docrep/fao/010/i0015b/i0015b01.pdf.*

1105.   "Sahel Drought (L.E.D.C.)," Droughts on Tripod, 2012, 4 24, 2012, *droughts.tripod.com/drought/id8.html.*

1106.   "The Sahel Crisis," Food and Agriculture Organization of the United Nations. 2012, 4 24, 2012, *www.fao.org/crisis/sahel/the-sahel-crisis/en/.*

1107.   "Horn of Africa drought: 'A vision of hell,'" BBC News: Africa, 7 8, 2011, 4 25, 2012, *www.bbc.co.uk/news/uk-14078074.*

1108.   Will Ross, "Somalia's hungry head for a war zone," BBC News: Africa, 7 22, 2011, 4 25, 2012, *www.bbc.co.uk/news/world-africa-14248940.*

1109.   Farouk Chothia, "Could Somali famine deal a fatal blow to al-Shabab?" BBC News Africa, 6 9, 2011, 4 25, 2012, *www.bbc.co.uk/news/world-africa-14373264.*

1110.   Saeed Shah, Pakistan floods: people return home to find nothing left, nothing at all," *The Guardian*, 8 24, 2010, 4 25, 2012, *www.guardian.co.uk/world/2010/aug/24/pakistan-floods-villages-destruction?intcmp=239.*

1111.   Ibid.

1112.   Mark Leon Goldberg, Pakistan Floods Facts and Figures, UN Dispatch, 8 16, 2010, 4 25, 2012, *www.undispatch.com/pakistan-floods-facts-and-figures.*

1113.   Doug Gurian-Sherman, "Failure to Yield: Evaluating the Performance of Genetically Engineered Crops," *Union of Concerned Scientists*, 3, 2009, 12 27, 2012, *www.ucsusa.org/food_and_agriculture/our-failing-food-system/genetic-engineering/failure-to-yield.html*

1114.   Thayer, 64.

1115.   Thayer, 282–83.

1116.   Justin Champion, "The annual Bill of Mortality for London and its environs, 1665," Medical history, 1993, 5 3, 2012, *www.history.ac.uk/ihr/Focus/Medical/epichamp2.html.*

1117.   Ibid.

1118.   Ibid.

1119.   "The top 10 causes of death," World Health Organization Media centre, 6 2011, 5 6, 2012, *www.who.int/mediacentre/factsheets/fs310/en/index.html.*

1120.   "The top 10 causes of death."

1121.   Champion, "The annual Bill of Mortality."

1122.   "Metabolic syndrome; Insulin resistance syndrome; Syndrome X," PubMed Health; National Center for Biotechnology Information, U.S. National Library of Medicine, 6 28, 2012, 5 9, 2012, *www.ncbi.nlm.nih.gov/pubmedhealth/PMH0004546/.*

1123.   "High blood pressure and heart disease," University of Iowa Health Care, 2005, 5 6, 2012, *www.uihealthcare.com/topics/cardiovascularhealth/card4301.html.*

1124.   "Obesity: Halting the Epidemic by Making Health Easier," Centers for Disease Control and Prevention, 2011, 5 8, 2012, *www.cdc.gov/chronicdisease/resources/publications/AAG/obesity.htm.*

1125. Serena Gordon, "Today's Kids May Be Destined for Adult Heart Disease," US News, 5 4, 2012, 5 6, 2012, *health.usnews.com/health-news/news/articles/2012/05/04/todays-kids-may-be-destined-for-adult-heart-disease.*

1126. "Study: Global obesity rates double since 1980," WSA Today, 2 3, 2011, 5 10, 2012, *www.usatoday.com/news/health/story/health/story/2011/02/Study-Global-obesity-rates-double-since-1980/43253168/1.*

1127. "Corn Subsidies in the United States," Environmental Working Group, 2007-2012, 11 14, 2012 *farm.ewg.org/progdetail.php?fips=00000&progcode=corn.*

1128. Kenner, *Food, Inc.*

1129. Metea Gold, "Kids watch more than a day of TV each week," *The Los Angeles Post*, 4 5, 2012 5 3, 2012, *articles.latimes.com/2009/oct/27/entertainment/et-kids-tv27.*

1130. Roni Caryn Rabin, "Proximity to Fast Food a Factor in Student Obesity," *The New York Times*, 3 25, 2009, 5 8, 2012, *www.nytimes.com/2009/03/26/health/nutrition/26obese.html?_r=1.*

1131. Sanjay Gupta, "If we are what we eat, Americans are corn and soy," CNN, 9 22, 2012, 2 12, 2012, *articles.cnn.com/2007-09-22/health/kd.gupta.column_1_high-fructose-corn-syrup-corn-refiners-association-soybean-oil?_s=PM:HEALTH.*

1132. R. S. Bailey, "Genetically Modified Organisms: Grassroots Backlash," *The Los Angeles Post*, 4 5, 2012, 5 3, 2012, *www.thelosangelespost.org/gmo-grassroots-backlash/.*

1133. Mark Hyman, "5 Reasons High Fructose Corn Syrup Will Kill You," Dr. Mark Hyman's blog, 5 13, 2011, 5 10, 2012, *drhyman.com/blog/conditions/5-reasons-high-fructose-corn-syrup-will-kill-you/.*

1134. Robert H. Lustig, "Sugar: The Bitter Truth," lecture, YouTube, 430, 2009, 5 14, 2012, *www.youtube.com/watch?feature=player_embedded&v=dBnniua6-oM.*

1135. Taylor Orr, "High-Fructose Corn Syrup's Health Risks Remain Sticky," *Pacific Standard Magazine*, 1 25, 2011, 5 10, 2012, *www.psmag.com/health/high-fructose-corn-syrups-health-risks-remain-sticky-27633/?gclid=CLXZudL67q8CFSdjTAodplHDqA.*

1136. William M. Davis, *Wheat Belly: Lose the Wheat, Lose the Weight, and Find Your Path Back to Health* (New York: Rodale, 2011), 72

1137. Ibid., xi.

1138. "Infant Formula." Truth in Labeling, 7 3, 2004, 5 13, 2012, *www.truthinlabeling.org/formulacopy.html.*

1139. Russell Blaylock, "Sudden Cardiac Death and Food Excitotoxin Additives," Russell Blaylock, M.D., 4 23, 2009, 5 13, 2012, *www.russellblaylockmd.com/.*

1140. J. W. Olney, "Excitotoxins in foods," *Neurotoxicology* 15:3 (Fall 1994) 535–44.

1141. "The top 10 causes of death."

1142. "Asbestos Exposure and Cancer Risk," National Cancer Institute, 2012, 5 13, 2012, *www.cancer.gov/cancertopics/factsheet/Risk/asbestos.*

1143. "Formaldehyde and Cancer Risk," National Cancer Institute, 2012, 5 13, 2012, *www.cancer.gov/cancertopics/factsheet/Risk/formaldehyde.*

1144. "Hair Dyes and Cancer Risk," National Cancer Institute, 2012, 5 13, 2012, *www.cancer.gov/cancertopics/factsheet/Risk/hair-dyes.*

1145. "Anyone Can Get Skin Cancer," National Cancer Institute, 2012, 5 13, 2012, *www.cancer.gov/cancertopics/prevention/skin/anyone-can-get-skin-cancer.*

1146. "Smoking: Tobacco Facts," National Cancer Institute, 2012, 5 13, 2012, *www.cancer.gov/cancertopics/tobacco/smoking.*

1147. Bill Rankin, "Nuclear Explosions since 1945," Radical Cartography, 2007, 5 14, 2012, *www.radicalcartography.net/.*

1148. Kenner, *Food, Inc.*

1149. "Animal rights," *Encyclopædia Britannica*, 2012, web, 8 26, 2012.

1150. "Wolf reintroduction in Yellowstone," *Wikipedia*, 12 5, 2012, web, 12 28, 2012.

1151. T.R. Mader, "Fact Sheet—Wolf Reintroduction in the United States," *Abundant Wildlife Society of North America*, 2012, 12 28 2012, *www.aws. vcn.com/fact.html*

1152. "CDC Plague Home Page," Center of Disease Control and Prevention, 6 25, 2009, 5 15, 2012, *www.cdc.gov/ncidod/dvbid/plague/.*

1153. "2009 H1N1 Flu ("Swine Flu") and You," Center of Disease Control and Prevention, 2 10, 2010, 5 15, 2012, *www.cdc.gov/h1n1flu/qa.htm.*

1154. "Swine influenza," *Wikipedia*, 5 14, 2012, web, 5 15, 2012.

1155. "Avian influenza," *Wikipedia*, 5 14, 2012, web, 5 15, 2012.

1156. "West Nile virus," *Wikipedia*, 5 9, 2012, web, 5 15, 2012.

1157. "Mad Cow Disease, MedicineNet, 2012, 5 15, 2012, *www.medicinenet. com/mad_cow_disease/article.htm.*

1158. "Ebola," *Wikipedia*, 5 15, 2012, web, 5 15, 2012.

1159. Edwin Brock, "Five Ways to Kill a Man," Poetry Archive (Enitharmon, 1997), 5 15, 2012, *www.poetryarchive.org/poetryarchive/singlePoem. do?poemId=7497.*

1160. "Obese children will die younger than their parents: report," CBC News—Health, 3 27, 2007, 5 15, 2012, *www.cbc.ca/news/health/ story/2007/03/27/obesity-child.html.*

1161. Pam Belluck, "Children's Life Expectancy Being Cut Short by Obesity," *The New York Times*, 3 16, 2005, 5 15, 2012, *www.nytimes. com/2005/03/17/health/17obese.html.*

1162. Rosa Prince, "Children will die younger than their parents, minister warns," *The Telegraph*, 7 23, 2008, 5 15, 2012, *www.telegraph.co.uk/health/2449040/ Children-will-die-younger-than-their-parents-minister-warns.html.*

1163. Blue Letter Bible, "Dictionary and Word Search for dĕchal (Aramaic) (Strong's 1763)," Blue Letter Bible, 1996–2012, 5 17, 2012, *www. blueletterbible.org/lang/lexicon/lexicon.cfm?Strongs=H1763&t=KJV.*

1164. Blue Letter Bible, "Dictionary and Word Search for 'emtaniy (Aramaic) (Strong's 574)," Blue Letter Bible, 1996–2012, 5 17, 2012, *www. blueletterbible.org/lang/lexicon/lexicon.cfm?Strongs=H574&t=KJV.*

1165. Brown, Driver, and Briggs, 608.

1166. "Equipment," Legion XXIV Media Atlantia, 10 23, 2003, 5 16, 2012, *www.legionxxiv.org/equipment/.*

1167. Adam Cohen, "What Your Cell Phone Could Be Telling the Government," *Time* magazine, 8 15, 2010, 5 16, 2012, *www.time.com/time/nation/article/0,8599,2019239,00.html.*

1168. Blue Letter Bible, "Dictionary and Word Search for 'akal (Aramaic) (Strong's 399)," Blue Letter Bible, 1996–2012, 5 17, 2012, *www.blueletterbible.org/lang/lexicon/lexicon.cfm?Strongs=H399&t=KJV.*

1169. Blue Letter Bible, "Dictionary and Word Search for děqaq (Aramaic) (Strong's 1855)," Blue Letter Bible, 1996–2012, 5 17, 2012, *www.blueletterbible.org/lang/lexicon/lexicon.cfm?Strongs=H1855&t=KJV.*

1170. Blue Letter Bible, "Dictionary and Word Search for rěphac (Aramaic) (Strong's 7512)," Blue Letter Bible, 1996–2012, 5 17, 2012, *www.blueletterbible.org/lang/lexicon/lexicon.cfm?Strongs=H7512&t=KJV.*

1171. Brown, Driver, and Briggs, 952.

1172. Bat Ye'or, "Dhimmitude: History: Dhimmitude," Dhimmitude.org, 2001–2006, 5 17, 2012, *www.dhimmitude.org/d_history_dhimmitude.html.*

1173. Blue Letter Bible, "Dictionary and Word Search for sh na' (Aramaic) (Strong's 8133)," Blue Letter Bible, 1996–2012, 5 17, 2012, *www.blueletterbible.org/lang/lexicon/lexicon.cfm?Strongs=H8133&t=KJV.*

1174. Mesarović and Pestel, *Mankind a the Turning Point,* 40–41.

1175. Mihajlo Mesarovic and Eduard Pestel, "Regionalized and Adaptive Model of the Global World System: Report on the Progress in the Strategy for Survival Project of the Club of Rome," Conspiracy Wiki, 9 17, 1973, 5 18, 2012, *conspiracywiki.com/documents/club-of-rome-report-regionalized-and-adaptive-model-of-the-global-world.pdf.*

1176. Daniel S. Burt, *The Biography Book: a Reader's Guide to Nonfiction, Fictional and Film Biographies of More Than 500 of the Most Fascinating Individuals of All Time* (Westport, CT: Oryx Press, 2001), 315.

1177. Blue Letter Bible, "Text Commentaries—Isaac Newton," Blue Letter Bible, 1996–2012, 5 30, 2012, *www.blueletterbible.org/commentaries/comm_author.cfm?AuthorID=11.*

1178. Isaac Newton, *Observations upon the Prophesies of Daniel, and the Apocalypse of St. John,* 1733, 5 30, 2012, *www.isaacnewton.ca/daniel_apocalypse/pt2ch01.html.*

1179. J. P. Green, *The Interlinear Hebrew-Greek-English Bible* (USA: Hendrickson Publishers, 1985), 679.

1180. Toby Westerman, "Silent Holocaust of Christian Martyrs—A Warning of Things to Come?" International News Analysis Today, 1 13, 2010, 5 20, 2012, *www.inatoday.com/christianmartyrs1132010.htm.*

1181. Tom Quiner, "The 21st century's epidemic of Christian martyrs," Quiner's Diner: A Heapin' Plate of Conservative Politics & Religion, 10 24, 2011, 5 20, 2012, *quinersdiner.com/2011/10/24/the-21st-centurys-epidemic-of-christian-martyrs/.*

1182. Mary Fairchild, "Christianity Today—General Statistics and Facts of Christianity," About.com, 2012, 5 20, 2012, *christianity.about.com/od/denominations/p/christiantoday.htm.*

1183. "Sociologist: Every 5 Minutes a Christian is Martyred," Zenit—the World Seen From Rome, 6 3, 2011, 5 20, 2012, *www.zenit.org/article-32747?l=english.*

1184. George Weigel, "Christian Number-Crunching," First Things: on the Square, 2 9, 2011, 5 20, 2012, *www.firstthings.com/onthesquare/2011/02/christian-number-crunching.*

1185. Franklin D. Roosevelt, "'Only Thing We Have to Fear Is Fear Itself:' FDR's First Inaugural Address," History Matters, 1933, 5 20, 2012, *historymatters.gmu.edu/d/5057/.*

1186. "Stages of labor: Baby, it's time!" Mayo Clinic, 4 9, 2011, 5 20, 2012, *www.mayoclinic.com/health/stages-of-labor/PR00106.*

1187. Ibid.

1188. "The stages of childbirth," Baby Center Medical Advisory Board, 11 2009, 7 8, 2012, *www.babycentre.co.uk/pregnancy/labourandbirth/labour/stagesofchildbirth/.*

1189. Thayer, 644.

CPSIA information can be obtained at www.ICGtesting.com
Printed in the USA
BVOW080611010513

319545BV00003B/7/P